The Audubon Society
Field Guide to
North American Wildflowers

A Chanticleer Press Edition

The Audubon Society Field Guide to North American Wildflowers

Eastern Region

William A. Niering,
Professor of Botany,
Connecticut College, New London
and Nancy C. Olmstead,
Research Associate,
Connecticut Arboretum

Visual Key by
Susan Rayfield and Carol Nehring

Alfred A. Knopf, New York

This is a Borzoi Book
Published by Alfred A. Knopf, Inc.

Prepared and produced by
Chanticleer Press, Inc., New York.

Color reproductions by Nievergelt
Repro AG, Zurich, Switzerland.
Type set in Garamond by
Dix Type Inc., Syracuse, New York.
Printed and bound in Japan.

Published June 29, 1979
Reprinted eight times
Tenth Printing, October 1988

Library of Congress Catalog Card
Number 78-20383
ISBN 0-394-50432-1

CONTENTS

THE AUDUBON SOCIETY FIELD GUIDE SERIES

Also available in this unique all-color, all-photographic format:

Birds (*Eastern Region*)

Birds (*Western Region*)

Butterflies

Fishes, Whales, and Dolphins

Fossils

Insects and Spiders

Mammals

Mushrooms

Reptiles and Amphibians

Rocks and Minerals

Seashells

Seashore Creatures

Trees (*Eastern Region*)

Trees (*Western Region*)

Wildflowers (*Western Region*)

THE AUDUBON SOCIETY

The National Audubon Society is among the oldest and largest private conservation organizations in the world. With over 560,000 members and more than 500 local chapters across the country, the Society works in behalf of our natural heritage through environmental education and conservation action. It protects wildlife in more than seventy sanctuaries from coast to coast. It also operates outdoor education centers and ecology workshops and publishes the prizewinning AUDUBON magazine, AMERICAN BIRDS magazine, newsletters, films, and other educational materials. For further information regarding membership in the Society, write to the National Audubon Society, 950 Third Avenue, New York, New York 10022.

AUTHORS

William A. Niering is Katharine Blunt Professor of Botany at Connecticut College, New London, and Director of the Connecticut Arboretum. He has written many technical and popular articles on flowers and other ecological subjects and is the author of a book, *The Life of the Marsh*.

Nancy C. Olmstead is Research Associate at the Connecticut Arboretum and has been co-author of several Connecticut Arboretum bulletins on tidal marshes and estuaries.

ACKNOWLEDGMENTS

This book has evolved with the aid of many references and the invaluable assistance of numerous persons. The deep interest and involvement of Harry Ahles in checking the species identification and reading the text has greatly enhanced the quality of this guide. We also wish to acknowledge the continued assistance of Richard Spellenberg, author of the Western Wildflowers, for contributing to the overall organization and writing the family descriptions and glossary. The assistance of Catherine Niering in typing much of the manuscript is also acknowledged.

It has been a great pleasure to work with the staff of Chanticleer Press. We would especially like to thank Paul Steiner and Gudrun Buettner for their most helpful contributions and guidance. The dedication of Susan Rayfield has been invaluable, as well as the continued support and encouragement of Milton Rugoff. The efforts of others who added immeasurably to this work—Carol Nehring, Richard Christopher, Mary Beth Brewer, Helga Lose and Ray Patient—are also acknowledged with our deepest appreciation.

William A. Niering, Nancy C. Olmstead

INTRODUCTION

In the past decade there has been a tremendous increase in interest in the natural world. We have come to realize that we are part of a much larger sphere of life and that we share this fragile planet with a diversity of other living forms. Some of these, the wildflowers are among the most beautiful of nature's works. The reader need not have access to a natural area to begin observing and identifying some of the more common ones. A lawn, a city sidewalk, or a vacant lot often provides a rich display of interesting species. Since several thousand species of flowering plants occur within this ecologically diverse region, even such an ample guide as this can only include those species most typical or representative.

Nonetheless, we have attempted to represent not only most of the common wildflowers of the forests and grasslands but some subtropical flora as well. We also include many so-called weeds of lawn and garden and many of the showy or more interesting vines and shrubs. Though few wildflower books cover grass-like plants, we describe some distinctive grasses, sedges, and rushes, to acquaint our readers with these interesting, perhaps less showy yet often common, flowering plants.

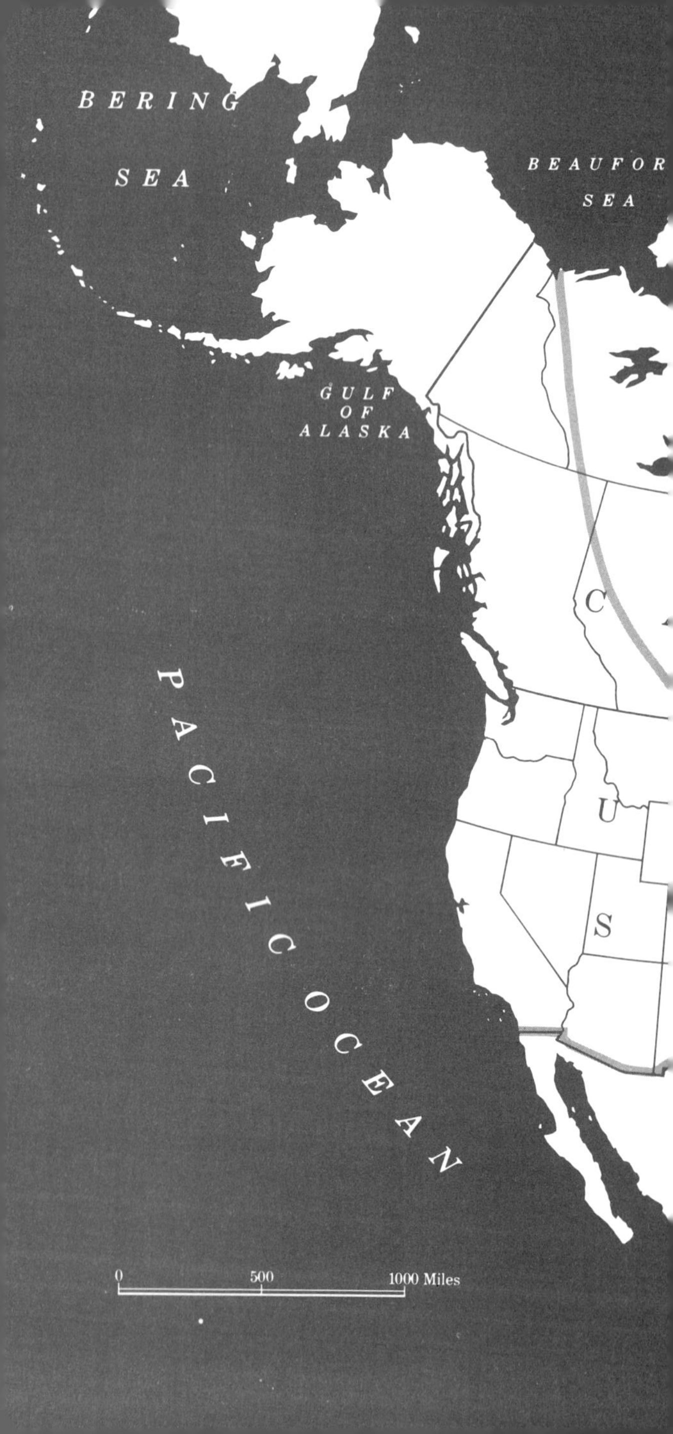
BERING
SEA
BEAUFOR
SEA
GULF
OF
ALASKA
C
U
S
PACIFIC OCEAN
0
500
1000 Miles

There is also some attempt to sample flowers from such less familiar habitats as bogs and alpine zones.

An effective aid in examining a flower more closely is a hand lens. With it you will become aware of the microscopic beauty and perfection of many flowers, such as the Common Dandelion or roadside Chicory.

Geographic Scope:
Many field guides covering the Eastern and Western United States have arbitrarily used the 100th meridian as a dividing line between the two regions. We have chosen, instead, what we consider a somewhat more natural boundary (see map), which more or less parallels this demarcation line but extends from the eastern base of the Rockies in Montana southward across Wyoming and Colorado and through western Texas.

Major Eastern Habitats:
The eastern sector includes the extensive deciduous forest region from the East Coast westward to Minnesota, eastern Iowa, southern Missouri, and eastern Texas. From the northeast the deciduous forest stretches southward through the Appalachians but is replaced on the coastal plains by extensive evergreen pine forests. The southern tip of Florida is subtropical and has many Caribbean species.

With decreasing precipitation as one moves westward, forest vegetation is replaced by grassland with a rich diversity of prairie flowers. Although sporadic remnants of tall-grass prairie occur as far east as Ohio, the vast continuous grasslands begin in Kansas and Oklahoma. As aridity increases to the west, tall-grass prairie tends to give way to mid-height grasses and, ultimately, to short-grass plains near the Rocky Mountains.

Photographs:
Many flower books are illustrated with drawings or paintings, but we have

chosen to use color photographs because they show flowers as you see them in nature, rather than as interpreted by an artist. In using the work of America's leading wildflower photographers, we believe we are adding an exciting new dimension to what generally appears in guides as drawings. A good photograph captures the natural color of a wildflower in its natural setting, making identification that much easier. Finally there is the beauty itself of pictures taken by outstanding photographers: this guide is meant to be a delight to look at as well as use. In selecting the photographs, we have tended to emphasize the flowers themselves, but leaves and other identifying features are also shown in many instances. Where useful, a number of line drawings are included among the text descriptions.

Captions: The caption under each photograph gives the common name of the flower and height data for the plant. It also gives one of the following flower dimensions: the average flower width (*w.*) or flower length (*l.*); approximate cluster length (*cl.*) or approximate cluster width (*cw.*). [For further details, see note preceding the color plates.] This information is especially helpful where flowers are shown larger or smaller than life-size. Plant height is not given for plants classified as aquatics, epiphytes, vines, or creepers. The term "creeper" is used here not in the botanical sense of a prostrate plant rooting at the nodes but, more loosely, to describe any trailing or sprawling plant. The caption ends with the page number of the species description.

Arrangement by Color: Since most inexperienced wildflower enthusiasts notice the color of a flower first, we have grouped the flowers by color, though we realize that this, like any identification technique, has its limitations. The color groups are in the following order:

Green
White (includes Cream)
Yellow
Orange
Brown
Red
Pink (includes Lavender)
Blue (includes Purple)

Where a flower has more than one prominent color, it may be shown in two different color sections. Where a plant has a conspicuously colored or unusual fruit, the fruit may also be shown.

Flower Subgroups: Within the larger color groups, such as Yellow, we have further organized the flowers according to similar structure or form. To accomplish this, we have devised seven basic subgroups: Simple-shaped flowers; Daisy- and Dandelion-like Flowers; Odd-shaped Flowers; Elongated Clusters; Rounded Clusters; Vines and Shrubs; Seeds and Fruit. These subgroups will be described in more detail later in this Introduction.

Flower Types: If one looks directly into the face of a flower, its overall symmetry is evident.

Those with 4 or 5 or more petals radiating in a wheel-like fashion are referred to as regular or radially symmetrical flowers (a). When divided in half, such a flower always separates into two equal parts. In contrast, a

bilaterally symmetrical flower (b), often called irregular, usually has a lip, and will yield two equal parts only if divided along one particular axis.

Flower Parts: Most flowers consist of four parts: the outer green sepals; the showy, colored petals; the pollen-bearing stamens; and the pistil, or pistils, at the center of the flower. Sometimes the sepals are petal-like and true petals are absent. Collectively, the sepals are called the calyx, and the petals are the corolla. In some flowers the petals may be separate; that is, one petal may be removed without removing the others. In another type (e.g., an Orchid), all the petals may be fused, so that the entire set of petals is removed if one attempts to pull off a single lobe of the corolla.

The stamen, or male part of a flower, usually consists of a pronounced stalk or filament with a small pollen-bearing body, the anther. When the anther breaks open, wind or insects facilitate pollination—the carrying of pollen from the anther to the tip of a pistil. The pistil, the seed-bearing organ, usually consists of a tip, called the stigma, which intercepts the pollen; a neck, or style; and a lower portion, the ovary. Within the ovary are produced tiny ovules which, following fertilization, will form the seeds. The ovary matures into a dry or fleshy fruit. The floral parts may be attached at the top of the ovary ("inferior position") or at its base ("superior position").

Flower Forms: Flowers are borne in various forms. In one type, such as the Daisy Family, many individual florets are arranged in a head, and a set of ray or strap-like flowers radiates from, or encloses, a set of disk or tubular flowers in the center. Around the outside of the head, green bracts make up the involucre. Various flowers may be borne separately (solitary form), in elongated spikes, in rounded clusters, or in varied types of inflorescences. Some are borne in such a distinctive manner they can be distinguished by their flower cluster alone. An example of this is the Carrot Family, in which all the flowers originate from one point at the end of the floral stalk—an arrangement known

Parts of a Flower

Petal
Pistil
stigma
style
ovary
Sepal

Stamen
anther
filament

Disk Flower   Ray Flower

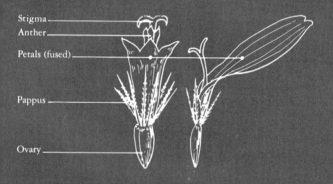

Stigma
Anther
Petals (fused)
Pappus
Ovary

Composite Flower

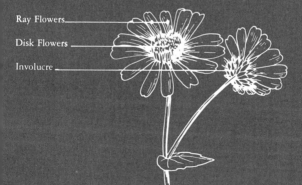

Ray Flowers
Disk Flowers
Involucre

Arum

Spathe

Spadix

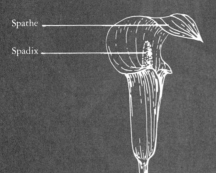

Pea Flower

Banner

Wing

Keel

Iris

Standard (petal)

Petal-like Style

Crest

Fall (sepal)

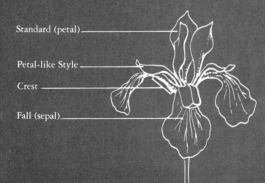

Cluster Types

Umbel

Corymb

Cyme

Panicle

Raceme

Spike

as an umbel. Such commonly used botanical terms are defined in the Glossary and appear in labeled drawings.

Leaves: The leaf form of wildflowers may be highly variable. Many wildflowers have underground stems, and only their leaves rise above the ground in spring; these are referred to as basal leaves. Leaves may be simple or compound. Simple leaves have a single blade and stalk (or petiole); compound leaves have a set of leaflets that may be organized in two rows (pinnately compound) or radiate like a fan (palmately compound). Sometimes a compound leaf is further compounded. The margins (edges) of a leaf are also highly variable, ranging from smooth to toothed or lobed. Similarly, leaf textures may be thin, thick, smooth or hairy. Leaves can be arranged opposite each other along the stem or, more commonly, alternately. If three or more leaves are arranged in a ring around the stem, they are said to be whorled. If the leaf arrangement is not mentioned in the text, it may be assumed that it is alternate. Opposite leaf arrangement will always be indicated.

Classification and Names: Flowers are classified by families, within a family by genera, and within a genus by species. In a given family most genera and species have certain characteristics in common. For example, a member of the Mint Family can usually be recognized by its square stem, bilaterally symmetrical flowers, and minty odor. By studying family characteristics and flower structure, the reader will soon be able to recognize plants by families.

Most plant species have a common name. However, since a given plant may have several common names—or different names in different regions—it is also given a scientific name, which is the same all over the world. This

Leaf Types

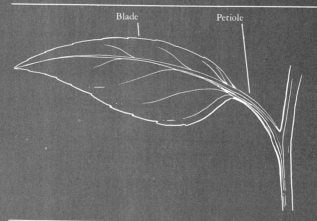

Blade   Petiole

Entire   Toothed   Lobed

Linear   Lanceolate   Ovate

Leaf Arrangements

Opposite Basal Alternate

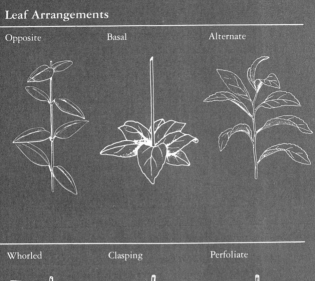

Whorled Clasping Perfoliate

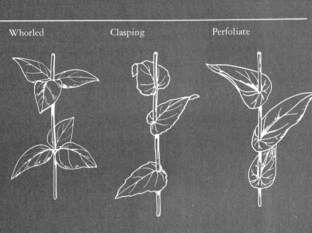

Palmate Once Pinnate Twice Pinnate

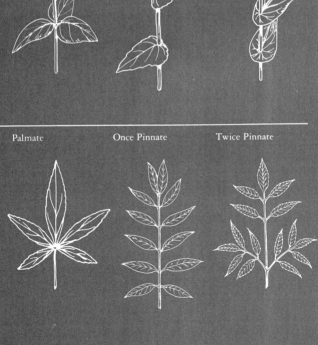

uniform system of naming all plants and animals was invented by the Swedish naturalist Carolus Linnaeus in the 18th Century; since Latin was still a language known to educated people everywhere, he gave all the scientific names a Latin form (many with descriptive Greek roots, however). Each scientific name consists first of a genus name (always capitalized), followed by a species name (lowercase). Thus, the flower with the common name Turk's-cap Lily has the scientific name *Lilium superbum*, which indicates it belongs to the genus *Lilium* and within that genus to the species *superbum*. When a genus name is followed by the abbreviation "spp.," we are referring to any one of a number of species within the genus. The scientific names generally convey information about the nature of the plant. The scientific names used here are based primarily on *Gray's Manual of Botany*, 8th edition; H. W. Rickett, *Wild Flowers of the United States*, Volume 2; and A. E. Radford, H. E. Ahles, and C. R. Bell, *Manual of the Vascular Flora of the Carolinas*.

Text
Descriptions:
The text contains descriptions of each species shown in the color plates. The species descriptions are arranged alphabetically by scientific name within genera, and the genera within families. This arrangement tends to put closely related species nearby, thus allowing for easy comparison of similar species. The following details are given in each of the species accounts:

Description:
The opening statement characterizes the main visible features of the plant, so that the user can quickly determine whether this is most likely the species being sought. This is followed by more specific details concerning the plant: its flowers, leaves, fruit, height, and sometimes other distinctive features. As an additional aid, prominent features are italicized.

Flowering: The period in which the plant blooms varies considerably, depending on climatic conditions. Also, plants of a species in southern locations tend to bloom earlier than those in more northerly sites. Therefore, we have given the overall maximum limits, which may be relevant only in certain parts of the plant's range.

Habitat: Some species are quite restricted in their habitat, the type of locale where the plant tends to occur in nature. Thus Queen Anne's Lace is found mainly in open sunny fields; Pink Lady's Slipper is typical of shady woods; and Skunk Cabbage and Marsh Marigold prefer wetlands. Knowing the typical habitat can often help in identification.

Range: The geographical range of each species is usually given from north to south, starting in Canada or the northeastern United States and moving clockwise: that is, southward, then westward, and finally northward again.

Comments: These notes give additional information about the plant, such as the origin of its names, its uses, and various other legend and lore.

Endangered Species: Many wildflowers may be picked without depleting the population; however, some groups such as Orchids and Gentians should never be picked. And no wildflower should ever be pulled out by the roots. We have indicated a few wildflowers that are presently in these categories. *Endangered and Threatened Plants of the United States* by Edward S. Ayensu and Robert A. DeFillipps, published in 1978 by the Smithsonian Institution and the World Wildlife Fund, gives the most recent survey of information concerning such flowers.

How to Find the Flower: In using this guide, first determine which of the color groups the flower belongs to.

To make it easy to locate each color group, and the shapes within the larger color groups, a thumb tab showing the color and shape is provided. Since flowers are complicated structures, if you fail to find your flower in one likely subgroup, try another subgroup in the same color category.

Turn to the plates of the appropriate color section and see if the flower matches the photograph. The small color groups—Green, Orange, and Brown—have only a few species and so are not further subdivided; they are indicated by the General Flower Thumb Tab only. The larger color groups—White, Yellow, Pink, and Blue—are further divided, according to flower or plant shape, into seven subgroups as follows:

Simple-shaped Flowers: The individual flowers tend to stand out separately; most flowers are radially symmetrical, usually with 4 or 5 petals (occasionally 3 or 6).

Daisy- and Dandelion-like Flowers: Flower head with a button-like center and many radiating, strap-like petals (actually ray flowers), or with many ray flowers and no button-like center.

Odd-shaped Flowers: Flowers or plants with an unusual overall appearance (generally bilaterally symmetrical); often difficult to classify in terms of shape.

Elongated Clusters: Elongated masses of flowers either tightly or somewhat loosely arranged along the stalk; individual flowers may be symmetrical or asymmetrical.

Rounded Clusters: Rounded masses of flowers either tightly or somewhat loosely arranged on a stalk; individual flowers may be symmetrical or asymmetrical.

Vines and Shrubs: Climbers and multistemmed woody plants.

Seeds and Fruit: The dried or fleshy reproductive parts of a flower.

If the flower and the photograph seem to match, read the caption beneath the picture and refer to the text description to confirm your identification.

An inexpensive hand lens is useful in studying the flower, and will also expand your appreciation of the minute perfection and beauty of the individual flower parts.

HOW TO USE THIS GUIDE

Example 1
Yellow Flower
in an Open Field

In an open field you have found a yellow flower that stands out by itself, is radially symmetrical, and has 5 showy yellow petal-like structures.

1. Turn to the color plate section marked *Yellow Simple-shaped Flowers*. Among the 38 photographs in this group are several Buttercups resembling your flower. The captions under the photographs give information about height, and the size of the flower or flower cluster, as well as the page numbers of the species descriptions.

2. On reading the species descriptions of the various Buttercups, you find that your plant matches the one with backward-curving sepals and that the terminal lobe of its 3-part leaf is stalked. The root, you find, is bulbous, as indicated by its common name. It is the Bulbous Buttercup, which grows in open fields.

Example 2
Yellow Flower
in a Wetland

In a wet area you have found a plant with yellow star-like flowers grouped together in an elongated cluster and with lanceolate, opposite leaves.

1. Turn to the color plates labeled *Yellow Elongated Clusters*. Among these, your flower resembles one of the Loosestrifes.

2. Turn to the descriptions of the various species of Loosestrife. There you find that the description of Swamp Candles matches your example.

Example 3 In a moist, wooded area you have found
Red Berry-like a bright red, berry-like fruit on a plant
Fruit in Moist growing close to the ground with
Woods round, shiny green, opposite leaves.

1. Turn to the color plates labeled *Red
   Seeds and Fruit*. Among the many plants
   with red berry-like fruits in this
   section, only two are labeled as *creepers:*
   the Partridgeberry and the Cranberry.
   Closer examination of the photographs
   shows that only the Partridgeberry has
   round, shiny green, opposite leaves.
2. Reading the species description
   confirms your identification.

Part I
Color Plates

Key to the Color Plates

The color plates on the following pages
are divided into eight color groups:

Green
White (includes Cream)
Yellow
Orange
Brown
Red
Pink (includes Lavender)
Blue (includes Purple)

Within the larger color groups—
White, Yellow, Pink, and Blue—the
flowers are further divided by shape and
form into seven subgroups:

Simple-shaped Flowers
Daisy- and Dandelion-like Flowers
Odd-shaped Flowers
Elongated Clusters
Rounded Clusters
Vines and Shrubs
Seeds and Fruit

Thumb Tabs Each subgroup is indicated by a colored
symbol on a thumb tab at the left edge
of each double-page of plates. The
smaller color groups—Green, Orange,
Brown, and Red—are represented by
the General Flower Thumb Tab, with
the Red color group having an
additional thumb tab for seeds and
fruit.

Symbol	Subgroup

Simple-shaped Flowers

The individual flowers tend to stand out separately; most flowers are radially symmetrical, usually with 4–5 petals (occasionally 3 or 6).

Daisy- and Dandelion-like Flowers

Flower head with a button-like center and many radiating, strap-like petals (actually ray flowers), or with many ray flowers and no button-like center.

Odd-shaped Flowers

Flowers or plants with an unusual overall appearance (generally bilaterally symmetrical); often difficult to classify in terms of shape.

Elongated Clusters

Elongated masses of flowers either tightly or somewhat loosely arranged along the stalk; individual flowers may be symmetrical or asymmetrical.

Rounded Clusters

Rounded masses of flowers either tightly or somewhat loosely arranged on a stalk; individual flowers may be symmetrical or asymmetrical.

Examples

Wood Poppy

Violet

Trillium

Daisy

Hawkweed

Dandelion

Iris

Clover

Bellwort

Goldenrod

Larkspur

Blazing Star

Milkweed

Queen Anne's Lace

Mint

Symbol	Subgroup

Vines and Shrubs

Climbers and multistemmed woody plants.

Seeds and Fruit

The dried or fleshy reproductive parts of a flower.

General Flower Thumb Tab

Used for the Green, Orange, Brown, and Red color groups. Whenever possible, the flowers and fruit within these groups are arranged according to similar shapes.

Examples

Dodder

Rhododendron

Honeysuckle

Bittersweet Berries

Dandelion Seeds

Milkweed Pod

How to Read the Captions under the Plates

Example:

274   Downy Yellow Violet, 6–16″, *w.* ¾″, *p. 821*

1— 2———————————— 3—— 4—— 5——

w. (width)	refers to average *width* of the flower. In Sunflowers or Clovers it is the width of the entire flower head.
l. (length)	refers to average *length* of the flower. Given for some tubular and pendant flowers as well as some extremely recurved flowers where the length of the flower in profile is its most noticeable dimension. In Sunflowers and Clovers it is the length of the entire flower head.
cw. (cluster width)	refers to range of *cluster width*. Given for broad clusters, usually umbels, compound umbels, corymbs and cymes.
cl. (cluster length)	refers to range of *cluster length*. Given for elongated clusters, usually spikes, racemes and panicles.

1 Plate number.
2 Common name of plant.
3 Height of typical mature plant. Usually a range is given; if only one figure is shown, it refers to maximum height.
4 Dimensions of the flower (see chart below).
5 Page number of species description.

Sunflower

Lily

Bunchberry
(bracts conspicuous)

Coneflower

Orchid (lip)

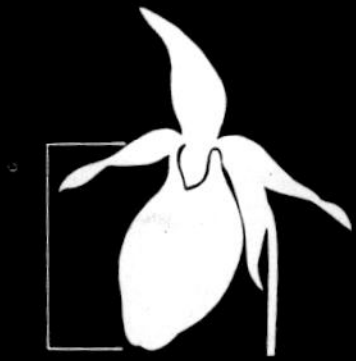

Bellwort

Dwarf Ginseng

Queen Anne's Lace

Sensitive Brier

Smartweed

False Hellebore

White Sweet Clover

1   Ginseng, 8–24″, *cw.* ½–¾″, *p. 346*

2   Wild Sarsaparilla, 8–15″, *cw.* 1½–2″, *p. 345*

3   Indian Cucumber Root, 1–2½′, *l.* ½″, *p.* 604

4   Smooth Solomon's Seal, 8–36″, *l.* ⅔″, *p.* 605

5 Alumroot, 2–3′, *l.* ¼″, *p.* 777

6 Bluebead Lily, 6–15″, *l.* 1″, *p.* 597

7   Greenfly Orchid, 2½–16″, *w.* ⅓″, *p. 654*

8   Ragged Fringed Orchid, 1–2′, *l.* ½″, *p. 658*

9   Jack-in-the-pulpit, 1–3′, *cl.* 2–3″, *p. 340*

10   Water Lettuce, *aquatic, p. 343*

11 Arrow Arum, *aquatic, cl. 4–7", p. 343*

12 Green Dragon, 1–3', *cl. 4–8", p. 340*

13   Water Pennywort, *creeper, w. ¹⁄₁₆″, p. 332*

14   Swamp Saxifrage, *1–3′, w. ¹⁄₆″, p. 780*

15 Thorny Pigweed, 1–4′, *cl.* 5–6″, *p. 320*

16 Black Snakeroot, 2–6′, *cl.* ½–¼″, *p. 322*

17 Ditch Stonecrop, 8–24″, *w.* ⅙″, *p. 479*

18 Green Violet, 1–3′, *l.* ¼″, *p. 817*

19 Lamb's Quarters, 1–6′, *w.* ¹⁄₁₆″, *p. 464*

20 Marijuana, 3–10′, *w.* ⅛″, *p. 443*

21 Clearweed, 4–20″, *l.* ⅙″, *p. 812*

22 Stinging Nettle, 2–4′, *l.* 1/12″, *p. 813*

23 Wood Nettle, 1½–4′, *l.* ⅙″, *p. 812*

24 False Nettle, 1½–3′, *l.* 1/12″, *p. 811*

25 Great Ragweed, 2–15′, *cl.* 1–10″, *p. 356*

26 Common Ragweed, 1–5′, *cl.* 1–6″, *p. 355*

27 False Hellebore, 2–7′, *cl.* 8–20″, *p. 614*

28 Pigweed, 2–4′, *cl.* 2–2½″, *p. 319*

29 Kentucky Bluegrass, 1–3′, *cl.* 5–6″ *p. 691*

30 Wool Grass, 3–5′, *cw.* 3–6″, *p. 485*

31 Smooth Crabgrass, 6–16″, *cl.* 3–4″, *p. 687*

32 Timothy, 1½–3′, *cl.* 6–7″, *p. 689*

33 Common Plantain, 6–18″, *cl.* 1–8″, *p. 681*

34 Slender Glasswort, 6–18″, *cw.* 1/16–1/8″, *p. 465*

35   Staghorn Sumac, 3–30′, *cl.* 7–8″, *p. 326*

36   Smooth Sumac, 2–10′, *cl.* 3–5″, *p. 325*

37   Winged Sumac, 3–30′, *cl.* 5–6″, *p. 324*

38 Virgin's Bower, *vine, cw.* 2–2½", *p. 733*

39 Spanish Moss, *epiphyte, l.* ½", *p. 434*

40 Carrion Flower, *vine, cw.* ½–1½", *p. 606*

41   Bur Reed, 1–3′, *cw.* ¾–1½″, *p. 807*

42   Rattlesnake Master, 2–6′, *cw.* ¼–¾″, *p. 330*

43   Bur Cucumber, *vine, l. 1–2″, p. 481*

44   Cocklebur, 1–6′, *l. 1″, p. 411*

45   Diapensia, 1–3″, *w.* ½″, *p. 488*

46   Pyxie, *creeper, w.* ¼″, *p. 489*

47   Mountain Sandwort, 2–5″, *w.* ½″, *p. 454*

48   Chickweed, 3–8″, *w.* ¼″, *p. 461*

49   Mouse-ear Chickweed, 6–12″, *w.* ¼″, *p. 455*

50   Star Chickweed, 6–16″, *w.* ½″, *p. 462*

51 Whitlow Grass, 8″, w. ⅙″, p. 429

52 Oconee Bells, 2–8″, w. 1″, p. 490

53 Bloodroot, 10″, w. 1½″, p. 674

54 Wood Anemone, *4–8″, w. 1″, p. 728*

55 Rue Anemone, *4–8″, w. 1″, p. 729*

56 False Rue Anemone, *4–16″, w. ½″, p. 737*

57 Swamp Dewberry, *creeper, w. ¾", p. 758*

58 Common Strawberry, *creeper, w. ¾", p. 749*

59 False Violet, *creeper, w. ½", p. 748*

60 Bunchberry, 3–8″, *w.* 1½″, *p.* 477

61 Starflower, 4–8″, *w.* ½″, *p.* 721

62 Goldthread, 3–6″, *w.* ¼″, *p.* 733

63 Round-leaved Sundew, 4–9″, *w.* ¼″, *p. 495*

64 Canada Violet, 8–16″, *w.* 1″, *p. 818*

65 Sweet White Violet, 3–5″, *w.* ½″, *p. 818*

66　Thimbleweed, 2–3′, *w.* 1″, *p. 728*

67　Spotted Wintergreen, 3–9″, *w.* ⅔″, *p. 722*

68　One-flowered Cancer Root, 3–10″, *l.* ¾″, *p. 665*

69 Evening Lychnis, 1–3′, *w*. 1″, *p. 456*

70 Starry Campion, 2–3′, *w*. ¾″, *p. 460*

71 Bladder Campion, 8–30″, *w*. 1″, *p. 460*

72 Cheeses, *creeper, w. ½", p. 629*

73 Grass-of-Parnassus, *6–20", w. 1", p. 778*

74 Partridgeberry, *creeper, l. ⅔", p. 766*

75 Nodding Trillium, 6–24″, *w.* 1½″, *p. 609*

76 Painted Trillium, 8–20″, *w.* 2¼″, *p. 612*

77 Large-flowered Trillium, 8–18″, *w.* 3″, *p. 610*

78 Cranberry, *creeper*, l. ½″, p. 509

79 Common Nightshade, 1–2½′, *w.* ⅓″, p. 804

80 Horse Nettle, 1–3′, *w.* 1″, p. 805

81 Floating Hearts, *aquatic, w.* ⅔", *p. 547*

82 Fragrant Water Lily, *aquatic, w.* 4", *p. 639*

83 Carolina Anemone, 4–10", *w.* 1½", *p. 726*

84 White Prickly Poppy, 1–3′, *w.* 3″, *p. 670*

85 Easter Lily, 1′, *w.* 3½″, *p. 323*

86 Jimsonweed, 1–5′, *w.* 3½″, *p. 802*

87   Mayapple, 12–18″, *w*. 2″, *p*. 417

88   Twinleaf, 5–10″, *w*. 1″, *p*. 417

89   Bowman's Root, 2–3′, w. 1½″, p. 751

90   Swamp Lily, 3′, w. 4″, p. 321

91   Oxeye Daisy, 1–3′, *w.* 1¾″, *p.* 371

92   Mayweed, 1–2′, *w.* 1″, *p.* 357

93   Daisy Fleabane, 1–5′ *w*. ½″, *p*. 376

94   Common Fleabane, 6–36″, *w*. ¾″, *p*. 377

95   Shepherd's Needle, 1–3′, *w.* 1″, *p.* 369

96   Salt-marsh Aster, 1–2′, *w.* 1″, *p.* 365

97   White Wood Aster, 1–3′, *w.* 1″, *p. 359*

98   Flat-topped White Aster, 1–7′, *w.* ⅔″, *p. 365*

99 Panicled Aster, 2–5′, *w.* 1″, *p. 363*

100 Bushy Aster, 1–3′, *w.* ¾″, *p. 359*

101   Small-flowered White Aster, 2–5′, *w.* ⅓″, *p.* 367

102   Calico Aster, 1–5′, *w.* ½″, *p.* 361

103   White-topped Sedge, 8–24″, *w.* 3″, *p.* 484

104   Spider Lily, 1½′, *w.* 7″, *p.* 322

105 Showy Orchis, 5–12″, *l.* 1″, *p. 660*

106 Nodding Mandarin, 8–24″, *l.* 1″, *p. 598*

White Odd-shaped Flowers

107 English Plantain, 6–20″, *cw.* ½–¾″, *p. 680*

108 Common Pipewort, *aquatic, cw.* ¼–½″, *p. 511*

109 Water Arum, *aquatic, cl.* ¾–1″, *p. 341*

110 Featherfoil, *aquatic, cw.* 1–1½″, *p. 716*

111   Lawn Orchid, 2–7″, *l.* ¼″, *p.* 663

112   Indian Pipe, 3–9″, *l.* ¾″, *p.* 635

113   Turtlehead, 1–3′, *l.* 1¼″, *p.* 786

114   Dutchman's Breeches, 4–12″, *l.* ¾″, *p.* 672

115 Smooth Solomon's Seal, 8–36″, *l.* ⅔″, *p.* 605

116 Cow Wheat, 6–18″, *l.* ½″, *p.* 790

117 Goldenseal, 1–1¼′, *w.* ½″, *p.* 736

118 **Prairie Acacia,** 1–5′, *cw.* ½–¾″, *p. 517*

119 **Prairie Mimosa,** 2–4′, *cw.* ¼–½″, *p. 527*

120 **White Clover,** *creeper,* *w.* ¾″, *p. 542*

121   Lizard's Tail, 2–5′, *cl.* 5–6″, *p. 775*

122   False Solomon's Seal, 1–3′, *cl.* 2–3″, *p. 605*

123   Foamflower, 6–12″, *cl.* 2–3″, *p. 781*

124 Devil's Bit, 1–4', *cl.* 4–5", *p.* 596

125 Canada Mayflower, 2–6", *cl.* 1½–2", *p.* 603

126 Thyme-leaved Speedwell, 2–10", *cl.* ⅛", *p.* 800

127 Colicroot, 1–3′, *cl.* 4–8″, *p. 591*

128 Rattlesnake Plantain, 18″, *cl.* 2–5″, *p. 654*

129 Miterwort, 8–18″, *cl.* 3–5″, *p. 777*

130 Beetleweed, 1–2½′, *cl.* 3–4″, *p. 489*

131 Nodding Ladies' Tresses, 6–24″, *cl.* 2–4″, *p. 662*

132 Shinleaf, 5–10″, *cl.* 2–4″, *p. 723*

133   Culver's Root, 3–6′, *cl.* 4–8″, *p. 800*

134   Black Cohosh, 3–8′, *cl.* 1–2½′, *p. 731*

135 White Sweet Clover, 3–8′, *cl.* 7–8″, *p. 534*

136 Camas, 1–4′, *cl.* 3–5″, *p. 616*

137 Death Camas, 1–2½′, *w.* ½″, *p.* 617

138 Fly Poison, 1–4′, *w.* ½″, *p.* 595

139 Turkey Beard, 2–4′, *w.* ½″, *p. 614*

140 Yucca, 2–10′, *w.* 1½″, *p. 615*

141   Canadian Burnet, 1–5′, *cl.* 5–6″ *p.* 760

142   Featherbells, 3–5′, *cl.* 1–2′, *p.* 607

143   Pokeweed, 10′, w. ¼″, p. 679

144   Spring Cress, 6–24″, w. ½″, p. 428

145   Lopseed, 1–3′, *l.* ¼″, *p.* 678

146   Prairie False Indigo, 2–5′, *l.* 1″, *p.* 522

147   Vervain, 2–4′, *w.* ¼″, *p. 815*

148   Illinois Tick Trefoil, 2–5′, *l.* ½″, *p. 528*

149   Arrowhead, *aquatic*, w. ⅔", p. 318

150   Moth Mullein, 2–4', w. 1", p. 797

151 White Fringed Orchid, 1–2′, *l.* 1½″, *p.* 655

152 Prairie Larkspur, 1–3′, *l.* 1″, *p.* 735

153 Goatsbeard, 3–6′, *w*. ⅙″, *p.* 747

154 False Goatsbeard, 2–6′, *l*. ⅙″, *p.* 776

155   Silverrod, 1–3′, *l.* ¼″, *p. 401*

156   Horseweed, 1–7′, *w.* ¼″, *p. 377*

157   Wild Leek, 6–20″, *cw.* 1–1½″, *p. 594*

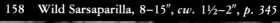

158   Wild Sarsaparilla, 8–15″, *cw.* 1½–2″, *p. 345*

159   Early Saxifrage, 4–16″, *cw.* 1–2″, *p. 781*

160 Dwarf Ginseng, 4–8″, *cw.* ½″, *p. 347*

161 Red Baneberry, 1–2′, *cw.* 1–1½″, *p. 726*

162 White Baneberry, 1–2′, *cw.* ½–¾″, *p. 725*

163   Bouncing Bet, 1–2½', *w.* 1", *p. 458*

164   Cut-leaved Toothwort, 8–16", *w.* ¾", *p. 428*

165   Tread-softly, 6–36", *w.* 1", *p. 512*

166　Virginia Waterleaf, 1–2½′, *l.* ⅓″, *p.* 555

167　White Lettuce, 2–5′, *l.* ½″, *p.* 397

168　Early Meadow Rue, 8–30″, *l.* ¼″, *p.* 741

169   Sweet Cicely, 1½–3′, *w.* ¹⁄₁₆″, *p. 332*

170   Enchanter's Nightshade, 1–3′, *w.* ¼″, *p. 640*

171   Cleavers, *creeper, w.* 1/8″, *p. 764*

172   Pennywort, 3–6″, *l.* 1/2″, *p. 547*

173 Shepherd's Purse, 6–18″, *cw.* ¾–1″, *p.* 427

174 Peppergrass, 6–24″, *cw.* ¼–½″, *p.* 430

175 Honewort, 1–3′, *w.* ⅛″, *p. 329*

176 Venus Flytrap, 4–12″, *w.* 1″, *p. 491*

177   Lyre-leaved Rock Cress, 4–16″, *w.* ¼″, *p. 424*

178   True Watercress, *aquatic, cw.* ½–¾″, *p. 430*

179   White-flowered Gilia, 1–2′, *l.* 2″, *p. 694*

180 Bastard Toadflax, 6–16″, *w.* ¹⁄₆″, *p. 769*

181 Wild Madder, 1–3′, *w.* ⅙″, *p. 765*

182 Northern Snow Bedstraw, 8–36″, *w.* ¼″, *p. 764*

183 Catnip, 1–3′, *cl.* ¾–2½″, *p.* 577

184 Water Horehound, 6–24″, *cl.* ¼″–½″, *p.* 573

185   Hoary Mountain Mint, 1–3′, *cw.* 1½″, *p.* 579

186   Wild Mint, 1–2′, *w.* ⅛″, *p.* 574

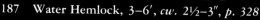

187 Water Hemlock, 3–6′, *cw.* 2½–3″, *p. 328*

188 Water Parsnip, 2–6′, *cw.* 2–3″, *p. 333*

189   White Snakeroot, 1–3′, *cw.* 1½–2″, *p. 379*

190   White Milkweed, 1–3′, *cw.* 2½–3″, *p. 352*

191 Queen Anne's Lace, 1–3′, *cw.* 3–5″, *p.* 330

192 Yarrow, 1–3′, *cw.* 2–3″, *p.* 354

193   Cow Parsnip, 4–9′, *cw.* 4–8″, *p. 331*

194   B   3–6′   6–5″   *p. 370*

White Rounded Clusters

195   Smaller Pussytoes, 6–18″, *cw.* 1–2″, *p.* 357

196   Pearly Everlasting, 1–3′, *cw.* 3–4″, *p.* 356

197   Sweet Everlasting, 1–2′, *cw.* 2–4″, *p.* 381

198 Flowering Spurge, 10–36″, *w.* ⅜″, *p. 513*

199 Water Plantain, *aquatic,* *w.* ⅙″, *p. 317*

200 Tall Meadow Rue, 2–8′, *w.* ½″, *p. 742*

201   Japanese Honeysuckle, *vine, l.* 1½", *p. 445*

202   Dodder, *vine, w.* ⅛", *p. 473*

203   Climbing Boneset, *vine, cw.* ¾–1¼", *p. 396*

204 Common Moonseed, *vine, cl.* ¾–1″, *p. 633*

205 Bur Cucumber, *vine, w.* ⅔″, *p. 481*

206 Virgin's Bower, *vine, w.* 1″, *p. 733*

207   Tartarian Honeysuckle, 4–10′, *l.* ¾″, *p. 447*

208   Swamp Honeysuckle, 3–9′, *l.* 1¾″, *p. 508*

209   Labrador Tea, 1–4′, *cw.* ¾–1″, *p. 501*

210   **Great Laurel,** 5–35′, *w.* 1¾″, *p.* 506

211   **Multiflora Rose,** 6–15′, *w.* 1¼″, *p.* 755

212   **Mountain Laurel,** 3–15′, *w.* ¾″, *p.* 500

213 Arrowwood, 3–15′, *cw.* 2–3″, *p. 452*

214 Maple-leaved Viburnum, 3–6′, *cw.* 2–3″, *p. 450*

215 Hobblebush, 3–10′, *cw.* 2–6″, *p. 451*

216　Witherod, 3–12′, *cw.* 3–4″, *p. 452*

217　Elderberry, 3–12′, *cw.* 2–10″, *p. 447*

218　Red Chokeberry, 3–12′, *cw.* ¾–2″, *p. 754*

219 **Meadowsweet**, 2–5′, *cl.* 4–7″, *p.* 760

220 **Groundsel Tree**, 6–9′, *l.* ½″, *p.* 367

221 Sweet Pepperbush, 3–10′, *cl.* 2–8″, *p. 468*

222 Titi, 25′, *cl.* 2½–6″, *p. 487*

223 Japanese Bamboo, 3–7′, *cl. 2–3″, p. 706*

224 Poison Ivy, *vine, cl. 1–3″, p. 325*

225 New Jersey Tea, 3–4′, *cw. ¼–½″, p. 744*

226   Winterberry, 3–10′, *cw.* ¼–½″, *p. 337*

227   Buttonbush, 3–10′, *cw.* 1–1½″, *p. 763*

228   Maleberry, 3–12′, *w.* ⅛″, *p. 503*

229   Teaberry, *creeper, l. ⅓", p. 499*

230   Bearberry, *creeper, l. ⅕", p. 496*

231 Leatherleaf, 1–4′, *l.* ¼″, *p. 497*

232 Highbush Blueberry, 5–15′, *l.* ⅓″, *p. 508*

233 Tawny Cotton Grass, 1½–4′, *w.* 1″, *p. 484*

234 Common Milkweed, 2–6′, *p. 351*

235   Common Dandelion, 2–18″, *w.* 1½″, *p. 408*

236   Oyster Plant, 2–4′, *w.* 3″, *p. 409*

237 Red Osier, 3–10', *p. 478*

238 White Baneberry, 1–2', *p. 725*

239 Mistletoe, 1′, *p. 621*

240 Snowberry, 1–4′, *p. 449*

241 Many-spined Opuntia, 2–24″, *w.* 3″, *p.* 436

242 Prickly Pear, 2–12″, *w.* 2–3″, *p.* 436

243 Rafinesque's Prickly Pear, 2–24″, *w.* 2½″, *p.* 437

244 Yellow Pond Lily, *aquatic, w. 2″, p.* 637

245 American Lotus, *aquatic, w. 8″, p.* 636

246 Yellow Water Lily, *aquatic, w. 4½″, p.* 638

247 Rough-fruited Cinquefoil, 1–2′, *w.* ¾″, *p.* 753

248 Punctureweed, *creeper, w.* ½″, *p.* 825

249 Silverweed, *creeper, w.* 1″, *p.* 752

250   Dwarf Cinquefoil, ½–2″, *w.* ⅓″, *p. 754*

251   Indian Strawberry, *creeper, w.* ¾″, *p. 748*

252   Canadian Dwarf Cinquefoil, 2–6″, *w.* ½″, *p. 752*

253   Wood Poppy, 1–1½', *w.* 1¾", *p.* 675

254   Celandine, 1–2', *w.* ⅔", *p.* 671

255   Globeflower, 12–20", *w.* 1¼", *p.* 743

256   Velvetleaf, 1–6′, *w.* 1″, *p. 625*

257   Seedbox, 2–3′, *w.* ½″, *p. 643*

258   Frostweed, 8–18″, *w.* 1″, *p. 466*

259 Kidneyleaf Buttercup, 6–24″, *w.* ¼″, *p.* 738

260 Yellow Water Buttercup, *aquatic, w.* 1″, *p.* 740

261 Moneywort, *creeper, w.* 1″, *p.* 718

262 Bulbous Buttercup, 1–2′, *w.* 1″, *p.* 739

263 Swamp Buttercup, 1–3′, *w.* 1″, *p.* 741

264 Common Buttercup, 2–3′, *w.* 1″, *p.* 738

265   Yellow Wood Sorrel, 6–15″, *w.* ½″, *p. 667*

266   Purslane, *creeper, w.* ¼″, *p. 713*

267   Muskflower, 8–16″, *l.* ¾″, *p. 791*

268   Pineweed, 4–20″, w. ⅛″, p. 559

269   Yellow-eyed Grass, 2–3′, w. ½″, p. 823

270   Yellow Star Grass, 3–6″, w. ¾″, p. 322

271 Swollen Bladderwort, *aquatic, w. ⅔", p. 589*

272 Yellow Butterwort, 5–18", *w.* 1", p. 587

273   Clammy Ground Cherry, 1–3′, *w.* ¾″, *p.* 803

274   Downy Yellow Violet, 6–16″, *w.* ¾″, *p.* 821

275 Barren Strawberry, 3–8″, *w*. ½″, *p*. 762

276 Marsh Marigold, 1–2′, *w*. 1¼″, *p*. 730

277   Canada Lily, 2–5′, *w.* 2½″, *p.* 600

278   Trout Lily, 4–10″, *w.* 1″, *p.* 598

279   Sneezeweed, 2–5', *w.* 1½", *p. 383*

280   Prairie Coneflower, 1½–5', *l.* 2", *p. 398*

281   Black-eyed Susan, 1–3′, *w.* 2½″, *p.* 399

282   Garden Coreopsis, 2–4′, *w.* 1¼″, *p.* 376

283 Jerusalem Artichoke, 5–10′, *w.* 3″, *p.* 386

284 Giant Sunflower, 3–12′, *w.* 2″, *p.* 384

285   Woodland Sunflower, 3–7', *w.* 3", *p.* 385

286   Common Sunflower, 3–10', *w.* 4½", *p.* 383

287 Tickseed Sunflower, 1–5′, *w.* 1½″, *p. 368*

288 Nodding Bur Marigold, 1–3′, *w.* 2″, *p. 369*

289   Golden Ragwort, 1–2′, *w*. ¾″, *p. 399*

290   Maximilian's Sunflower, 3–10′, *w*. 2½″, *p. 385*

291   Camphorweed, 1–3′, *w.* ⅔″, *p.* 387

292   Hairy Golden Aster, 1–2′, *w.* 1″, *p.* 372

293 Compass Plant, 3–12′, *w.* 3″, *p. 400*

294 Lance-leaved Coreopsis, 1–2′, *w.* 2½″, *p. 375*

295   Yellow Goatsbeard, 1–3′, *w.* 2″, *p. 408*

296   Elecampane, 2–6′, *w.* 3″, *p. 390*

297   Coltsfoot, 3–18″, *w.* 1″, *p. 410*

298 Gumweed, 6–36″, *w. 1″, p. 381*

299 Spiny-leaved Sow Thistle, 1–6′, *w. 1″, p. 406*

300 Wild Lettuce, 2–10′, *w. ¼″, p. 391*

301   Rattlesnake Weed, 1–2½′, *w.* ⅔″, *p. 389*

302   Mouse-ear Hawkweed, 3–12′, *w.* 1″, *p. 388*

303   Two-flowered Cynthia, 1–2′, *w.* 1½″, *p. 391*

304   **Prickly Lettuce,** 2–5′, *w.* ¼″, *p. 393*

305   **Common Dandelion,** 2–18″, *w.* 1½″, *p. 408*

306   **Yellow Hawkweed,** 1–3′, *w.* ½″, *p. 389*

307   Squawroot, 3–10″, *cl.* 2–8″, *p. 664*

308   Golden Club, *aquatic, cl.* 1–2″, *p. 342*

309   Common Cattail, 3–9′, *cl.* 5–6″, *p. 809*

310   Sweetflag, *aquatic, cl.* 2–3½″, *p. 339*

311 Hooded Pitcher Plant, 6–24″, *w.* 2″, *p.* 773

312 Trumpets, 1½–3½′, *w.* 4″, *p.* 771

313   Horned Bladderwort, 2–12″, *l.* ¾″, *p. 588*

314   Yellow Flag, 2–3′, *w.* 3″, *p. 564*

315 Pale Touch-me-not, 3–6′, *l.* 1½″, *p.* 414

316 Hop Clover, 6–18″, *w.* 1″, *p.* 540

317 Yellow Thistle, 1–5′, *w.* 2½″, *p.* 374

318 Wild Oats, 6–12″, *l.* 1″, *p. 613*

319 Small Whorled Pogonia, 4–10″, *l.* ¾″, *p. 659*

320 Yellow Lady's Slipper, 4–28″, *l.* 2″, *p. 652*

321   Garden Loosestrife, 2–3′, *w.* ¾″, *p.* 719

322   Whorled Loosestrife, 1–3′, *w.* ½″, *p.* 719

323   Agrimony, 1–6′, *w.* ¼″, *p. 746*

324   Swamp Candles, 1–3′, *w.* ½″, *p. 720*

325   Prince's Plume, 1–4′, *cl.* 3–6″, *p. 432*

326   Yellow Sweet Clover, 2–5′, *cl.* 2–6″, *p. 534*

327   Showy Rattlebox, 2–3′, *l.* 1″, *p. 526*

328   Wild Indigo, 3′, *l.* ½″, *p. 522*

329   Horse Balm, 2–4′, *l.* ½″, *p. 570*

330   Wild Senna, 3–6′, *w.* ¾″, *p. 523*

331 Butter-and-eggs, 1–3′, *l.* 1″, *p. 789*

332 Yellow Rattlebox, 4–32″, *l.* ½″, *p. 795*

333   Downy False Foxglove, 1–5′, *w.* 1″, *p.* 785

334   Smooth False Foxglove, 1–5′, *w.* ¾″, *p.* 784

335   Moth Mullein, *2–4′, w. 1″, p. 797*

336   Common Mullein, *2–6′, w. 1″, p. 798*

337 Blue-stemmed Goldenrod, 1–3′, *l.* ¼″, *p. 402*

338 Seaside Goldenrod, 1–8′, *l.* ⅓″, *p. 405*

339 Lance-leaved Goldenrod, 2–4′, *l.* ⅕″, *p. 403*

340 Stiff Goldenrod, 1–5′, *l.* ⅓″, *p. 404*

341 Showy Goldenrod, 2–7′, *l.* ¼″, *p. 406*

342 Sweet Goldenrod, 2–3′, *l.* ⅙″, *p. 403*

343　Tall Goldenrod, 2–7′, *l.* ⅛″, *p. 401*

344　Rough-stemmed Goldenrod, 1–6′, *l.* ⅙″, *p. 404*

345   Common Winter Cress, 1–2′, *cw.* 1–1½″, *p. 425*

346   Black Mustard, 2–3′, *cw.* ¼ – ½″, *p. 426*

347   Hedge Mustard, 1–1⅔′, *cw.* ½–¾″, *p. 431*

348 Yellow Milkwort, 5–16″, *cw.* 5–6″, *p. 701*

349 Golden Alexanders, 1–3′, *cw.* 1½–2″, *p. 334*

350 Cypress Spurge, 6–12″, *cw.* 1–1½″, *p. 513*

351 St. Peterswort, 1–3′, *w.* 1″, *p.* 560

352 Common St. Johnswort, 1–2½′, *w.* ¾″, *p.* 558

353 Fringed Loosestrife, 1–4′, *w.* ¾″, *p.* 717

354 Evening Primrose, 2–5', *w.* 1½", *p.* 644

355 Common Tansy, 2–3', *w.* ½", *p.* 407

356 Birdsfoot Trefoil, 6–24", *l.* ½", *p.* 531

357   Yellow Jessamine, *vine, w.* 1″, *p. 619*

358   Bush Honeysuckle, *4–5′, l.* ¾″, *p. 444*

359 Witch Hazel, 10–15′, *cw.* 1–2″, *p. 553*

360 Japanese Honeysuckle, *vine, l.* 1½″, *p. 445*

361 Kalm's St. Johnswort, 2–3′, *w.* 1″, *p.* 557

362 Common Barberry, 3–10′, *cl.* 1–2″, *p.* 415

363 Beach Heath, 3–8″, *w.* ¼″, *p.* 467

364 **Pussy Willow,** 2–20′, *l.* 2″, *p. 768*

365 **Spicebush,** 6–17′, *cw.* ½–¾″, *p. 585*

366 **Broom Snakeweed,** 6–20″, *w.* ¼″, *p. 382*

367   Turk's-cap Lily, 3–7′, *l.* 2½″, *p. 602*

368   Canada Lily, 2–5′, *w.* 2½″, *p. 600*

369 Blackberry Lily, 1½–4′, w. 2″, p. 562

370 Day Lily, 2–4′, w. 3½″, p. 600

371   Wood Lily, *1–3′, w. 2″, p. 601*

372   Carolina Mallow, *creeper, w. ½″, p. 629*

373   Scarlet Pimpernel, *4–12″, w. ¼″, p. 715*

374 Orange Hawkweed, 1–2′, *w.* ¾″, *p. 387*

375 Hoary Puccoon, 6–18″, *w.* ½″, *p. 421*

376 Spotted Touch-me-not, 2–5′, *l.* 1″, *p. 413*

377   Orange Milkwort, 6–12″, *cw.* ½–¾″, *p. 700*

378   Yellow Fringed Orchid, 1–2½′, *l.* ¾″, *p. 656*

379   Butterfly Weed, 1–2½′, *cw.* 1½–2″, *p. 352* °

380 Flame Azalea, *15', w. 2", p. 504*

381 Trumpet Creeper, *vine, l. 2½", p. 419*

382 Climbing Bittersweet, *vine, p. 463*

383   Toadshade, 4–12″, *l.* 1½″, *p. 611*

384   Purple Trillium, 8–16″, *w.* 2½″, *p. 610*

385   Red Iris, 2–5′, *w.* 3″, *p. 563*

386 Wild Ginger, 6–12″, *w.* 1½″, *p. 349*

387 Dutchman's Pipe, *vine, l.* 2″, *p. 348*

388 Blue Cohosh, 1–3′, *w.* ½″, *p. 416*

389 Maryland Figwort, 3–8′, *l.* ¼″, *p.* 796

390 Jack-in-the-pulpit, 1–3′, *cl.* 2–3″, *p.* 340

391 Skunk Cabbage, 1–2′, *cl.* 3–6″, *p.* 344

392   Spotted Coralroot, 6–20″, *l.* ¾″, *p.* 649

393   Beechdrops, 6–18″, *l.* ½″, *p.* 665

394   Large Twayblade, 4–10″, *l.* ½″, *p.* 659

395   Soft Rush, 1½–4′, *cw.* 1–1½″, *p. 568*

396   Shining Cyperus, 4–16″, *cw.* ¾–1″, *p. 483*

397   Wood Rush, 6–16″, *cw.* ¾–1½″, *p. 569*

398 Grama Grass, 6–20″, *cl.* 1½–2″, *p.* 687

399 Sweet Vernal Grass, 12–28″, *cl.* 2½–3″, *p.* 686

400 Little Bluestem Grass, 1½–4½′, *cl.* 2–2½″, *p.* 685

401 Indian Grass, 3–8′, *cl.* 9–10″, *p.* 692

402 Barnyard Grass, 6–48″, *cl.* 4–12″, *p.* 688

403   Redtop, 8–30″, *cl.* 8–9″, *p. 684*

404   Bottlebrush Grass, 2–5′, *cl.* 9–10″, *p. 689*

405 Sea Oats, 3–7′, *cl.* 8–16″, *p.* 693

407 Leafy Three-square, 1–5′, *cw.* 1–1½″, *p.* 486

408 Prairie Smoke, 6–16″, *l.* ¾″, *p.* 750

409   Smooth Sumac, 2–10′, *cl. 3–5″, p. 325*

410   Staghorn Sumac, 3–30′, *cl. 7–8″, p. 326*

411   Winged Sumac, 3–30′, *cl. 5–6″, p. 324*

412 Groundnut, *vine, l. ½″, p. 520*

413 Seedbox, *2–3′, p. 643*

414 Poison Sumac, *6–20′, p. 327*

415 Fire Pink, 6–24″, *w.* 1½″, *p.* 461

416 Maltese Cross, 2–3′, *w.* 1″, *p.* 457

417 Annual Phlox, 8–18″, *w.* 1″, *p.* 696

418　Small Red Morning Glory, *vine, w.* ¾″, *p. 474*

419　Indian Blanket, 8–16″, *w.* 2″, *p. 380*

420　Hibiscus, 3–10′, *w.* 7″, *p. 626*

421   Pinesap, 4–16″, *l.* ½″, *p. 634*

422   Striped Coralroot, 8–20″, *l.* 1¼″, *p. 650*

423 Northern Pitcher Plant, 8–24", *w.* 2", *p.* 773

424 Crimson Pitcher Plant, 2–3', *w.* 2½", *p.* 772

425 Indian Pink, 1–2′, *w.* 1″, *p. 620*

426 Wild Columbine, 1–2′, *l.* 1½″, *p. 730*

427 Wild Coffee, 2–4', *l.* ¾", *p.* 449

428 Scarlet Gilia, 2–6', *l.* 1", *p.* 695

429   Salvia, 1–2′, *l.* 1″, *p.* 580

430   Cardinal Flower, 2–4′, *l.* 1½″, *p.* 439

431 Trumpet Honeysuckle, *vine, l. 1½", p. 446*

432 Coral Bean, *2–5', l. 2", p. 529*

433   Indian Paintbrush, 1–2′, *l.* 1″, *p.* 785

434   Bee Balm, 2–5′, *cw.* 2–3½″, *p.* 575

435 Wild Poinsettia, 2–3′, *cw.* ¾–1″, *p.* 514

436 Wood Betony, 6–18″, *cw.* 1–2″, *p.* 792

437 Slender Glasswort, 6–18″, *cw.* ⅟₁₆–⅛″, *p. 465*

438 Wild Pine, 1–2′, *epiphyte, cl.* 3–6″, *p. 433*

439 Curly Dock, 2–4′, *cw.* 1½–2½″, *p.* 709

440 Sheep Sorrel, 6–12″, *cw.* ¼–½″, *p.* 708

441 Ginseng, 8–24″, *p. 346*

442 Red Baneberry, 1–2′, *p. 726*

443 Jack-in-the-pulpit, 1–3′, *p. 340*

444 **Bearberry**, 6–12″, *p. 496*

445 **Partridgeberry**, *creeper, p. 766*

446 **Bunchberry**, 3–8″, *p. 477*

447   Red-berried Elder, 2–10′, *p. 448*

448   Bittersweet Nightshade, *vine, p. 805*

449   Crab's-eye, *vine, p. 516*

450 Yaupon, 5–15′, *p. 338*

451 Winterberry, 3–10′, *p. 337*

452 Cranberry, *creeper, p. 509*

453   Rose Moss, 2–8″, *w.* ⅔″, *p.* 714

454   Alpine Azalea, *creeper, w.* ¼″, *p.* 502

455   Purple Saxifrage, ¾–4″, *w.* ½″, *p.* 779

456 Sand Myrtle, 4–20″, *w.* ¼″, *p. 502*

457 Moss Campion, 1–3″, *w.* ½″, *p. 459*

458 Moss Phlox, *creeper, w.* ¾″, *p. 697*

459   Spring Beauty, 6–12″, *w.* ½″, *p.* 712

460   Common Wood Sorrel, 3–6″, *w.* ¾″, *p.* 668

461   Herb Robert, 1–2′, *w.* ½″, *p.* 552

462   Storksbill, 6–12″, *w.* ½″, *p. 550*

463   Violet Wood Sorrel, 4–8″, *w.* ¾″, *p. 669*

464   Round-lobed Hepatica, 4–6″, *w.* ¾″, *p. 736*

465   Hairy Willow Herb, 2–5′, *w.* 1″, *p. 642*

466   Wild Geranium, 1–2′, *w.* 1¼″, *p. 551*

467   Musk Mallow, 8–24″, *w.* 1½″, *p. 628*

468 Showy Evening Primrose, 8–24″, *w. 3″, p. 645*

469 Corn Cockle, 1–3′, *w. 2″, p. 454*

470 Swamp Rose Mallow, 3–8′, *w. 6″, p. 626*

471   Sea Rocket, 6–20″, *w. ¼″, p. 426*

472   Marsh St. Johnswort, 8–24″, *w. ⅔″, p. 561*

473   Salt-marsh Pink, 6–18″, *w.* 1″, *p. 548*

474   Deptford Pink, 6–24″, *w.* ½″, *p. 456*

475   Thread-leaved Sundew, 4–12″, w. ½″, p. 494

476   Wild Petunia, 1–2′, l. 2″, p. 316

477 Virginia Meadow Beauty, 1–2', *w.* 1¼", *p. 631*

478 Catesby's Trillium, 8–20", *w.* 2½", *p. 608*

479   New England Aster, 3–7′, *w.* 1½″, *p.* 362

480   Wavy-leaved Aster, 1–3½′, *w.* ¾″, *p.* 366

481   Showy Aster, 1–2′, *w.* 1½″, *p.* 364

482   Oyster Plant, 2–4′, *w.* 3″, *p.* 409

483   Common Fleabane, 6–36″, *w.* ¾″, *p.* 377

484   Daisy Fleabane, 1–5′, *w.* ½″, *p.* 376

485   Canada Thistle, 1–5′, *w.* 1″, *p. 373*

486   Spotted Knapweed, 2–3′, *w.* 1″, *p. 371*

487   Common Burdock, 1–5′, *w.* ¾″, *p. 358*

488 Nodding Thistle, 2–9′, *w.* 2″, *p. 370*

489 Bull Thistle, 2–6′, *w.* 1¾″, *p. 374*

490 Teasel, 2–6′, *l.* ½″, *p. 492*

491   Calypso, 3–8″, *l.* 1¾″, *p.* 648

492   Swamp Pink, 5–10″, *l.* 2″, *p.* 647

493 Pink Lady's Slipper, 6–15″, *l.* 2½″, *p. 651*

494 Showy Lady's Slipper, 1–3′, *l.* 1½″, *p. 653*

495　Rose Pogonia, 3–24″, *l.* 1¾″, *p. 661*

496　Fringed Polygala, 3–7″, *l.* ¾″, *p. 701*

497 Rosebud Orchid, 1–2′, *l.* 2″, *p. 649*

498 Grass Pink, 6–20″, *l.* 1½″, *p. 647*

499   Water Willow, 1–3', *l.* ½", *p. 315*

500   Ragged Robin, 1–3', *w.* ½", *p. 458*

501   Wild Bleeding Heart, 10–18", *l.* ¾", *p. 673*

502   Eyebright, 4–15″, *l.* ⅓″, *p. 788*

503   Three-birds Orchid, 3–12″, *l.* ¾″, *p. 662*

504   Showy Orchis, 5–12″, *l.* 1″, *p. 660*

505 Rose Twisted-stalk, 1–3′, *l.* ⅓″, *p. 608*

506 Twinflower, *creeper, l.* ½″, *p. 445*

507 Pine Hyacinth, 1–2′, *l.* 1½″, *p. 732*

508 Shooting Star, 8–20″, *l.* 1″, *p. 716*

509   Butterfly Pea, 1–3′, *l.* 2″, *p. 525*

510   Beach Pea, 1–2′, *l.* ¾″, *p. 529*

511 Wild Bergamot, 2–4′, *cw.* 2–3″, *p.* 576

512 Lyon's Turtlehead, 1–3′, *l.* 1″, *p.* 787

513　Sensitive Brier, *creeper, cw.* ¾–1″, *p. 538*

514　Swamp Pink, 1–3′, *cl.* 1–3″, *p. 599*

515　Purple Prairie Clover, 1–3′, *cl.* 2″, *p. 536*

516   Red Clover, 6–24″, *w.* ¾″, *p. 541*

517   Field Milkwort, 5–15″, *cl.* ½–¾″, *p. 702*

518   Rabbit-foot Clover, 6–18″, *l.* ¾″, *p. 541*

519   Large-flowered Beardtongue, 2–4′, *l. 2″, p. 794*

520   Purple Gerardia, 1–4′, *l. 1″, p. 783*

521   Seashore Mallow, 1–3′, *w.* 2″, *p. 627*

522   Seaside Gentian, 1–3′, *w.* 1½″, *p. 544*

523 Common Speedwell, *creeper, w.* ¹/₅″, *p. 799*

524 Goat's Rue, *1–2′, l.* ¾″, *p. 539*

525   Large Purple Fringed Orchid, 2–4′, *l.* 1″, *p.* 657

526   Locoweed, 4–12″, *l.* ¾″, *p.* 535

527   Swamp Smartweed, *aquatic, cl.* 1½–7″, *p. 705*

528   Lady's Thumb, 8–32″, *cl.* ⅔–2″, *p. 707*

529   Pennsylvania Smartweed, 4′, *cl.* ½–2½″, *p. 706*

530   Long-bristled Smartweed, 3′, *cl.* ¾–1½″, *p. 704*

531   Woolly Locoweed, 8–18″, *l.* 1″, *p. 521*

532   Hairy Vetch, 3′, *l.* ⅔″, *p. 543*

533 Showy Tick Trefoil, 2–6′, *l.* ½″, *p.* 527

534 Cow Vetch, 4′, *l.* ½″, *p.* 542

535   Wood Sage, 1–3′, *cl.* 2–6″, *p.* 583

536   Obedient Plant, 1–4′, *l.* 1″, *p.* 578

537   Plains Bee Balm, 6–12″, *cw.* 1–2″, *p.* 576

538   Slender Bush Clover, 1–3′, *cw.* ¼–½″, *p.* 531

539 Steeplebush, 2–4′, *cl.* 4–6″, *p. 761*

540 Crazyweed, 8–12″, *l.* ¾″, *p. 535*

541 Fireweed, 2–6′, *w. 1″, p. 641*

542 Purple Loosestrife, 2–4′, *w. ⅔″, p. 624*

543 Large Blazing Star, 1–5′, w. 1″, p. 395

544 Rough Blazing Star, 1⅓–4′, w. ¾″, p. 393

45 Prairie Blazing Star, 2–5′, *w.* ½″, *p. 394*

546 Dense Blazing Star, 1–6′, *w.* ¼″, *p. 395* °

547   Common Milkweed, 2–6′, *cw.* 2″, *p. 351*

548   Swamp Milkweed, 1–4′, *cw.* 1½–2″, *p. 350*

549   Garden Phlox, 2–6′, *cw.* 1½–2″, *p. 697*

550   Rose Vervain, 6–18″, *cw.* 1¼–1½″, *p. 814*

551   Autumn Wild Onion, 1–2′, *cw.* 2–2½″, *p. 593*

552   Live Forever, 8–18″, *w.* ⅓″, *p. 480*

553 Wild Garlic, 8–24″, *w.* ⅓″, *p. 592*

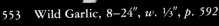

554 Nodding Wild Onion, 8–24′, *l.* ¼″, *p. 593*°

555 Hairy Beardtongue, 1–3′, *l.* 1″, *p.* 794

556 Gray Beardtongue, 1–3′, *l.* 1¼″, *p.* 793

557 Spreading Dogbane, 1–4′, *w.* ⅓″, *p. 335*

558 Wild Basil, 8–20″, *l.* ½″, *p. 581*

559 Motherwort, 2–4′, *cw.* ½–¾″, *p.* 572

560 Peppermint, 1–3′, *cw.* ½–¾″, *p.* 574

561 Wild Mint, 6–24″, *cw.* ½–¾″, *p.* 574

562 Swamp Loosestrife, 8′, *cw.* 1–1½″, *p.* 623

563   Salt-marsh Fleabane, 1–3′, *cw.* 1–2″, *p. 396*

564   Spotted Joe-Pye Weed, 2–6′, *cw.* 4–5½″, *p. 378*

565   New York Ironweed, 3–6′, *cw.* 3–4″, *p. 411*

566   Queen-of-the-Prairie, 3–6′, *cw.* 1½–2½″, *p. 750*

567 Mountain Cranberry, *creeper, l. ¼″, p. 510*

568 Trailing Arbutus, *creeper, w. ½″, p. 498*

569 Morning Honeysuckle, *2–5′, w. ¼″, p. 643*

570 Pale Corydalis, 5–24″, *l.* ½″, *p.* 671

571 Henbit, 4–16″, *l.* ⅔″, *p.* 572

572 Crown Vetch, 1–2′, *cw.* ¾–1″, *p.* 525

573   Creeping Bush Clover, *creeper, l. ¼", p. 530*

574   Spurred Butterfly Pea, *vine, l. 1¼", p. 524*

575   Hog Peanut, *vine, l.* ½″, *p. 519*

576   Kudzu Vine, *vine, l.* 1″, *p. 538*

577   Glades Morning Glory, *vine, l. 3″, p. 476*

578   Railroad Vine, *vine, l. 2″, p. 475*

579 Hedge Bindweed, *vine, l.* 2½", *p.* 472

580 Common Morning Glory, *vine, l.* 2½", *p.* 475

581   Virginia Rose, 1–6′, *w.* 2½″, *p.* 757

582   Rugosa Rose, 4–6′, *w.* 2½″, *p.* 756

583 Purple-flowering Raspberry, 3–6′, *w.* 1½″, *p.* 759

584 Prairie Rose, 2′, *w.* 2″, *p.* 757

585   Sheep Laurel, 1–3′, *w.* ½″, *p.* 499

586   Mountain Laurel, 3–15′, *w.* ¾″, *p.* 500

587   Mountain Rosebay, 3–20′, *w.* 2″, *p.* 505

588　Pinxter Flower, 2–6′, *w*. 1¾″, *p*. 507

589　Rhodora, 1–3′, *l*. ¾″, *p*. 504

590　Lapland Rosebay, 4–12″, *w*. ⅔″, *p*. 506

591   Corn Speedwell, 2–16″, *w.* ¹/₅″, *p. 798*

592   Round-lobed Hepatica, 4–6″, *w.* ¾″, *p. 736*

593 Bluets, 3–6″, *w.* ½″, *p.* 766

594 Pointed Blue-eyed Grass, 4–20″, *w.* ½″, *p.* 566

595   Dog Violet, 2–6″, *w.* ¾″, *p. 819*

596   Common Butterwort, 2–6″, *w.* ⅓″, *p. 588*

597   Common Blue Violet, 3–8″, w. ⅔″, p. 820

598   Bird-foot Violet, 4–10″, w. 1½″, p. 821

599 Periwinkle, 6–8″, *w.* 1″, *p.* 336

600 Wild Flax, 1–2′, *w.* 1¼″, *p.* 618

601 Venus's Looking-glass, 6–18″, *w.* ¾″, *p.* 442

602 Pasqueflower, 6–16″, *w.* 2½″, *p.* 727

603   New England Aster, 3–7′, *w.* 1½″, *p. 362*

604   Smooth Aster, 2–4′, *w.* 1″, *p. 360*

605　Chicory, 1–4', *w.* 1½", *p.* 372

606　Florida Lettuce, 2–7', *w.* ½", *p.* 392

607   Tall Ironweed, 3–7′, w. ¼″, p. 410

608   Stiff Aster, 8–18″, w. 1″, p. 361

609 New York Aster, 8–36″, w. 1¼″, p. 362

610 Tansyleaf Aster, 1–2′, w. 1½″, p. 364

611 Asiatic Dayflower, *creeper, w. ½″, p. 469*

612 Blue Curls, 6–30″, *l. ⅔″, p. 583*

613 Monkshood, 2–4′, *l. ¾″, p. 724*

614   Spiderwort, 8–24″, *w.* 1½″, *p. 470*

615   Pinewoods Lily, 1–2½′, *w.* 1½″, *p. 566*

616   Monkeyflower, 1–3′, *l.* 1″, *p. 791*

617   Fringed Gentian, 1–3′, *l.* 2″, *p.* 545

618   Harebell, 6–20″, *l.* ¾″, *p.* 439

619 Crested Dwarf Iris, 4–9″, *w.* 2½″, *p. 563*

620 Blue Flag, 2–3′, *w.* 3″, *p. 565*

621   Wild Hyacinth, 6–24″, *w.* 1″, *p.* 596

622   Spring Larkspur, 4–24″, *w.* ¾″, *p.* 734

623   Pickerelweed, *aquatic, cl.* 2–6″, *p. 711*

624   Water Hyacinth, *aquatic, w.* 2″, *p. 710*

625   Tall Bellflower, 2–6′, *w.* 1″, *p.* 438

626   Jacob's Ladder, 1½–3′, *w.* ¾″, *p.* 699

627   Blue Toadflax, 6–24″, *l.* ⅓″, *p. 788*

628   Lyre-leaved Sage, 1–2′, *l.* 1″, *p. 581*

629 Blue Vervain, 2–6′, *w.* ⅛″, *p. 815*

630 Viper's Bugloss, 1–2½′, *l.* ¾″, *p. 420*

631 Indigobush, 5–17′, *cl.* 3–6″, *p.* 519

632 Leadplant, 1–3′, *cl.* 3–4″, *p.* 518

633 Indian Tobacco, 1–3′, *l.* ¼″, *p.* 440

634 Spiked Lobelia, 1–4′, *l.* ½″, *p.* 441

635   Blue Salvia, 2–5′, *l.* ¾″, *p. 580*

636   Great Lobelia, 1–4′, *l.* 1″, *p. 441*

637 Silverleaf Scurf Pea, 1–2′, *l*. ⅓″, *p*. 537

638 Hyssop Skullcap, 1–2½′, *l*. 1″, *p*. 582

639   Texas Bluebonnet, 12–15″, *l.* ½″, *p.* 533

640   Wild Lupine, 8–24″, *l.* ⅔″, *p.* 532

641   Greek Valerian, 1–1½′, *w.* ½″, *p.* 698

642   True Forget-me-not, 6–24″, *cw.* ½–¾″, *p.* 422

643   Fringed Phacelia, 8–16″, *w.* ½″, *p.* 556

644   Wild Blue Phlox, 10–20″, *w.* 1″, *p.* 695

645　Blue-eyed Mary, 6–18″, *l.* ½″, *p.* 787

646　Heal-all, 6–12″, *l.* ½″, *p.* 578

647 Gray Beardtongue, 1–3′, *l.* 1¼″, *p.* 793

648 Ground Ivy, *creeper, l.* ⅔″, *p.* 571

649   Virginia Bluebells, 8–24″, *l.* 1″, *p. 421*

650   Closed Gentian, 1–2′, *l.* 1¼″, *p. 546*

651   Sea Lavender, 1–2′, *w.* ⅛″, *p. 682*

652   Passionflower, *vine, w. 2″, p. 676*

653   Bittersweet Nightshade, *vine, w. ½″, p. 805*

654   Ivy-leaved Morning Glory, *vine, w. 1½″, p. 474*

655   Carrion Flower, *vine, p. 606*

656   Pokeweed, 10′, p. 679

657 Highbush Blueberry, 5–15′, *p. 508*

658 Bluebead Lily, 6–15″, *p. 597*

The numbers preceding the species
descriptions in the following pages
correspond to the plate numbers in the
color section.

ACANTHUS FAMILY
(Acanthaceae)

Herbs or shrubs with seeds borne on characteristic hooked projection.
Flowers: often bilaterally symmetrical, with showy bracts. Corolla with 4–5 united petals, usually with 2-lobed upper lip and 3-lobed lower lip; sepals 4–5, stamens 2 or 4; all these parts attached at base of the ovary.
Leaves: simple, opposite, smoothly margined, with pale streaks or bumps.
Fruit: 2-celled capsule.
Throughout the world about 250 genera and 2,600 species are native to temperate and tropical regions. Many are cultivated as ornamentals.

499 Water Willow
(*Justicia americana*)
Acanthus Family (Acanthaceae)

Description:	An emergent water plant with *bicolored flowers* borne in dense head-like or spike-like clusters on long, slender flower stalks rising from the leaf axils. Flowers: to ½" (1.3 cm) long, 2-lipped; 3-lobed lower lip, white spotted with purple; upper lip pale violet or white, arching over the lower. Only *2 stamens, with purplish-red anthers*. Leaves: 3–6" (7.5–15 cm) long, narrow, opposite, *willow-like*. Fruit: a brown capsule. Height: 1–3' (30–90 cm).
Flowering:	June–October.
Habitat:	Margins of shallow streams, lakes, and ponds; wet shores.
Range:	Ontario and Quebec; Vermont and New York south to Georgia; west to Texas; north to Missouri, Kansas, and Wisconsin.
Comments:	This plant has underground stems and forms colonies. *J. ovata,* a similar species found from Virginia to Florida, has more loosely flowered spikes.

476 **Wild Petunia; Stalked Ruellia**
(*Ruellia pedunculata*)
Acanthus Family (Acanthaceae)

Description: Violet *trumpet-shaped flowers* rise on
short, hairy stems from the leaf axils.
Flowers: to 2″ (5 cm) long, with 5
long, narrow, *thread-like calyx lobes;*
below each flower is a pair of *leaf-like
bracts.*
Leaves: to 2″ (5 cm) long, opposite,
elliptic, short-stalked, downy.
Height: 1–2′ (30–60 cm).

Flowering: June–September.

Habitat: Rich woods, especially limestone sites.

Range: Illinois and Missouri south to Arkansas
and Louisiana; west to eastern Texas
and Oklahoma.

Comments: Seven other members of this somewhat
petunia-like genus, all typical of warm
climes, occur in our range. This one is
recognized by the long-pointed calyx
lobes and bracts under the flower.

WATER PLANTAIN FAMILY
(Alismataceae)

Aquatic or marsh herbs with long-stalked, simple basal leaves and a leafless stalk that bears whorls of small flowers in a much-branched inflorescence or raceme.
Flowers: radially symmetrical; sepals 3, green; petals 3, delicate, white or pinkish; stamens 6 to many; pistils 6 to many, separate.
Leaves: prominently veined, with bases sheathing the stem.
Fruit: hard, 1-seeded.
The family includes about 13 genera and 90 species, widely distributed in shallow freshwater or muddy habitats in warm and temperate climates.

199 Water Plantain
(*Alisma subcordatum*)
Water Plantain Family (Alismataceae)

Description: Tall, *spindly, many-branched plant* with small white (rarely pink) *flowers arranged in whorls.*
Flowers: ⅛" (4 mm) wide, with 3 petals, 3 green sepals.
Leaves: basal, 2–6" (5–15 cm) long, olive-green, distinctly veined, elliptical.
Height: 4–36" (10–90 cm).
Flowering: June–October.
Habitat: Shallow water in freshwater marshes, sluggish streams, edges of ponds and lakes.
Range: Quebec; south to New York; west to Wisconsin.
Comments: In this typical emergent aquatic plant, the lower part is often submerged, while the upper part is exposed. If leaves are submerged, they are ribbon-like, not elliptical. Submerged root-like structure is edible; it was dried and eaten by the Indians.

149 **Arrowhead**
(*Sagittaria latifolia*)
Water Plantain Family (Alismataceae)

Description: Aquatic plant with a tall stalk rising
from *large basal leaves,* with white
flowers in whorls of 3.
Flowers: ⅔″ (1.6 cm) wide, with 3
white petals, 3 sepals; 7–10 stamens.
Leaves: 2–16″ (5–40 cm) long, arrow-
shaped, vary from broad to narrow,
unlobed to lobed (with 2 long
backward-projecting lobes).
Height: 1–4′ (30–120 cm).
Flowering: July–September.
Habitat: Wet sites or shallow water along lake
and stream margins, marshes, and
swamps.
Range: Throughout.
Comments: This aquatic is closely related to Water
Plantain. Several similar species with
arrow-shaped leaves are distinguished
from one another by number of stamens
and petal size. Beneath the muck,
rhizomes produce edible starchy tubers,
utilized by ducks and muskrats and
known as "duck potatoes." Indians are
said to have opened muskrat houses to
get at their cache of roots.

AMARANTH FAMILY
(Amaranthaceae)

Mostly herbs with inconspicuous flowers, usually in spike-like or head-like clusters, often with brightly colored bracts.
Flowers: radially symmetrical, unisexual or bisexual. Calyx has 2–5 sepals, often scaly and brightly colored; petals absent; stamens 5 or fewer; all these parts attached at base of the ovary.
Leaves: simple, alternate or opposite.
Fruit: 1-seeded.
The family includes about 60 genera and 900 species; most are abundant in warm regions. Some with conspicuous colored bracts, such as Cockscomb (*Celosia*), are cultivated; others may be considered troublesome, allergy-causing weeds.

28 Pigweed; Green Amaranth
(*Amaranthus retroflexus*)
Amaranth Family (Amaranthaceae)

Description: Rough, hairy stem bears clusters of tiny greenish flowers.
Flowers: on terminal spikes to 2½" (6.3 cm) long and in axillary clusters, intermingled with elongate, bristle-like bracts.
Leaves: 3–6" (7.5–15 cm) long, oval to lanceolate, stalked and untoothed.
Height: 2–4' (60–120 cm).
Flowering: August–October.
Habitat: Waste ground, roadsides, cultivated soil.
Range: Throughout.
Comments: The growth of these generally unattractive "Pigweeds" is prolific over a broad range of habitats.

15 **Thorny Pigweed**
(Amaranthus spinosus)
Amaranth Family (Amaranthaceae)

Description: Tiny yellow-green flowers on a stout,
much-branched, *reddish stem*.
Flowers: the male mostly in slender
terminal spikes up to 6″ (15 cm) long,
the female mostly in dense, globular
clusters; *intermingled with bristly bracts* a
long as the sepals.
Leaves: 1–3″ (2.5–7.5 cm) long, ovate
to lanceolate, with a *pair of rigid spines*
in each leaf axil.
Height: 1–4′ (30–120 cm).
Flowering: July–October.
Habitat: Waste places, disturbed ground,
cultivated soil.
Range: New England south to Florida; west
along Gulf Coast to Mexico; north to
Minnesota.
Comments: Amaranths, though regarded as
common weeds, produce tremendous
numbers of seeds, and are an important
food for many songbirds.

AMARYLLIS FAMILY
(Amaryllidaceae)

Herbs or (rarely) woody plants, growing from bulbs or underground stems, with narrow basal leaves and a long, leafless flowering stalk.
Flowers: radially symmetrical; sepals 3 and petals 3, colored alike and united below into a tube, sometimes with additional parts in the center forming a crown; stamens 6; all these parts attached above the ovary.
Leaves: grass-like or rigid blades, sharply pointed and with teeth along edges.
Fruit: capsule or berry.
Members of this family are mostly native of tropical and warm regions. About 86 genera and 1,300 species exist; among them, Daffodils, Jonquils, and Amaryllis are highly prized ornamentals.

---

90 **Swamp Lily**
(*Crinum americanum*)
Amaryllis Family (Amaryllidaceae)

Description: Small cluster of fragrant, *stringy white flowers* on a leafless stalk which rises from basal leaves.
Flowers: 4″ (10 cm) wide; 6 narrow, petal-like lobes attached to a long green floral tube; stamens 6, *reddish-purple filaments*.
Leaves: to 4′ (1.2 m) long, 1–3″ (2.5–7.5 cm) wide, strap-like.
Height: to 3′ (90 cm).
Flowering: Periodically throughout the year, chiefly spring–fall.
Habitat: Marshes and stream banks.
Range: Along coastal plain, Florida to Texas.
Comments: Despite its common name, this beautiful flower is not a true Lily but a member of the Amaryllis Family. Its floral parts are attached above the ovary rather than below as in Lilies.

104 Spider Lily
(*Hymenocallis liriosme*)
Amaryllis Family (Amaryllidaceae)

Description: Few *spidery white flowers* borne on 2-edged stalk above basal leaves.
Flowers: to 7″ (17.5 cm) wide, each a long slender tube with 6 radiating lobe (comprising 3 petals and 3 petal-like sepals), inside which is a cup, or crown of white gauzy tissue from which 6 stamens issue.
Leaves: to ½″ (1.3 cm) wide, 1′ (30 cm) or more long, strap-like, deeply grooved.
Height: 1½′ (45 cm).
Flowering: March–May.
Habitat: Marshes, ditches.
Range: Louisiana west to Texas.
Comments: A showy southern member of the Amaryllis Family whose cup-like structure, the "hymen" or membrane, from which the stamens arise, is distinctive, as is the spidery appearance of the long, narrow petaloid parts. The species name means "fragrant lily." In the southeastern United States, 11 species of *Hymenocallis* occur.

270 Yellow Star Grass
(*Hypoxis hirsuta*)
Amaryllis Family (Amaryllidaceae)

Description: Small grass-like plant with *star-shaped yellow flowers* (often in threes) at the tip of a hairy stem.
Flowers: ¾″ (2 cm) wide; 6-pointed, 3 petals and 3 sepals similar, 6 stamens.
Leaves: 4–12″ (10–30 cm) long, basal, narrow, hairy, grass-like.
Height: 3–6″ (7.5–15 cm).
Flowering: March–September.
Habitat: Open woods and dry meadows.
Range: Maine south to Florida; west to Texas; north to North Dakota.
Comments: This small plant, which contrasts sharply with the large, showy Amaryllis

of the same family, can easily be
confused with a grass unless its
distinctive flower is seen.

85 Easter Lily; Atamasco Lily; Zephyr Lily
(*Zephyranthes atamasco*)
Amaryllis Family (Amaryllidaceae)

Description: From an underground bulb grow
several flat leaves; leafless flowerstalk,
usually single and about as tall as the
leaves, bears *white lily-like flower,* tinged
with pink.
Flowers: 3½″ (9 cm) wide; 6 petaloid
parts, widest toward the tip, curving
outward slightly; stamens shorter than
style.
Leaves: to 14″ (35 cm) long, basal,
narrow, sharp-edged.
Height: to 1′ (30 cm).

Flowering: April–June.

Habitat: Rich woods and damp clearings.

Range: Virginia south to Florida; west to
Mississippi.

Comments: The generic name alludes to Zephyrus,
in Greek myth the west wind and
husband of Chloris, goddess of flowers.
Blooming generally around Eastertime,
they are popularly known as Easter
Lilies. The species name, derived from
an Indian word meaning "stained with
red," describes the parti-colored flower.
The leaves and bulbs are poisonous, as
are the bulbs of many members of the
Amaryllis Family.

CASHEW OR SUMAC FAMILY
(Anacardiaceae)

Shrubs or small trees with resinous or milky juice.

Flowers: small, bisexual or unisexual, mostly radially symmetrical; usually sepals 5, petals 5, and stamens 5 or 10; all these parts attached at base of the ovary.

Leaves: alternate, simple or pinnately compound.

Fruit: berry-like.

The family consists of about 60 genera and 400 species, mostly in the tropics but also in temperate regions. Some species are grown as ornamentals for landscape decoration, and some for their nuts. Others, such as Poison Ivy, contain a volatile oil that can cause severe skin irritation.

37, 411 Winged Sumac
(*Rhus copallina*)
Cashew Family (Anacardiaceae)

Description: A shrub or small tree with hairy twigs, milky sap, and small greenish flowers.
Flowers: clusters to 6" (15 cm) long, dense pyramidal, terminal.
Leaves: hairy, pinnately compound, with *winged midrib* between untoothed shiny leaflets 3" (7.5 cm) long.
Fruit: berry-like, reddish-brown, covered with short hairs.
Height: 3–30' (90–900 cm).
Flowering: July–September.
Habitat: Dry woods and clearings.
Range: New York south to Florida; west to Texas; north to Kansas and Wisconsin.
Comments: Like the Smooth (*R. glabra*) and Staghorn (*R. typhina*) Sumacs, this plant is cropped by deer and moose. The fruits are rich in Vitamin A and, though apparently not much relished by birds, are a valuable food source in winter when other fruits are scarce.

36, 409 Smooth Sumac
(*Rhus glabra*)
Cashew Family (Anacardiaceae)

Description: Shrub with *whitish bloom on its smooth
twigs,* bearing small yellowish-green
flowers.
Flowers: clusters 3–5" (7.5–12.5 cm)
long, pyramidal arrangement, terminal.
Leaves: compound, pinnately divided
into numerous sharply toothed leaflets,
each 2–4" (5–10 cm) long.
Fruit: berry-like, reddish-brown,
velvety, and clustered.
Height: 2–10' (60–300 cm).
Flowering: June–July.
Habitat: Dry soil.
Range: Throughout.
Comments: The Fragrant Sumac (*R. aromatica*) has
only 3 leaflets, bears brilliant red fruits,
and occurs from southeastern Quebec
and western Vermont south to
northwest Florida, west to eastern
Texas, and north to Nebraska. *R.
michauxii,* a southern species (southern
North Carolina to Georgia), resembles a
dwarf *R. typhina,* but its leaflets are
green and downy on the underside.

224 Poison Ivy
(*Rhus radicans*)
Cashew Family (Anacardiaceae)

Description: Upright, climbing, or trailing shrub
that bears small yellowish-white flower
clusters; old stems, covered with fibrous
roots, look hairy.
Flowers: ⅛" (3 mm) wide, in loose
clusters 1–3" (2.5–7.5 cm) long at
lower leaf axils.
Leaves: compound, divided into 3 *glossy
or dull green leaflets,* each 2–4" (5–10
cm) long.
Fruit: to ¼" (6 mm) wide, *clustered,
white,* berry-like.
Height: vine.
Flowering: May–July. Fruit appears August–

November, persisting through winter.

Habitat: Open woods, thickets, fence rows, roadsides, and waste places.

Range: Throughout.

Comments: All parts of plant contain volatile oil that can cause severe skin inflammation, itching, and blistering on direct contact or if borne by sooty smoke. Washing thoroughly with soap or swabbing with alcohol immediately on exposure removes oil irritant. The plant is extremely variable in form, occurring as a ground cover along roadsides, an erect shrub (especially in sandy coastal areas), or a large vine on trees. Red fall foliage is especially conspicuous. Valuable winter forage for wildlife, its fruits are eaten by many songbirds and game birds with no harmful effects.

35, 410 Staghorn Sumac
(*Rhus typhina*)
Cashew Family (Anacardiaceae)

Description: Shrub or small tree with *branches and twigs covered with velvety hairs* and small green flowers in terminal clusters.
Flowers: clusters to 8″ (20 cm) long, pyramidal.
Leaves: compound, with opposite, lanceolate, toothed leaflets 2–5″ (5–12.5 cm) long, dark green above, paler below.
Fruit: berry-like, reddish-brown, *covered with bright red hairs*.
Height: 3–30′ (90–900 cm).

Flowering: June–July.

Habitat: Fields, clearings, dry ground.

Range: Ontario and Nova Scotia; New England south to North Carolina, and in mountain regions to Georgia; west to Kentucky, Illinois, Iowa; north to Canada.

Comments: Soft hairy covering on the branches, resembling that on a deer's antlers when "in velvet," accounts for the common name. Species name indicates supposed resemblance of the branches to Cattails (*Typha* spp.). Its bark and leaves are a source of tannin, and the downy fruits are eaten by many songbirds and game birds, particularly in winter.

414 Poison Sumac
(*Rhus vernix*)
Cashew Family (Anacardiaceae)

Description: The smooth, gray, black-speckled branches of this *poisonous tall shrub or small tree* bear small, yellowish-green flowers on purplish leafstalks, in loose clusters arising from lower leaf axils.
Flowers: less than ⅛" (4 mm) long.
Leaves: to 1' (30 cm) long, with 7–13 pointed leaflets, *not toothed.*
Fruit: whitish, berry-like, in clusters.
Height: 6–20' (1.8–6 m).

Flowering: May–July.

Habitat: Swamps.

Range: Ontario and Quebec; New England south to Florida; west to eastern Texas; north to Minnesota.

Comments: Touching this poisonous plant can result in serious skin irritation, with inflammation, itching, and blistering. The shrubs, easily recognized by their whitish fruit and restriction to wet sites, are a valuable winter food source for many songbirds and game birds, since their fruits persist when other food is scarce.

CARROT OR PARSLEY FAMILY
(Apiaceae or Umbelliferae)

Usually aromatic herbs with hollow stems and fern-like leaves. Small flowers in umbels, further grouped into a compound umbel.
Flowers: radially symmetrical, with those near edge of the compound umbel sometimes bilaterally symmetrical; sepals 5 small; petals 5; stamens 5; all these parts attached at top of the ovary.
Leaves: alternate, pinnately compound.
Fruit: splits into 2 halves, each 1-seeded.
About 300 genera and 3,000 species, mostly in the Northern Hemisphere. Nearly a quarter of genera are native to the United States, with several large genera in the West. The family is important for such foods as carrots, parsnips, and celery and such spices and seasonings as coriander seeds, caraway, anise, parsley, and dill. Some native species are very poisonous.

187 **Water Hemlock**
(*Cicuta maculata*)
Parsley Family (Apiaceae)

Description: Smooth, erect, highly branched plant bearing dome-shaped, loose clusters of small white flowers. The sturdy *stem is magenta-streaked.*
Flowers: florets about ⅙″ (4 mm) long; no bracts beneath flattened umbels, 3″ (7.5 cm) wide.
Leaves: lower ones to 1′ (30 cm) long, doubly divided, sharp-pointed, toothed, *veins ending at notches between the teeth.*
Fruit: round, flat, with thick ridges.
Height: 3–6′ (90–180 cm).
Flowering: June–September.
Habitat: Wet meadows, thickets, freshwater swamps.
Range: Southern Ontario to Nova Scotia; south

through New England to Florida; west to Texas; north through Missouri to Canada.

Comments: Only a very small quantity of this *highly poisonous* plant can cause death. Its roots have been mistaken for parsnips and other common root crops, with fatal results; cattle, horses, and sheep have died from grazing on it. The plant is not related to true Hemlock (*Tsuga* spp.), but to Poison Hemlock (*Conium maculatum*), the plant used to poison Socrates. In our range it grows as an introduced species, which has a more finely cut compound leaf.

175 Honewort; Wild Chervil
(*Cryptotaenia canadensis*)
Parsley Family (Apiaceae)

Description: Small uneven clusters of tiny white flowers, borne on stalks of varying lengths.
Flowers: florets about ⅛″ (3 mm) wide, lacking visible sepals, clusters of variable size.
Leaves: 3–6″ (7.5–15 cm) long, palmately divided into 3 toothed leaflets, often lobed.
Fruit: blackish, oblong, *ribbed*.
Height: 1–3′ (30–90 cm).
Flowering: June–September.
Habitat: Moist woods, thickets.
Range: Manitoba to New Brunswick; south from New England to Georgia; west to Texas; north through Nebraska and beyond.
Comments: Honewort, though not a showy wildflower because of its minute, irregularly clustered florets, does have sizable distinctive fruits. Its young leaves and stems may be used as a seasoning like parsley or as a boiled green; the roots may be cooked and eaten like parsnips.

191 **Queen Anne's Lace; Wild Carrot**
(*Daucus carota*)
Parsley Family (Apiaceae)

Description: Plant having lacy, flat-topped clusters
of tiny cream-white flowers, with one
dark *reddish-brown floret* usually at center
of umbel.
Flowers: in clusters (compound
umbels) 3–5" (7.5–12.5 cm) wide,
with stiff *3-forked,* leaf-like bracts
below.
Leaves: 2–8" (5–20 cm) long, very
finely cut, fern-like.
Fruit: *bristly,* not barbed; umbels curled
inward, forming "bird's nest."
Height: 1–3' (30–90 cm).
Flowering: May–October.
Habitat: Dry fields, waste places.
Range: Throughout.
Comments: An attractive, hairy biennial, wild
carrot is considered a troublesome
weed. It was the ancestor of the garden
carrot, and its long, first-year taproot
can be cooked and eaten. The plant has
been reproduced from one embryonic
cell in tissue culture and has actually
flowered, with even the usual central
red floret present.

42 **Rattlesnake Master**
(*Eryngium yuccifolium*)
Carrot Family (Apiaceae)

Description: Smooth, rigid stem bearing thistle-like
flower heads made up of small greenish-
white florets mingled with pointed
bracts.
Flowers: head ¾" (2 cm) wide, slightly
ovoid, surrounded by larger pointed
bracts.
Leaves: to 3' (90 cm) long, linear,
sharp-pointed, parallel-veined, bristly
clasping stem.
Height: 2–6' (60–180 cm).
Flowering: July–August.
Habitat: Prairies, open woods, and thickets.

Range: Southern Connecticut south to Florida; west to Texas and Kansas; north to Minnesota, Wisconsin, and Michigan.

Comments: Their spiny leaves make walking through clumps of these plants difficult, and also make them unpalatable to grazing livestock. They were once credited with a variety of curative powers. Their flower heads develop a bluish cast with maturity.

193 Cow Parsnip
(*Heracleum lanatum*)
Parsley Family (Apiaceae)

Description: This very tall plant has huge leaves and flat clusters of numerous white flowers; stem is grooved, woolly, and hollow.
Flowers: to ½″ (1.3 cm) wide, in clusters 4–8″ (10–20 cm) wide; asymmetrical notched petals, often tinged with purple.
Leaves: *in 3 segments,* each 3–6″ (7.5–15 cm) wide, lobed and toothed, the whole leaf with *inflated sheath* at base of stalk.
Fruit: broad, flat, oval.
Height: 4–9′ (1.2–2.7 m).

Flowering: June–August.

Habitat: Moist ground.

Range: Across Canada; south from New England to mountains of Georgia; west to Missouri, Kansas, and beyond.

Comments: The young stems and the roots of this plant can be cooked and eaten, but because the flowers resemble those of Water Hemlock (*Cicuta maculata*), which is extremely poisonous, great care must be taken in identifying it.

13 Water Pennywort
(*Hydrocotyle americana*)
Parsley Family (Apiaceae)

Description: Creeping or weakly erect marsh plant
with clusters of tiny greenish-white
flowers arising from the leaf axils.
Flowers: about ⅟₁₆″ (1.5 mm) wide,
5-parted, in clusters of 1–5.
Leaves: ½–1¾″ (1.3–4.4 cm) wide,
roundish, doubly scalloped, deep basal
notch.
Height: *creeper,* with runners arising
from leaf axils.

Flowering: June–September.

Habitat: Damp woods, meadows.

Range: Newfoundland and Nova Scotia; south
through New England to Maryland and
upland North Carolina; west to
Tennessee; northwesterly to Minnesota.

Comments: There are numerous species of
Pennyworts in our range. Their
distinctive, rounded, "penny-like"
leaves, on stems that creep or float,
account for their popular name.

169 Sweet Cicely
(*Osmorhiza claytoni*)
Parsley Family (Apiaceae)

Description: Sparse, flat-topped clusters of this hairy
plant have small white flowers.
Flowers: less than ⅟₁₆″ (1.6 mm) wide,
5-petaled.
Leaves: alternate, fern-like, divided
into blunt-toothed or lobed leaflets
⅔–3½″ (1.6–9 cm) long.
Fruit: tapered, blackish, covered with
stiff, clinging hairs; style short,
persistent.
Height: 1½–3′ (45–90 cm).

Flowering: May–June.

Habitat: Woods.

Range: Saskatchewan to Nova Scotia; south
through New England to Georgia; west
to Texas; north to Kansas and Missouri.

Comments: The roots of this plant have a licorice-like odor when bruised. Several species of this genus occur in our range, among them Aniseroot (*O. longistylis*).

16 Black Snakeroot
(Sanicula canadensis)
Parsley Family (Apiaceae)

Description: Inconspicuous greenish flowers bloom in small clusters on stalks of differing lengths.
Flowers: sepals ¹⁄₁₂″ (2 mm) long, narrow, lanceolate, exceeding tiny white petals; leafy bracts beneath *uneven umbels.*
Leaves: *palmately divided* into 3–5 wedge-shaped to narrow oblong leaflets, to 3″ (7.5 cm) long, *sharply toothed.*
Fruit: small, oval, covered with hooked bristles.
Height: 1–4′ (30–120 cm).
Flowering: May–July.
Habitat: Dry open woods.
Range: New Hampshire and Massachusetts; south to Florida; west to Texas and Oklahoma; north through Missouri to southern Minnesota.
Comments: The generic name of this widely distributed species, derived from the Latin *sanare* ("to heal"), refers to some once-reputed medicinal powers of the plant. Several closely related species are distinguished only by minor traits.

188 Water Parsnip
(Sium suave)
Parsley Family (Apiaceae)

Description: Fragrant, sometimes aquatic plant with flat clusters of tiny dull-white flowers and strongly ridged stems.
Flowers: in clusters (compound umbels) 2–3″ (5–7.5 cm) wide, with *narrow, leaf-like bracts below umbels.*
Leaves: 4–10″ (10–25 cm) long,

pinnately compound; divided into 3–7 pairs of lanceolate, toothed leaflets, with basal ones often submerged and finely cut, 2½–5½" (6.3–14 cm) long. Fruit: tiny, ovate, with prominent ribs. Height: 2–6' (60–180 cm).

Flowering: July–September.

Habitat: Wet meadows and thickets, muddy shores.

Range: Throughout.

Comments: The roots of this plant can be boiled and eaten as a cooked vegetable, but because of the plant's resemblance to the deadly Water Hemlock (*Cicuta maculata*) they are best left alone.

349   Golden Alexanders
(*Zizia aurea*)
Parsley Family (Apiaceae)

Description: The plant bears flat-topped clusters of small bright yellow flowers, the middle flower of each umbel being stalkless. Flowers: in clusters (compound umbels), about 2" (5 cm) wide. Leaves: twice divided, with usually 3–7 long, pointed, *toothed leaflets,* each 1–2" (2.5–5 cm) long. Height: 1–3' (30–90 cm).

Flowering: April–June.

Habitat: Meadows, shores, moist woods and thickets.

Range: Saskatchewan to New Brunswick; south to Georgia; west to Texas; north to Oklahoma and Missouri.

Comments: Other yellow-flowering members of the Parsley Family include: Heart-leaved Meadow Parsnip (*Z. aptera*), with simple heart-shaped basal leaves; and Yellow Pimpernel (*Taenidia integerrima*), with compound leaves and untoothed leaflets. A common southern Meadow Parsnip of a different genus (*Thaspium trifoliatum*), sometimes called Golden Alexanders as well, has only 3 lanceolate, toothed leaflets.

DOGBANE FAMILY (Apocynaceae)

Herbs or shrubs (trees in tropical
regions) with solitary or clustered
flowers and milky juice.
Flowers: radially symmetrical; calyx
with 5 united sepals; corolla with 5
united petals; corolla lobes often
twisted in the bud; stamens 5; all these
parts attached at base of the ovary.
Leaves: simple, opposite, whorled, or
alternate.
Fruit: 2 pods, often attached at tip by
the style.
There are about 200 genera and 2,000
species, most abundant in the tropics
and subtropics. Among them, Oleander
and Periwinkle are popular ornamentals; other species produce valuable
fruits; many are poisonous.

557 **Spreading Dogbane**
(*Apocynum androsaemifolium*)
Dogbane Family (Apocynaceae)

Description: Bushy plant with numerous small pink,
nodding, bell-like flowers, fragrant and
striped inside with deeper pink. *Milky
juice* exudes from broken stems and
leaves.
Flowers: ⅓" (8 mm) wide; clustered at
top or rising from leaf axils.
Leaves: smooth, opposite, ovate, blue-
green, 2–4" (5–10 cm) long.
Fruit: 2 long, slender seed pods, 3–8"
(7.5–20 cm) opening along one side,
with seeds ending in a tuft of hair.
Height: 1–4' (30–120 cm).
Flowering: June–August.
Habitat: Borders of dry woods, thickets, and
fields; roadsides.
Range: Nearly throughout.
Comments: These plants are relatives of the
milkweeds. Indian Hemp (*A.
cannabinum*), a slightly smaller species
with erect clusters of greenish-white

flowers, is also found in fields and is *poisonous.* Clasping-leaved Dogbane (*A. sibiricum*), found widely throughout the Northeast in sandy or gravelly habitats such as stream banks, has stalkless or nearly stalkless leaves.

---

599   Periwinkle; Myrtle
(*Vinca minor*)
Dogbane Family (Apocynaceae)

Description: Low, evergreen, *trailing plant* with *purplish-blue flowers* borne singly in the leaf axils.
Flowers: to 1″ (2.5 cm) wide; corolla funnel-shaped, 5-lobed, with *whitish star* in center.
Leaves: 1½″ (4 cm) long, *shiny, dark green, opposite.*
Height: 6–8″ (15–20 cm).
Flowering: April–May.
Habitat: Borders of woods, roadsides, abandoned sites.
Range: Throughout.
Comments: This introduced plant, now escaped from cultivation, frequently forms extensive patches in woods. Its Latin name, *pervinca* (from the root "to bind"), is the source for both the present generic and common names. In the southern United States the erect Old Maid (*Vinca rosea*), with either pink or white flowers, often becomes well established.

ARUM FAMILY (Araceae)

Erect, prostrate, or climbing herbs with numerous small flowers crowded on a fleshy spike (spadix), surrounded by an often showy bract (spathe).

Flowers: bisexual or unisexual; sepals and petals absent or represented by 4–6 segments; stamens usually 4–6; all these parts attached at base of the ovary.

Leaves: simple or compound, long-petioled.

Fruit: berry.

More than 115 genera and about 2,000 species are found in shady, damp or wet places, most numerous and varied in the tropics. Many such as the Calla Lily, Philodendron, Dieffenbachia or Dumbcane are cultivated as ornamentals. Hawaiian *poi* is made from Taro root.

310 **Sweetflag; Calamus**
(*Acorous calamus*)
Arum Family (Araceae)

Description: This plant emerges from the water with a 2-edged stalk, with an *outward-jutting club-like spadix* bearing tiny, greenish-yellow flowers.
Flowers: clustered in diamond-shaped patterns on a spadix 2–3½" (5–9 cm) long; typical spathe lacking.
Leaves: 1–4' (30–120 cm) long, stiff, light green, *sword-like.*
Fruit: small, gelatinous berries that eventually dry.
Height: aquatic, leaves above water 1–4' (30–120 cm).
Flowering: May–August.
Habitat: Swamps, marshes, riverbanks, small streams.
Range: Nova Scotia; south to North Carolina; west to Texas and Oregon coast.
Comments: This plant, which grows partly in and partly out of the water, reproduces by

underground rootstalks that have a
sweet odor and flavor, once used for
making candy. All parts of the plant
are fragrant when bruised.

12   Green Dragon
(*Arisaema dracontium*)
Arum Family (Araceae)

Description: Solitary greenish inflorescence similar to
Jack-in-the-pulpit, but with a less
dominant hood (spathe) and a curious
long-tipped spadix (the "dragon's
tongue") protruding several inches
beyond the narrow spathe.
Flowers: tiny greenish-yellow male and
female flowers at base of spadix 4–8"
(10–20 cm) long.
Leaves: single, compound, long-
stalked, with 5–15 pointed, dull-green
leaflets, central ones to 8" (20 cm) long.
Fruit: orange-red and green berries.
Height: 1–3' (30–90 cm).

Flowering: May–June.

Habitat: Wet woodlands, low rich ground,
stream banks, in neutral or basic soils.

Range: Southern Ontario and Quebec; Vermont
south to Florida; west to Texas; north
to Wisconsin and Minnesota.

Comments: As with Jack-in-the-pulpit, the
tuberous taproot of this plant can burn
the mouth severely if ingested
uncooked. Far less common than Jack-
in-the-pulpit, Green Dragon is
considered comparatively rare.

9, 390, 443   Jack-in-the-pulpit; Indian Turnip
(*Arisaema triphyllum*)
Arum Family (Araceae)

Description: Distinctive "Jack-in-the-pulpit"
formation grows beneath large leaves.
Flowers: curving ridged hood (the
spathe or "pulpit"), green or purplish-

brown, often streaked or mottled, envelops an erect club (the spadix or "Jack") 2–3″ (5–7.5 cm) long. Spadix bears tiny separate male and female flowers at the base.
Leaves: 1 or usually 2, long-stemmed, 3-parted, veined, dull green.
Fruit: cluster of shiny red berries on spadix in late summer and fall.
Height: 1–3′ (30–90 cm).
Flowering: April–June.
Habitat: Damp woods and swamps.
Range: Southern Quebec and New Brunswick; south through Appalachians and coastal plain to Florida; west to Louisiana and eastern Texas.
Comments: Some authorities recognize one species, and others three, based on minor differences in leaves, spathe, and size. Because of needle-like calcium oxalate crystals in the underground tuber, it is peppery to the taste and causes a strong burning reaction if eaten raw. This unpleasant property can be eliminated by cooking, and American Indians gathered the fleshy taproots (corms) as a vegetable.

109 Water Arum; Wild Calla
(*Calla palustris*)
Arum Family (Araceae)

Description: Growing in water among oblong heart-shaped leaves, is a *broad white spathe* around a spadix covered with tiny yellow flowers.
Flowers: clustered on yellow spadix 1″ (2.5 cm) long, inside white, rolled-edge spathe 2″ (5 cm) long.
Leaves: commonly up to 6″ (15 cm) long, numerous, long-stemmed, glossy dark green.
Fruit: red clustered berries in late summer and autumn.
Height: aquatic, stem above water 6–12″ (15–30 cm).

Flowering: Late May–August.
Habitat: Cool, boggy wetlands and pond edges.
Range: Across southeast Canada; south from New England to Pennsylvania; west to Indiana; northwest into Minnesota.
Comments: This perennial, a more northerly specie than the other arums in our range, is also found in Eurasia. It is very showy when in flower and, later, when bearing its fruit. The genus name *Calla*, its meaning uncertain, was used by Pliny; the species epithet *palustris* means "of marshes."

---

308 Golden Club
(*Orontium aquaticum*)
Arum Family (Araceae)

Description: An aquatic with long-stalked leaves, and a *golden yellow, club-like spadix.*
Flowers: minute, clustered on spadix, 1–2″ (2.5–5 cm) long, with 4–6 sepals, 6 stamens; undeveloped spathe appears as narrow leaf sheath.
Leaves: blades 5–12″ (13–30 cm) long, elliptical, veined, dark green, extending above or floating upon water.
Fruit: blue-green, bladder-like.
Height: aquatic, 1–2′ (30–60 cm) above waterline.
Flowering: April–June.
Habitat: Shallow waters of marshes, swamps, and ponds.
Range: Massachusetts and central New York south to Florida and west to Louisiana, chiefly along coastal plain; inland to Kentucky and West Virginia.
Comments: This emergent perennial is of striking beauty, especially when seen against the backdrop of dark open waters in southern swamps. Its Latin generic name derives from a plant that grows in the Orontes River of Syria.

11 **Arrow Arum**
(*Peltandra virginica*)
Arum Family (Araceae)

Description: Aquatic plant with large, long-stalked
fleshy leaves and a green, wavy-
margined, *tapering, leaf-like spathe*
curled around a rod-like spadix.
Flowers: spathe 4–7″ (10–17.5 cm)
long; female flowers at base of club-like
spadix, male above.
Leaves: 1–2′ (30–60 cm) long,
arrowhead shape, with prominent
veining.
Fruit: black or blackish-green berries in
clusters.
Height: 1–2′ (30–60 cm).

Flowering: May–July.

Habitat: Shallow waters of ponds and slow-
moving rivers, swamps, and marshes.

Range: Southern Ontario and Quebec; southern
Maine south to Florida; west to Texas;
north to Michigan.

Comments: This aquatic is especially common in
and along shallow waterways, where it
may occur in large colonies. The genus
name derives from the Greek *pelte*
("small shield") and *aner* ("stamen"),
referring to the shield-like contour of
stamens. The common name, of course,
derives from the pronounced leaf shape.

10 **Water Lettuce**
(*Pistia stratiotes*)
Arum Family (Araceae)

Description: Small *floating* aquatic plant with
inconspicuous white flowers on a spadix
embedded in a *rosette of green leaves.*
Flowers: male florets at apex of spadix;
female at base. Spathe small, greenish-
white, about ½″ (1.3 cm) long.
Leaves: 2–10″ (5–25 cm) long, velvety,
parallel-ribbed; rosette about 6″
(15 cm) wide.
Height: aquatic, to 10″ (25 cm) above
water

Flowering: April.
Habitat: Still waters of ponds, ditches, and swamps; slow-moving streams.
Range: Florida west to Texas.
Comments: This aggressive plant rapidly covers vast expanses of open water in southern wetlands, especially cypress swamps. It growth is so dense and compact that it gives the illusion it can be walked upon. It is sometimes used as an aquarium plant.

391 Skunk Cabbage
(Symplocarpus foetidus)
Arum Family (Araceae)

Description: Emerging from moist earth in early spring, a large brownish-purple and green, mottled, *shell-like spathe* enclosing a knob-like spadix covered with tiny flowers. By late spring a tight roll of fresh green leaves beside the spathe unfolds to form huge, dark green, cabbagy leaves that may carpet an area.
Flowers: floral leaf (spathe) 3–6″ (7.5–15 cm) long.
Leaves: 1–2′ (30–60 cm) long, to 1′ (30 cm) wide, veined, on stalks rising directly from ground.
Height: 1–2′ (30–60 cm).
Flowering: February–May.
Habitat: Open swamps and marshes, along streams, wet woodlands.
Range: Much of southern Canada; throughout U.S. Northeast; south to upland Georgia; west to Iowa.
Comments: This distinctive plant of marshy woods sprouts so early in spring that the heat of cellular respiration resulting from its rapid growth actually melts snow or ice around it. Its strong fetid odor, especially when the plant is bruised, resembles decaying flesh and lures insects that pollinate it.

GINSENG FAMILY (Araliaceae)

Trees, shrubs, vines, or herbs with occasionally simple but, more usually, compound leaves, and small flowers in umbels or head-like clusters.
Flowers: radially symmetrical; bisexual or unisexual; calyx absent or reduced to 4–5 points; usually petals 5 and stamens 5; all these parts attached at top of the ovary.
Leaves: alternate or whorled, generally pinnately or palmately compound, with 3–5 leaflets each.
Fruit: berry or berry-like stone fruit.
There are more than 50 genera and about 500 species, found in both temperate and tropical regions. Some members, such as English Ivy, are cultivated as ornamentals or are important drug or flavoring sources.

2, 158 **Wild Sarsaparilla**
(*Aralia nudicaulis*)
Ginseng Family (Araliaceae)

Description: The leafless flower stem, topped with clusters of greenish-white flowers, is beneath a *large, umbrella-like leaf.*
Flowers: hemispherical clusters 1½–2″ (3.8–5 cm) wide; flowers with highly reflexed, tiny petals, 5 green stamens.
Leaves: single, long-stalked, 8–15″ (20–38 cm) tall; rising above the flower stalk in 3 branching parts, each with 3 to 5 ovate, finely toothed leaflets.
Fruit: purple-black berries, in clusters.
Height: 8–15″ (20–38 cm).
Flowering: July–August.
Habitat: Upland woods.
Range: British Columbia to Newfoundland; south to Georgia; west through Tennessee and Illinois to Missouri, Nebraska, and in places even farther westward.
Comments: The aromatic rhizomes of this plant are used as a substitute for sarsaparilla. The

species name, from the Latin *nudus* ("naked") and *cauli* ("stalk"), refers to the leafless flowerstalk. Devil's-walking-stick (*A. spinosa*), a small tree or large shrub, has leaves and stems covered with spines. Bristly Sarsaparilla (*A. hispida*), to 4' (1.2 m) tall, is bristly only at the base. Spikenard (*A. racemosa*) lacks spines and has numerous flower umbels in large clusters.

1, 441 Ginseng
(*Panax quinquefolium*)
Ginseng Family (Araliaceae)

Description: An umbel of small, greenish-white or yellow-green flowers, scented like Lily-of-the-valley, rises from the center of *3 large compound leaves* arranged in a circle.
Flowers: about $\frac{1}{12}$" (2 mm) wide, with 5 petals.
Leaves: 5–12" (12.5–30 cm) long, each with 5 leaflets, pointed and toothed.
Fruit: cluster of red berries.
Height: 8–24" (20–60 cm).
Flowering: May–August.
Habitat: Cool, moist woods.
Range: Manitoba to Quebec; south to Florida; west through Alabama to Louisiana and Oklahoma.
Comments: The root of this species is highly prized by the Chinese as an alleged aphrodisiac and heart stimulant. It is also in demand here as a tonic, which has resulted in overcollection, so that the plant is now considered rare. It is classified as a threatened species in 31 states in our range. The common name, corruption of the Chinese *Jin-chen* ("man-like"), refers to the often forked, trouser-shaped fleshy root.

160 Dwarf Ginseng
(*Panax trifolium*)
Ginseng Family (Araliaceae)

Description: An umbel of tiny, dull white flowers (fading to pink) rises above a *whorl of 3 compound leaves; round white tuberous root.*
Flowers: about $\frac{1}{12}''$ (2 mm) wide, 5 petals.
Leaves: with 3–5 stalkless, toothed, ovate leaflets, each 1–1½" (2.5–3.8 cm) long.
Fruit: cluster of yellowish berries.
Height: 4–8" (10–20 cm).

Flowering: April–June.

Habitat: Moist woods and damp clearings.

Range: Southern Quebec to Nova Scotia; New England south through mountains to Georgia; west through Indiana to Nebraska and Minnesota.

Comments: This tiny woodland perennial looks like a small version of Ginseng (*P. quinquefolium*). Its distinctive tuber can be eaten raw or boiled.

BIRTHWORT FAMILY
(Aristolochiaceae)

Herbs or woody vines with commonly heart-shaped leaves and medium-to-large, bizarre, often carrion-scented flowers.
Flowers: bilaterally or radially symmetrical; calyx 3-lobed or bent with united red, purple, or brown sepals; no petals; stamens usually 6 or more; all these parts attached to top of the ovary.
Leaves: alternate, stalked or basal, untoothed.
Fruit: capsule with 4–6 chambers.
This is a small family of about 6 genera and 400 species, widely distributed in tropical and temperate regions. Some are aromatic; a few are cultivated.

387 Dutchman's Pipe
(*Aristolochia durior*)
Birthwort Family (Aristolochiaceae)

Description: A tall climbing vine with pipe-shaped, or *S-shaped, brownish-purple flowers.*
Flowers: 2″ (5 cm) long; calyx flares into 3 short lobes.
Leaves: large, untoothed, *heart-shaped,* green underside, 6–15″ (15–38 cm)
Height: vine.
Flowering: April–June.
Habitat: Rich, moist woods and stream banks.
Range: Southwestern Pennsylvania and West Virginia; south to uplands of Georgia and Alabama.
Comments: A characteristic plant of the southern Appalachian hardwood forests, Dutchman's Pipe is often cultivated eastward to New Jersey and north to New England. Flowers of this family were once used as an aid in childbirth, since they were thought to resemble a human fetus. The similar Pipe Vine (*A. tomentosa*) has a yellowish calyx with a purple orifice and leaf undersurfaces that are downy and whitish.

386 Wild Ginger
(*Asarum canadense*)
Birthwort Family (Aristolochiaceae)

Description: *Growing at ground level* in the crotch between 2 leafstalks is a single darkish red-brown to green-brown flower.
Flowers: 1½″ (3.8 cm) wide, cup-shaped, with 3 pointed lobes.
Leaves: a pair; large, *hairy, heart-shaped,* each 3–6″ (7.5–15 cm) wide, overshadowing the flower.
Height: 6–12″ (15–30 cm).

Flowering: April–May.

Habitat: Rich woods.

Range: Quebec to New Brunswick; south to South Carolina; west through Kentucky to Missouri; north to Minnesota.

Comments: The root of this spring flower has a strong ginger-like odor and, when cooked with sugar, can be used as a substitute for ginger. A southern species with greenish-purple flowers (*A. arifolium*) has more triangular, evergreen leaf blades.

MILKWEED FAMILY
(Asclepiadaceae)

Herbs, shrubs, or vines usually with thick milky juice, opposite or whorled leaves, flowers in umbel-like clusters (cymes), and tufted seeds in pods.
Flowers: radially symmetrical in flat or round clusters; sepals 5; corolla of 5 united petals with reflexed lobes and a 5-lobed crown between corolla and stamens; stamens 5; all parts attached at base of the 2 ovaries.
Leaves: simple, mostly paired or in whorls of 4.
Fruit: 2 pods often joined at tips by style filled with many silky-haired seeds.
There are about 250 genera and 2,000 species, widely distributed but most abundant in tropical and subtropical regions. The unusual structure of the flower regulates pollination. Sacs of pollen snag on insects' legs, are pulled from the stamens, and then must be precisely inserted in slits behind the crown. If inserted backwards, pollen grains germinate in the wrong direction and are wasted. This may explain why so few pods occur on most plants. Insects too small to pull free die trapped on the flower.

548 **Swamp Milkweed**
(*Asclepias incarnata*)
Milkweed Family (Asclepiadaceae)

Description: Deep pink flowers clustered at the top of a tall, branching stem, bearing numerous *narrow, lanceolate leaves.*
Flowers: ¼″ (6 mm) broad, typical of the milkweeds, with 5 recurved petals and elevated central crown divided into 5 parts.
Leaves: to 4″ (10 cm) long, opposite.
Fruit: an elongated pod, 2–4″ (5–10 cm) long, opening along one side.

Height: 1–4' (30–120 cm).
Flowering: June–August.
Habitat: Swamps, shores, and thickets.
Range: Manitoba, Quebec, and Nova Scotia; from New England south to Georgia; west to Louisiana, and Texas; north to North Dakota.
Comments: The juice of this wetland milkweed is less milky than that of other species. The genus was named in honor of Aesculapius, Greek god of medicine, undoubtedly because some species have long been used to treat a variety of ailments. The Latin species name means "flesh-colored."

234, 547 **Common Milkweed**
(*Asclepias syriaca*)
Milkweed Family (Asclepiadaceae)

Description: A tall, *downy* plant with slightly drooping purplish to pink flower clusters.
Flowers: ½" (1.3 cm) wide, with 5 downward-pointing petals and a conspicuous 5-part central crown; in clusters 2" (5 cm) wide.
Leaves: 4–10" (10–25 cm) long, opposite, broad-oblong, light green with *gray down beneath,* exude a milky juice when bruised.
Fruit: rough-textured pod that splits open on one side, filled with many overlapping seeds, each covered with tuft of silky hairs.
Height: 2–6' (60–180 cm).
Flowering: June–August.
Habitat: Old fields, roadsides, and waste places.
Range: Saskatchewan to New Brunswick; south to Georgia; west through Tennessee to Kansas and Iowa.
Comments: This plant differs from Showy Milkweed, (*A. speciosa*), in having an unbranched stem. The plant contains cardiac glycosides, allied to digitalins used in treating some heart disease. These glycosides, when absorbed by

monarch butterfly larvae, whose sole
source of food is milkweed foliage,
make the larvae and adult butterflies
toxic to birds and other predators.

379 **Butterfly Weed; Pleurisy Root**
(*Asclepias tuberosa*)
Milkweed Family (Asclepiadaceae)

Description: Small *bright orange* clustered flowers
crown the leafy, hairy stem.
Flowers: ⅜″ (9 mm) wide, with 5
curved-back petals and a central crown,
in clusters about 2″ (5 cm) wide.
Leaves: alternate, oblong, narrow, 2–6″
(5–15 cm) long, with *juice that is
watery, not milky.*
Fruit: spindle-shaped, *narrow, hairy,
erect pods.*
Height: 1–2½′ (30–75 cm).
Flowering: June–September.
Habitat: Dry open soil, roadsides, and fields.
Range: Ontario to Newfoundland; New
England south to Florida; west to
Texas; north through Colorado to
Minnesota.
Comments: This showy plant is frequently grown
from seed in home gardens. Its brilliant
flowers attract butterflies. Because its
tough root was chewed by the Indians
as a cure for pleurisy and other
pulmonary ailments, Butterfly Weed
was given its other common name,
Pleurisy Root.

190 **White Milkweed**
(*Asclepias variegata*)
Milkweed Family (Asclepiadaceae)

Description: Small white flowers with purplish
centers are crowded into globular
terminal clusters.
Flowers: ¼–½″ (6–13 mm) long, with
5 petals below elevated 5-part crown,
in clusters 2½–3″ (6–7.5 cm) wide.

Leaves: 3–6″ (7.5–15 cm) long, dark green above and *pale beneath;* opposite, oval to oblong.

Fruit: capsule ¾″ (2 cm) thick, spindle-shaped.

Height: 1–3′ (30–90 cm).

Flowering: May–July.

Habitat: Open woods and thickets.

Range: Connecticut south to Florida; west to Texas and Oklahoma; north to Missouri and Illinois.

Comments: The stem of this plant has the milky juice typical of Milkweeds. The Latin species name describes the parti-colored flowers, which are quite showy in masses.

SUNFLOWER OR DAISY FAMILY
(Asteraceae or Compositae)

Herbs, sometimes shrubs or vines, rarely trees, with simple or compound, alternate or opposite leaves. Flowers small, but organized into larger heads resembling a single, radially symmetrical flower cupped by a ring of green bracts. Flower-like heads: tiny, radially symmetrical central flowers form the disk; larger flowers around the edge, the rays, strap-shaped and resembling petals (however, all flowers in one head may be disk flowers or rays).
Flowers: calyx absent, or modified into hairs, bristles, scales, or a crown, which often persist atop the fruits; corolla has 5 united petals, 5 stamens; all these parts attached to top of the ovary.
Leaves: simple or compound, opposite, alternate or whorled.
Fruit: 1-seeded, with hard shell.
In this large, worldwide, family there are about 920 genera and 19,000 species. Cosmos, Sunflower, Zinnia, Dahlia, and many others are grown as ornamentals; Lettuce, Sunflowers, and Artichokes provide food. Safflower oil is obtained from this family.

---

192 **Yarrow**
(*Achillea millefolium*)
Sunflower Family (Asteraceae)

Description: Flat-topped clusters of small, whitish flowers grow at the top of a gray-green, leafy, usually hairy, stem.
Flowers: heads about ¼″ (6 mm) across, composed of 4–6 ray flowers surrounding tiny central disk flowers.
Leaves: 6″ (15 cm) long, *very finely dissected, gray-green, fern-like,* aromatic; lanceolate in outline, stalkless. Basal leaves longer.
Height: 1–3′ (30–90 cm).

Flowering: June–September.
Habitat: Old fields, roadsides.
Range: Throughout.
Comments: Yarrow was formerly used for medicinal
purposes: to break a fever by increasing
perspiration, to treat hemorrhaging,
and as a poultice for rashes. A tea used
by the Indians to cure stomach
disorders was made by steeping the
leaves. The foliage has a pleasant smell
when crushed.

26 Common Ragweed
(*Ambrosia artemisiifolia*)
Sunflower Family (Asteraceae)

Description: Coarse, hairy-stemmed annual with
inconspicuous flowers in elongated
clusters.
Flowers: *male,* small yellow-green,
packed with yellow stamens, borne in
heads of 15–20 florets each, arranged
on slender clusters 1–6″ (2.5–15 cm)
long, near top of plant (hundreds of
heads per plant); *female,* small, green,
stalkless, borne in small clusters at leaf
axils.
Leaves: highly dissected, light green,
up to 4″ (10 cm) long.
Fruit: small, top-shaped, capped with 6
short spines.
Height: 1–5′ (30–150 cm).
Flowering: July–October.
Habitat: Cultivated fields or old fields, waste
places, and roadsides.
Range: Throughout.
Comments: This plant, not Goldenrod, is a cause of
hay fever, recognized by all who suffer
the discomfiting allergy. Pollination is
by wind, as indicated by the drabness
of the flowers, which do not attract
insects. The best control is to permit
perennial plants to crowd this annual
out. Since the seeds persist into winter
and are numerous and rich in oil, they
are relished by songbirds and upland
game birds.

25 Great Ragweed
(*Ambrosia trifida*)
Sunflower Family (Asteraceae)

Description: A tall, rough, hairy plant with
nodding heads of minute green flowers
arranged in *elongated clusters*.
Flowers: similar to those of Common
Ragweed; clusters 1–10″ (2.5–25 cm)
long.
Leaves: up to 8″ (20 cm) long,
opposite, palmately 3-lobed.
Fruit: beaked, with 4–10 short points.
Height: 2–15′ (60–450 cm).

Flowering: June–October.

Habitat: Waste places, fields, and roadsides.

Range: Throughout.

Comments: This is the giant among the Ragweeds.
The pollen of this species, like that of
other Ragweeds, is spread by the wind
and is a principal cause of hay fever.

196 Pearly Everlasting
(*Anaphalis margaritacea*)
Sunflower Family (Asteraceae)

Description: Erect plant with a white woolly stem,
bearing a *flat cluster of white globe-shaped
heads*.
Flowers: heads about ¼″ (6 mm) wide,
small, of all disk flowers, with petal-
like bracts.
Leaves: 3–5″ (7.5–13 cm) long,
alternate, narrow, greenish-white
above, with dense white wool below.
Height: 1–3′ (30–90 cm).

Flowering: July–September.

Habitat: Dry pastures, roadsides, and waste
places.

Range: Across Canada; south through New
England to the mountains of Virginia;
west to West Virginia and Ohio; north
to the Dakotas.

Comments: The pure white flowers of this most
showy of Everlastings are often used in
dried flower arrangements. Male and
female flowers grow on separate plants.

195 Smaller Pussytoes
(*Antennaria neodioica*)
Sunflower Family (Asteraceae)

Description: Densely grouped low plants each with a slender, erect *woolly stem* bearing a terminal cluster of fuzzy white flower heads.
Flowers: heads up to ½" (1.3 cm) wide, all disk flowers, enclosed by greenish or brownish bracts with white tips; calyx represented by long bristles.
Leaves: basal leaves ½–1" (1.3–2.5 cm) long, arranged in a rosette, white-woolly, single-veined, spoon-shaped, tips upturned, ending in a small abrupt point; 5–14 small stem leaves, linear, pointed.
Height: 6–18" (15–45 cm).
Flowering: May–July.
Habitat: Lawns, pastures, and open woods.
Range: Ontario to Nova Scotia; New England south to Virginia; west through Indiana and Illinois; north to Wisconsin and Minnesota.
Comments: Bristly flower heads are crowded together into a cluster resembling a cat's paw; hence the common name. Male and female flowers are on different plants, and in some species, including Smaller Pussytoes, the male flowers are rare. Plantain-leaved Pussytoes (*A. plantaginifolia*) has broader and longer basal leaves, up to 3" (7.5 cm) long, with 3 main veins.

92 Mayweed
(*Anthemis cotula*)
Sunflower Family (Asteraceae)

Description: Daisy-like plant with white ray flowers surrounding a dome-shaped yellow disk.
Flowers: heads to 1" (2.5 cm) wide.
Leaves: 1–2½" (2.5–6.3 cm) long, *finely dissected,* fern-like, with *unpleasant odor* and acrid taste.

Height: 1–2′ (30–60 cm).
Flowering: June–October.
Habitat: Waste places and roadsides.
Range: Throughout.
Comments: An introduced bushy annual with
foliage that may cause skin irritation if
handled, Mayweed resembles a plant
from which chamomile tea is made;
hence its other common name, Stinking
Chamomile. The similar Corn
Chamomile (*A. arvensis*) has flower
heads up to 1½″ (3.8 cm) wide and
grayish, hairy stems, but is scentless.
Yellow Chamomile (*A. tinctoria*) is the
only yellow ray-flowered species,
occurring sporadically from Quebec
south to New Jersey and westward to
Minnesota.

487   Common Burdock
(*Arctium minus*)
Sunflower Family (Asteraceae)

Description: Large, bushy plant with globular
prickly, pink to lavender flower heads.
Flowers: heads ¾″ (2 cm) wide,
overlapping green bracts with hooked
tips, enclosing the numerous, tubular,
purplish florets.
Leaves: up to 18″ (45 cm) long, ovate,
lower ones heart-shaped, dark green,
woolly underneath, with hollow
leafstalks.
Height: 1–5′ (30–150 cm).
Flowering: July–October.
Habitat: Old fields and waste places.
Range: Across Canada; south through New
England to Georgia; west to
Mississippi; north to Missouri, Kansas,
and beyond.
Comments: The prickly heads of this Old World
weed easily catch on fur and clothing,
thus providing an excellent mechanism
for seed dispersal. Its young leaves and
leafstalks, roots, and flower stalks can
all be prepared in various ways and
eaten. The Great Burdock (*A. lappa*), a

larger plant up to 9′ (2.7 m) tall, has bigger flower heads on solid, grooved leafstalks.

97 White Wood Aster
(*Aster divaricatus*)
Sunflower Family (Asteraceae)

Description: Often zigzag stem bears somewhat flat-topped clusters of white flower heads.
Flowers: heads to 1″ (2.5 cm) wide, with 6–10 ray flowers and a center disk that turns bronzy-purple. Bracts under flower heads whitish with green tips.
Leaves: 2–7″ (5–17.5 cm) long, smooth-stalked, *heart-shaped,* long-tapering, coarsely toothed.
Fruit: dry, seed-like, tipped with whitish bristles.
Height: 1–3′ (30–90 cm).
Flowering: July–October.
Habitat: Dry open woods.
Range: New England south to Georgia; west to Alabama; north to Tennessee and Ohio.
Comments: This white Aster is a typical late summer-early fall bloomer in open woodlands. Among the related species in our range, the taller Large-leaved Aster (*A. macrophyllus*) has large, thick, rough leaves, lavender flowers, and rough, glandular flower stalks. The very young leaves of this species may be cooked and eaten as greens.

100 Bushy Aster
(*Aster dumosus*)
Sunflower Family (Asteraceae)

Description: Rather stiff plant having leafy branches that bear numerous terminal flower heads, with white or pale lavender ray flowers and pale yellow or brownish disk flowers.
Flowers: heads ½–¾″ (1.3–2 cm)

wide; individual heads relatively *long-stalked.*
Leaves: stem leaves 1–3″ (2.5–7.5 cm) long, firm, linear to narrow lanceolate, with rough margins; *branch leaves smaller, numerous, and bract-like.*
Height: 1–3′ (30–90 cm).

Flowering: August–October.

Habitat: Sandy open sites; occasionally marshy ground.

Range: Southeast Ontario; Maine south to Florida and west to Texas, mainly coastal; north through Illinois and Indiana to Michigan.

Comments: This species of Aster is most widely found in southern states, and elsewhere is more locally restricted to shoreline areas, such as around the Great Lakes.

604 Smooth Aster
(*Aster laevis*)
Sunflower Family (Asteraceae)

Description: A *smooth-leaved* perennial with many rich lavender-blue ray and yellow disk flowers and a *light grayish-white bloom* on its stem.
Flowers: to 1″ (2.5 cm) wide, green-tipped bracts around flower head.
Leaves: 1–4″ (2.5–10 cm) long, thick, slightly toothed, elliptic or lanceolate, lower ones stalked, upper unstalked and clasping the stem.
Fruit: dry, 1–seeded, often with reddish bristles.
Height: 2–4′ (60–120 cm).

Flowering: August–October.

Habitat: Fields, open woods and roadsides.

Range: Southern Ontario to New Brunswick; Maine south to Georgia; west to Louisiana; north to Kansas.

Comments: One of the most attractive blue Asters, it has bright green foliage that is very smooth to the touch. At least 11 other related species are found within our range.

102 Calico Aster
(*Aster lateriflorus*)
Sunflower Family (Asteraceae)

Description: Several small flower heads of white or pale purple ray flowers surrounding *yellow or purple disk flowers* are on one side of straggly, divergent branches.
Flowers: less than ½″ (1.3 cm) wide with 9–15 ray flowers surrounding the central disk, bracts under flower heads with greenish midrib.
Leaves: 2–6″ (5–15 cm) long, lanceolate to elliptic, coarsely toothed.
Height: 1–5′ (30–150 cm).

Flowering: August–October.

Habitat: Fields, thickets.

Range: Ontario to Nova Scotia south through New England to Georgia; west to Tennessee and Arkansas; north to Minnesota.

Comments: This is one of a group of closely related white, narrow-leaved Asters which presumably interbreed and are difficult to distinguish. The common name refers to the fact that the heads are at first yellow and later turn purplish-red, so that flowers on one plant and even a single head may include both colors at the same time.

608 Stiff Aster; Bristly Aster
(*Aster linariifolius*)
Sunflower Family (Asteraceae)

Description: *Stiff, leafy stalk* is terminated by several flower heads with blue ray flowers and yellow center disk flowers that turn bronzy.
Flowers: heads to 1″ (2.5 cm) wide.
Leaves: to 1½″ (3.8 cm) long, dark green, *linear*.
Fruit: dry, 1-seeded, with tawny, silky bristles.
Height: 8–18″ (20–45 cm).

Flowering: August–October.

Habitat: Dry clearings, rocky banks.

Range: Southern Ontario to New Brunswick; New England south to northwest Florida; west to Louisiana and eastern Texas; north to Minnesota.

Comments: Numerous short stems form a mound of flowers in colors ranging from deepest lavender to pinks and whites.

479, 603 New England Aster
(Aster novae-angliae)
Sunflower Family (Asteraceae)

Description: Large, stout, hairy, leafy plant with bright lavender to purplish-blue flower heads clustered at ends of branches.
Flowers: heads 1–2″ (2.5–5 cm) wide; ray flowers 35–45; disk flowers yellowish; bracts beneath flower heads narrow, hairy, *sticky;* flowerstalk with sticky hairs (glandular).
Leaves: 1½–5″ (3.8–12.5 cm) long, lanceolate, toothless, *clasping* large stem.
Height: 3–7′ (90–210 cm).

Flowering: August–October.

Habitat: Wet thickets, meadows, and swamps.

Range: Across southern Canada; south from New England to Maryland, upland to western North Carolina; west to Arkansas, Kansas, and beyond.

Comments: The flower color is variable, ranging from lavender to blue to white. A pink variety of this species is sometimes grown commercially.

---

609 New York Aster
(Aster novi-belgii)
Sunflower Family (Asteraceae)

Description: A branching plant with slender, mostly smooth stems which bear narrow leaves and numerous flower heads with violet-blue ray flowers surrounding the central yellow or reddish disk flowers.
Flowers: heads 1–1¼″ (2.5–3 cm)

wide. Ray flowers 20–40. Bracts under
flower heads whitish green with
spreading or backward-curving tips.
Leaves: 2–6″ (5–15 cm) long, oblong
to linear-lanceolate. Upper leaves partly
clasp the stem.
Height: 8–36″ (20–90 cm).

Flowering: July–October.

Habitat: Shores, damp thickets and meadows.

Range: Quebec, Newfoundland, and Nova
Scotia south to Georgia, mostly near
the coast.

Comments: The large, purple-flowered Aster is very
abundant in low areas along the coast.
There are many forms, among them a
white and a rose. The species name,
Latin for "of New Belgium," is from
the early name for New York.

99 Panicled Aster
(*Aster simplex*)
Sunflower Family (Asteraceae)

Description: Tall stem bears a loose cluster of white,
occasionally violet-tinged, flower heads.
Flowers: heads ¾–1″ (2–2.5 cm) wide;
ray flowers numerous, bracts
surrounding the flower heads narrow,
green-tipped.
Leaves: lanceolate, sharp-pointed; lower
leaves 3–6″ (7.5–15 cm) long, upper
ones smaller.
Height: 2–5′ (60–150 cm).

Flowering: August–October.

Habitat: Damp thickets, meadows, and shores.

Range: Across southern Canada to Nova Scotia;
south to Virginia and upland North
Carolina; west to Texas; north to
Kansas and North Dakota.

Comments: This plant spreads by underground
rootstocks to form colonies. It has many
varieties, differing in color, size of the
ray flowers, leaf form, and serration.

481 Showy Aster
(*Aster spectabilis*)
Sunflower Family (Asteraceae)

Description: Open clusters of showy flower heads
with *bright lavender ray flowers*
surrounding the central yellow disk
flowers. Stiff, rough stem, often
branched toward the top.
Flowers: heads to 1½″ (3.8 cm) wide;
bracts under heads oblong, sticky, with
spreading green tips.
Leaves: lower ones, 3–5″ (7.5–12.5
cm) long, light green, elliptical,
stalked, with shallow teeth; upper ones,
linear, oblong, stalkless, and mostly
untoothed.
Height: 1–2′ (30–60 cm).

Flowering: August–October.

Habitat: Dry clearings and sandy woods.

Range: Massachusetts south to South Carolina.

Comments: This very showy, large-flowered Aster
with a short stem is easily cultivated
and makes a fine display in late
summer. Its distribution is mainly
coastal, especially in pine barrens.

610 Tansyleaf Aster
(*Aster tanacetifolius*)
Sunflower Family (Asteraceae)

Description: A hairy, often *sticky*, plant with lobed,
bristle-tipped leaves and numerous flower
heads with violet-blue ray flowers
surrounding the central yellow disk
flowers.
Flowers: heads 1–2″ (2.5–5 cm) wide;
ray flowers 15–25; bracts surrounding
flower heads with whitish base and
spreading green tips.
Leaves: 1–2″ (2.5–5 cm) long,
pinnately cut into 2–3 linear-oblong,
bristle-tipped lobes.
Height: 1–2′ (30–60 cm).

Flowering: June–August.

Habitat: Dry soil.

Range: South Dakota south through Texas to

Mexico; prevalent farther west.

Comments: The common and species names refer to the fact that its lobed leaves are somewhat like those of Common Tansy (*Tanacetum vulgare*). It is distinct from most Asters in having finely dissected leaves.

96 Salt-marsh Aster
(*Aster tenuifolius*)
Sunflower Family (Asteraceae)

Description: This weak, straggly plant with widely spreading branches has only a *few flower heads,* with numerous white or pale purple ray flowers.
Flowers: head ½–1″ (1.3–2.5 cm) wide.
Leaves: up to 6″ (15 cm) long, sparse, *fleshy,* narrow, tapering at both ends.
Height: 1–2′ (30–60 cm).
Flowering: August–October.
Habitat: Salt or brackish marshes.
Range: Coastal from New Hampshire to Florida; west to Mississippi.
Comments: Although a very few-flowered plant, this perennial Aster forms conspicuous masses in the brackish tidal marshes where all other large-flowered species are absent. The Annual Salt-marsh Aster (*A. subulatus*) has many flower heads, which are only ¼–½″ (6–13 mm) wide.

98 Flat-topped White Aster
(*Aster umbellatus*)
Sunflower Family (Asteraceae)

Description: The rigid, upright stem has a *flat-topped* cluster of white flower heads.
Flowers: heads ½–¾″ (1.3–2 cm) wide, with 10–15 ray flowers, tending to curve downward or backward.
Leaves: to 6″ (15 cm) long, lanceolate or elliptic, tapering at both ends, *toothless.*

Height: 1–7′ (30–210 cm).
Flowering: August–September.
Habitat: Moist thickets and woods; edge of swamps.
Range: Ontario to Newfoundland and Nova Scotia; south from New England to North Carolina and upland Georgia; west to Kentucky; north to Iowa and Minnesota.
Comments: This very conspicuous Aster of wet meadows, with an extremely wide, flat top—almost 1′ (30 cm) across—is one of the first Asters to bloom.

480 Wavy-leaved Aster
(*Aster undulatus*)
Sunflower Family (Asteraceae)

Description: A stiff, very rough stem has spreading branches with diffuse clusters of lavender, violet to pale blue flower heads.
Flowers: heads about ¾″ (2 cm) wide, with 12–20 ray flowers surrounding central yellow disk flowers; downy bracts beneath flower heads pale, with green tips.
Leaves: 2–6″ (5–15 cm) long, with *wavy or shallow toothed margins,* ovate, somewhat hoary; lower ones often with *dilated leafstalk bases* that clasp the stem; upper ones stalkless.
Fruit: dry, 1-seeded, with tan to whitish bristles.
Height: 1–3½′ (30–105 cm).
Flowering: August–November.
Habitat: Dry woods, thickets, and clearings.
Range: Ontario to Nova Scotia; Maine south to Florida; west to Louisiana; north to Minnesota.
Comments: There are several varieties of this plant, differing only in the outline of the leaves. The broad winged leafstalks are particularly noteworthy.

101 Small-flowered White Aster
(*Aster vimineus*)
Sunflower Family (Asteraceae)

Description: Numerous white flower heads are *mostly clustered along one side of widely diverging branches* on a smooth, slender, purple-tinged stem.
Flowers: head about ⅓" (8 mm) wide; ray flowers 15–30; green-tipped bracts beneath heads.
Leaves: stem leaves 3–5" (7.5–12.5 cm) long, linear to lanceolate, untoothed; branch leaves smaller.
Height: 2–5' (60–150 cm).

Flowering: August–October.

Habitat: Dry to moist fields, meadows and shores.

Range: Southern Ontario and Quebec; Maine south to Georgia; west to Texas; north to Michigan.

Comments: One of the many small-flowered Asters found in our range, this species closely resembles the Bushy Aster (*A. dumosus*), which occurs near the coast and inland along rivers.

220 Groundsel Tree
(*Baccharis halimifolia*)
Aster Family (Asteraceae)

Description: A *salt marsh shrub* with greenish-white flower heads and *angled twigs*.
Flowers: heads ½" (1 cm) long, all disk flowers, in clusters of 1–5, with male and female flowers on different plants.
Leaves: up to 2½" (6.3 cm) long, *alternate*, egg-shaped; lower, irregularly and bluntly toothed; upper, toothless.
Fruit: female bristles *very white-silky*.
Height: 6–9' (1.8–2.7 m).

Flowering: August–September.

Habitat: Borders of salt marshes.

Range: Along coast from Massachusetts south to Florida; west to Texas and Mexico.

Comments: The female plants are especially showy in the fall due to the silky bristles of

the numerous flower heads. Groundsel
Tree is one of two shrubs associated
with coastal wetlands. The other is the
Marsh Elder, (*Iva frutescens*), an
opposite-leaved shrub that often forms a
belt at the edge of the marsh and
invades even the marsh itself along
mosquito ditches.

---

287 Tickseed Sunflower
(*Bidens aristosa*)
Sunflower Family (Asteraceae)

Description: Slender, leafy, much-branched stems
bear several Daisy-like flower heads
with yellow ray and disk flowers.
Flowers: heads 1–2″ (2.5–5 cm) wide;
rays long in relation to width of center
disk.
Leaves: to 6″ (15 cm) long, opposite,
pinnately divided, segments toothed.
Fruit: dry, *flat,* ovoid, usually with
2 spines.
Height: 1–5′ (30–150 cm).
Flowering: August–October.
Habitat: Wet meadows, roadside ditches,
abandoned fields, and low ground.
Range: New England south to Virginia; west
to Louisiana and Texas; north through
Missouri to Minnesota.
Comments: The fruits of this plant are the very
common, 2-pronged stickers that cling
to one's clothing during autumn walks.
They can be removed easily with the
flat edge of a knife blade. Two similar
species, differing in minute fruit
characteristics, are *B. polylepis,* with
round-margined fruit, and the Southern
Tickseed (*B. coronata*), with narrow,
straight-sided fruit.

288 Nodding Bur Marigold
(*Bidens cernua*)
Sunflower Family (Asteraceae)

Description: Numerous yellow *flower heads nod*
increasingly as the flowers mature.
Flowers: heads to 2″ (5 cm) wide,
usually with 6–8 yellow ray flowers,
short in comparison to diameter of
darker yellow disk; ray flowers
occasionally lacking.
Leaves: 2–6″ (5–15 cm) long, *simple,*
smooth, opposite, stalkless, *narrowly
lanceolate to elliptic.*
Fruit: seed-like, 4-pronged, toothed.
Height: 1–3′ (30–90 cm).

Flowering: August–October.

Habitat: Swamps and wet ground.

Range: Nova Scotia; in the east, mainly coastal
to North Carolina; occurs inland on a
local basis.

Comments: The species name is Latin for
"nodding." Bur Marigold seeds are
sometimes eaten by ducks. Where the
range of this species and Smooth Bur
Marigold (*B. laevis*) overlap in coastal
areas, *B. cernua* is much less prevalent.

95 Shepherd's Needle
(*Bidens pilosa*)
Sunflower Family (Asteraceae)

Description: A *square-stemmed* plant with flowering
heads having white to pale yellow, or
purplish, ray flowers and yellow disk
flowers on stalks rising from the leaf
axils.
Flowers: heads to 1″ (2.5 cm) wide.
Leaves: opposite, divided into
lanceolate to ovate toothed segments
1–4″ (2.5–10 cm) long.
Fruit: dry, 1-seeded, spindle-shaped,
with 2 backward- or downward-
pointing barbs.
Height: 1–3′ (30–90 cm).

Flowering: March–frost.

Habitat: Waste places, roadsides, and lawns.

Range: Southeastern North Carolina south to Florida; west to Texas.

Comments: The barbed seeds of this plant adhere to clothing and the fur of animals, thus providing an excellent means of dispersal. The plant is also found in Central America.

488 Nodding Thistle, Musk Thistle
(*Carduus nutans*)
Aster Family (Asteraceae)

Description: A *nodding,* rose-purple, thistle-like flower head is borne alone on a long floral stalk at the end of the main stem and its branches. A cobweb-like covering may be present on the stem.
Flowers: heads 1½–2½″ (3.8–6.3 cm) wide, surrounded by *broad, pointed, purple bracts,* the outer ones curving *outward.*
Leaves: to 10″ (25 cm) long, lanceolate, deeply lobed, *very spiny,* with bases extending up and down the stem as prickly wings.
Fruit: seed-like, with long, white, minutely barbed bristles.
Height: 2–9′ (60–270 cm).

Flowering: June–October.

Habitat: Waste places, fields.

Range: New Brunswick south through New England to South Carolina; west to Missouri and Iowa.

Comments: This European introduction spread rapidly into the rangeland of the Midwest. It differs from the closely related genus *Cirsium* in lacking the white matted hairs on the leaves and in having outward-pointing bracts around the flower heads.

486 **Spotted Knapweed**
(*Centaurea maculosa*)
Sunflower Family (Asteraceae)

Description: A highly branched, wiry-stemmed
plant with lavender heads composed
entirely of disk flowers; stem has soft
hairs.
Flowers: heads to 1″ (2.5 cm) wide,
with *harsh, prickly, black-tipped bracts.*
Leaves: 4–8″ (10–20 cm) long at base
of plant, smaller above, highly
dissected into linear segments.
Height: 2–3′ (60–90 cm).
Flowering: June–August.
Habitat: Fields, waste places, and roadsides
preferably on basic or neutral soil.
Range: Across southern Canada; south through
New England to northwest South
Carolina; west to Tennessee, Missouri,
Kansas, and beyond.
Comments: Its spiny, thistle-like flower bracts are a
prominent feature. Two similar annuals
are Cornflower (*C. cyanus*), with bright
blue flower heads, and Star Thistle,
(*C. americana*), a showy southwestern
species with larger, pink disk flowers
and smaller white disk flowers.

91 **Oxeye Daisy**
(*Chrysanthemum leucanthemum*)
Sunflower Family (Asteraceae)

Description: The common white-and-yellow Daisy of
the fields, with solitary flower heads on
slender, erect stems.
Flowers: heads 1–2″ (2.5–5 cm) wide;
ray flowers white, all female; disk
flowers yellow, both male and female;
disk depressed at center.
Leaves: dark green, coarsely toothed or
pinnately lobed, basal ones to 6″ (15
cm) long, upper ones to 3″ (7.5 cm).
Height: 1–3′ (30–90 cm).
Flowering: June–August.
Habitat: Waste places, meadows, pastures, and
roadsides.

Range: Throughout, but less abundant
southward.

Comments: This species—the "day's eye"—is
disliked by farmers because it can
produce an unwanted flavor in milk if
eaten by cattle. Though an extremely
common, even weed-like species, the
Oxeye Daisy was originally introduced
in North America from Europe.

---

292 **Hairy Golden Aster; Prairie Golden
Aster**
(*Chrysopsis camporum*)
Sunflower Family (Asteraceae)

Description: The stiff, rough, hairy and leafy stem
bears few flower heads with golden-
yellow ray flowers and slightly darker
disk flowers that turn brown with age.
Flowers: heads 1″ (2.5 cm) or more
wide.
Leaves: 1–3″ (2.5–7.5 cm) long,
oblong to lanceolate, covered with short
hairs; upper leaves stalkless, lower
leaves narrowed into short leafstalks.
Fruit: seed-like, ovate, tipped with soft
hairs.
Height: 1–2′ (30–60 cm).

Flowering: July–September.

Habitat: Dry plains and prairies.

Range: Manitoba south to Wisconsin, western
Indiana and eastern Missouri.

Comments: The heights of these plants vary greatly
with environmental conditions. At least
16 related species occur in the eastern
United States.

---

605 **Chicory**
(*Cichorium intybus*)
Sunflower Family (Asteraceae)

Description: A stiff stem bears several stalkless,
showy *blue* flower heads, with *square-
tipped, fringed ray flowers.*
Flowers: heads to 1½″ (3.8 cm) wide,

disk flowers absent; two-part style is
surrounded by dark blue, fused anthers.
Leaves: basal leaves 3–6" (7.5–15 cm)
long, dandelion–like. Stem leaves
much smaller, oblong to lanceolate,
clasping.
Height: 1–4' (30–120 cm).

Flowering: June–October.
Habitat: Fields, roadsides, and waste places.
Range: Throughout.
Comments: Only a few flower heads open at a time,
and each lasts only a day. While this
Old World weed has in some places
proliferated to become a plant pest, it is
also sought for its food uses and is
cultivated as well. The roots can be
roasted and ground as a coffee
substitute or additive. (A European
form is cultivated for this purpose, and
millions of pounds are used here and
abroad.)

485 Canada Thistle
(*Cirsium arvense*)
Aster Family (Asteraceae)

Description: Numerous fragrant pale magenta or
lavender flower heads top this highly-
branched, smooth-stemmed plant.
Flowers: heads 1" (2.5 cm) wide,
all disk type, heads surrounded by
spine-tipped bracts.
Leaves: 5–8" (12.5–20 cm) long, gray-
green with matted hairs, *spiny*,
lanceolate, deeply cut, wavy-edged,
mostly stalkless.
Height: 1–5' (30–150 cm).

Flowering: June–October.
Habitat: Pastures, roadsides, waste places.
Range: Throughout.
Comments: This is a European introduction that
reached us by way of Canada, hence the
common name. Its smaller flowering
heads and non-spiny stem distinguish it
from the Bull Thistle (*C. vulgare*).

317 **Yellow Thistle**
(*Cirsium horridulum*)
Sunflower Family (Asteraceae)

Description: A tall branching stem with large yellow
flower heads and very *spiny, clasping
leaves.*
Flowers: heads 2½" (6.3 cm) wide, made
up of tiny, 5–parted, tubular disk
flowers enclosed in weakly-spined
bracts. Heads surrounded by erect,
narrow, spiny bract-like leaves.
Leaves: 6–10" (15–25 cm) long,
lanceolate in outline, pinnately lobed,
stalkless and clasping the stem, with
spiny margins and tips.
Height: 1–5' (30–150 cm).
Flowering: May–August.
Habitat: Shores, marshes, sandy or peaty fields.
Range: Coastal Plain from southern Maine to
Florida; west to Texas.
Comments: Often found along the edges of salt
marshes, it is also a pasture weed in the
South, where it is frequently red-purple
instead of yellow. Prairie Thistle (*C.
plattense*) also yellow, has leaves white
and velvety beneath and grayish above
with leaf bases extending, wing-like,
down the stem. It is typical of
overgrazed western pastures.

489 **Bull Thistle**
(*Cirsium vulgare*)
Sunflower Family (Asteraceae)

Description: This very *prickly* plant has a *spiny-
winged stem* and large rose-purple flower
heads, composed entirely of disk flowers
and surrounded by spiny, yellow-tipped
bracts.
Flowers: heads 1½–2" (3.8–5 cm)
wide.
Leaves: 3–6" (7.5–15 cm) long,
coarsely pinnately lobed, spiny.
Height: 2–6' (60–180 cm).
Flowering: June–September.
Habitat: Roadsides, pastures, and waste places.

Range: Throughout.
Comments: This, our spiniest thistle, should be
handled only with gloves. A biennial,
it produces a rosette of leaves the first
year, and an upright flowering stalk the
second year. The "thistledown," or
bristles on the fruits, serve as
parachutes to carry the light seeds.
Within our range 15 additional
biennial species with purple flower
heads occur.

294 Lance-leaved Coreopsis; Tickseed
(*Coreopsis lanceolata*)
Sunflower Family (Asteraceae)

Description: Solitary yellow daisy-like flower heads
bloom on long stalks.
Flowers: heads 2–2½″ (5–6.3 cm)
wide; 8 yellow ray flowers with 3–4
notches at tips and numerous yellow disk
flowers; outer bracts surrounding flower
head shorter than inner ones.
Leaves: lower and basal 3–6″ (7.5–15
cm) long, short-stalked, elliptic to
linear, occasionally lobed; upper leaves
few, opposite, unstalked, linear to
oblong.
Fruit: 1-seeded, dry, winged, with 2
terminal scales.
Height: 1–2′ (30–60 cm).
Flowering: May–July.
Habitat: Sandy or rocky soil, disturbed areas.
Range: Virginia south to Florida; west to
Louisiana; north to Missouri, Illinois,
and Michigan. Escaped from cultivation
north to New England.
Comments: This native species has branching stems
at base and often forms sizable colonies
along roadsides and in old fields. A
southern species, Greater Tickseed
(*C. major*), 2–3′ (60–90 cm) tall, has
sunflower-like flower heads 1–2″ (2.5–
5 cm) wide and opposite leaves deeply
segmented into 3 parts, appearing as a
whorl of 6. Within our range 11 other
perennial yellow-flowered species occur.

282 Garden Coreopsis
(*Coreopsis tinctoria*)
Sunflower Family (Asteraceae)

Description: Numerous, smooth, slightly angled
branches have showy yellow daisy-like
flowers with reddish-purple disks.
Flowers: heads to 1¼" (3 cm) wide.
Ray flowers 5–7, 3–toothed, blotched
with reddish brown at the base; bracts
surrounding in 2 sets.
Leaves: 2–4" (5–10 cm) long, opposite
highly dissected into linear segments.
Height: 2–4' (60–120 cm).
Flowering: June–September.
Habitat: Low ground, roadsides and waste
places.
Range: Minnesota and Nebraska south to
Louisiana and Texas.
Comments: A prevailing Western species that
escapes cultivation in the East. This is
widespread western and southern
annual in disturbed areas such as moist
ditches. Due to its showiness, the
flower is cultivated extensively; hence
its common name.

93, 484 Daisy Fleabane
(*Erigeron annuus*)
Sunflower Family (Asteraceae)

Description: An erect *stem covered with spreading hairs*
bears flower heads with 40 or more
tightly packed white to pale pink ray
flowers surrounding the central yellow
disk flowers.
Flowers: heads ½" (1.3 cm) wide;
length of *ray flowers short in comparison to
diameter of disk;* head surrounded by
single set of bracts.
Leaves: to 5" (12.5 cm) long, hairy,
lanceolate, toothed.
Height: 1–5' (30–150 cm).
Flowering: June–October.
Habitat: Fields, roadsides, and waste places.
Range: Throughout.
Comments: The descriptive common name

originated from a belief that dried
flowers could rid a dwelling of fleas.

156 Horseweed
(*Erigeron canadensis*)
Sunflower Family (Asteraceae)

Description: A *coarse weed* with erect bristly-haired
stem that has branching clusters of
small, cup-like, greenish-white flower
heads arising from upper leaf axils. The
minute white rays do not spread and
thus are not showy; the numerous disk
flowers are yellow.
Flowers: heads less than ¼" (6 mm)
wide.
Leaves: 1–4" (2.5–10 cm) long, dark
green, linear to narrow lanceolate,
hairy, usually slightly toothed.
Fruit: tiny, 1-seeded, with numerous
bristles that aid seed dispersal.
Height: 1–7' (30–210 cm).
Flowering: July–November.
Habitat: Fields, roadsides, and waste places.
Range: Throughout.
Comments: An annual that thrives on bare soil,
Horseweed is soon crowded out as
perennials become established.
Originally a North American plant, it
has spread to Europe, where it colonizes
open disturbed sites. Indians and early
settlers used a preparation of its leaves
to treat dysentery and sore throat.

94, 483 Common Fleabane; Philadelphia
Fleabane
(*Erigeron philadelphicus*)
Sunflower Family (Asteraceae)

Description: Small aster-like flower heads, with
numerous white to pink ray flowers
surrounding a large yellow disk.
Flowers: heads ½–1" (1.3–2.5 cm)
wide.
Leaves: hairy basal ones to 6" (15 cm)

long, oblong to narrowly ovate; hairy
stem leaves smaller, toothed, *clasping.*
Height: 6–36" (15–90 cm).

Flowering: April–August.

Habitat: Rich thickets, fields, and open woods.

Range: Throughout.

Comments: The generic name, from Greek *eri*
("early") and *geron* ("old man"),
presumably refers to the fact that the
plant flowers early and has a hoary
down suggesting an old man's beard.
Robin's Plaintain (*E. pulchellus*) is
slightly shorter and has fewer, but
larger, lilac or violet flower heads, as
well as stem leaves that are sparse and
stalkless but do not clasp the stem; it is
insect-pollinated and also spreads
actively by runners.

---

564 Spotted Joe-Pye Weed
(*Eupatorium maculatum*)
Sunflower Family (Asteraceae)

Description: Atop a sturdy *purple or purple-spotted
stem,* hairy above, is a large pinkish-
purplish, *flat-topped cluster of fuzzy flower
heads.*
Flowers: heads ⅓" (8 mm) wide, in
clusters 4–5½" (10–14 cm) wide, of all
disk flowers.
Leaves: 2½–8" (6.3–20 cm) long, *in
whorls of 3–5*, thick, lanceolate,
coarsely toothed.
Height: 2–6' (60–180 cm).

Flowering: July–September.

Habitat: Damp meadows, thickets, and shores.

Range: Across southern Canada and northern
U.S.; in mountain areas south to North
Carolina.

Comments: This is one of several similar species
found in our range. Sweet Joe-Pye
Weed (*E. purpureum*) has a greenish
stem, a dome-shaped cluster of dull
pink flower heads, and foliage that
smells like vanilla when crushed.
Hollow Joe-Pye Weed (*E. fistulosum*) has
a hollow stem, and *E. dubium* is a

smaller species with ovate leaves. Folklore tells that an Indian, "Joe Pye," used this plant to cure fevers and that the early American colonists used it to treat an outbreak of typhus.

---

194 Boneset
(*Eupatorium perfoliatum*)
Sunflower Family (Asteraceae)

Description: Hairy plant with dense flat-topped clusters of many dull-white flowers.
Flowers: heads to ¼" (6 mm) long.
Leaves: 4–8" (10–20 cm) long, opposite, lanceolate, wrinkled, toothed; united at base as to *completely surround stem.*
Height: 2–4' (60–120 cm).
Flowering: July–October.
Habitat: Low woods and wet meadows.
Range: Throughout.
Comments: As suggested by the Latin species name, the stem appears to be growing through the leaf. To early herb doctors, this indicated the plant would be useful in setting bones, so its leaves were wrapped with bandages around splints. The dried leaves have also been used to make a tonic, boneset tea, thought effective in treating colds, coughs, and constipation. Upland Boneset (*E. sessilifolium*) is somewhat similar, but its leaves are not fused at the base.

---

189 White Snakeroot
(*Eupatorium rugosum*)
Sunflower Family (Asteraceae)

Description: Solitary or clustered firm stems bear flat-topped clusters of small fuzzy white flower heads composed entirely of disk flowers.
Flowers: heads about ⅕" (5 mm) long and ⅙" (4 mm) wide.
Leaves: 2½–7" (6–18 cm) long,

opposite, ovate, *stalked,* coarsely or sometimes sharply toothed.

Fruit: tiny, seed-like, bearing white bristles.

Height: 1–3' (30–90 cm).

Flowering: July–October.

Habitat: Woods and thickets.

Range: Southern Ontario to New Brunswick; south through New England to Virginia and upland Georgia; west to Louisiana and northeast Texas; north to Wisconsin.

Comments: When eaten by cows, this toxic plant results in milk that can be fatal to humans. Smaller White Snakeroot (*E. aromaticum*), a nonaromatic plant despite its name, has less coarsely toothed leaves, the upper ones stalkless; Late-flowering Thoroughwort (*E. serotinum*) has long-stalked lanceolate leaves with a 3–5 main veins; and Hyssop-leaved Thoroughwort (*E. hyssopifolium*) has very narrow leaves in whorls of 3–4.

419 **Indian Blanket; Showy Gaillardia**
(*Gaillardia pulchella*)
Sunflower Family (Asteraceae)

Description: Branching hairy stems bear solitary flower heads with *reddish ray flowers, tipped with yellow,* surrounding central disk flowers.

Flowers: heads 1–3" (2.5–7.5 cm) wide; ray flowers occasionally all yellow; disk flowers same color as rays.

Leaves: 1–3" (2.5–7.5 cm) long, bristly-haired or downy, mostly stalkless; lower bluntly lobed, upper lanceolate.

Height: 8–16" (20–40 cm).

Flowering: June–July.

Habitat: Prairies, sandy fields, and roadsides.

Range: Southeast Virginia south to Florida; west to Texas and beyond; north to Minnesota.

Comments: This lovely annual may produce many

color variants and combinations in the
red-pink-yellow range, as well as
structural differences in the transition
between disk and ray flowers. If ray
flowers are absent, entire heads may
consist of enlarged disk flowers.

197 Sweet Everlasting; Catfoot
(*Gnaphalium obtusifolium*)
Sunflower Family (Asteraceae)

Description: Erect, *cottony stem* bears branched
clusters of whitish-yellow, round,
fragrant flower heads.
Flowers: heads about ¼" (6 mm) long,
made up of tiny tubular disk flowers
with bristles; overlapping bracts under
flower heads, white or tinged with
yellow, persisting.
Leaves: 1–4" (2.5–10 cm) long,
whitish-woolly beneath, narrow,
pointed, stalkless; not mostly basal as
in Pussytoes (*Antennaria* spp.)
Height: 1–2' (30–60 cm).
Flowering: August–November.
Habitat: Dry clearings, fields, and edges of
woods.
Range: Throughout.
Comments: The genus name *Gnaphalium,* derived
from the Greek *gnaphallon* ("tuft of
wool"), refers to the nature of the
flower heads. This is one of the more
common among the 12 species within
our range.

298 Gumweed; Tarweed; Sticky Heads
(*Grindelia squarrosa*)
Sunflower Family (Asteraceae)

Description: Stout erect stem bears several branches
with yellow daisy-like flower heads.
Flowers: heads about 1" (2.5 cm) wide,
with ray flowers encircling darker
central disk flowers; entire head
surrounded by pointed, outward-

curling, green bracts that produce *sticky*
material.

Leaves: 1–2½″ (2.5–6.3 cm) long,
oblong, stalkless, toothed, covered with
translucent dots.

Height: 6–36″ (15–90 cm)

Flowering: July–September.

Habitat: Prairies and waste places.

Range: Native in west and southwest of our
range, but spread eastward to the Mid-
Atlantic states and north to Ontario
and Quebec.

Comments: This tough but short-lived perennial, a
common invader of overgrazed
rangeland in the West, has now spread
to dry waste places in the East. Because
of its bitter taste it is not eaten by
cattle. Indians used its flowers and
leaves for treating bronchitis and
asthma and for healing sores. The
powdered flower heads were once used
in cigarettes to relieve asthma.

366 Broom Snakeweed; Turpentine Weed
(*Gutierrezia sarothrae*)
Sunflower Family (Asteraceae)

Description: Oblong yellow flower heads of this
sticky bushy plant occur in clusters at
ends of the smooth branches.

Flowers: heads ¼″ (6 mm) wide, in
clusters of 2–5.

Leaves: about 1½″ (3.8 cm) long,
alternate, narrow, untoothed.

Height: 6–20″ (15–50 cm).

Flowering: July–September.

Habitat: Dry plains and prairies.

Range: Southern Manitoba; Minnesota south to
Texas; very prevalent through
Southwest.

Comments: The fine, brittle stems of this shrubby
perennial, which are somewhat broom-
like, account for its common name;
they die back nearly to the ground each
year. It is poor grazing fodder, and the
new spring growth may be toxic to

animals. Since it tends to increase with overgrazing, its abundance often indicates overused rangeland.

279 Sneezeweed
(*Helenium autumnale*)
Sunflower Family (Asteraceae)

Description: *Winged stem* bears yellow daisy-like flower heads with fan-shaped *ray flowers that droop backward;* disk flowers form conspicuous, greenish-yellow, ball-like structure at center of head.
Flowers: heads 1–2″ (2.5–5 cm) wide; ray flowers 3-lobed.
Leaves: to 6″ (15 cm) long, alternate, lanceolate, toothed, with bases forming winged extensions down the stem.
Height: 2–5′ (60–150 cm).
Flowering: August–November.
Habitat: Swamps and wet meadows.
Range: Throughout.
Comments: As the species name implies, Sneezeweed flowers in late summer or fall. The common name is based on the use of its dried leaves in making snuff, inhaled to cause sneezing that would supposedly rid the body of evil spirits. Other species include Purple-headed Sneezeweed (*H. nudiflorum*), with a purplish-brown ball of disk flowers.

286 Common Sunflower
(*Helianthus annuus*)
Sunflower Family (Asteraceae)

Description: Rough erect stem bears from one to several terminal flower heads, with sterile, overlapping, yellow ray flowers and *brownish disk flowers* that produce the fruit.
Flowers: heads 3–6″ (7.5–15 cm) wide; bracts enclosing heads edged with bristles.

Leaves: 3–12" (7.5–30 cm) long, *ovate to nearly triangular,* pointed, with rough stiff hairs, mostly alternate.
Fruit: dry, seed-like, with a white seed inside.
Height: 3–10' (90–300 cm).
Flowering: July–November.
Habitat: Prairies and rich soils, but spread to waste places and roadsides.
Range: Throughout.
Comments: This native annual is appreciably smaller than the familiar cultivated variety. The Common Sunflower was much used by the Indians for bread flour made from its ground seeds and for oil used in cooking and for dressing hair. In the 19th century it was believed that plants growing near a home would protect from malaria. Recent uses include making silage from the plant and extracting the oil to make soap. Closely related is the Prairie Sunflower (*H. petiolaris*), found throughout the Great Plains.

---

284 Giant Sunflower; Tall Sunflower
(*Helianthus giganteus*)
Sunflower Family (Asteraceae)

Description: Tall rough reddish stem bears several to many light-yellow flower heads.
Flowers: heads 1½–3" (3.8–7.5 cm) wide, with 10–20 ray flowers and numerous yellow disk flowers; bracts beneath heads narrow, thin, green.
Leaves: 3–7" (7.5–17.5 cm) long, mostly alternate; *rough,* lanceolate, pointed, finely toothed, occasionally opposite.
Height: 3–12' (90–360 cm).
Flowering: July–October.
Habitat: Swamps, wet thickets, and meadows.
Range: Nearly throughout.
Comments: Considering its name, the flowers of this plant are comparatively small; the "Giant" in its common name actually refers to the plant's overall height.

290 Maximilian's Sunflower
(*Helianthus maximiliani*)
Sunflower Family (Asteraceae)

Description: Heads of yellow ray and disk flowers
rise from upper half of stalk on one or
more rough stems.
Flowers: heads 2–3″ (5–7.5 cm) wide.
Leaves: 4–6″ (10–15 cm) long, stiff,
narrow, tapering at both ends, *rough on
both sides,* often folded lengthwise and
curved downward at tips, mostly
alternate.
Height: 3–10′ (90–300 cm).
Flowering: July–October.
Habitat: Prairies.
Range: Saskatchewan and Manitoba; Minnesota
south to Missouri, Oklahoma, and
Texas; escaped from cultivation
eastward to Atlantic states.
Comments: A native perennial, associated with the
bluegrass prairie, it is a desirable range
plant, eaten by many livestock. A
heavy crop of seeds is produced; thus it
is a valuable plant for wildlife. It was
named for the naturalist Prince
Maximilian of Wied Neuwied, who led
an expedition into the American West
in the 1830s. Another bluegrass prairie
species, the Willow-leaved Sunflower
(*H. salicifolius*), has numerous long,
narrow, drooping leaves covered with
soft hairs and a purple-brown disk and
is typical of rocky outcrops with heavy
soil.

285 Woodland Sunflower
(*Helianthus strumosus*)
Sunflower Family (Asteraceae)

Description: Yellow flower heads on branches from a
smooth or slightly rough main stem.
Flowers: 2½–3½″ (6.3–9 cm) wide,
with 9–15 ray flowers surrounding
yellow disk flowers.
Leaves: 3–8″ (7.5–20 cm) long, mostly
opposite, ovate to broadly lanceolate,

shallow-toothed or entire; rough above
*pale to whitish and somewhat hairy
underneath.*
Height: 3–7′ (90–210 cm).
Flowering: August–September.
Habitat: Woods, thickets, and clearings.
Range: Quebec; New England south to
Georgia; west to Oklahoma; north to
North Dakota.
Comments: This is one of approximately 20 species
of Sunflowers with yellow disk flowers
that bloom in our range.

283 Jerusalem Artichoke
(*Helianthus tuberosus*)
Sunflower Family (Asteraceae)

Description: Stout, rough branching stems bear *large
golden-yellow flower heads.*
Flowers: heads to 3″ (7.5 cm) wide,
with 10–20 ray flowers; bracts beneath
heads narrow, spreading.
Leaves: to 4–10″ (10–25 cm) long,
ovate to lanceolate, *thick and rough,*
toothed, opposite below and alternate
above, *with winged stalks, 3 main veins.*
Height: 5–10′ (150–300 cm).
Flowering: August–October.
Habitat: Moist soil.
Range: Spread from cultivation throughout our
range.
Comments: This large, coarse Sunflower was
cultivated by the Indians and has spread
eastward. The edible tuber is highly
nutritious and, unlike potatoes,
contains no starch, but rather
carbohydrate in a form that is
metabolized into natural sugar. In 1805
Lewis and Clark dined on the tubers,
prepared by a squaw, in what is now
North Dakota. Today they are sold in
produce markets or "health food" stores
and, when boiled or roasted like
potatoes, are delicious. Raw, they have
a sweet, nut-like taste. The common
name is a corruption of the Italian
girasole, meaning "turning to the sun."

291 Camphorweed
(*Heterotheca subaxillaris*)
Sunflower Family (Asteraceae)

Description: Yellow daisy-like flower heads on tall, hairy stems; plant often has one-sided, unbalanced look.
Flowers: heads ½–¾" (1.3–2 cm) wide.
Leaves: alternate, oblong; basal ones 2–3" (5–7.5 cm) long, stalked; *upper ones smaller, wavy-edged, clasping stem.*
Height: 1–3' (30–90 cm).

Flowering: July–November.

Habitat: Sandy soils of prairies, waste places, and roadsides.

Range: New Jersey and Delaware south to Florida; west to Texas; north to Kansas and Illinois.

Comments: This native annual or biennial has been extending its range northward. It is unpalatable to grazing livestock on open rangeland.

374 Orange Hawkweed; Devil's Paintbrush
(*Hieracium aurantiacum*)
Sunflower Family (Asteraceae)

Description: A slender, hairy, usually leafless floral stalk bears dandelion-like orange flower heads.
Flowers: heads ¾" (2 cm) wide, with all ray flowers, each having 5 teeth (tips of fused petals); disk flowers absent; green bracts around flower head covered with *black, gland-tipped hairs.*
Leaves: 2–5" (5–12.5 cm) long, in basal rosette, elliptic, coarsely hairy.
Height: 1–2' (30–60 cm).

Flowering: June–August.

Habitat: Fields, clearings, and roadsides.

Range: Newfoundland and Nova Scotia; south through New England to North Carolina; west to Iowa; north to Minnesota.

Comments: This showy, introduced Hawkweed is

found across the northern part of our range, particularly New England. Farmers, who saw it as a troublesome weed, named it Devil's Paintbrush. Th name Hawkweed derives from a folk belief that hawks ate the flowers to aid their vision.

302 Mouse-ear Hawkweed
(*Hieracium pilosella*)
Sunflower Family (Asteraceae)

Description: Small plant with a solitary yellow, dandelion-like flower head on a leafless, *hairy,* and glandular stalk.
Flowers: head 1″ (2.5 cm) wide, with all ray flowers; disk flowers absent; bracts surrounding flower head covered with black hairs and glands.
Leaves: basal 1–5″ (2.5–12.5 cm) long, oblong, covered with stiff, long hairs; *white bloom on underside.*
Fruit: small, seed-like, with slender bristles.
Height: 3–12′ (90–360 cm).

Flowering: June–September.

Habitat: Pastures, fields, and lawns.

Range: Newfoundland and Nova Scotia; south from New England to North Carolina; west to Ohio and beyond; north to Minnesota.

Comments: This European introduction to the Northeast has spread south to North Carolina and west to Minnesota; it has even been seen as far away as Oregon. The plant spreads rapidly by leafy runners as well as by its numerous, dandelion-like seeds. The common name and the species name relate to the hairy nature of the leaves. Large Mouse-ear (*H. flagellare*), which has 2–5 flower heads and leaves with green undersides, occurs from Prince Edward Island south to Virginia and west to Michigan.

306 Yellow Hawkweed; King Devil
(*Hieracium pratense*)
Sunflower Family (Asteraceae)

Description: Hairy mostly leafless stalk bears several heads of bright yellow ray flowers.
Flowers: heads ½" (1.3 cm) wide, each surrounded by bracts covered with gland-tipped *black hairs.*
Leaves: basal leaves 2–10" (5–25 cm) long, oblong, untoothed, covered with stiff hairs.
Height: 1–3' (30–90 cm).

Flowering: May–August.

Habitat: Pastures and roadsides.

Range: Southern Ontario and Quebec to Nova Scotia; New England south to upland Georgia; west to Tennessee.

Comments: This perennial is similar to the Orange Hawkweed (*H. aurantiacum*), differing primarily in flower color. Both introduced from Europe, they are considered weeds by farmers since they spread quickly by leafy runners. New England meadows covered with a mixture of both flowers, however, are a beautiful sight. The very similar *H. floribundum,* found from Newfoundland to Connecticut and west to Ohio, differs in having upper leaf surfaces with only a few hairs near the margin. *H. florentinum,* occurring from Newfoundland south to North Carolina, northwest to Iowa and Ontario, has no runners, essentially smooth leaves, and few black hairs on the bracts. These last two species were also European introductions.

301 Rattlesnake Weed
(*Hieracium venosum*)
Sunflower Family (Asteraceae)

Description: Numerous yellow, dandelion-like flower heads in open clusters top a long, usually leafless floral stalk.
Flowers: heads ½–¾" (1.3–2 cm)

wide, with all ray flowers.
Leaves: basal, 1½–6″ (3.8–15 cm)
long, elliptic, green with *reddish-purple
veins.*
Fruit: dry, with yellowish bristles.
Height: 1–2½′ (30–75 cm).

Flowering: May–September.

Habitat: Dry open woods, thickets, and
clearings.

Range: New England south to Florida; west to
Louisiana; north through Missouri and
beyond.

Comments: This native woodland flower is
relatively widespread but most common
in parts of our range where rattlesnakes
occur; hence the common name.
Within our range 11 other yellow-
flowered species, 9 of them native, are
found.

296 Elecampane
(*Inula helenium*)
Sunflower Family (Asteraceae)

Description: Yellow Sunflower-like heads with long,
narrow, straggly ray flowers surrounding a
darker central disk atop a tall, hairy
stem.
Flowers: 2–4″ (5–10 cm) wide.
Leaves: large, rough, toothed leaves,
white-woolly beneath; *stem leaves
stalkless, clasp stem;* basal leaves up to
20″ (50 cm) long, with long leafstalks.
Height: 2–6′ (60–180 cm).

Flowering: July–September.

Habitat: Fields and roadsides.

Range: Southern Ontario to Nova Scotia; south
to North Carolina; west to Missouri;
north to Minnesota and beyond.

Comments: Perhaps of Asian origin, Elecampane
was introduced to Europe, then
brought to America by early colonists.
In the 19th century a tincture of its
roots was thought useful in reducing
fevers and as a diuretic, but it may have
caused more illness than it cured.

303 Two-flowered Cynthia
(*Krigia biflora*)
Sunflower Family (Asteraceae)

Description: Yellow-orange Dandelion-like flower
heads top a smooth, forking stem.
Flowers: heads up to 1½" (3.8 cm)
wide, 2–6, of all ray flowers.
Leaves: single, (occasionally 2), small,
oval, *clasp stem below fork;* basal leaves,
2–7" (5–17.5 cm) long, elliptic
stalked.
Height: 1–2' (30–60 cm).

Flowering: May–August.

Habitat: Open woods and meadows.

Range: Manitoba to New England; south to
Georgia; west to Tennessee and
Missouri; (southwestward beyond our
range).

Comments: This native perennial is related to the
Hawkweeds. The smaller Dwarf
Dandelion (*K. virginica*), of sandy sites,
has a solitary flower rising from a set of
toothed or lobed basal leaves and is less
than 1' (30 cm) tall. Potato Dandelion
(*K. dandelion*), which has a large solitary
head on a leafless stem and a tuber
½–1" (1.3–2.5 cm) long just below
the surface, is found from southern
New Jersey to Florida, west to Texas,
and north to Missouri.

300 Wild Lettuce
(*Lactuca canadensis*)
Sunflower Family (Asteraceae)

Description: *Tall plant* with elongated cluster of
small pale yellow flower heads; foliage
exudes milky juice when crushed; slight
bloom present on stem and leaves.
Flowers: heads ¼" (6 mm) wide.
Leaves: to 1' (30 cm) long, variable,
from nearly toothless and lanceolate to
deeply lobed, stalkless.
Fruit: dry, flat, 1-seeded, with bristly
"parachute" that aids in seed dispersal.
Height: 2–10' (60–300 cm).

Flowering: July–September.
Habitat: Clearings, thickets, and edges of woods.
Range: Throughout.
Comments: This rather large biennial is frequently found in disturbed sites. Its flowers are insignificant, and the leaves lack the spines of the similar Prickly Lettuce (*L. scariola*). Young leaves can be used in salads or as cooked greens, but have a slightly bitter taste.

606 Florida Lettuce; False Lettuce
(*Lactuca floridana*)
Sunflower Family (Asteraceae)

Description: Atop a leafy stem is loose cluster of numerous blue, sometimes whitish, flower heads.
Flowers: heads ¼–½″ (6–13 mm) wide; 11–17 ray flowers.
Leaves: blades 4–12″ (10–30 cm) long, deeply cut, dandelion-like; terminal segment triangular; lateral segments lanceolate to oval, all toothed.
Fruit: 1-seeded, crowned with *shiny white hairs*.
Height: 2–7′ (60–210 cm).
Flowering: August–October.
Habitat: Rich woods, thickets, and clearings.
Range: Massachusetts and New York south to Florida; west to Texas; north to Nebraska and Minnesota.
Comments: There are several species of Blue Lettuce, among them a more western species, Large-flowered Blue Lettuce (*L. pulchella*), with larger and fewer flower heads than this species and foliage covered with a white, waxy bloom. Tall Blue Lettuce (*L. biennis*), found from southern Canada to North Carolina and west to Iowa, has crowded flower clusters and tan fruit bristles. Wild Lettuce is related to garden lettuce; if the latter is allowed to go to seed, the floral resemblance can be seen.

304 Prickly Lettuce
(*Lactuca scariola*)
Sunflower Family (Asteraceae)

Description: Loose clusters of small, yellow,
Dandelion-like flower heads are borne
on *erect stem with very prickly leaves:*
foliage exudes milky juice when
broken.
Flowers: ¼″ (6 mm) wide, usually with
16–24 ray flowers; disk flowers absent.
Leaves: 2–12″ (5–30 cm) long, oblong,
lobed or unlobed, *prickly-edged,* bristly
on undersurface along midrib, clasping
the stem at base; often *set on edge* and
oriented in one plane.
Fruit: dry, 1-seeded, with white
bristles that aid seed dispersal.
Height: 2–5′ (60–150 cm).
Flowering: June–October.
Habitat: Roadsides and waste places.
Range: Throughout.
Comments: The leaves of this introduced species are
arranged distinctively, often in a flat,
north-south plane. It was once
mistakenly thought its juice could be
used as an opium substitute.

544 Rough Blazing Star
(*Liatris aspera*)
Sunflower Family (Asteraceae)

Description: *Rounded lavender flowers* in a loose spike-
like cluster on stiff, erect stem covered
with grayish hairs.
Flowers: heads about ¾″ (2 cm) wide,
all disk flowers, both stalkless and
stalked; bracts beneath heads *broadly
rounded,* flaring, with pinkish
translucent margins.
Leaves: rough, lanceolate to linear;
lower leaves 4–12″ (10–30 cm) long,
upper ones progressively smaller.
Height: 16–48″ (40–120 cm).
Flowering: August–October.
Habitat: Open plains and thin woods, in sandy
soil.

Range: Southern Manitoba and Ontario; North
Carolina south to Florida; west to
Texas; north through Oklahoma and
Missouri to North Dakota and beyond.

Comments: This species is distinguished by its
roughness and rounded floral bracts.
The origin of the genus name is
unknown; *aspera* is Latin for "rough."

545 Prairie Blazing Star
(*Liatris pycnostachya*)
Sunflower Family (Asteraceae)

Description: Rose-purple, cylindric, stalkless flower
heads made up of all disk flowers,
densely crowded on a coarse, hairy, very
leafy stem.
Flowers: heads about ½" (1.3 cm) wide
in spike-like clusters; bracts beneath
heads with long-pointed purplish tips,
spreading or bent backward.
Leaves: lower 4–12" (10–30 cm) long,
upper much smaller, punctate, linear.
Height: 2–5' (60–150 cm).

Flowering: July–October.

Habitat: Damp prairies.

Range: Wisconsin south to Kentucky and
Louisiana; west to Texas and
Oklahoma; north to South Dakota and
Minnesota.

Comments: One of the most popular of the Blazing
Stars, this is sometimes grown as an
ornamental. The species name, from
the Greek for "crowded," describes
both the leaves and the flower heads. A
dry prairie species, Dotted Blazing Star
(*L. punctata*), has leaves covered with
resinous dots and long, pointed and flat
bracts beneath the flower heads.

543 Large Blazing Star
(*Liatris scariosa*)
Sunflower Family (Asteraceae)

Description: Spike of pink-lavender flower heads in
interrupted clusters on a tall smooth or
downy stem.
Flowers: heads to 1″ (2.5 cm) wide,
composed entirely of disk flowers, on
diverging stalks; overlapping bracts
surrounding flower heads are in 5–6
series.
Leaves: to 10″ (25 cm) long, numerous,
soft-hairy to rough; lower ones ovate to
lanceolate; upper ones smaller, linear.
Height: 1–5′ (30–150 cm).
Flowering: August–September.
Habitat: Dry woods and clearings.
Range: Pennsylvania south to Georgia;
northwesterly to Illinois and Nebraska.
Comments: The flower heads and broad leaves with
stalks well separated are characteristic
of 4 very similar species in our range,
which may eventually prove variants of
a single species.

546 Dense Blazing Star
(*Liatris spicata*)
Sunflower Family (Asteraceae)

Description: Rose-purple *flower heads closely set* on a
spike 1′ (30 cm) or more in length.
Flowers: heads ¼″ (6 mm) wide,
stalkless, all disk flowers; long styles
protrude beyond corolla lobes; thin
scale-like bracts beneath flower heads,
blunt, with purple edges.
Leaves: numerous, linear, crowded, 1′
(30 cm) or more in length at base of
plant, decreasing in size upward.
Height: 1–6′ (30–180 cm).
Flowering: July–September.
Habitat: Moist, low ground.
Range: Long Island south to Florida; west to
Louisiana; north to Michigan and
Wisconsin; escaped from cultivation in
southern New England and New York.

Comments: The species name describes the
elongated inflorescence, with its
crowded stalkless flower heads. The
protruding styles give the flower an
overall feathery appearance; hence its
occasional alternate name, Gay Feather.

203 Climbing Boneset; Climbing Hempweed
(*Mikania scandens*)
Sunflower Family (Asteraceae)

Description: Twining *vine* with flat-topped clusters
of white or pinkish flower heads rising
from the leaf axils.
Flowers: heads about ¼″ (6 mm) wide,
made up of 4 disk flowers, surrounded
by scale-like bracts.
Leaves: 1–3″ (2.5–7.5 cm) long,
opposite, ovate to triangular, with
wavy-toothed or untoothed margins.
Fruit: tiny, dried, seed-like, with tuft
of whitish bristles.
Height: vine, variable.
Flowering: July–October (throughout year in the
South).
Habitat: Stream banks, moist thickets, swamps.
Range: Southern Ontario; New England south
to Florida; west to Texas.
Comments: This species forms a sizable growth over
other plants in moist woods and
thickets. Its flower resembles that of
Boneset (*Eupatorium perfoliatum*).
Two similar Hemp Vines (*M.
batatifolia: M. cordifolia*) are found
in Florida.

563 Salt-marsh Fleabane
(*Pluchea purpurescens*)
Sunflower Family (Asteraceae)

Description: Erect annual with *flat-topped clusters* of
pink-lavender flower heads; plant has a
faint camphor fragrance.
Flowers: heads about ⅕″ (5 mm) wide;

all disk flowers, ray flowers absent; pink
or purple bracts under flower heads.
Leaves: 2–6″ (5–15 cm) long, short
stalks or stalkless, ovate to lanceolate,
slightly toothed, scalloped, or smooth.
Fruit: tiny, dry, 1-seeded, with circle
of bristles.
Height: 1–3′ (30–90 cm).
Flowering: July–October.
Habitat: Saline to brackish marshes.
Range: Southern Maine south to Florida,
largely coastal; west to Texas and
beyond.
Comments: This typical brackish-marsh plant adds
a flash of pink to marsh grasses at the
end of the growing season. Its dense
pinkish flower masses are often used in
dried flower arrangements.

167 White Lettuce; Rattlesnake Root
(*Prenanthes alba*)
Sunflower Family (Asteraceae)

Description: Tall, slender perennial with white or
pinkish *drooping flower heads* in clusters
along the stem; smooth stem, usually
purplish with whitish bloom, has milky
juice when crushed.
Flowers: heads about ½″ (1.3 cm) long,
made up of 8–12 ray flowers; disk
flowers absent; stamens prominent,
cream-colored.
Leaves: variable up to 8″ (20 cm) long,
smooth; lower ones triangular, lobed or
unlobed; uppermost often lanceolate.
Fruit: dry, seed-like, with tan or
reddish-brown bristles.
Height: 2–5′ (60–150 cm).
Flowering: August–September.
Habitat: Rich woods and thickets.
Range: Across southeast Canada; New England
south to upland Georgia; northwesterly
to Missouri and South Dakota.
Comments: The alternate common name
Rattlesnake Root suggests the plant
was used as a remedy for snakebite. A
bitter tonic was made from the roots

and thought useful in treating dysentery. This is one of several species of Rattlesnake Root, all of which have drooping flower heads, distinctly lobed leaves, and milky juice. Lion's Foot (*P. serpentaria*) is similar but has white bristles on its fruit and the stem lacks bloom. Gall-of-the-earth (*P. trifoliata*) has very deeply divided 3-part leaves and a waxy reddish stem. Tall White Lettuce (*P. altissima*) has only 5 main bracts surrounding the flower heads. Smooth White Lettuce (*P. racemosa*) has pinkish flowers in a spike, clasping elongated leaves, and yellow bristles.

280 Prairie Coneflower; Gray-headed Coneflower
(*Ratibida pinnata*)
Sunflower Family (Asteraceae)

Description: Slender, hairy-stemmed plant having flower heads with *drooping yellow ray flowers* and disk flowers forming a cylindrical cone shorter than the rays; *grayish cone* darkens to brown as ray flowers fall.
Flowers: rays 1–2½″ (2.5–6.3 cm) long; disk cone ¾″ (2 cm) long.
Leaves: about 5″ (12.5 cm) long, compound, pinnately divided into lanceolate, coarsely toothed segments.
Height: 1½–5′ (45–150 cm).
Flowering: June–September.
Habitat: Dry woods and prairies.
Range: Southern Ontario; western New York south to Georgia, mainly inland; west to Oklahoma and Nebraska; north to Minnesota.
Comments: A similar species, *R. columnifera* is a shorter plant. Since these perennials are palatable to livestock, they tend to diminish with overgrazing of rangeland. When bruised, disk exudes an anise scent.

281 Black-eyed Susan
(*Rudbeckia hirta*)
Sunflower Family (Asteraceae)

Description: Coarse, rough-stemmed plant with daisy-like flower heads made up of showy golden-yellow ray flowers, with disk flowers forming a *brown central cone.*
Flowers: head 2–3″ (5–7.5 cm) wide.
Leaves: 2–7″ (5–17.5 cm) long, lanceolate to ovate, rough, hairy; lower ones untoothed or scantily toothed, with 3 prominent veins and winged leafstalks.
Fruit: tiny, dry, seed-like, lacking the typical bristles.
Height: 1–3′ (30–90 cm).
Flowering: June–October.
Habitat: Fields, prairies, and open woods.
Range: Nearly throughout.
Comments: This native prairie biennial forms a rosette of leaves the first year, followed by flowers the second year. It is covered with hairs that give it a slightly rough texture. The Green-headed Coneflower (*R. laciniata*) has yellow ray flowers pointing downward, a greenish-yellow disk, and irregularly divided leaves.

289 Golden Ragwort
(*Senecio aureus*)
Sunflower Family (Asteraceae)

Description: Smooth plant with yellow daisy-like flower heads in flat-topped clusters.
Flowers: ¾″ (2 cm) wide, each head with 8–12 yellow ray flowers and yellow central disk flowers.
Leaves: basal leaves ½–6″ (1.3–15 cm) long, *heart-shaped,* with long stalks, rounded teeth; upper stem leaves 1–3½″ (2.5–9 cm) long, pinnately lobed.
Height: 1–2′ (30–60 cm).
Flowering: April–July.
Habitat: Wet meadows, swamps, moist woods.

Range: Southern Ontario to Newfoundland; New England south to South Carolina and upland Alabama; west to Missouri; north to North Dakota.

Comments: Of the 16 species in our range, an upland forest species, Squaw Weed (*S. obovatus*), has spatulate leaves tapering at the base. Westward, on dry bluffs and prairies, Prairie Ragwort (*S. plattensis*) has basal leaves woolly on the underside. Woolly Ragwort (*S. tomentosus*), found in open woods and fields along the coastal plain from New Jersey to Texas, has long, narrow, woolly basal leaves, especially when young.

---

293 Compass Plant
(*Silphium laciniatum*)
Sunflower Family (Asteraceae)

Description: Tall plant with heads made up of yellow ray and disk flowers enclosed by large, hairy-edged, green bracts; stem exudes resinous juice.
Flowers: heads to 3″ (7.5 cm) wide.
Leaves: 12–18″ (30–45 cm) long, alternate, rough, *large, deeply divided,* vertical, *edges mostly oriented in north-south direction,* unstalked or short-stalked.
Height: 3–12′ (90–360 cm).
Flowering: July–September.
Habitat: Prairies.
Range: Michigan and Indiana south to Alabama; west to Texas; north to North Dakota.
Comments: Compass Plant is one of a group of tall, mostly prairie Sunflowers, some with very large leaves. The common name refers to the north-south orientation of the leaves. The species name is related to its deeply incised leaves. The hardened sap of this plant can be chewed like gum. Rosinweed (*S. integrifolium*) has opposite, very rough, stalkless leaves, untoothed or

slightly toothed, and is 2–5′ (60–150 cm) tall. Cup Plant (*S. perfoliatum*) has opposite leaves that envelop its square stem, forming a "cup" around it. Prairie Dock (*S. terebinthinaceum*) has large ovate or heart-shaped basal leaves, up to 2′ (60 cm) long, with very tall stalks.

343 Tall Goldenrod
(*Solidago altissima*)
Sunflower Family (Asteraceae)

Description: Small yellow flower heads on *outward-arching* branches form a pyramidal cluster atop a *grayish, downy* stem.
Flowers: heads about ⅛″ (3 mm) long.
Leaves: lanceolate, rough above, hairy below, sometimes toothed; lower ones up to 6″ (15 cm) long, upper ones smaller.
Height: 2–7′ (60–210 cm).
Flowering: August–November.
Habitat: Thickets, roadsides, and clearings.
Range: Southern Ontario and Quebec; New York south to Florida; west to Texas; north to Minnesota and beyond.
Comments: Two other similar species with arching flowerstalks are Late Goldenrod (*S. gigantea*), smooth-stemmed, often with a whitish bloom, and flower heads up to ¼″ (6 mm) high, and Canada Goldenrod (*S. canadensis*), with sharply toothed leaves and very small flower heads, only ⅛″ (3 mm) high.

155 Silverrod
(*Solidago bicolor*)
Sunflower Family (Asteraceae)

Description: Elongated spike of *white flower heads* on short stalks atop a hairy, grayish stem.
Flowers: heads about ¼″ (6 mm) long, with small yellow disk flowers

surrounded by 7–9 white ray flowers.
Leaves: basal and lower leaves 2–4″
(5–10 cm) long, oblong, stalked,
toothed; upper ones smaller, narrower,
often without stalks or teeth.
Height: 1–3′ (30–90 cm).

Flowering: July–October.

Habitat: Thin woods or dry, open soil.

Range: Southern Ontario to Nova Scotia; south
to Georgia; west to Arkansas; north to
Wisconsin.

Comments: This is the only goldenrod species with
white rays. Hairy Goldenrod
(*S. hispida*) has yellow ray flowers; it is
found south through New England to
Georgia, west to Arkansas, and north
to Minnesota.

337 Blue-stemmed Goldenrod
(*Solidago caesia*)
Sunflower Family (Asteraceae)

Description: Smooth *purplish,* frequently arching
stem covered with *whitish bloom* and
bearing *scattered clusters* of yellow flower
heads in the leaf axils, with a large
terminal cluster.
Flowers: heads about ¼″ (6 mm) long.
Leaves: 2½–5″ (6–12.5 cm) long,
stalkless, elliptic, tapering at both
ends, toothed, sharply pointed.
Height: 1–3′ (30–90 cm).

Flowering: August–October.

Habitat: Woods, thickets, and clearings.

Range: Southern Ontario to Nova Scotia;
Maine south to Florida; west to Texas;
north to Wisconsin.

Comments: Other Goldenrods with scattered flower
clusters include the Wand-like
Goldenrod (*S. stricta*), found in sandy
sites from New Jersey southward, with
a wand-like flowerstalk and narrow
scale-like leaves pressed against the
stem. Zigzag Goldenrod (*S. flexicaulis*)
has a zigzag stem and broad ovate
leaves. Downy Goldenrod (*S. puberula*),
found in dry sites along the East Coast,

has a very leafy stem covered with fine,
spreading hairs.

339 Lance-leaved Goldenrod
(*Solidago graminifolia*)
Sunflower Family (Asteraceae)

Description: Smooth or finely downy stem branches
above the middle, with each branch
bearing a *flat-topped cluster* of small
yellow flower heads.
Flowers: heads about ⅕" (5 mm) long,
with 10–20 ray flowers and 8–12 disk
flowers.
Leaves: 3–5" (7–12.5 cm) long, *narrow,
elongated, pointed,* with 3–5 veins.
Height: 2–4' (60–120 cm).

Flowering: July–October.

Habitat: Roadsides, fields, and thickets.

Range: Across southern Canada; New England
south to North Carolina; northwesterly
to South Dakota and Minnesota.

Comments: The flat-topped floral arrangement and
narrow leaves of this Goldenrod are
distinctive. Slender Fragrant Goldenrod
(*S. tenuifolia*) has grass-like leaves with
tiny resin dots and only one rib or vein.
The similar, still smaller Narrow-leaved
Bushy Goldenrod (*S. microcephala*) has
leaves less than ⅛" (3 mm) wide, with
tufts of minute leaves in the axils.

342 Sweet Goldenrod
(*Solidago odora*)
Sunflower Family (Asteraceae)

Description: Smooth, tall, *anise-scented* plant bears
crowded, cylindrical, yellow flower
clusters, with flower heads arranged
along one side of slightly arching
branches.
Flowers: heads about ⅙" (4 mm) long.
Leaves: 1–4" (2.5–10 cm) long,
smooth, narrow, stalkless, with small
translucent dots.

Height: 2–3′ (60–90 cm).
Flowering: July–September.
Habitat: Dry fields and open woods.
Range: New England south to Florida; west to Texas and north to Ohio.
Comments: The crushed leaves of Sweet Goldenrod give off a licorice scent that readily identifies this widespread species. A tea can be brewed from its leaves.

---

340 Stiff Goldenrod; Hard-leaved Goldenrod
(*Solidago rigida*)
Sunflower Family (Asteraceae)

Description: Tall, coarse, hairy stem bears a dense, rounded or flat-topped, terminal group of large, dark yellow, bell-shaped flower heads.
Flowers: heads about ⅓″ (8 mm) long, each with 7–10 ray flowers, 20–30 disk flowers.
Leaves: basal rough, elliptic, long-stalked, the blade up to 10″ (25 cm) in length; upper leaves oval, clasping, *rigid, rough*.
Height: 1–5′ (30–150 cm).
Flowering: August–October.
Habitat: Prairies, thickets, and open woods.
Range: Massachusetts south to Georgia; west to Texas; north to Canada.
Comments: This deep-rooted species is usually found in clumps. There are 4 similar species with relatively broad leaves and flat-topped clusters, but they have smooth stems.

---

344 Rough-stemmed Goldenrod
(*Solidago rugosa*)
Sunflower Family (Asteraceae)

Description: Tall, *rough, hairy stem* bears divergent, or arching, branches with small, light yellow flower heads concentrated on the upper side.

Flowers: heads about ⅛″ (4 mm) long, each with 6–11 ray flowers and 4–7 disk flowers.
Leaves: 1½–5″ (3.8–12.5 cm) long, rough, *sharply toothed, very hairy, and wrinkled.*
Height: 1–6′ (30–180 cm).
Flowering: July–October.
Habitat: Fields, roadsides, and borders of woods.
Range: Ontario to Nova Scotia and Newfoundland; New England south to Florida; west to Texas; north to Michigan.
Comments: This highly variable Goldenrod can form large masses in fields that were once cultivated. Physicians in ancient times believed that Goldenrod had healing powers; in recent times these plants have been popularly blamed for causing hay fever, but its irritating symptoms are actually caused by Ragweed, whose pollen is abundant when Goldenrod is in flower.

338 Seaside Goldenrod
(*Solidago sempervirens*)
Sunflower Family (Asteraceae)

Description: Succulent-leaved salt-marsh Goldenrod with arching branches that bear *one-sided clusters* of large, bright yellow flower heads.
Flowers: heads about ⅓″ (8 mm) long, each with 7–10 ray flowers.
Leaves: *fleshy,* lanceolate to oblong, toothless; upper, 2–8″ (5–20 cm) long; basal, to 1′ (30 cm).
Height: 1–8′ (30–240 cm).
Flowering: July–November.
Habitat: Edges of saline or brackish marshes, and sandy sites.
Range: Coastal, Newfoundland south to Florida; west along Gulf Coast to Texas and Mexico.
Comments: Plants found from Florida to Texas and Mexico are recognized by some experts as a different species (*S. mexicana*), but

as another variety of this single species by others. It also hybridizes regularly with Rough-stemmed Goldenrod (*S. rugosa*).

341 **Showy Goldenrod**
(*Solidago speciosa*)
Sunflower Family (Asteraceae)

Description: Stout stem, smooth below and rough above, bears a dense *pyramidal or club-shaped terminal cluster* of small yellow flower heads.
Flowers: heads about ¼" (6 mm) long.
Leaves: elliptical, obscurely toothed; lower and basal leaves 4–10" (10–25 cm) long, stalked; upper much smaller, unstalked.
Height: 2–7' (60–210 cm).

Flowering: August–October.

Habitat: Open woods, prairies, and thickets.

Range: New Hampshire south to North Carolina; west to Louisiana; north to Minnesota and beyond.

Comments: This is one of the showiest members among the approximately 125 species of Goldenrods occurring in all sections of the country, but most common in the Eastern U.S.

299 **Spiny-leaved Sow Thistle**
(*Sonchus asper*)
Sunflower Family (Asteraceae)

Description: On a smooth, angled stem containing milky juice are borne yellow dandelion-like flower heads.
Flowers: heads 1" (2.5 cm) wide, made up of all ray flowers; bracts beneath flower heads lanceolate, green-margined.
Leaves: up to 10" (25 cm) long, *prickly-edged,* usually rounded at the base and deeply lobed, but may be undivided.
Fruit: soft and *white,* with hair-like bristles.

Height: 1–6' (30–180 cm).
Flowering: June–October.
Habitat: Waste places and roadsides.
Range: Throughout.
Comments: This annual species closely resembles the Common Sow Thistle (*S. oleraceus*). The succulent leaves of this Old World plant were once used as a potherb. Field Sow Thistle (*S. arvensis*) and *S. uliginosus* are perennials with larger heads, the former with numerous gland-tipped hairs on the bracts and the latter with smooth bracts.

355 Common Tansy
(*Tanacetum vulgare*)
Sunflower Family (Asteraceae)

Description: Erect perennial with flat-topped clusters of bright orange-yellow, *button-like flower heads.*
Flowers: heads ½" (1.3 cm) wide, composed entirely of disk flowers with occasional ray-like extensions developing from marginal flowers.
Leaves: 4–8" (10–20 cm) long, pinnately divided into linear, toothed segments, *strongly aromatic.*
Height: 2–3' (60–90 cm).
Flowering: July–September.
Habitat: Roadsides and edges of fields (escaped from gardens).
Range: Throughout.
Comments: For centuries this plant was used medicinally to cause abortions, with sometimes fatal results. The bitter-tasting leaves and stem contain tanacetum, an oil toxic to humans and animals. The fresh young leaves and flowers, however, can be used as a substitute for sage in cooking.

235, 305 Common Dandelion
(Taraxacum officinale)
Sunflower Family (Asteraceae)

Description: Slender stalks bear solitary flower
heads, each with numerous yellow ray
flowers; stem juice is milky.
Flowers: heads about 1½" (3.8 cm)
wide; ray flowers strap-like, with 5 tiny
lobes (petals); bracts under flower heads
narrow, pointed, with outer ones bent
backward.
Leaves: basal, 2–16" (5–40 cm) long,
deeply and irregularly toothed and
lobed.
Fruit: dry, 1-seeded, with long white
bristles on top; fruiting mass becomes
silky, downy, globular head when ripe.
Height: 2–18" (5–45 cm).

Flowering: March–September.

Habitat: Fields, roadsides, and lawns.

Range: Throughout; but rare in extreme
southeastern U.S.

Comments: The Dandelion is probably known by
most as a lawn weed. Its common name
refers to the likeness of the leaf teeth to
those of a lion.

295 Yellow Goatsbeard
(Tragopogon dubius)
Sunflower Family (Asteraceae)

Description: Smooth stems bear grass-like leaf blades
and single yellow flower heads that
open in the morning and usually close
by noon; *stems swollen* just below flower
heads.
Flowers: heads 1–2½" (2.5–6.3 cm)
wide, with all ray flowers, surrounded
at base by *long-pointed green bracts.*
Leaves: to 1' (30 cm) long, broad at
base where they clasp the stem, then
narrow to long sharp tip.
Fruit: *heads large and plumose,* with seed-
like fruits bearing parachute of bristles.
Height: 1–3' (30–90 cm).

Flowering: May–August.

Habitat:	Fields and waste places.
Range:	Massachusetts south to Virginia; west to Texas and beyond; north to Illinois.
Comments:	The basal leaves of this plant can be eaten raw in salads or as cooked greens. The closely related Meadow Salsify (*T pratensis*), found from Nova Scotia south to Georgia, west to Missouri and Kansas, and north to Ontario, lacks the stem swelling.

236, 482 Oyster Plant; Salsify
(Tragopogon porrifolius)
Sunflower Family (Asteraceae)

Description:	Showy plant with branched stems, each topped by a large solitary pink head of all ray flowers; stem swollen and hollow just below flower head. Flowers: heads 2–4″ (5–10 cm) wide; bracts beneath flower heads long-pointed and longer than the rays. Leaves: to 1′ (30 cm) long, linear, grass-like, clasping the stem. Fruit: seed-like with *plumose bristles* 2″ (5 cm) long. Height: 2–4′ (60–120 cm).
Flowering:	May–July.
Habitat:	Fields and roadsides.
Range:	Ontario to Nova Scotia; south to Georgia, west to Kansas; north to Canada.
Comments:	This is a most striking plant when in fruit, with its beige ball of fluff. Its roots can be boiled and eaten, and the taste is somewhat like that of oysters. The spring leaves can be used in salads or cooked as greens. The genus name, derived from Greek *tragos* ("goat") and *pogon* ("beard"), refers to the resemblance of the fruiting heads to a goat's beard.

297 Coltsfoot
(*Tussilago farfara*)
Sunflower Family (Asteraceae)

Description: Low dandelion-like plant with a solitary
yellow flower head on a scaly stalk.
Flowers: heads 1″ (2.5 cm) wide, with
thin ray flowers surrounding the disk
flowers.
Leaves: basal, 2–7″ (5–17.5 cm) long
and broad, *heart-shaped,* slightly
toothed, upright, *whitish beneath.*
Height: 3–18″ (8–45 cm).

Flowering: February–June.

Habitat: Roadsides and waste places.

Range: Newfoundland to Nova Scotia; New
England south to New Jersey; west to
Ohio; northwesterly to Minnesota.

Comments: The common and species names refer to
the supposed resemblance of the leaf to
a colt's foot. The generic name alludes
to the plant's reputation as a cure for
coughs. An extract of fresh leaves can
be used for making cough drops or hard
candy, and its dried leaves can be
steeped for a tea.

607 Tall Ironweed
(*Vernonia altissima*)
Sunflower Family (Asteraceae)

Description: Tall erect stem bears deep purple-blue
flower heads in loose terminal clusters.
Flowers: heads about ¼″ (6 mm) wide,
with 13–30 5-lobed disk flowers; ray
flowers absent; bracts beneath flower
heads *blunt-tipped,* usually purple.
Leaves: 6–10″ (15–25 cm) long, thin,
lanceolate, pointed, *lower surfaces downy.*
Fruit: seed-like, with a double set of
purplish bristles.
Height: 3–7′ (90–210 cm).

Flowering: August–October.

Habitat: Damp, rich soil.

Range: New York south to Georgia; west to
Louisiana; north to Missouri, Illinois,
and Michigan.

Comments: The common name refers to the
toughness of the stem. The genus name
honors the English botanist William
Vernon, who did fieldwork in North
America. At least 6 additional species
are found in the East; some were once
used for treating stomach ailments.

---

565 New York Ironweed
(*Vernonia noveboracensis*)
Sunflower Family (Asteraceae)

Description: Tall erect stem branches toward the
summit, with each branch bearing a
cluster of deep lavender to violet flower
heads; together, clusters form a loose
spray.
Flowers: clusters 3–4″ (7.5–10 cm)
wide, each head about ⅓″ (8 mm)
wide, with 30–50 5-lobed disk flowers;
ray flowers absent; bracts surrounding
flower heads with *long hair-like tips*.
Leaves: 4–8″ (10–20 cm) long,
alternate, finely toothed, lanceolate,
pointed.
Fruit: seed-like, with double set of
purplish bristles.
Height: 3–6′ (90–180 cm).
Flowering: August–October.
Habitat: Moist low ground and stream margins.
Range: Massachusetts and New York south to
Georgia; west to Mississippi; north to
West Virginia and Ohio.
Comments: This often roughish plant is common in
wet open bottomland fields. It typically
has more flowers per head than Tall
Ironweed.

---

44 Cocklebur; Clotbur
(*Xanthium strumarium*)
Sunflower Family (Asteraceae)

Description: Rough-stemmed plant with separate
greenish male and female flower heads.
Flowers: *female* form spiny, nonhairy,

ovoid burs, ½–1½" (1.3–3.8 cm) long, in leaf axils; *male,* on short spikes.

Leaves: 2–6" (5–15 cm) long, maple-like, coarsely toothed, long-stalked.

Height: 1–6' (30–180 cm).

Flowering: August–October.

Habitat: Waste places, roadsides, and low ground.

Range: Throughout.

Comments: · The only other species occurring in our range is Spiny Clotbur (*X. spinosum*), which has tapering, shiny, veined leaves and distinctive 3-branched orangish spines at the point of each leaf attachment.

TOUCH-ME-NOT FAMILY
(Balsaminaceae)

Often soft and somewhat succulent
herbs with leafy, pale, translucent
stems.
Flowers: bilaterally symmetrical,
commonly nodding; sepals 3–5, often
resembling petals, one forming a
backward-projecting nectar-bearing
spur; petals 5, the pairs at the sides
united, lower ones larger than upper;
stamens 5, joined and forming a cap
over pistil.
Leaves: simple, opposite or whorled.
Fruit: capsule with sides usually elastic
at maturity, opening explosively and
throwing seeds from the 5 chambers.
There are 2 genera and about 500
species. Several species of *Impatiens* are
grown as ornamentals.

376 Spotted Touch-me-not; Jewelweed
(*Impatiens capensis*)
Touch-me-not Family (Balsaminaceae)

Description: Tall, leafy plant with *succulent
translucent stems* and pendent *golden-
orange flowers* splotched with reddish-
brown.
Flowers: 1″ (2.5 cm) long; 1 calyx lobe
colored as petals, with a *sharply spurred
sac* ¼″ (6 mm) long; other 2 sepals
green; 3 petals, 2 of them 2-lobed,
open out at mouth.
Leaves: 1½–3½″ (3.8–8.8 cm) long,
thin, ovate, pale and glaucous
underneath.
Fruit: swollen capsule that explodes
at maturity when touched, expelling
seeds.
Height: 2–5′ (60–150 cm).
Flowering: July–October.
Habitat: Shaded wetlands.
Range: Saskatchewan to Newfoundland; south
to Georgia; west to Oklahoma; north to
Missouri.

Comments: An annual that often occurs in dense
stands, it is especially adapted to
hummingbird visitation; but bees and
butterflies are also important
pollinators. If the leaves are submerged
they have a silvery look. The stem juice
is said to relieve itching from poison
ivy and has also been used to treat
athlete's foot. Scientific data confirm
the fungicidal qualities.

---

315 Pale Touch-me-not; Jewelweed
(*Impatiens pallida*)
Touch-me-not Family (Balsaminaceae)

Description: Similar to Spotted Touch-me-not, but
with larger pale *yellow flowers* with only
occasional brown spots; *stem translucent,*
with watery juice.
Flowers: 1½" (3.8 cm) long, with calyx
tube ending in *short, hooked spur.*
Leaves: 1–4" (2.5–10 cm) long, thin,
ovate, toothed.
Fruit: fragile, swollen, elliptical
capsule; pops when mature, dispersing
its seeds.
Height: 3–6' (90–180 cm).
Flowering: June–October.
Habitat: Wet woods and meadows; often on
mountainsides in wet, shady, limestone
or neutral sites.
Range: Across southern Canada to
Newfoundland; south to North
Carolina and upland Georgia; west to
Missouri; north to Canada.
Comments: This soft-stemmed annual is less
common than Spotted Touch-me-not
(*I. capensis*). The sensitive triggering of
seeds from the ripe capsule inspired the
common name Touch-me-not. A large
purple-flowered species (*I. glandulifera*)
is found from Ontario across to Nova
Scotia and down to Massachusetts.

BARBERRY FAMILY
(Berberidaceae)

Herbs or shrubs, with flowers in clusters or racemes and often with spiny leaves.
Flowers: radially symmetrical, single; sepals 4–6, often petal-like; petals 4–6; stamens 4–18, in two circles, with pollen sacs opening by little flaps.
Leaves: simple or compound.
Fruit: berry.
There are about 9 genera and nearly 600 species. A few Barberry species are cultivated as ornamentals. Common Barberry is a necessary host in the complex life cycle of wheat rust, a destructive parasitic fungus.

362 Common Barberry
(*Berberis vulgaris*)
Barberry Family (Berberidaceae)

Description: *Spiny, gray-twigged shrub* bears *pendulous clusters* of small yellow flowers and clustered leaves; 3-pronged thorns.
Flowers: about ¼" (6 mm) wide; 6 sepals, 6 petals with 2 glandular spots inside, 6 stamens, and a circular and depressed stigma.
Leaves: 1–3" (2.5–7.5 cm) long, bristle-toothed.
Fruit: elliptical berries, *scarlet when mature.*
Height: 3–10' (90–300 cm).
Flowering: May–June.
Habitat: Pastures and thickets.
Range: Southern Ontario to Nova Scotia; south to Delaware and Pennsylvania; west to Missouri; north to Minnesota.
Comments: Barberry is very susceptible to the black stem rust of wheat, a fungus that spends part of its life cycle on these shrubs and the remainder on the grain. Japanese Barberry (*B. thunbergii*), with untoothed leaves and simple thorns, is a common hedge that often escapes to

pastures and other open spots, as far south as North Carolina and west to Michigan. Its flowers are solitary or in small clusters in the leaf axils. American Barberry (*B. canadensis*), found in southern mountains, has brown branches, widely toothed leaves, 3-pronged thorns, and yellow flowers with notched petals in few-flowered clusters.

---

388 Blue Cohosh
(*Caulophyllum thalictroides*)
Barberry Family (Berberidaceae)

Description: Inconspicuous purplish-brown to yellow-green flowers borne in a loosely branched cluster.
Flowers: ½" (1.3 cm) wide; 6 pointed sepals, 6 smaller hood-shaped petals.
Leaves: 2, compound, alternate; lower one large, usually highly divided into 27 leaflets, each 1–3" (2.5–7.5 cm) long; upper one small, with 9–12 leaflets; at apex of leaflets are 3–5 pointed lobes; young plants covered with white, waxy bloom.
Fruit: *deep blue berry-like seeds* on small, *inflated stalks.*
Height: 1–3' (30–90 cm).
Flowering: April–June.
Habitat: Moist woods.
Range: Nearly throughout, but mainly limited to mountainous areas farther south.
Comments: The 6 stamens and central pistil of this early spring flower mature at different times, assuring cross-pollination. The petals bear fleshy nectar glands that are visited by early solitary bees. The seeds are reportedly used as a coffee substitute. The foliage resembles the Meadow Rues (*Thalictrum*); hence the species name, *thalictroides.*

88 Twinleaf
(*Jeffersonia diphylla*)
Barberry Family (Berberidaceae)

Description: Solitary white flower atop a leafless stalk.
Flowers: 1″ (2.5 cm) wide, with 4 early-falling sepals and 8 petals.
Leaves: 3–6″ (7.5–15 cm) long, basal, long-stemmed, *parted lengthwise into two wings*.
Fruit: large, dry, pear-shaped pod with tiny, hinged lid.
Height: 5–10″ (12.5–25 cm) when in flower; increasing to 18″ (45 cm) as fruit matures.

Flowering: April–May.

Habitat: Rich, damp, open woods, usually with limestone soil.

Range: Southern Ontario; western New York south to Virginia; west to Iowa; north to Wisconsin.

Comments: The flower somewhat resembles Bloodroot, but the leaf is 2-lobed. The genus was named in honor of Thomas Jefferson by his friend and fellow botanist William Bartram. Only one other species occurs in the world: *J. dubia*, found in Japan.

87 Mayapple; Mandrake
(*Podophyllum peltatum*)
Barberry Family (Berberidaceae)

Description: *Solitary, nodding flower* borne in the crotch between a *pair of large, deeply lobed leaves*.
Flowers: 2″ (5 cm) wide, with 6–9 *waxy white petals*.
Leaves: to 1′ (30 cm) wide.
Fruit: large, fleshy, *lemon-like berry*.
Height: 12–18″ (30–45 cm).

Flowering: April–June.

Habitat: Rich woods and damp, shady clearings.

Range: Southern Ontario and western Quebec; south to Florida; west to Texas; north to Minnesota.

Comments: The common name refers to the May
blooming of its apple-blossom-like
flower. Although the leaves, roots, and
seeds are poisonous if ingested in large
quantities, the roots were used as a
cathartic by the Indians. The edible
ripe golden-yellow fruits can be used in
jellies. The alternate popular name
"Mandrake" rightly belongs to an
unrelated Old World plant with a
similar root.

TRUMPET CREEPER FAMILY
(Bignoniaceae)

Trees, shrubs, or woody vines,
occasionally herbs, with large, showy,
clustered flowers. About 100 genera
and over 600 species, mostly in tropics.
Flowers: in clusters at ends of branches
or at axils; bilaterally symmetrical;
calyx 5-lobed; corolla funnelform, bell-
shaped, or tubular, 5-lobed and often
2-lipped; stamens 2 or 4. All these
parts attached at base of ovary.
Leaves: usually opposite, simple or
pinnately or palmately compound.
Fruit: 2-valved capsule.

381 Trumpet Creeper
(*Campsis radicans*)
Trumpet Creeper Family (Bignoniaceae)

Description: *Woody vine* with *trumpet-shaped,
reddish-orange flowers.*
Flowers: 2½″ (6.3 cm) long; corolla
5-lobed.
Leaves: pinnately compound, with 7–
11 toothed, ovate, pointed leaflets, each
about 2½″ (6.3 cm) long
Fruit: capsule 6″ (15 cm) long.
Height: vine.

Flowering: July–September.

Habitat: Low woods and thickets.

Range: New Jersey south to Florida; west to
Texas; north to Iowa, but naturalized
north to Massachusetts and Michigan.

Comments: This attractive vine is often cultivated.
Aerial rootlets from the stem are used
for climbing. Can be undesirably
aggressive in the South.

FORGET-ME-NOT OR BORAGE FAMILY (Boraginaceae)

Generally herbs, often covered with bristly hairs.
Flowers: radially symmetrical, often borne along one side of branches or at tip of stem coiled like a fiddleneck; sepals 5, united at base; petals 5, united into a narrow tube and an abruptly flared top; around the small entry to the tube usually 5 small *pads;* stamens 5. All these parts attached near base of ovary.
Leaves: simple.
Fruit: separates into 4 hard seed-like sections (nutlets); or in a few species, fruit is a berry.
There are about 100 genera and 2,000 species, found mostly in warm or temperate regions. Forget-me-nots are grown as ornamentals.

630 Viper's Bugloss; Blueweed
(*Echium vulgare*)
Forget-me-not Family (Boraginaceae)

Description: Hairy plant with showy, tubular blue flowers, each with *protruding red stamens,* in 1-sided clusters on lateral branches; clusters uncoil as flowers bloom.
Flowers: ¾" (2 cm) long; corolla 5-lobed; stamens 5.
Leaves: 2–6" (5–15 cm) long, hairy, oblong to lanceolate.
Fruit: rough nutlets.
Height: 1–2½' (30–75 cm).
Flowering: June–October.
Habitat: Fields, roadsides, and waste places, often preferring limestone soils.
Range: Throughout, except south of South Carolina and Tennessee.
Comments: A European species introduced as early as 1683, this plant is considered a weed by some and a desirable wildflower by others. Its common name may derive from the resemblance of the nutlets to a

snake's head, or else because the dried
plant was an alleged remedy for
snakebite. Bugloss is from the ancient
Greek for "ox-tongue," which its leaves
were thought to resemble.

375 Hoary Puccoon
(*Lithospermum canescens*)
Forget-me-not Family (Boraginaceae)

Description: *Hairy, grayish* plant with terminal
cluster of yellow-orange tubular
flowers; leaves and stems covered with
fine, soft hairs that give plant a "hoary"
look.
Flowers: ½" (1.3 cm) wide; corolla with
5 flaring lobes.
Leaves: ½–1½" (1.3–3.8 cm) long,
alternate, narrow, mostly stalkless.
Fruit: 4 nutlets.
Height: 6–18" (15–45 cm).
Flowering: March–June.
Habitat: Dry, rocky sites; edges of grasslands.
Range: Saskatchewan to southern Ontario;
south from Virginia to Georgia and
Alabama (absent in northeastern U.S.);
west to Texas; frequent in lower
Mississippi Valley.
Comments: *Puccoon* is an Indian name for a number
of plants that yield colored dyes.
Among the other species in our range,
L. caroliniense has harsher, longer hairs;
Corn Gromwell (*L. arvense*), found
throughout the United States, has
inconspicuous white flowers among its
upper leaf axils.

649 Virginia Bluebells; Virginia Cowslip
(*Mertensia virginica*)
Forget-me-not Family (Boraginaceae)

Description: Erect plant with smooth gray-green
foliage and nodding clusters of pink
buds that open into light *blue trumpet-
shaped flowers.*

Flowers: about 1″ (2.5 cm) long; coroll 5-lobed.

Leaves: basal leaves 2–8″ (5–20 cm) long; stem leaves smaller, alternate, oval, untoothed.

Height: 8–24″ (20–60 cm).

Flowering: March–June.

Habitat: Moist woods; rarely, meadows; especially on floodplains.

Range: Southern Ontario; western New York south to northern North Carolina and Alabama; west to Arkansas and eastern Kansas; north to Minnesota.

Comments: When it grows in masses, this species makes a spectacular show, especially in the Midwest. A smaller, trailing, rosy-pink-flowered species, Sea Lungwort (*M. maritima*), occurs on beaches from Newfoundland to Massachusetts. Tall Lungwort (*M. paniculata*), a western species with a hairy stem, enters our range in Wisconsin, northeast Iowa, and Minnesota. The genus is named for the German botanist Franz Karl Mertens (1764–1831).

642 **True Forget-me-not**
(*Myosotis scorpioides*)
Forget-me-not Family (Boraginaceae)

Description: Sprawling plant with several tiny, *light. blue tubular flowers with golden eyes,* growing on small, curving, divergent branches that uncoil as the flowers bloom.

Flowers: ¼″ (6 mm) wide, corolla 5-lobed.

Leaves: 1–2″ (2.5–5 cm) long, oblong, blunt, hairy, mostly stalkless.

Height: 6–24″ (15–30 cm).

Flowering: May–October.

Habitat: Stream borders and wet places.

Range: Nearly throughout.

Comments: This European introduction, which was once extensively cultivated, has now been naturalized around lakes, ponds, and streams. In bud, the tightly coiled flower cluster resembles a scorpion; hence the species name. The Tufted Forget-me-not (*M. sylvatica*) is now commonly cultivated and is becoming established in drier habitats of the northeastern United States. The Smaller Forget-me-not (*M. laxa*), with much smaller flowers, is native to North America, particularly in wet places. Two native white species, Spring Forget-me-not (*M. verna*) and *M. macrosperma,* also occur in the eastern United States.

MUSTARD FAMILY
(Brassicaceae or Cruciferae)

Herbs, often with peppery sap.
Flowers: usually radially symmetrical,
in racemes; 4 separate sepals; 4 separate
petals, the base of each often long and
slender; stamens usually 6, with *2 outer
shorter than the inner 4.* All these parts
attached near base of ovary; ovary
superior in position, divided into 2
chambers by parchment-like partition.
Leaves: usually simple, but sometimes
pinnately divided.
Fruit: pod, either long and narrow
(silique) or short and relatively broader
(silicle).
There are about 375 genera and 3,200
species, found mostly in cooler regions
of the Northern Hemisphere. The
family is economically important,
providing vegetables, spices, and
ornamentals. Some species are
unwelcome weeds, a few poisonous
to livestock.

---

177 **Lyre-leaved Rock Cress**
(*Arabis lyrata*)
Mustard Family (Brassicaceae)

Description: Erect stem rising from a rosette of basal
leaves has terminal cluster of small
white or greenish-white flowers.
Flowers: about ¼" (6 mm) wide,
4-petaled.
Leaves: basal, ¾–1½" (2–3.8 cm)
long, *deeply lobed;* stem, linear or
spatulate.
Fruit: seedpod to 1¼" (3 cm), narrow,
upcurving.
Height: 4–16" (10–40 cm).
Flowering: April–May.
Habitat: Cliffs, ledges and sandy places in
gravelly or sandy soil.
Range: Across southern Canada; Vermont south
to Georgia; west through Tennessee to
Missouri; north to Minnesota.

Comments: Other common members of this family
are Hairy Rock Cress (*A. hirsuta*), with
a basal rosette of hairy, oblong leaves,
clasping stem leaves, and pods that are
erect or pressed against the stem; and
Smooth Rock Cress (*A. laevigata*), with
smooth, lanceolate clasping leaves and
seed pods that either curve downward
or are horizontal.

---

345 **Common Winter Cress**
(*Barbarea vulgaris*)
Mustard Family (Brassicaceae)

Description: Tufted plant with elongated clusters of
small *bright yellow flowers* atop erect leafy
stems.
Flowers: ⅓″ (8 mm) wide, with 4
petals forming a cross; 6 stamens.
Leaves: lower ones 2–5″ (5–12.5 cm)
long, with stalks, *pinnately divided into
5 segments, terminal one large and rounded;*
upper leaves lobed, clasping the stem.
Fruit: erect seedpod, ¾–1½″
(2–3.8 cm) long, with a short beak.
Height: 1–2′ (30–60 cm).
Flowering: April–August.
Habitat: Moist fields, meadows, and brooksides.
Range: Ontario to Nova Scotia; south to
Virginia; west to Missouri and Kansas;
north to Canada.
Comments: This introduced early-blooming
mustard frequently forms showy yellow
patches in open fields. The young leaves
can be used in salads or cooked as
greens. Another introduced species,
Early Winter Cress (*B. verna*) has lower
leaves with 4–10 lobes and longer
capsules. Now naturalized from
Massachusetts southward, it is
sometimes grown as a winter salad
green called Scurvy Grass.

346 Black Mustard
(*Brassica nigra*)
Mustard Family (Brassicaceae)

Description: Widely branched plant with deeply lobed lower leaves and narrow clusters of small yellow flowers toward the top of the stem.
Flowers: each about ½" (1.3 cm) wide, 4-petaled.
Leaves: 1½–3" (3.8–7.5 cm) long, with *large terminal lobe* and usually 4 lateral lobes; upper ones lanceolate, toothed, but not lobed.
Fruit: beaked, 4-sided seed pod, ½" (1.3 cm) long, *closely pressed to the stem.*
Height: 2–3' (60–90 cm).
Flowering: June–October.
Habitat: Fields and waste places.
Range: Throughout; but very rare in Southeast.
Comments: This European immigrant is a member of the genus that includes some common garden vegetables: cabbage, cauliflower, broccoli, and Brussel sprouts. The very young lower leaves and unopened flower buds can be eaten cooked. The seeds are used for seasoning in pickle recipes and in making mustard sauce; they are favored by songbirds and sometimes sold as food for caged birds. At least 6 species occur in our range.

471 Sea Rocket
(*Cakile edentula*)
Mustard Family (Brassicaceae)

Description: Low, *fleshy,* branching beach plant with pale lavender flowers.
Flowers: ¼" (6 mm) wide, 4-petaled.
Leaves: 3–5" (7.5–12.5 cm) long, ovate to lanceolate, wavy-toothed or lobed.
Fruit: *2-jointed seed pod,* to ¾" (2 cm) long, the upper joint longer than the lower, ovoid, *with a short beak.*
Height: 6–20" (15–50 cm).

Flowering: July–September.

Habitat: Beaches.

Range: Southern Labrador south along coast to Florida; local around Great Lakes (also present on Pacific Coast).

Comments: This annual, found on the ridge of wind-blown sand behind the high-tide line of beaches, gets its common name from the rocket-like shape of the seed pods. The succulent young stems and leaves have a pungent taste, somewhat like horseradish. Harper's Sea Rocket (*C. harperi*), occurring from North Carolina to Florida, has much more angulate fruits. European Sea Rocket (*C. maritima*), introduced from Europe and occurring along our northern beaches, has very deeply lobed leaves.

173 Shepherd's Purse
(*Capsella bursa-pastoris*)
Mustard Family (Brassicaceae)

Description: Erect plant with *triangular seed pods* and terminal cluster of tiny white flowers.
Flowers: only ¹⁄₁₂″ (2 mm) long, with 4 petals *arranged as a cross;* 6 stamens.
Leaves: those of basal rosette deeply toothed, *dandelion-like,* 2–4″ (5–10 cm) long; stem leaves smaller, arrowhead-shaped, clasping.
Fruit: triangular pod, ¼–½″ (6–13 mm) wide, indented at tip.
Height: 6–18″ (15–45 cm).

Flowering: March–December.

Habitat: Disturbed areas, cultivated land, lawns, and waste places.

Range: Throughout.

Comments: This annual weed has wide distribution throughout the world. The distinctive wedge-shaped fruit pods, slightly puffed out along the sides, resemble a medieval shepherd's purse, thus accounting for the common and Latin species names.

144 Spring Cress; Bitter Cress
(*Cardamine bulbosa*)
Mustard Family (Brassicaceae)

Description: Small white flowers, with *4 petals
arranged as a cross,* in cluster atop
smooth, erect stem.
Flowers: ½" (1.3 cm) wide, with petals
much longer than the 4 sepals;
6 stamens.
Leaves: basal 1–1½" (2.5–3.8 cm)
long, oval or roundish, with long
stalks; stem leaves oblong to lanceolate,
usually toothed, without stalks.
Fruit: seedpod 1" (2.5 cm) long,
erect, narrow.
Height: 6–24" (15–60 cm).
Flowering: March–June.
Habitat: Alongside springs and brooks, swamps,
and wet clearings.
Range: Southern Ontario and Quebec; south to
Florida; west to Texas, north to South
Dakota and Minnesota.
Comments: Cuckoo Flower (*C. pratensis*), with
white or pinkish flowers, has pinnately
divided leaves. Pennsylvania Bittercress
(*C. pensylvanica*), with very tiny flowers,
also has pinnately divided leaves.
Mountain Watercress (*C. rotundifolia*),
also white-flowered, has oval leaves
with tiny projections on the leafstalk.
True Watercress, which occurs in
streams and around springs, belongs to
the genus *Nasturtium* of this family.

164 Cut-leaved Toothwort
(*Dentaria laciniata*)
Mustard Family (Brassicaceae)

Description: Terminal cluster of white or pink
flowers on erect stem with *deeply cleft
leaves.*
Flowers: ¾" (2 cm) wide; 4 petals,
arranged in a cross shape.
Leaves: 2–5" (5–12.5 cm) wide, deeply
lobed and sharply toothed, in *whorl of 3*
above middle of stem.

Fruit: narrow, upward-angled capsule.
Height: 8–16″ (20–40 cm).
Flowering: April–May.
Habitat: Moist low woodlands and damp thickets.
Range: Quebec; south to Florida; west to Louisiana; north through Kansas and Nebraska to Minnesota.
Comments: Toothworts are spring flowers. Two-leaved Toothwort (*D. diphylla*) has only two, nearly opposite, deeply dissected leaves, with three toothed lobes. The common name refers to the tooth-like projections on its underground stems or rhizomes.

51 Whitlow Grass
(*Draba verna*)
Mustard Family (Brassicaceae)

Description: Tiny plant with rosette of flattened basal leaves, from which rise slender *leafless stalks* bearing miniature white flowers.
Flowers: ⅛″ (4 mm) wide, with 4 petals so deeply notched as to appear 8.
Leaves: ½–1″ (1.3–2.5 cm) long, hairy, oblong to spatulate.
Fruit: elliptical pod on stalk longer than pod.
Height: to 8″ (20 cm).
Flowering: March–June.
Habitat: Fields, roadsides, and open places.
Range: Massachusetts south to Georgia; west to Mississippi; north to Illinois.
Comments: The species name suggests the early spring (vernal) blooming of this very small introduced annual, often seen in garden soils. The plant was reputedly useful in treating finger sores known as "whitlows"; hence its common name. Within our range 10 other species, all native, occur.

174 Peppergrass; Poor-man's Pepper
(Lepidium virginicum)
Mustard Family (Brassicaceae)

Description: Tiny white flowers with 4 petals and *only 2 stamens,* arranged in elongated clusters.
Flowers: 1/12" (2 mm) wide, with petals arranged in a cross form.
Leaves: basal about 2" (5 cm) long, toothed, with large terminal lobe and several small side lobes; stem leaves lanceolate, unstalked, or else lower ones stalked.
Fruit: dry, *rounded, flattened pods,* slightly notched at the top.
Height: 6–24" (15–60 cm).

Flowering: June–November.

Habitat: Waste places and roadsides.

Range: Throughout.

Comments: This prolific weed is one of the most common Peppergrasses. Its seeds have a peppery taste and can be used to season soups and stews; the young leaves are used in salads or cooked as greens. The hairy Field Peppergrass (*L. campestre*) has six stamens, leaves that clasp the stem, and fruiting pods longer than broad. *L. perfoliatum* is a striking species with minute yellow flowers, basal and lower leaves that are finely cut and fern-like, and circular upper leaves that wrap around the stem.

178 True Watercress
(Nasturtium officinale)
Mustard Family (Brassicaceae)

Description: Aquatic plant with stems that *float* in water or *creep* over mud, compound leaves partly or completely submerged, and small white flowers.
Flowers: 1/8" (4 mm) wide, with 4 petals.
Leaves: 3/4–6" (2–15 cm) long, with 5–9 oval segments, the terminal one larger than the side ones.

Fruit: seed pod to 1″ (2.5 cm) long,
slightly curving upward.
Height: 4–10″ (10–25 cm).
Flowering: April–October.
Habitat: Brooks, streams, and springs.
Range: Throughout.
Comments: Naturalized from Europe and often
cultivated there and in this country,
this plant is highly prized for its
slightly pungent, pepper-flavored
leaves. High in vitamins A and C, the
plant was long used as a treatment for
scurvy; thus it is sometimes known as
Scurvy Grass. Our native Watercress,
the edible Pennsylvania Bittercress
(*Cardamine pensylvanica*), is more erect.

347 Hedge Mustard
(*Sisymbrium officinale*)
Mustard Family (Brassicaceae)

Description: Clusters of small, pale yellow flowers
terminate stiffly diverging branches:
Flowers: each about ⅙″ (4 mm) wide,
with 4 petals in a cross-like pattern.
Leaves: 1–6″ (2.5–15 cm) long,
triangular, deeply lobed, toothed
or wavy-edged.
Fruit: pods to ¾″ (2 cm) long, hairy,
linear, *closely pressed against stem.*
Height: 12–32″ (30–80 cm).
Flowering: May–October.
Habitat: Disturbed areas.
Range: Throughout.
Comments: This weedy annual is an introduced
mustard. Tumble Mustard
(*S. altissimum*) is troublesome in grain
fields, especially in the West. It has
pale yellow flowers, finely dissected
leaves, and elongate thread-like
seed pods.

325 Prince's Plume
(*Stanleya pinnata*)
Mustard Family (Brassicaceae)

Description: *Showy* sulfur-yellow flowers appear in elongated terminal clusters.
Flowers: ¾–1″ (2–2.5 cm) long, each with 4 petals; stamens and pistil extend beyond petals.
Leaves: 5–8″ (12.5–20 cm) long, pale green, smooth, fleshy, sometimes divided or lobed.
Fruit: seedpod 2–3″ (5–7.5 cm) long, narrow, curving downward.
Height: 1–4′ (30–120 cm).

Flowering: May–July.

Habitat: Plains, dry soil.

Range: South Dakota and Nebraska (and throughout Southwest).

Comments: This beautiful species and others in the same genus are accumulators of selenium, a soil element absorbed by plants that is poisonous to livestock if sufficiently concentrated.

PINEAPPLE FAMILY
(Bromeliaceae)

Epiphytic (rarely terrestrial) scurfy
herbs, with generally stiff, long leaves
and flowers, often in long clusters with
conspicuously colored bracts.
Flowers: often bilaterally symmetrical,
in dense spikes or heads; sepals 3 and
petals 3; stamens 6. All these parts
attached either at base or at top of
ovary.
Leaves: often with spiny margins and
bases that sheath the stem.
Fruit: berry or capsule to which remains
of calyx and corolla adhere.
The family contains about 59 genera
and more than 1,300 species, mostly
native of tropical America. Some have
been introduced into other warm
regions and cultivated for use as
ornamentals or for their edible fruit.

---

438 Wild Pine
(*Tillandsia fasciculata*)
Pineapple Family (Bromeliaceae)

Description: An *air plant* with inconspicuous flowers
in the axils of *showy bracts,* which are
usually red.
Flowers: 2" (5 cm) long, with violet
petals and protruding stamens and
style; arranged in numerous spikes up
to 6" (15 cm) long on stalks about as
long as the leaves; bracts about 1½"
(3.8 cm) long, ranging in color from
yellow to red or green.
Leaves: 12–20" (30–50 cm) long, in
rosettes, grayish-green with brown bases,
lanceolate to linear, *stiff.*
Height: epiphyte.
Flowering: January–August.
Habitat: Cypress swamps; in hammocks, usually
on cypress trees.
Range: Florida.
Comments: This is the most common of the Wild
Pines that occur as epiphytes, especially

on Bald Cypress. Although they grow on the trees, they get their nourishment from the air, rain, and minerals leached from the host tree. Among the 15 other erect species of *Tillandsia* that occur in Florida are: Ball Moss (*T. recurvata*), with narrow leaves forming grayish, ball-like clusters on branches of deciduous trees, especially oaks; Needle-leaved Wild Pine (*T. setacea*), with very narrow, needle-like leaves; *T. pruinosa,* with a distinctive coat of hoary scales; and Giant Wild Pine (*T. utriculata*), the largest species in the United States, with leaves reaching 2′ (60 cm) in length and a flowerstalk up to 6′ (1.8 m) tall. The flowers are white.

39 Spanish Moss
(*Tillandsia usneoides*)
Pineapple Family (Bromeliaceae)

Description: *Cascading* masses of slender *stems covered with gray scales,* with a solitary inconspicuous flower at the end of short axillary branches.
Flowers: ½–¾″ (1.3–2 cm) long, with 3 short, narrow, pale green petals that fade to yellow; short bracts.
Leaves: 1–2″ (2.5–5 cm) long, thread-like, also covered with scales.
Height: epiphyte.
Flowering: April–June.
Habitat: Hangs from Live Oak and other tree branches and telephone wires.
Range: Primarily coastal, Virginia south to Florida; west to Texas.
Comments: Spanish Moss is an air plant (epiphyte), not a parasite, because it photosynthesizes its own energy from the sun. The scales help the plant absorb water and nutrients, most of which come from minerals leached from the foliage of the host tree.

CACTUS FAMILY (Cactaceae)

Succulent, mostly leafless, commonly spiny herbs and shrubs with globose, cylindrical, or flat stems that are sometimes jointed.

Flowers: often showy, radially symmetrical, blooming singly on sides or near top of stem; many separate sepals, often petal-like; many separate petals, the bases of both may be fused into a long tube above the ovary; many stamens. All these parts attached near top of ovary.

Leaves: simple and obviously leaf-like in primitive tropical species, but very small and dropping early, or not even present in most desert species; in leaf axils (or where leaves would be) clusters of spines often develop.

Fruit: usually fleshy, often edible, with many seeds.

About 140 genera have perhaps 2,000 species, mostly in the warm parts of the Americas. Most species favor dry, hot environments and exhibit several adaptations aiding survival. The shape reduces surface area and thereby water loss. Root systems are shallow, absorbing from brief showers water that is stored in the succulent stems. Pores (stomates) in the skin (epidermis) open during the cool night, allowing entry of carbon dioxide, which is chemically stored; during the day the carbon dioxide is used in photosynthesis. Spines discourage eating of the plants by animals in regions where there is little other green growth for food; they reflect light and heat, and also shade the surface, aiding to keep the plant cool. Many are grown as succulent novelties, and collecting of cacti, a popular hobby, has brought some rarer species near extinction.

242 Prickly Pear
(*Opuntia humifusa*)
Cactus Family (Cactaceae)

Description: Few yellow flowers, often with reddish
centers, bloom on *flat, fleshy green pads;*
plant spreads and forms clumps to 3'
(90 cm) wide and to 1' (30 cm) tall;
pads covered with clusters of short,
reddish-brown, barbed bristles (glochids);
spines lacking, or only 1 or 2.
Flowers: 2–3″ (5–7.5 cm) wide;
numerous sepals, petals, and stamens.
Leaves: small, brown; soon deciduous.
Fruit: green to dull purple, edible
berry.
Height: to 1' (30 cm).

Flowering: May–August.

Habitat: Sandy areas and open rocky sites:

Range: Massachusetts south to Florida and
upland Alabama; west to Oklahoma;
north to Minnesota.

Comments: This showy native plant is the only
cactus widespread in the East and is
occasionally transplanted into northern
gardens. Care should be taken in
handling it, since the barbed glochids
can be more troublesome than the
spines typical of most cacti. The East
Coast variety (*O. compressa*) usually has
yellow flowers, while the variety that
grows inland has reddish centers.
Brittle Prickly Pear (*O. fragilis*), found
in Illinois, Iowa, and Kansas, and
Drummond's Prickly Pear
(*O. drummondii*), occurring in the
Southeast, have stems only slightly
flattened.

241 Many-spined Opuntia
(*Opuntia polyacantha*)
Cactus Family (Cactaceae)

Description: Fleshy, sprawling perennial with pale
yellow flowers and *flat pads* having
groups of 5–12 *whitish spines,*
1″ (2.5 cm) long, with tufts of bristles

above the spines; may form clumps
8–12′ (2.4–3.6 m) in width.

Flowers: 2–3″ (5–8 cm) wide, stalkless
with numerous sepals, petals, and
stamens; stamens much shorter
than petals.

Leaves: tiny; soon deciduous.

Fruit: 1″ (2.5 cm) long; reddish prickly
berry with edible flesh.

Height: 2–24″ (5–60 cm).

Flowering: May–June.

Habitat: Plains and dry soil.

Range: Missouri northwest to Nebraska and
South Dakota (and farther west).

Comments: This plant spreads as a result of drought
and overgrazing; its seeds are also
carried by rodents. It is one of several
"Prickly Pears" with yellow or orange
flowers found on plains and prairies in
the West and Southwest. The larger
spines and finer glochids are very
painful and difficult to extract; but
with the skin and seeds removed, the
fruits can be eaten raw or used to make
cactus candy.

243 Rafinesque's Prickly Pear
(*Opuntia rafinesquei*)
Cactus Family (Cactaceae)

Description: Low-spreading cactus with flat pads
bearing yellow flowers and clusters of
short, reddish-brown, barbed bristles;
spines present on upper half of pads.

Flowers: 2–3″ (5–7.5 cm) wide; sepals,
petals, and stamens numerous.

Leaves: tiny; soon deciduous.

Fruit: juicy, edible berry.

Height: 2–24″ (5–60 cm).

Flowering: May–August.

Habitat: Dry, shady, rocky soil.

Range: Wisconsin southwest to Texas (and
beyond to Arizona).

Comments: This species has often been grouped
with the very similar Prickly Pear
(*O. compressa*), but it differs in having
more spines.

BLUEBELL FAMILY
(Campanulaceae)

Usually herbs, rarely trees or shrubs, with commonly blue, lavender, or white flowers, solitary or clustered. Flowers: radially symmetrical, with corolla tubular or bell-shaped, having 5 lobes; or bilaterally symmetrical, with corolla conspicuously 2-lipped; stamens 5. All these parts attached at top of ovary.
Leaves: alternate, simple, sometimes deeply divided.
Fruit: berry or capsule.
There are about 35 genera and 900 species, widely distributed in tropical and temperate regions. Many are used as ornamentals. An exception to the usual blue or lavender flower color is the scarlet Cardinal Flower.

625 Tall Bellflower
(*Campanula americana*)
Bluebell Family (Campanulaceae)

Description: Light blue flowers, in clusters or solitary in the axils of upper leaves, form an elongated, spike-like cluster. Flowers: ¾–1" (2–2.5 cm) wide; clusters 1–2' (30–60 cm) long; *corolla flat, deeply 5-cleft* or sometimes tubular; style long, curving and recurving, protruding; bracts beneath lower flowers leaf-like, upper ones awl-shaped.
Leaves: 3–6" (7.5–1.5 cm) long, thin, ovate to lanceolate, toothed.
Height: 2–6' (60–180 cm).
Flowering: June–August.
Habitat: Rich, moist thickets and woods.
Range: Southern Ontario; New York south to Florida and Alabama; west to Missouri; north to Minnesota.
Comments: In spite of the common name and the genus name (from Latin *campana,* "bell"), the flowers of this species are

usually flat, not bell-shaped as are many others in the genus.

618 Harebell
(*Campanula rotundifolia*)
Bluebell Family (Campanulaceae)

Description: Blue, *bell-like flowers* borne singly or in clusters on *nodding thread-like stalks.*
Flowers: ¾″ (2 cm) long, 5-lobed; with 3-part stigma, not protruding beyond petals, and 5 lavender stamens.
Leaves: stem leaves to 3″ (7.5 cm) long, numerous, narrow; basal leaves, when present, broadly ovate.
Fruit: nodding capsule.
Height: 6–20″ (15–50 cm).

Flowering: June–September.

Habitat: Rocky banks and slopes, meadows, and shores.

Range: Northern Canada south through northeastern and midwestern states; west to Texas and beyond.

Comments: The characteristics of this perennial vary considerably, depending on habitat conditions. Among other common species are the Southern Harebell (*C. divaricata*), with wider leaves and smaller, white or pale lavender flowers, typical of wet, grassy meadows. The common garden Bellflower (*C. rapunculoides*), which frequently escapes from cultivation, has flowers usually borne on one side of the stems and lanceolate or heart-shaped leaves.

430 Cardinal Flower
(*Lobelia cardinalis*)
Bluebell Family (Campanulaceae)

Description: Many *brilliant red, tubular flowers* in an elongated cluster on an erect stalk.
Flowers: 1½″ (3.8 cm) long, 5-petaled with 2 lips; upper with 2 lobes, lower with 3; *united stamens* form a tube

around style and extend beyond corolla; narrow leaf-like bracts beneath flowers.
Leaves: to 6″ (15 cm) long, alternate, lanceolate, toothed.
Height: 2–4′ (60–120 cm).

Flowering: July–September.

Habitat: Damp sites, especially along streams.

Range: Southern Ontario and Quebec to New Brunswick; south to Florida; west to eastern Texas; north to Minnesota.

Comments: One of our handsomest deep red wildflowers, Cardinal Flower is pollinated chiefly by hummingbirds, since most insects find it difficult to navigate the long tubular flowers. Although relatively common, overpicking has resulted in its scarcity in some areas. Its common name alludes to the bright red robes worn by Roman Catholic cardinals.

---

633 Indian Tobacco
(*Lobelia inflata*)
Bluebell Family (Campanulaceae)

Description: Slightly hairy stems may be simple or branched and have several tiny lavender or blue-violet flowers in terminal, leafy, elongated clusters.
Flowers: ¼″ (6 mm) long, 2-lipped, lower lip bearded; after flowering, *calyx* surrounding fruit becomes distinctly *inflated and balloon-like*, up to ⅓″ (8 mm) across.
Leaves: 1–2½″ (2.5–6.3 cm) long, thin, light green, alternate, ovate, wavy-toothed.
Fruit: ribbed capsule enclosed in swollen calyx.
Height: 1–3′ (30–90 cm).

Flowering: June–October.

Habitat: Fields, open woods, and roadsides.

Range: Across southern Canada; south to Georgia; west to Arkansas and eastern Kansas.

Comments: This acrid poisonous annual is found in a variety of sites, often in poor soil. The

American Indians were said to have
smoked and chewed its leaves; hence
the common name. Though once used
as an emetic, the root should not be
eaten, for if taken in quantity it can
be fatal.

636 Great Lobelia
(*Lobelia siphilitica*)
Bluebell Family (Campanulaceae)

Description: Showy, *bright blue flowers* are in the axils
of leafy bracts and form an elongated
cluster on a leafy stem.
Flowers: about 1″ (2.5 cm) long,
2-lipped, the lower-lip striped with
white; calyx hairy, with 5 pointed
lobes; stamens 5, forming a united
tube around style.
Leaves: 2–6″ (5–15 cm) long, oval to
lanceolate, untoothed or irregularly
toothed.
Height: 1–4′ (30–120 cm).
Flowering: August–September.
Habitat: Rich lowland woods and meadows,
swamps.
Range: Western New England south to eastern
Virginia and uplands of North Carolina
and Alabama, west to eastern Kansas
and Minnesota.
Comments: This blue counterpart of the Cardinal
Flower is a most desirable plant for
wildflower gardens. The unfortunate
species name is based on the fact that it
was a supposed cure for syphilis. The
root contains alkaloids which cause
vomiting.

634 Spiked Lobelia
(*Lobelia spicata*)
Bluebell Family (Campanulaceae)

Description: Small purplish-blue to bluish white
flowers are in an *elongated, slender,
spikelike cluster* on a leafy stem that is

often reddish and hairy at the base, smooth above.

Flowers: ⅓–½" (8–13 mm) long, 2-lipped.

Leaves: basal ones 1–3½" (2.5–8.8 cm) long, lanceolate to elliptic, light green becoming smaller, up the stem, sessile eventually reduced to bracts under flowers.

Height: 1–4' (30–120 cm).

Flowering: June–August.

Habitat: Fields, woodlands, and rich meadows; dry sandy soil.

Range: New Brunswick south to Georgia, west to Arkansas, north to Minnesota.

Comments: A highly variable species with several varieties recognized by botanists.

---

601 Venus's Looking-glass
(*Specularia perfoliata*)
Bluebell Family (Campanulaceae)

Description: *Wheel-shaped,* blue-violet flowers set singly in the *axils of leaves that clasp the stem.*

Flowers: ¾" (2 cm) wide, with 5 petals; flowers in lower leaf axils fail to open.

Leaves: ¼–1" (6–25 mm) wide, *scallop-toothed, shell-shaped.*

Height: 6–18" (15–45 cm).

Flowering: May–August.

Habitat: Dry woods and fields; often in poor soils.

Range: Southern Ontario and Quebec; south to Florida; west to Texas; northwesterly to the Dakotas and beyond our range.

Comments: The genus and common names, derived from Latin *specularius* ("pertaining to mirrors"), may refer to the somewhat shiny seeds. This distinctive annual can appear in any open spot, even in cultivated flower gardens. A very similar species, *S. biflora,* which has less clasping leaves and open flowers only at the very tip of the stem, occurs from southeastern Virginia to Florida and west to the Pacific coast.

HEMP FAMILY (Cannabinaceae)

Coarse, aromatic herbs with watery juice and axillary clusters of small flowers.

Flowers: staminate ("male") in long, loose clusters, with 5 sepals, 5 stamens, and petals absent; pistillate ("female") in dense clusters, each flower having a single sepal and closely associated with bracts.

Leaves: simple or palmately compound, toothed.

Fruit: small and seed-like.

Only 2 genera and 4 species are known. *Humulus,* widely distributed through the north temperate zone, is of economic importance in the production of hops, used in beermaking. *Cannabis,* from which marijuana and hemp fibers are derived, is native to central Asia.

---

20 Marijuana; Hemp
(*Cannabis sativa*)
Hemp Family (Cannabinaceae)

Description: *Coarse, branching plant* with erect stems and clusters of small greenish flowers in the leaf axils.
Flowers: to ⅛" (3 mm) wide; male and female on separate plants.
Leaves: *palmately divided,* hairy, with 5–7 long, *narrow, coarsely toothed, tapering leaflets* 2–6" (5–15 cm) long.
Height: 3–10' (90–300 cm).
Flowering: June–October.
Habitat: Waste places and roadsides.
Range: Ontario to New Brunswick; south to Virginia; west to Tennessee and Kansas; north to Minnesota.
Comments: This annual was introduced from Asia; the narcotic marijuana is obtained by extracting resin from its female flowers. Its leaves are dried and smoked like tobacco for their euphoric effect.

HONEYSUCKLE FAMILY
(Caprifoliaceae)

Mostly shrubs, sometimes vines or herbs, commonly with showy flowers. Flowers: radially or bilaterally symmetrical, usually in a branched or forked cluster; sepals 5 small; corolla with 5 petals united into a slender tube, flared into a trumpet-shaped end or forming an upper and lower lip; stamens usually 5. All these parts attached at top of ovary.
Leaves: opposite, simple or compound.
Fruit: berry, drupe, or capsule.
There are about 15 genera and 400 species in north temperate regions and in tropical mountains. Snowberries, honeysuckle, and elderberries are grown as ornamentals, and elderberries are also eaten or made into jelly and wine.

358 Bush Honeysuckle
(Diervilla sessilifolia)
Honeysuckle Family (Caprifoliaceae)

Description: A low shrub with sulfur-yellow flowers in terminal or axillary clusters of 3–7 flowers. Branchlets nearly square.
Flowers: ¾" (2 cm) long; tubular, with 5 lobes, 3 pointed forward and 2 backward.
Leaves: 2–5" (5–12.5 cm) long; opposite, *stalkless,* ovate to lanceolate, toothed.
Height: 4–5' (1.2–2.5 m).
Flowering: June–August.
Habitat: Upland woods.
Range: Virginia south to Georgia; west to Alabama and Tennessee.
Comments: A similar species, Northern Bush Honeysuckle (*D. lonicera*) has round branchlets, stalked leaves, and the clusters are mostly made up of only 3 flowers.

506 Twinflower
(*Linnaea borealis*)
Honeysuckle Family (Caprifoliaceae)

Description: A low, delicate evergreen plant with
trailing stems having short, upright
branches, each terminated by *2 pinkish-
white, nodding bell-shaped flowers.* Stems
hairy.
Flowers: ½" (1.3 cm) long; corolla five-
lobed, hairy inside.
Leaves; about ½" (1 cm) wide and ½–
1" (1.3–2.5 cm) long; opposite,
rounded, light green, with toothed
edges; low on flower stalks.
Height: creeper, with flowering
branches 3–6" (7.5–15 cm) high.
Flowering: June–August.
Habitat: Cool woods and bogs.
Range: Alaska to Greenland; south to New
England, Maryland, and West
Virginia; west to Ohio, Indiana, and
South Dakota.
Comments: A beautiful trailing plant of the North,
this is the American variety of the
European plant. It was named after
Carolus Linnaeus (1707–1778), the
father of modern botany, who was so
fond of the flower he had his portrait
painted with it.

201, 360 Japanese Honeysuckle
(*Lonicera japonica*)
Honeysuckle Family (Caprifoliaceae)

Description: This vine has *fragrant, tubular flowers,*
white (turning yellow with age), in
pairs in the leaf axils. Twigs hairy.
Flowers: 1½" (3.8 cm) long; long,
curved stamens project from 2-lipped,
5-lobed corolla.
Leaves: to 3" (7.5 cm) long; opposite,
ovate, *untoothed,* evergreen, hairy.
Fruit: a black berry.
Height: *vine.*
Flowering: April–July, occasionally into fall.
Habitat: Thickets, roadsides, and woodlands.

Range: Massachusetts, New York, and Ohio; south to Florida; west to Texas and Kansas.

Comments: This woody vine, introduced from Asia, has escaped from cultivation. A fast-growing climber that can engulf a woodland and strangle trees, it is a serious competitor with the native flora. It is reported to grow as much as 30′ (9 m) in a single year and is difficult to eradicate. Sweet nectar can be milked from the base of the corolla.

431 Trumpet Honeysuckle
(*Lonicera sempervirens*)
Honeysuckle Family (Caprifoliaceae)

Description: This *vine* has showy, *trumpet-shaped flowers,* red outside, yellow inside, in several *whorled clusters* at the ends of the stems.
Flowers: 1–2″ (2.5–5 cm) long; corolla 5-lobed.
Leaves: 1½–3″ (3.8–7.5 cm) long; opposite, the uppermost pairs so united that stem seems to pierce them, oblong, deep green, with whitish bloom beneath.
Fruit: scarlet berries.
Height: vine.

Flowering: April–August.

Habitat: Woods and thickets.

Range: Massachusetts and New York; south to Florida; west to Texas, Ohio, Iowa, and Nebraska. Those farther north may have escaped cultivation.

Comments: This beautiful, slender, climbing vine is frequently visited by hummingbirds. The species name refers to its evergreen habit, especially in the South. Upper leaves are united. Five additional species also have upper leaves united. They differ from *L. sempervirens* in having wide spreading flower lobes.

207 Tartarian Honeysuckle
(*Lonicera tatarica*)
Honeysuckle Family (Caprifoliaceae)

Description: A hollow-branched, erect shrub with
pink or white, *paired, deeply lobed,*
tubular flowers arising from leaf axils.
Flowers: ¾″ (2 cm) long; corolla
5-lobed, hairy inside.
Leaves: 1–2½″ (2.5–6.3 cm) long;
smooth, ovate, opposite.
Fruit: a red berry.
Height: 4–10′ (1.2–3 m).
Flowering: May–June.
Habitat: Thickets, borders of fields.
Range: Ontario and Quebec; south to New
England, New Jersey, and Kentucky;
west to Iowa.
Comments: Two very similar species are Morrow's
Honeysuckle (*L. Morrowi*), the white
flowers of which turn yellow with age,
and European Fly Honeysuckle
(*L. xylosteum*), with whitish-yellow
flowers.

217 Elderberry
(*Sambucus canadensis*)
Honeysuckle Family (Caprifoliaceae)

Description: Smooth-stemmed shrub with *pinnately*
compound leaves and *flat-topped clusters* of
tiny, white, fragrant flowers; twigs
have large white pith and prominent
lenticels.
Flowers: ⅛″ (4 mm) wide, in clusters
2–10″ (5–25 cm) wide; corolla
5-lobed.
Leaves: opposite, pinnately cut into
5–11 elliptic to lanceolate, toothed
leaflets, each 2–6″ (5–15 cm) long.
Fruit: purplish-black, berry-like
drupes, in clusters.
Height: 3–12′ (90–360 cm).
Flowering: June–July.
Habitat: Low ground, wet areas, and borders of
fields and copses.
Range: Manitoba to Nova Scotia; south from

New England to Florida; west to Louisiana and Oklahoma; north to Minnesota.

Comments: This soft, woody species yields fruit which makes tasty jelly and wine. It is also an important food source for many songbirds and game birds. The genus name comes from Greek *sambuce,* an ancient musical instrument, and refers to the soft pith, easily removed from the twigs and used to make flutes and whistles.

447   Red-berried Elder
(*Sambucus pubens*)
Honeysuckle Family (Caprifoliaceae)

Description: A shrub with downy twigs and leaves and concave or *pyramidal clusters* of small white flowers.
Flowers: ¼″ (6 mm) wide; petals 5.
Leaves: opposite, pinnately compound, with 5–7 oval or ovate-lanceolate, sharply toothed leaflets, each 2–5″ (5–12.5 cm) long.
Fruit: *bright red* berry-like drupes in clusters.
Height: 2–10′ (60–300 cm).
Flowering: April–July.
Habitat: Rich woods, clearings.
Range: Across Canada; south to Pennsylvania and in mountains to Georgia; west to Indiana, Illinois, South Dakota, and westward.
Comments: The fruits of this species have a disagreeably bitter taste and are said to cause digestive upsets if eaten in quantity. However, they are a favorite food of birds.

240 Snowberry
(*Symphoricarpos albus*)
Honeysuckle Family (Caprifoliaceae)

Description: This hollow-stemmed shrub has tiny, pinkish-white, *bell-shaped flowers* in small terminal or axillary clusters.
Flowers: ¼" (6 mm) long; corolla 5-lobed.
Leaves: 1–2" (2.5–5 cm) long; opposite, oval, dull gray-green.
Fruit: a white, waxy, berry-like drupe, ½" (1.3 cm) wide, persisting into early winter.
Height: 1–4' (30–120 cm).

Flowering: May–July.

Habitat: Rocky banks and roadsides.

Range: Quebec and western Massachusetts south to Pennsylvania and West Virginia; west to Minnesota, Nebraska, and Colorado.

Comments: This plant escaped from old-fashioned dooryard gardens; variety *laevigatus* of this shrub is also cultivated. Two other species are often encountered: Coralberry (*S. orbiculatus*), with sessile, axillary, purplish-green flowers and showy clusters of pink berries; and Wolfberry (*S. occidentalis*) a dry prairie shrub with pale pink flowers, leathery, oval leaves, and greenish-white fruit.

427 Wild Coffee; Feverwort; Tinker's-weed
(*Triosteum perfoliatum*)
Honeysuckle Family (Caprifoliaceae)

Description: A coarse plant with hairy, sticky stems and few-flowered clusters of small, *tubular, red to greenish flowers* in the axils of the upper leaves.
Flowers: ¾" (2 cm) long, with 5-lobed corolla and 5 *long sepals*.
Leaves: 4–10" (10–25 cm) long; opposite, lanceolate to ovate, unstalked. *Bases of paired leaves so united* they appear to be pierced by the stem.

Fruit: hairy, *yellow-orange berries* with persistent 5-lobed calyx and 3 seeds.
Height: 2–4' (60–120 cm).

Flowering: May–July.

Habitat: Open, rocky woods and thickets.

Range: Massachusetts and eastern New York south to Georgia; west to West Virginia, Michigan, Wisconsin, Minnesota, Nebraska and eastern Kansas.

Comments: The fruits can be dried, roasted, ground, and used as a coffee substitute. The genus name refers to the trio of bony seeds in the fruits. A closely related species with a similar range, Horse Gentian (*T. aurantiacum*) has opposite leaves and a smooth stem. Narrow-leaved Horse Gentian (*T. angustifolium*) has yellow flowers and leaves to 2" (5 cm).

214 Maple-leaved Viburnum
(*Viburnum acerifolium*)
Honeysuckle Family (Caprifoliaceae)

Description: A shrub with *maple-like leaves* and small, white flowers of uniform size in flat topped clusters.
Flowers: ¼" (6 mm) wide; clusters 2–3" (5–7.5 cm) wide; corolla 5-lobed.
Leaves: 2–5" (5–12.5 cm) long, opposite, *3-lobed,* maple-like, hairy, with minute black dots beneath.
Fruit: purplish-black, berry-like drupes.
Height: 3–6' (90–180 cm).

Flowering: May–August.

Habitat: Shrub layer of moist, upland, hardwood forests.

Range: Quebec south to New England and Florida; west to Tennessee, Michigan, and Minnesota.

Comments: The distinctive, purplish-pink autumn foliage makes this one of our handsomest shrubs. Another native Viburnum with 3-lobed leaves, Highbush Cranberry (*V. trilobum*) has large, showy, white, sterile outer flowers in each cluster and in late summer and autumn bears red fruits suitable for jam. Few-flowered Cranberry Bush (*V. edule*), with red fruit and only slightly lobed leaves, occurs at high elevations in the Northeast, extending far north into Canada.

215 Hobblebush; Moosewood
(*Viburnum alnifolium*)
Honeysuckle Family (Caprifoliaceae)

Description: This shrub has fragrant, flat-topped clusters of small, white flowers, the *outer flowers larger* than the inner ones.
Flowers: marginal ones to 1″ (2.5 cm) wide; showy petals 5; no stamens or pistils. Clusters 2–6″ (5–15 cm) wide.
Leaves: 3–8″ (7.5–20 cm) wide, opposite, heart-shaped, with prominent veins, finely *saw-toothed margins,* and star-like, rusty hairs beneath.
Fruit: berry-like drupes, at first red, turning almost black.
Height: 3–10′ (90–300 cm).

Flowering: May–June.

Habitat: Shrub layer of cooler Northeast forests and higher elevations southward.

Range: Ontario to Nova Scotia; south to New England, northern New Jersey, and in the mountains of Georgia and Tennessee; west to Michigan.

Comments: This straggly shrub has beautiful bronze-red or purple-pink autumn coloration and is used by wildlife for food and cover. Its branches often bend and take root, tripping or "hobbling" passers-by; hence its common name.

216 **Witherod; Wild Raisin**
(*Viburnum cassinoides*)
Honeysuckle Family (Caprifoliaceae)

Description: A shrub with flat-topped, *stalked clusters* of small, white, scented flowers.
Flowers: about ¼" (6 mm) wide in clusters about 4" (10 cm) wide; petals 5.
Leaves: 2–4" (5–10 cm) long; opposite, thick, dull green, oval to ovate, the *margins usually wavy* or toothed, occasionally untoothed, with brownish hairs beneath.
Fruit: a blue-black, raisin-like drupe with sweet pulp.
Height: 3–12' (30–360 cm).

Flowering: May–early August.

Habitat: Wet thickets, swamps and clearings, borders of woods.

Range: Ontario to Nova Scotia, south to New England, Delaware, Maryland, uplands to Georgia, Alabama and Tennessee, north to Ohio, northern Indiana and Wisconsin.

Comments: This is one of several relatively similar Viburnums with edible fruits. Black Haw (*V. prunifolium*) is more tree-like, growing to 20' (6 m), with finely toothed, oval leaves and many short, twiggy branches borne at right angles to the stem. Nannyberry (*V. lentago*) is a shrub or tree, growing to 30' (9 m) in height, with long, tapering leaf tips and winged petioles; the heartwood has an unpleasant, goat-like smell; fruit is raisin-like.

---

213 **Arrowwood**
(*Viburnum dentatum*)
Honeysuckle Family (Caprifoliaceae)

Description: A shrub with downy twigs, *coarsely toothed leaves,* and flat-topped clusters of small, white flowers.
Flowers: ⅕" (5 mm) wide, in clusters 2–3" (5–7.5 cm) wide; petals 5.

Leaves: 1½–3″ (3.8–7.5 cm) long; rounded or heart-shaped at the base, opposite, ovate, or egg-shaped, with *saw-like teeth*.

Fruit: purplish-black or blue-gray berry-like drupes.

Height: 3–15′ (90–450 cm).

Flowering: May–August.

Habitat: Wet or dry thickets and borders of woods.

Range: Ontario to New Brunswick; south to Florida; west to Texas.

Comments: Some botanists recognize two separate species for this highly variable plant, the other being northern Arrowwood (*V. recognitum*) with smooth twigs.

PINK OR CARNATION FAMILY
(Caryophyllaceae)

Herbs with swollen nodes on the stems
and flowers blooming singly or in a
branched or forked cluster.
Flowers: sepals 5, free from one another
or united; petals 5, each often with a
slender portion at base and fringed or
toothed at end; stamens 5 or 10. All
these parts attached at base of ovary.
Leaves: opposite, simple.
Fruit: usually a capsule.
There are about 80 genera and 2,000
species, primarily in the Northern
Hemisphere, especially in cool regions.

469 Corn Cockle
(Agrostemma githago)
Pink Family (Caryophyllaceae)

Description: Tall, *densely hairy plant* with showy
pink flowers at tips of long stalks.
Flowers: 2″ (5 cm) wide; calyx with
10 prominent ribs and 5 narrow sepals
longer than the 5 wide petals.
Leaves: to 4″ (10 cm) long, opposite,
narrow, pale green.
Height: 1–3′ (30–90 cm).

Flowering: June–September.

Habitat: Grain fields, roadsides, and waste
places.

Range: Throughout.

Comments: This European introduction is especially
bothersome in grain fields, because its
seeds contain poisonous enzymes like
those of Bouncing Bet.

47 Mountain Sandwort
(Arenaria groenlandica)
Pink Family (Caryophyllaceae)

Description: *Mat-forming plants* with many small
white flowers at tips of slender stalks,
rising from tufts of basal leaves.

Flowers: ½″ (1.3 cm) wide, translucent;
petals 5, separate, slightly notched.
Leaves: ½″ (1.3 cm) long, opposite,
narrow or needle-like.
Height: 2–5″ (5–12.5 cm).

Flowering: June–August.
Habitat: Granite crevices and gravelly sites,
often in higher mountains.
Range: Greenland down to northern New
England; New York south to Georgia.
Comments: This delicate plant with arctic affinities
is often tucked into rock outcrops. On
Mt. Washington, New Hampshire, it
is called Mountain Daisy.

49 Mouse-ear Chickweed
(*Cerastium vulgatum*)
Pink Family (Caryophyllaceae)

Description: Low, horizontally spreading plant with
hairy sticky stems, fuzzy leaves, and small
white flowers in clusters at the top of
slender stalks.
Flowers: ¼″ (6 mm) wide; 5 *deeply
notched petals.*
Leaves: to ½″ (1.3 cm) long, paired,
oblong, stalkless.
Fruit: small cylindrical capsule.
Height: 6–12″ (15–30 cm).

Flowering: May–September.
Habitat: Waste places, fields, and roadsides.
Range: Throughout.
Comments: This naturalized European plant takes
its common name from the fuzzy
leaves. Although a troublesome weed in
the garden, its leaves can be boiled and
eaten as greens. Nine additional species
occur in our range: 3 native, the rest
introduced.

474 Deptford Pink
(*Dianthus armeria*)
Pink Family (Caryophyllaceae)

Description: *Deep pink* flowers in flat-topped clusters
at the top of stiff, erect stems.
Flowers: ½" (1.3 cm) wide; 5 petals,
with jagged edges and *tiny white spots;*
leaf-like bracts below flowers are
lanceolate or awl-shaped.
Leaves: 1–4" (2.5–10 cm) long,
narrow, erect, light green.
Height: 6–24" (15–60 cm).
Flowering: May–September.
Habitat: Dry fields and roadsides.
Range: Southern Ontario to Nova Scotia; south
to Georgia; northwest to Missouri.
Comments: This European introduction somewhat
resembles Sweet William. The common
name refers to Deptford, England (now
part of London), where the flower was
once abundant. A closely related
species, Maiden Pink (*D. deltoides*), has
larger, solitary, flowers.

69 Evening Lychnis; White Campion
(*Lychnis alba*)
Pink Family (Caryophyllaceae)

Description: Downy, much-branched plant having
white, (occasionally pinkish), *sweet-
scented* flowers with an inflated calyx.
Flowers: 1" (2.5 cm) wide, with 5 *deeply
notched* petals; female flower has 5
curved styles protruding from center,
inflated, sticky calyx with 20 veins and
5 sharp teeth; male flower has a slender
10-veined calyx and 10 stamens.
Leaves: 1½–4" (3.8–10 cm) long,
opposite, hairy, ovate or lanceolate.
Fruit: vase-shaped capsule.
Height: 1–3' (30–90 cm).
Flowering: July–October.
Habitat: Fields, roadsides, and waste places.
Range: Quebec; south to South Carolina; west
to Alabama; north to Missouri (and
beyond our range).

Comments: This European introduction, which has male and female flowers on separate plants, blooms at night and attracts moths that pollinate the flowers. It is quite similar to Night-flowering Catchfly (*Silene noctiflora*), another introduced species, also white and sticky, which has only 3 styles. Red Campion (*L. dioica*), which is quite rare, has pink flowers and is very similar to Evening Lychnis.

---

416 Maltese Cross
(*Lychnis chalcedonica*)
Pink Family (Caryophyllaceae)

Description: Scarlet flowers with *Y-shaped petals* are in round clusters at the top of leafy, hairy stems.
Flowers: about 1″ (2.5 cm) wide, with 5 deeply notched petals.
Leaves: 2–4″ (5–10 cm) long, opposite, lanceolate to ovate, rounded or heart-shaped at the base and often clasping the stem.
Height: 2–3′ (60–90 cm).

Flowering: June–August.
Habitat: Thickets, roadsides, and open woods.
Range: Prince Edward Island to southern New England; west to Minnesota.
Comments: Introduced from Asia and planted in gardens, this flower has escaped from cultivation. The common name reflects the similarity of the petal arrangement to the shape of the cross adopted by the Knights of Malta. The species name refers to Chalcedon, an ancient town on the Bosporus, an area where the flower occurs.

500   Ragged Robin
(*Lychnis flos-cuculi*)
Pink Family (Caryophyllaceae)

Description: Deep pink (sometimes white) flowers with *deeply cut* petals are in clusters at the ends of thin branching stalks; stem slightly sticky toward the top, downy below.
Flowers: ½" (1.3 cm) wide, 5 petals, each cut into four thin lobes, appearing ragged.
Leaves: opposite, lanceolate, decreasing in size as they go up the stem, the lower ones 2–3" (5–7.5 cm) long.
Height: 1–3' (30–90 cm).

Flowering: May–July.

Habitat: Moist fields, meadows, waste places.

Range: Quebec; south through New England to New York and Pennsylvania.

Comments: This plant, introduced from Europe, has become naturalized in the northeastern United States. The genus name *Lychnis*, derived from *lychnos* ("flame"), was originally used by the ancient Greeks for some flame-colored species. The species name *flos-cuculi* means "cuckoo flower," another common name for this pink. The somewhat similar Mullein Pink (*L. coronaria*) is a densely woolly white plant.

163   Bouncing Bet; Soapwort
(*Saponaria officinalis*)
Pink Family (Caryophyllaceae)

Description: Leafy, sparingly branched plant with smooth stems, *swollen at the nodes,* and terminal clusters of white or pinkish fragrant flowers.
Flowers: about 1" (2.5 cm) wide, with 5 delicate, *scalloped petals* with small appendages at their throats; occasionally double or with extra petals; calyx 5-lobed, the tube often splitting in double-flowered forms.

Leaves: 2–3″ (5–7.5 cm) long, opposite, oval, with 3–5 conspicuous veins.
Height: 1–2½′ (30–75 cm).
Flowering: July–September.
Habitat: Roadsides and disturbed areas.
Range: Throughout.
Comments: This attractive, phlox-like perennial, introduced from Europe, spreads by underground stems and forms sizable colonies. The plant contains poisonous saponins (soap-like substances) that inspired the genus name (from Latin *sapo,* meaning "soap") and the alternate common name Soapwort. Lather can be made from its crushed foliage. The common name, Bouncing Bet, is an old-fashioned nickname for a washerwoman.

457 Moss Campion
(*Silene acaulis*)
Pink Family (Caryophyllaceae)

Description: *Dwarf plant,* forming *dense tussocks,* with solitary pink to violet flowers at the ends of leafy branches.
Flowers: about ½″ (1.3 cm) across; 5 petals, entire to slightly notched.
Leaves: ⅓–½″ (8–13 mm) long, crowded, small, overlapping, linear.
Height: 1–3″ (2.5–7.5 cm).
Flowering: June–August.
Habitat: Alpine areas, barrens, and cliffs.
Range: Arctic regions; south in the eastern U.S. to mountaintops of New Hampshire.
Comments: This beautiful little mountain-dwelling wildflower forms extensive moss-like carpets in the western mountains but appears only locally in the East, where Mt. Washington in New Hampshire is its southern limit.

71 Bladder Campion
(*Silene cucubalus*)
Pink Family (Caryophyllaceae)

Description: White flowers with deeply notched petals and *globular calyx*, in loose clusters.
Flowers: 1″ (2.5 cm) wide, with 5 petals, each cut into 2 lobes; *calyx inflated, prominently veined*; styles 3.
Leaves: 1½–4″ (3.8–10 cm) long, opposite, lanceolate to oblong, often clasping the stem.
Height: 8–30″ (20–75 cm).
Flowering: April–August.
Habitat: Fields and roadsides.
Range: Across southern Canada to Newfoundland; south to Virginia and Tennessee; west to Missouri and beyond.
Comments: Its common name refers to the distinctive, balloon-like calyx. Two related white-flowered species found in our range are Night-Flowering Catchfly (*S. noctiflora*), which is hairy, sticky, and broader-leaved than Bladder Campion, and Forking Catchfly (*S. dichotoma*), which is also hairy but has slender leaves and stalkless flowers. Within our range, 8 other white-flowered species occur.

70 Starry Campion
(*Silene stellata*)
Pink Family (Caryophyllaceae)

Description: *Deeply fringed*, 5-petaled white flowers clustered atop tall slender stalks, with *leaves mostly in whorls of 4*.
Flowers: ¾″ (2 cm) wide; *sepals united and bell-shaped*.
Leaves: 1½–4″ (3.8–10 cm) long, lanceolate, smooth.
Height: 2–3′ (60–90 cm).
Flowering: June–September.
Habitat: Open woods.
Range: Massachusetts south to Georgia and

Alabama; west to eastern Texas and
Oklahoma; north to Minnesota.
Comments: This delicate wildflower is pollinated by
butterflies and many kinds of moths. It
is often grown in wildflower gardens.

415 Fire Pink
(*Silene virginica*)
Pink Family (Caryophyllaceae)

Description: *Bright red,* long-stalked flowers bloom
in loose clusters at tops of slender,
weak, or reclining stems.
Flowers: 1½" (3.8 cm) wide; 5 petals,
narrow, often deeply cleft; sepals united
into long sticky tube.
Leaves: basal 1½–4" (3.8–10 cm) long,
lanceolate to spatulate; stem leaves
opposite, unstalked, to 6" (15 cm)
long.
Height: 6–24" (15–60 cm).
Flowering: April–June.
Habitat: Open woods, thickets, rocky and sandy
slopes.
Range: Southern Ontario; south to Georgia;
west to Arkansas and Oklahoma; north
to Minnesota.
Comments: A common name for members of this
genus is Catchfly, which refers to the
sticky hairs or exudates which trap
insects. Another species with bright red
flowers is Royal Catchfly (*S. regia*),
found in Midwestern prairies and dry
woods; it has short-stalked flowers,
with petals that are only slightly
toothed or untoothed, and thicker
leaves.

48 Chickweed, Starwort
(*Stellaria media*)
Pink Family (Caryophyllaceae)

Description: A weak-stemmed, much-branched, *low
plant* with small white flowers with
deeply cleft petals, in terminal clusters or

solitary in leaf axils. Stems with a *single line of hairs* down the side.
Flowers: ¼" (6 mm) wide; petals 5, so deeply divided as to appear to be 10; sepals 5, green, *longer than the petals*.
Leaves: ½–1" (1.3–2.5 cm) long; relatively smooth, opposite, ovate, lower with petioles, upper without.
Height: 3–8" (7.5–20 cm), with trailing stem to 16" (40 cm) long.

Flowering: February–December.
Habitat: Lawns and disturbed areas.
Range: Throughout.
Comments: This highly variable annual, introduced from Eurasia, is a cosmopolitan weed. It can be eaten in a salad and is a favorite food of chickens and wild birds. There are a dozen or more chickweeds; those in the genus *Stellaria* have three styles, while those in the closely related genus *Cerastium* have five styles. The petals of the latter are deeply cleft, with sepals shorter than petals.

50 Star Chickweed
(*Stellaria pubera*)
Pink Family (Caryophyllaceae)

Description: White flowers with *deeply cleft petals* are in clusters at the top of an erect stem and arising from the leaf axils. Stems with *two lines of hairs*.
Flowers: ½" (1.3 cm) wide; petals 5, incised half their length or more, so that they appear 10; *sepals shorter than petals*.
Leaves: ¾–3" (2–7.5 cm) long; opposite, stalkless, elliptic.
Height: 6–16" (15–40 cm).

Flowering: March–May.
Habitat: Rich woods, rocky slopes.
Range: New Jersey south to northern Florida; west to Alabama; north to Illinois.
Comments: With its beautiful star-like flowers, this is the most showy of the many chickweeds.

STAFF TREE FAMILY
(Celastraceae)

Trees or shrubs, sometimes vine-like, with small flowers, solitary or in clusters growing in leaf axils or at tips of branches.

Flowers: radially symmetrical; bisexual or occasionally unisexual; calyx 4–5 lobed or parted; petals 4–5; stamens 4–5, growing from margin of a conspicuous fleshy disk at bottom of calyx; ovary embedded in the disk or separate from it.

Leaves: alternate or opposite, simple.

Fruit: capsule, berry or drupe.

There are about 40 genera and 400 species, occurring throughout the world, except the arctic regions.

382 Climbing Bittersweet
(*Celastrus scandens*)
Staff-Tree Family (Celastraceae)

Description: A *twining, woody vine* that produces small green flowers and distinctive bicolored fruits.
Flowers: ⅛″ (4 mm) wide, in terminal clusters up to 4″ (10 cm) long; petals 4–5.
Leaves: to 2–4″ (5–10 cm) long; ovate, pointed, finely serrated.
Fruit: *yellow-orange, opening upon maturing to expose the scarlet, berry-like interior* (actually the fleshy seeds).
Height: vine.
Flowering: May–June.
Habitat: Thickets, woods, riverbanks.
Range: Southern Manitoba and Quebec south to Georgia; west to Alabama, Louisiana, Oklahoma, and the Dakotas.
Comments: This native species is being replaced in the Northeast by the more aggressive Asiatic Bittersweet (*C. orbiculatus*) which has escaped from cultivation. It has flowers and showy scarlet fruit arising from the axils of the leaves.

GOOSEFOOT FAMILY
(Chenopodiaceae)

Mostly succulent herbs, rarely shrubs,
with minute clustered greenish flowers.
Flowers: usually radially symmetrical;
bisexual or unisexual; sepals 2–5 but
sometimes only 1 or even none; petals
absent; stamens 1–5. All these parts
attached at base of ovary.
Leaves: usually alternate, simple,
toothed or lobed, often with a grayish,
mealy surface.
Fruit: tiny, 1-seeded.
There are about 102 genera and 1,400
species, many found along seashores or
in other saline places. Some are used as
ornamentals, while many are weeds;
and some produce such garden
vegetables as beets, Swiss chard, and
spinach.

19 Lamb's Quarters; Pigweed
(*Chenopodium album*)
Goosefoot Family (Chenopodiaceae)

Description: On a branching plant, often with *red-streaked stems,* grow clustered spikes of
minute, *unstalked flowers.*
Flowers: less than 1/16" (1.5 mm) wide;
sessile, with greenish calyx; petals
lacking.
Leaves: 1–4" (2.5–10 cm) long;
triangular or diamond-shaped, coarsely
toothed, *mealy white beneath.*
Height: 1–6' (30–180 cm).
Flowering: June–October.
Habitat: Cultivated land, disturbed sites, and
roadsides.
Range: Throughout.
Comments: Many of the introduced members of
this family are weeds with non-showy
flowers that invade lawns and gardens.
Eighteen more species of this genus are
found in our range, two
of them aromatic: Mexican Tea
(*C. ambrosioides*) has oblong or

lanceolate leaves with wavy-toothed margins; Jerusalem-oak (*C. botrys*) has oak-like leaves.

34, 437 Slender Glasswort
(*Salicornia europaea*)
Goosefoot Family (Chenopodiaceae)

Description: A *fleshy, cylindrical, leafless,* opposite-branched plant with *stem joints longer than wide.*
Flowers: minute, green, borne in groups of three in the hollows of the upper joints in a spike ⅛″ (3 mm) wide.
Leaves: reduced to minute, opposite scales.
Height: 6–18″ (15–45 cm).
Flowering: August–November.
Habitat: Coastal salt marshes, especially on bare peat, salt licks, and inland salt marshes.
Range: Eastern New Brunswick and Nova Scotia south along the coast to Georgia; local in Michigan, Wisconsin, and Illinois.
Comments: This succulent turns reddish in the fall on northern tidal marshes. It is very salty and can be pickled or added raw to salads. Dwarf Glasswort (*S. bigelovii*) is usually unbranched, with joints wider than long; Woody Glasswort (*S. virginica*) has creeping stems that form extensive mats.

ROCKROSE FAMILY (Cistaceae)

Herbs or shrubs with flowers borne singly or in a branched cluster.
Flowers: radially symmetrical; calyx usually with 3 large sepals and 2 smaller ones, or small ones absent; petals 5 separate, sometimes fewer, occasionally none; numerous stamens. All these parts attached at base of ovary.
Leaves: alternate or opposite, simple.
Fruit: leathery or woody capsule with 3 or more chambers.
About 8 genera and 200 species mostly occur in dry, sunny locations, often in chalky or sandy soil. The family is found mostly in northern temperate regions, with a few species in South America. A few species are cultivated as ornamentals.

258 Frostweed
(*Helianthemum canadense*)
Rockrose Family (Cistaceae)

Description: A *solitary yellow flower* terminates a main stem, while later in the season clusters of inconspicuous, bud-like flowers are produced in the axils of branch leaves.
Flowers: ¾–1½" (2–3.8 cm) across; petals 5, *wedge-shaped;* many stamens. Flower lasts only 1 day and produces many seeds.
Leaves: about 1" (2.5 cm) long; narrow, dull green, and hoary with white hairs underneath.
Height: 8–18" (20–45 cm).
Flowering: May–July.
Habitat: Dry, sandy, or rocky open woods and openings.
Range: Southern Ontario to Nova Scotia south to North Carolina; west to Kentucky, Mississippi, Missouri, and Wisconsin.
Comments: This perennial of dry, open sites flower only in the sunlight, a fact which

explains the generic name, which is derived from the Greek *helios* ("the sun") and *anthemon* ("flower"). The common name relates to the ice crystals which form from sap exuding from cracks near the base of the stem in the late fall.

363 Beach Heath; False Heather; Poverty-Grass
(*Hudsonia tomentosa*)
Rockrose Family (Cistaceae)

Description: A low, matted, somewhat woody evergreen with numerous small, sulfur-yellow flowers at the tops of short branches.
Flowers: ¼" (6 mm) wide; petals 5, open only in sunlight and lasting 1 day.
Leaves: *tiny, scale-like, gray-woolly,* and pressed close to stems.
Height: 3–8" (7.5–20 cm).
Flowering: May–July.
Habitat: Sand dunes and poor soil openings.
Range: New Brunswick south along the coast to Northern Carolina; also Great Lakes region to Minnesota.
Comments: Golden Heather (*H. ericoides*), with greenish foliage and outward spreading leaves, is found in dry pinelands or sands from Newfoundland and Nova Scotia south to Delaware and South Carolina.

WHITE ALDER FAMILY
(Clethraceae)

Shrubs or small trees with fragrant, white or pinkish flowers in terminal racemes or panicles.
Flowers: calyx 5-part; corolla of 5 petals, slightly united at the base; stamens 10. All these parts attached at base of ovary.
Leaves: simple, alternate, toothed.
Fruit: capsule.
There are only 1 genus and about 30 species, occurring in tropical, subtropical, and temperate regions of both hemispheres. They are often used as ornamentals.

221 **Sweet Pepperbush**
(*Clethra alnifolia*)
White Alder Family (Clethraceae)

Description: A tall, many-branched, leafy shrub with spike-like, *upright clusters of fragrant white flowers.*
Flowers: each about ⅓″ (8 mm) wide; stamens 10, style protruding.
Leaves: up to 3″ (7.5 cm) long; wedge-shaped, sharply toothed above the middle, untoothed at base.
Fruit: small, globular capsules with persistent style.
Height: 3–10′ (90–300 cm).
Flowering: July–September.
Habitat: Wetlands, especially swamps, and sandy woods.
Range: Coastal, from southern Maine south to Florida; west to eastern Texas.
Comments: This shrub forms sizable patches. Its dry fruiting capsules remain long after flowering and help identify this plant in winter. Mountain Pepperbush (*C. acuminata*) has more pointed leaves and is found in southern mountains.

SPIDERWORT FAMILY
(Commelinaceae)

Herbs with more or less swollen nodes,
flowers arranged in clusters enveloped
in boat-shaped bracts.
Flowers: radially symmetrical; sepals 3;
petals 3; stamens 6, the stalks often
with colored hairs. All these parts
attached at base of ovary.
Leaves: alternate, simple, the base of
each forming a tubular sheath around
the stem.
Fruit: capsule with 3 chambers.
About 40 genera and 600 species are
known, found mostly in tropical and
subtropical regions. Dayflower,
Wandering Jew, and Moses-in-a-boat
are cultivated as ornamentals.

611 Asiatic Dayflower
(*Commelina communis*)
Spiderwort Family (Commelinaceae)

Description: The reclining stems have upright leafy
branches with deep blue flowers at the
top, protruding from a heart-shaped,
enfolding leaf.
Flowers: ½" (1.3 cm) wide; *2 rounded
blue petals, and a small white petal
beneath;* sepals 3, green; stamens 6.
Leaves: fleshy, oblong-lanceolate, 3–5"
(8–13 cm) long; pointed tips, with
rounded bases sheathing the stem.
Height: creeper, with reclining stem
1–3' (30–90 cm) long.

Flowering: June–October.

Habitat: Open disturbed areas, roadsides,
wooded borders.

Range: Massachusetts south to North Carolina
and Alabama; west to Arkansas and
eastern Kansas; north to Wisconsin.

Comments: This plant, introduced from Asia, has
flowers that bloom for only one day. It
often forms colonies by rooting from
the stem nodes; hence the species name
communis. The genus name refers to

three Dutch brothers named Commelin:
two (represented by the two larger
petals) became well-known botanists;
the third (represented by the small
petal) died without any achievements in
botany. Of the five other species found
in our range, the similar Slender
Dayflower (*C. erecta*) has an erect stem;
the Virginia Dayflower (*C. virginica*)
has an erect stem and 3 blue petals.

614 Spiderwort
(*Tradescantia virginiana*)
Spiderwort Family (Commelinaceae)

Description: Violet-blue flowers with *showy yellow
stamens* are in a terminal cluster above a
pair of long, narrow, leaf-like bracts.
Flowers: 1–2″ (2.5–5 cm) wide;
petals 3; *sepals 3, hairy, green;* stamens
6, hairy.
Leaves: to 15″ (37.5 cm) long; linear,
pointed, *folded lengthwise* forming a
channel.
Height: 8–24″ (20–60 cm).

Flowering: April–July.

Habitat: Wooded borders, thickets, meadows,
roadsides.

Range: Connecticut south to northwestern
Georgia; west to Tennessee and
Missouri; north to Wisconsin.

Comments: This is a showy spiderwort, so named
because the angular leaf arrangement
suggests a squatting spider. The flowers
open only in the morning; the petals
then wilt and turn to a jelly-like fluid.
The hairy stamens consist of a row of
thin-walled cells forming a chain. They
are a favorite subject for microscopic
examination in biology classes because
the flowing cytoplasm and nucleus can
be seen easily. Other spiderworts with
similar floral structure are: *T. subaspera,*
found from Virginia southward and
west to Missouri and Illinois, with blue
flowers and a markedly zigzag stem
reaching 3′ (90 cm) in height; Ohio

Spiderwort (*T. ohiensis*), occurring from Massachusetts to Florida and through the Midwest, with rose to blue flowers and a whitish bloom on the stem and leaves; and *T. hirsuticaulis,* found from North Carolina to Florida and west to Texas, a hairy plant with light blue flowers.

MORNING GLORY FAMILY
(Convolvulaceae)

Trees, shrubs, vines, or herbs, commonly with handsome, funnel-shaped flowers.
Flowers: radially symmetrical; sepals 5; corolla of 5 united petals, almost unlobed on the rim; stamens 5. Corolla attached at base of ovary.
Leaves: alternate, simple.
Fruit: capsule, berry, or nut.
About 50 genera and 1,400 species occur, mostly in temperate and tropical regions. Morning Glory refers either to *Convolvulus* or *Ipomoea:* the former has noxious weeds; the latter also has weeds, but some species are cultivated for their handsome flowers—and one, the sweet potato, for its edible underground fleshy stems.

579 Hedge Bindweed
(*Convolvulus sepium*)
Morning Glory Family
(Convolvulaceae)

Description: This smooth, *twining vine* has funnel-shaped flowers, pinkish with white stripes.
Flowers: 2–3″ (5–7.5 cm) long; petals 5, fused together; calyx 5-lobed, enclosed in 2 pale green bracts.
Leaves: 2–4″ (5–10 cm) long; *arrow-shaped or triangular.*
Height: vine, 3–10′ (90–300 cm) long.
Flowering: May–September.
Habitat: Moist soil along streams, thickets, roadsides, waste places.
Range: Throughout.
Comments: It resembles Morning Glory but differs in having 2 rounded stigmas, rather than 1. It can be a pest, twining among and engulfing desirable ornamentals, and is difficult to eradicate without removing the fleshy creeping roots. The

genus name is from the Latin *convolvere* ("to twine"); the species name means "of hedges." Field Bindweed (*C. arvensis*) has smaller flowers and leaves, without bracts, and usually grows on the ground. Erect Bindweed (*C. spithamaeus*) has oval leaves, may be trailing or erect, but does not twine.

202 Dodder
(*Cuscuta gronovii*)
Morning Glory Family
(Convolvulaceae)

Description:	A *climbing, parasitic vine* with dense clusters of small, white, bell-shaped, flowers on *orange-yellow stems.* Flowers: ⅛" (3 mm) wide; corolla 5-lobed. Leaves: reduced to a few minute scales. Height: vine.
Flowering:	July–October.
Habitat:	On a variety of plants in moist, low ground.
Range:	Manitoba, Quebec, and Nova Scotia; New England south to Florida; west to Texas and beyond.
Comments:	The seeds of this plant germinate in the soil, but the roots eventually die as it twines around a host plant and sends out suckers through which it obtains all its nourishment. The species name honors Dutch botanist Jan Fredrik Gronovius, teacher of Linnaeus. Other Dodders grow exclusively on such plants as flax or clover. At least 15 species are found in our area, and all are difficult to distinguish from one another.

418 Small Red Morning Glory
(*Ipomoea coccinea*)
Morning Glory Family
(Convolvulaceae)

Description: This twining vine bears *small scarlet flowers,* each with a flaring tube that flattens into 5 shallow lobes.
Flowers: about ¾" (2 cm) wide; *sepals 5, with bristle-like tips;* stamens and stigma protruding.
Leaves: 1½–4" (3.8–10 cm) long; heart-shaped, occasionally lobed.
Height: vine, 3–9' (90–270 cm) long.

Flowering: July–October.

Habitat: Thickets, disturbed areas, roadsides.

Range: New England south to Florida; west to Kansas and beyond.

Comments: This showy vine introduced as an ornamental from tropical America has now escaped in many areas. The scientific name derives from the Greek for "worm-like" and refers to its twining habit. The closely related Scarlet Cypress Vine (*I. quamoclit*) has leaves divided into very narrow segments, like teeth on a comb.

654 Ivy-leaved Morning Glory
(*Ipomoea hederacea*)
Morning Glory Family
(Convolvulaceae)

Description: This leafy, hairy vine has *3-lobed leaves,* and blue, funnel-shaped flowers (white on the inside) that turn rose-purple late in the day.
Flowers: about 1½" (3.8 cm) wide; corolla of 5 fused petals; sepals 5, with long tips and narrow hairy base.
Leaves: 2–5" (5–12.5 cm) long or wide; deeply indented into three lobes, tapering to points.
Height: vine, 3–6' (90–180 cm) long.

Flowering: July–October.

Habitat: Fields and disturbed areas.

Range: New England and New York south to

Florida; west to Texas and beyond;
north to North Dakota.

Comments: Introduced from tropical America, this
twining plant is often a troublesome
weed, especially in Alabama. The
species name refers to English Ivy,
which has similar leaves.

578 Railroad Vine
(*Ipomoea pes-caprae*)
Morning Glory Family
(Convolvulaceae)

Description: A vine with a creeping stem but erect
flower stalks with purple or reddish-
pink *funnel-shaped flowers*.
Flowers: about 2" (5 cm) long; corolla
of 5 fused petals.
Leaves: 1–4" (2.5–10 cm) long; round,
bright green, usually *folded along
midrib* and *notched at apex*.
Height: vine, to 20' (6 m) long.
Flowering: All year.
Habitat: Coastal sand dunes.
Range: Georgia and Florida west to Texas.
Comments: Introduced from the West Indies, this
showy vine sometimes grows across
beaches almost to water's edge. The
species name, meaning "goat's foot,"
refers to the shape of the leaf.

580 Common Morning Glory
(*Ipomoea purpurea*)
Morning Glory Family
(Convolvulaceae)

Description: A twining vine with hairy stems and
funnel-shaped flowers of purple, pink,
blue, or white in clusters of 1–5 rising
from the leaf axils.
Flowers: 2–3" (5–7.5 cm) long; corolla
of 5 fused petals; sepals narrow,
pointed, and hairy.
Leaves: 2–5" (5–12.5 cm) long; broad,
heart-shaped.

Height: vine, to 10′ (3 m) long.
Flowering: July–October.
Habitat: Cultivated fields, roadsides, disturbed areas.
Range: Throughout.
Comments: Originally introduced from tropical America as an ornamental, this plant has escaped from gardens and become naturalized. Its broad, heart-shaped leaves are distinctive.

577 Glades Morning Glory
(*Ipomoea sagittata*)
Morning Glory Family
(Convolvulaceae)

Description: A climbing vine with smooth stems and pink or bright purple *funnel-shaped flowers* solitary or in clusters of 2–3.
Flowers: to 3″ (7.5 cm) long; corolla of 5 fused petals.
Leaves: 1½–4″ (3.8–10 cm) long; *arrowhead-shaped,* with long diverging basal lobes.
Height: vine.
Flowering: All year.
Habitat: Sandy soil, particularly brackish.
Range: North Carolina south to Florida; west to Texas.
Comments: The leaves of this southern vine resemble those of the Arrowheads; both derive their names from the Latin word *sagitta* ("arrow"). The very large, high-climbing Manroot, or Man-of-the-earth (*I. pandurata*), which has white flowers with deep purple throats, is very abundant in the Midwest.

DOGWOOD FAMILY (Cornaceae)

Mostly trees or shrubs, rarely herbs, commonly with tiny flowers surrounded by petal-like bracts, so as to resemble a single large flower.

Flowers: bisexual or unisexual, radially symmetrical; sepals 4 or 5, small; petals 4 or 5; stamens 4 or 5. All these parts attached at top of ovary.

Leaves: alternate or opposite, simple.

Fruit: berry or berry-like drupe.

About 12 genera and 100 species are known, mostly in temperate regions. Many members of this family are grown as ornamentals.

60, 446 Bunchberry
(*Cornus canadensis*)
Dogwood Family (Cornaceae)

Description: Erect stems from a creeping rootstock have at their summits 4 *white, petal-like bracts* above a whorl of leaves.
Flowers: set of bracts (the "flower"), about 1½" (3.8 cm) wide, surround a globose cluster of tiny yellowish-green flowers.
Leaves: 1½–3" (3.8–7.5 cm) long; ovate, pointed, with veins curved into an arc. 1 or 2 pairs of reduced, scale-like leaves present on stem below whorled main leaves.
Fruit: tight cluster of *bright red berry-like drupes.*
Height: 3–8" (7.5–20 cm).

Flowering: May–July.

Habitat: Cool woods, damp openings.

Range: Across southern Canada to Labrador and southern Greenland; south to Maryland; west through West Virginia, Ohio, and Illinois to South Dakota; north to Minnesota.

Comments: This showy wildflower and Northern Dwarf Cornel (*C. suecica*) of the northern forests are the only herbs in the dogwood group, the other members being trees or shrubs. *C. suecica* occurs in Canada, south to the St. Lawrence River and east to Nova Scotia. It has small purple flowers surrounded by 4 bracts.

237 Red Osier
(*Cornus stolonifera*)
Dogwood Family (Cornaceae)

Description: This shrub has flat-topped clusters of small, creamy-white flowers and *deep red, smooth twigs with white pith.*
Flowers: clusters 1–2″ (2.5–5 cm) wide; petals 4.
Leaves: 2–4″ (5–10 cm) long; opposite ovate, pale beneath, with veins curving.
Fruit: cluster of white, berry-like drupes.
Height: 3–10′ (90–300 cm).

Flowering: May–August.

Habitat: Shores and thickets.

Range: Ontario to Newfoundland; south to West Virginia; west to Nebraska and beyond.

Comments: This is the most showy of the red-twigged dogwoods. The genus name comes from the Latin *cornu* ("horn") and alludes to the hardness of the wood. A European species has long been used for making butchers' skewers; hence the common name Dogwood, derived from the Old English word *dagge* ("dagger"). A closely related species, Silky Dogwood (*C. amomum*) has slightly hairy red twigs with tan pith and blue fruits. At least 8 other species occur in our range.

SEDUM FAMILY (Crassulaceae)

Succulent herbs or small shrubs, commonly with star-like flowers in branched clusters.

Flowers: sepals 4 or 5; petals 4 or 5, free or united, with a scale-like gland at the base of each; stamens as many, or twice as many, as petals; pistils 3 to several.

Leaves: simple, alternate or opposite, fleshy.

There are about 35 genera and 1,500 species. Many are cultivated as ornamentals or succulent novelties, including Jade Tree, Stonecrops, and Air Plant. Vegetative reproduction is common in the family, and in some members little plantlets grow along the leaves, drop to the ground, and root.

17 Ditch Stonecrop
(*Penthorum sedoides*)
Sedum Family (Crassulaceae)

Description: Inconspicuous, yellowish-green *flowers are clustered on one side of slender, diverging stalks.*
Flowers: about ⅛" (4 mm) wide; sepals 5, oblong-lanceolate, erect; petals 5, but often absent or falling early.
Leaves: 2–4" (5–10 cm) long; lanceolate to elliptic, sharply toothed.
Fruit: 5-horned capsule.
Height: 8–24" (20–60 cm).

Flowering: July–October.
Habitat: Ditches, streambanks, wet places.
Range: Ontario to New Brunswick; south to Florida; west to Texas; north to Nebraska.
Comments: The genus name is derived from the Greek *pente* ("five") and *horos* ("mark") and refers to the 5-part pattern of the flower. This wildflower resembles members of the genus *Sedum* (Stonecrops) in the Orpine family; hence the species name *sedoides*.

However, the Sedums have succulent leaves which the Ditch Stonecrop lacks.

---

552 Live-Forever
(*Sedum purpureum*)
Sedum Family (Crassulaceae)

Description: Small, pinkish-purple, *star-like flowers* are borne in clusters at the ends of *succulent stalks.*
Flowers: ⅓″ (8 mm) wide; petals 5; sepals short.
Leaves: 1–2½″ (2.5–6.3 cm) long; alternate, smooth, fleshy, elliptic, coarsely toothed.
Height: 8–18″ (20–45 cm).

Flowering: July–September.

Habitat: Disturbed areas, roadsides, open wood

Range: Ontario to Newfoundland; south to Maryland; west to Indiana; north to Wisconsin.

Comments: This coarse plant, a European introduction, frequently escapes from cultivation. It can regenerate from almost any fragment; hence the common name. Children like to separate outer leaf layers to form little "balloon purses." A native pink Sedum, American Orpine (*S. telephioides*), found on cliffs and rocky outcroppings from New York west to Illinois and in mountains south to Georgia, has pale pink flowers and oblong, glaucous leaves. Rock Moss (*S. pulchellum*), four from Virginia southwest to Texas and Kansas, has rose-pink flowers and linea leaves. Roseroot (*S. rosea*) inhabits rock coastal cliffs from Maine to the inland mountains of North Carolina. Its 4-petaled flowers form terminal clusters, with purple pistillate flowers and yellow staminate ones. Leaves are fleshy, overlapping, and spirally arranged.

CUCUMBER FAMILY
(Cucurbitaceae)

Herbs, often trailing or climbing by coiled tendrils.
Flowers: radially symmetrical; sepals 5; petals 5, united; some flowers have 5 stamens and no ovary; others have an ovary with all parts attached at the top, but lack stamens.
Leaves: alternate, usually simple, but sometimes deeply palmately lobed.
Fruit: berry with a leathery rind.
About 100 genera and 850 species occur in warm regions of the world. Melons, cucumbers, squash, and pumpkins are economically important members of the family.

43, 205 Bur Cucumber
(*Echinocystis lobata*)
Cucumber Family (Cucurbitaceae)

Description: A *climbing vine* with an angular stem and small, *greenish-white flowers*. The flower stalks and 3-forked tendrils arise in leaf axils.
Flowers: ½–⅔" (1.3–1.6 cm) wide; *6-petaled female and male flowers* separate but on same vine; the female usually solitary or in small clusters below a long stalk bearing numerous male flowers.
Leaves: about 3" (8 cm) long; *maple-like,* toothed, with 3–7 mostly triangular lobes.
Fruit: *single,* 4-seeded, fleshy berry, to 2" (5 cm) long, *covered with weak spines,* dry when mature.
Height: vine.
Flowering: June–October.
Habitat: Moist woods, stream banks.
Range: Saskatchewan to New Brunswick; south to Florida; west to Texas; but very rare in the Southeast.
Comments: As the common name suggests, the fruit is like a cucumber, but inedible.

A somewhat similar vine, the Star Cucumber (*Sicyos angulatus*), also has maple-like leaves, but 5-petaled flower and 1-seeded fruits in clusters of 10, each about ½″ (1.3 cm) long.

SEDGE FAMILY (Cyperaceae)

Often grass-like herbs of wet sites, with stems commonly 3-sided.
Flowers: bisexual or unisexual, radially symmetrical, nestled in the axil of a bract, aggregated into small compact spikes arranged in raceme-like, dense or openly branched clusters; sepals and petals are bristles or scales, or entirely absent; stamens 3 or 6; floral parts attached at base of ovary.
Leaves: long, narrow, with sheaths at base enclosing stem; in some, the leaf blade is absent.
Fruit: seed-like, lens-shaped or 3-sided.
There are about 90 genera and 4,000 species, found nearly throughout the world. Cottongrass, Bulrush, and Tule are in the family.

396 Shining Cyperus
(*Cyperus rivularis*)
Sedge Family (Cyperaceae)

Description: Spikelets with *reddish-brown scales* enclosing the tiny flowers are in umbels at the top of a slender, triangular stem.
Flowers: spikelets up to ½" (1.3 cm) long, in clusters of 1–5; *scales lustrous;* perianth lacking; stamens 3; style 2-cleft; 2–4 leaf-like bracts present beneath the inflorescence.
Leaves: about ⅛" (3 mm) wide, shorter than the stalk.
Height: 4–16" (10–40 cm).
Flowering: July–October.
Habitat: Wet fields, ditches, marshes, stream banks.
Range: Ontario and Quebec; south to Georgia; west to Texas; north to Minnesota.
Comments: Although the Sedges resemble grasses, they are not good forage plants and are of little economic value, with the exception of those species used in making commercial mattings. Their seeds are eaten by some birds.

103 White-topped Sedge
(*Dichromena colorata*)
Sedge Family (Cyperaceae)

Description: The spikelets are in a globose cluster enclosed at the base by a set of 5 or 6 long, *drooping, white bracts with green tips.* Stem triangular.
Flowers: enclosed in oblong, whitish scales in a spikelet about ¼" (6 mm) long. Spikelets in a cluster to ⅔" (1.6 cm) wide. Perianth lacking; stamens 6; style 2-cleft. Bracts under inflorescence widely spreading, unequal, to 3" (7.5 cm) long.
Leaves: about ¹⁄₁₂" (2 mm) wide; grass-like, shorter than the stalk.
Height: 8–24" (20–60 cm).
Flowering: March–November.
Habitat: Brackish or calcareous swamps and marshes, moist pinelands.
Range: Virginia south to Florida; west to Texas.
Comments: The whitish bracts on this sedge are sufficiently striking to make one think it has showy, daisy-like flowers. The generic name is from the Greek *dis* ("double") and *chroma* ("color") and alludes to the two-colored bracts. The showier *D. latifolia,* with 7 or more longer, wider bracts, is most conspicuous in wet pinelands and savannahs. It occurs on the coastal plain from North Carolina to Florida and west to Mississippi.

233 Tawny Cotton Grass
(*Eriophorum virginicum*)
Sedge Family (Cyperaceae)

Description: The tiny flowers are within *scales nestled in tufts of tawny or copper-colored or whitish, silky hairs.* The scales are in spikelets arranged in a *dense, head-like terminal cluster.* Stem triangular toward the top but round below.
Flowers: spikelets about ¾" (2 cm)

long, including bristles; clusters about
1″ (2.5 cm) wide; enclosed by 2 or 3
spreading or downward-turning, leaf-
like bracts 2–6″ (5–15 cm) long. Sepals
and petals lacking; stamen 1; style
3-cleft.
Leaves: about ⅙″ (4 mm) wide; flat,
grass-like, the upper ones often
overtopping the stem.
Height: 1½–4′ (45–120 cm).

Flowering: June–September.

Habitat: Bogs, wet meadows.

Range: Ontario to Nova Scotia; south through
New England to Georgia; west to
Tennessee and Nebraska; north to
Wisconsin and Minnesota.

Comments: There are numerous species of these
mostly northern Cotton Grasses
(actually Sedges), most with white
bristles instead of tan. They are
especially showy in open northern bogs.
The generic name is from the Greek
erion ("cotton" or "wool") and *phoros*
("bearing") and refers to the cottony
nature of the fruiting head, as does the
common name.

30 Wool Grass
(*Scirpus cyperinus*)
Sedge Family (Cyperaceae)

Description: A compound umbel, made up of many
spikelets on branching rays, is at the
top of a triangular or nearly round stem
and is surrounded by *spreading green,
leaf-like bracts; spikelets woolly* in fruit.
Flowers: spikelets about ¼″ (6 mm)
long, ovoid to cylindric, their
reddish to brownish scales ovate to
lanceolate, with 6 protruding bristles
representing the sepals and petals;
stamens 3; style 3-cleft. Bracts under
inflorescence unequal, drooping at
the tips.
Leaves: up to 2′ (60 cm) long and ½″
(1.3 cm) wide; rough-margined.
Height: 3–5′ (90–150 cm).

Flowering: August–October.
  Habitat: Swamps, wet meadows.
    Range: Newfoundland and Nova Scotia; south from New England to Florida; west to Texas; north to Minnesota.
Comments: This is one of several species of important wetland plants, many of them emergents, that provide food and cover for waterfowl and other wildlife. Nearly 30 species occur in the East.

407 Leafy Three-square; Salt-marsh Bulrush

(*Scirpus robustus*)
Sedge Family (Cyperaceae)

Description: The reddish-tan ovoid spikelets, made up of overlapping scales containing the inconspicuous florets, are clustered closely against the *sharply triangular stem.*
  Flowers: spikelets about 1½" (3.8 cm) long, ovoid to cylindric, stalkless or stalked; scales hairy, ovate, with a stiff terminal bristle; stamens 3; style 3-cleft.
  Leaves: 2–24" (5–60 cm) long and about ½" (1.3 cm) wide; dark green, smooth, 3-ranked, arising along each of the stem surfaces.
  Height: 1–5' (30–150 cm).
Flowering: July–October.
  Habitat: Brackish coastal marshes.
    Range: Massachusetts south to Florida; west to Texas and beyond.
Comments: The Three-squares are an important group of sedges for wildlife. Their seeds are among the most common food of ducks and marsh birds. Their stems and rootstocks are eaten by muskrats and geese, and they provide cover for many birds and animals. A larger marsh species (*S. olneyi*) reaches a height of 10' (3 m), and all of its small spikelets are gathered along one side of the stalk near the top.

CYRILLA FAMILY (Cyrillaceae)

Shrubs or small trees with small flowers in racemes.
Flowers: radially symmetrical; sepals 5; petals 5; stamens 5 or 10. All these parts attached at base of ovary.
Leaves: simple, alternate.
Fruit: capsule or berry-like drupe.
There are 3 genera and about 12 species, native of North and South America and the West Indies.

222 Titi; Leatherwood
(*Cyrilla racemiflora*)
Cyrilla Family (Cyrillaceae)

Description: A shrub or small tree with terminal, *finger-like clusters* of numerous small white flowers.
Flowers: about ⅕" (5 mm) wide; clusters 2½–6" (6.3–15 cm) long; petals 5, pointed; sepals 5, white.
Leaves: 2–5" (5–12.5 cm) long; shiny, elliptic, leathery.
Fruit: brownish-yellow, berry-like drupe.
Height: to 25' (7.5 m).

Flowering: June–July.

Habitat: Swamps, low pinelands, along watercourses.

Range: Coastal Plain, Virginia to Florida; west to Texas.

Comments: This shrub is particularly beautiful in the fall when its foliage turns scarlet or orange. Buckwheat Tree, or Black Titi (*Cliftonia monophylla*), which occurs in southern wetlands, has wider flower clusters and small 4-winged fruits.

DIAPENSIA FAMILY
(Diapensiaceae)

Evergreen herbs or small, tufted shrubs with solitary or clustered pink or white flowers.
Flowers: radially symmetrical; calyx and corolla each 5-lobed; stamens 5, sometimes united into a tube. All these parts attached at base of ovary.
Leaves: simple, alternate or opposite.
Fruit: capsule.
There are 6 genera and about 10 species, native of the Northern Hemisphere and often grown in alpine and rock gardens.

45 Diapensia
(*Diapensia lapponica*)
Diapensia Family (Diapensiaceae)

Description: A *low-growing plant*, occurring in dense tufts, with white, bell-shaped flowers borne singly on short stalks.
Flowers: about ½" (1.3 cm) wide; corolla with 5 spreading, roundish lobes; stamens 5, yellow, attached to corolla between the petals.
Leaves: up to ¾" (2 cm) long; leathery, evergreen, in tight basal rosettes.
Height: 1–3" (2.5–7.5 cm).
Flowering: June–July.
Habitat: Bare ledges and gravel patches, mountain summits.
Range: Newfoundland and alpine region of Quebec; south to northern New England and New York.
Comments: This plant is strikingly showy when in flower. The low, mat-forming habit is typical of plants in harsh arctic and alpine environments. Diapensia is especially common above the timberline on Mount Washington, New Hampshire. The species name refers to Lapland, where the plant also occurs.

130 Beetleweed; Galax
(*Galax rotundifolia*)
Diapensia Family (Diapensiaceae)

Description: Small milk-white flowers are in a spike-like cluster on a long *leafless floral stalk*.
Flowers: about ⅙″ (4 mm) wide; petals 5, united at base.
Leaves: 2–5″ (5–12.5 cm) wide, in basal tufts, *shiny, dark evergreen, heart-shaped*, with rounded teeth.
Height: 1–2½′ (30–75 cm).

Flowering: May–July.

Habitat: Open woods.

Range: Virginia and West Virginia south to Georgia and Alabama.

Comments: The long flower stalk rising from the roundish, evergreen leaves identifies this attractive southern wildflower. Along with its smaller relative, Oconee Bells (*Shortia galacifolia*), it is found only in the Southern Appalachians. Planted in naturalized gardens as far north as Massachusetts, it may escape from cultivation. The species name has recently been changed from *G. aphylla*. The generic name is from the Greek word *gala* ("milk") and refers to the flower color.

46 Pyxie
(*Pyxidanthera barbulata*)
Diapensia Family (Diapensiaceae)

Description: A small, *trailing plant* with unstalked, numerous white or pinkish upright flowers at the ends of short, leafy branches.
Flowers: ¼″ (6 mm) wide; 5 *wedge-shaped, spreading petals* and 5 conspicuous stamens arising between the petals.
Leaves: up to ⅓″ (8 mm) long; linear, sharp-pointed, crowded together toward the ends of branches.
Height: creeper.

Flowering: March–May.

Habitat: Sandy pine barrens.

Range: New Jersey and southeastern Virginia to South Carolina.

Comments: This moss-like plant, especially showy when in flower, is typical of dry, sandy areas such as the pine barrens of New Jersey. The generic name, from the Greek *pyxis* ("small box") and the Latin *anthera* ("anther"), refers to the fact that the anthers open by means of a lid-like structure. *P. brevifolia* has showy pink flowers and whitish, woolly leaves, and grows on the Carolina sand hills.

52 Oconee Bells
(*Shortia galacifolia*)
Diapensia Family (Diapensiaceae)

Description: White, bell-shaped, *solitary flowers* hang from erect, leafless stalks.
Flowers: about 1″ (2.5 cm) wide; 5 *irregularly toothed lobes*.
Leaves: to 3″ (7.5 cm) long; basal, evergreen, rounded, shiny, with scalloped margins.
Height: 2–8″ (5–20 cm).

Flowering: March–April.

Habitat: Moist woods, alongside streams.

Range: Appalachian Mountains of the Carolinas and Georgia.

Comments: Found only in a few areas in the mountains of Georgia and North and South Carolina, this species is of considerable interest to botanists. Extremely rare, it was not found again for almost a century after its discovery. Although it shows no signs of spreading, it grows well in gardens. The species name suggests its resemblance to Galax (*G. rotundifolia*), but its scalloped leaves are smaller, and the flowers are solitary, not in long spikes. The genus name honors a 19th-century Kentucky botanist, Dr. Charles Wilkins Short.

VENUS FLYTRAP FAMILY
(Dionaeaceae)

There is only one species in this family, which is described below.

---

176 Venus Flytrap
(*Dionaea muscipula*)
Venus Flytrap Family (Dionaeaceae)

Description: An insectivorous plant with a cluster of white flowers at the top of a leafless stalk that rises above a rosette of *bristly, folded, basal leaves.*
Flowers: about 1″ (2.5 cm) wide; sepals and petals 5; stamens usually 15. All these parts attached at base of ovary.
Leaves: 1½–6″ (3.8–15 cm) long; blades folded lengthwise into 2 hinged lobes, green on the outside and often orange on the inside, fringed with long, stout bristles up to ⅓″ (8 mm) long; leafstalks long, winged.
Height: 4–12″ (10–30 cm).
Flowering: May–June.
Habitat: Moist sandy areas, pinelands.
Range: Coastal plain of North Carolina and northeast South Carolina.
Comments: When insects or spiders disturb any 2 of the 6 tactile hairs on the upper surface of the folded leaves of this fascinating plant, the hinged halves snap shut, trapping the prey. A chemical secreted by the prey stimulates the plant's secretion of digestive enzymes (this does not take place if the plant is stimulated by an inert object such as a pencil tip). Following digestion of the prey, the nutrients are absorbed and the leaf is reset. This plant is classified as an endangered species in both North and South Carolina and is protected by state law in the former. This is the only species in this family. All the known locales are within a 50-mile radius of Wilmington, North Carolina.

TEASEL FAMILY (Dipsacaceae)

Herbs with flowers clustered in dense heads.
Flowers: bilaterally symmetrical, each associated with 2 united bracts forming a calyx-like structure; sepals 5; petals 5 united; stamens 4. All these parts attached at top of ovary.
Leaves: simple or deeply divided, opposite.
Fruit: seed-like.
There are about 10 genera and 270 species, native of the Old World. Bluebuttons and Pincushion Flower are grown as ornamentals, and the weedy Teasel is used in dried flower arrangements.

---

490 **Teasel**
(*Dipsacus sylvestris*)
Teasel Family (Dipsacaceae)

Description: Small lavender flowers are clustered in an *egg-shaped, thistle-like spike* on a *prickly stem.*
Flowers: less than ½" (1.3 cm) long, tubular; calyx 5-lobed; corolla 4-lobed; cluster 1½–4" (3.8–10 cm) long and 1–2" (2.5–5 cm) wide. Spiny bracts project between flowers and longer, horizontal or upward-curving spiny bracts surround base of flowering spike.
Leaves: 4–16" (10–40 cm) long; lanceolate, toothed, opposite, the upper ones fused at their bases around the stem.
Height: 2–6' (60–180 cm).
Flowering: July–October.
Habitat: Old fields and roadsides, in basic or neutral soils.
Range: Ontario to Quebec; New England south to North Carolina; west to Mississippi; north to Missouri and Michigan.
Comments: Originally brought from Europe, this biennial was cultivated by wool manufacturers. The dried flower heads

were placed on spindles and used to raise the nap, or tease the cloth; hence the common name. Another species (*D. laciniatus*), which has coarsely toothed leaves that surround the stem and form a cup, is responsible for the genus name, derived from the Greek *dipsa*, meaning "thirst." The progression of flowers opening on the spike in all species of *Dipsacus* is unique. They start in a belt around the center of the spike, and new ones open daily in both directions, in time forming 2 bands of flowers.

SUNDEW FAMILY (Droseraceae)

Insectivorous herbs, mostly of acidic
bogs, with flowers in a raceme or
openly branched clusters.
Flowers: radially symmetrical; sepals 5,
united; petals 5, separate; stamens 5.
All these parts attached at base of
ovary.
Leaves: covered with sticky glandular
hairs in which insects become trapped.
Fruit: capsule with 2–5 chambers.
There are 4 genera and about 100
species, which generally grow in very
poor soil, so that extra nutrients
obtained from digested insects may be
devoted mostly to seed production.

475 Thread-leaved Sundew
(*Drosera filiformis*)
Sundew Family (Droseraceae)

Description: Insectivorous plant with lavender-rose
flowers in a one-sided, elongated cluster
on a leafless floral stalk, curved at the
tip, which rises in the midst of *erect,
thread-like, sticky basal leaves.*
Flowers: about ½″ (1.3 cm) wide;
petals 5.
Leaves: to 12″ (30 cm) long; *covered with
stalked glands.*
Height: 4–12″ (10–30 cm).
Flowering: June–September.
Habitat: Wet sandy areas near coast.
Range: Massachusetts to southern New Jersey
and from South Carolina to northern
Florida; west to Louisiana.
Comments: This striking member of the Sundew
family is distinctive, with its stringy
leaves covered with glistening droplets
of sticky exudate. Insects trapped in the
sticky hairs are digested by plant
enzymes. Researchers have fed these
plants fruit flies labeled with the
radioactive isotope nitrogen-15 and
have found that substantial quantities
of protein from the insects end up in

the storage roots, demonstrating the importance of this source of nutrients. The southern plants are larger than the northern and are considered by some to be a separate species (*D. tracyi*). The genus name derives from the Greek *droseros* ("dewy") and refers to the sticky droplets on the leaves.

63 Round-leaved Sundew
(*Drosera rotundifolia*)
Sundew Family (Droseraceae)

Description: Insectivorous, with white flowers in an elongated, one-sided cluster on a leafless stalk rising above a rosette of *small, reddish, sticky basal leaves.*
Flowers: about ¼" (6 mm) wide; petals 5, often pink-tinged.
Leaves: blades about ½" (1.3 cm) long; *circular,* covered with glandular hairs that exude a sticky substance; leafstalks about 1½" (3.8 cm) long.
Height: 4–9" (10–22.5 cm).
Flowering: June–August.
Habitat: Bogs.
Range: Throughout.
Comments: Sundews are able to survive on nutrient-poor soils where other plants are at a disadvantage. A similar species, the Spatulate-leaved Sundew (*D. leucantha*), has oval or spoon-shaped leaves. The very similar northern *D. anglica* has much narrower leaves and only grows as far south as northern Maine, Michigan, and Wisconsin. The Dwarf Sundew (*D. brevifolia*), which has wedge-shaped leaves with shorter stalks in a more compact rosette, is a more southerly species, occurring in damp areas from southern North Carolina to Florida, and west to Tennessee, Arkansas, and Texas.

HEATH FAMILY (Ericaceae)

Usually shrubs or woody perennial herbs, often with showy flowers blooming singly or in clusters; sometimes trees.
Flowers: radially or bilaterally symmetrical; sepals 4 or 5, united; petals 4 or 5, united, often taking the shape of a miniature Chinese lantern; stamens twice as many as petals, each anther usually opening by a terminal pore. All these parts attached either at base or at top of ovary.
Leaves: simple, usually alternate, often leathery.
Fruit: capsule, berry, or drupe.
There are at least 50 genera and up to 2,500 species, mostly on acid soils in temperate regions. Numerous handsome ornamentals, including the spectacular Rhododendrons and Azaleas, come from this family, as do several edible fruits such as Blueberry, Huckleberry, and Cranberry.

230, 444 **Bearberry**
(*Arctostaphylos uva-ursi*)
Heath Family (Ericaceae)

Description: Low, trailing *evergreen shrub* with terminal clusters of white or pale pink, *bell-shaped flowers.*
Flowers: about ⅕" (5 mm) long; petals 5, fused.
Leaves: ½–1½" (1.3–3.8 cm) long; *wedge- or spatulate-shaped, smooth, leathery,* green on both sides.
Fruit: red, berry-like.
Height: creeper, with flowering branches 6–12" (15–30 cm) high.
Flowering: May–July.
Habitat: Exposed rocky and sandy sites.
Range: Arctic regions south to Virginia; west to Indiana and northern Illinois.
Comments: This ground-trailing shrub has the papery, reddish, exfoliating bark

typical of woody plants in northern climes. It is frequently seen as a ground cover in sandy areas of the Northeast, especially the New Jersey pine barrens. It is very common on Cape Cod, where it covers vast areas in open, sandy, pine-studded communities. It is a hardy shrub for landscaping rocky or sandy sites. An astringent tea can be made by steeping the dried leaves in boiling water (sometimes used as a laxative). The fruit is edible but mealy and tasteless; it is much favored by birds and other wildlife. The genus name, from the Greek *arctos* ("bear") and *staphyle* ("bunch of grapes"), and the species name, meaning "bear's grape" in Latin, both refer to the fruit. One other species, Alpine Bearberry (*A. alpina*), is found on New England mountaintops.

231 Leatherleaf
(*Chamaedaphne calyculata*)
Heath Family (Ericaceae)

Description: An evergreen shrub with white *bell- or urn-shaped flowers, hanging along one-sided racemes.*
Flowers: ¼" (6 mm) long.
Leaves: ¾–2" (2–5 cm) long, *leathery,* elliptical, dull green, and dotted with round, *scurfy scales,* heaviest on the underside. Older leaves are often brownish-bronze, yellowish beneath.
Fruit: globular capsule.
Height: 1–4' (30–120 cm).

Flowering: March–July.

Habitat: Sphagnum bogs, pond margins.

Range: Across southern Canada to Newfoundland and Nova Scotia; south through New England to Georgia; northwesterly to Iowa and Wisconsin.

Comments: One of many evergreen members of the Heath family, this low, erect, many-branched, circumpolar plant is typical of boggy wetlands and highly acidic sites. It can begin the development of a bog by forming floating mats around the edges of a lake. In Massachusetts the rate of its advance has been recorded at over 1 foot per decade. The genus name is from the Greek *chamai* ("on the ground") and *daphne* ("laurel").

---

568 Trailing Arbutus
(*Epigaea repens*)
Heath Family (Ericaceae)

Description: A trailing, evergreen plant with *sweet-scented pink or white flowers* in terminal and axillary clusters on hairy stems.
Flowers: about ½" (1.3 cm) wide; corolla tubular, hairy within, flaring into 5 lobes, each as long as the corolla tube.
Leaves: ¾–3" (2–7.5 cm) long; *leathery*, oval, with hairy margins.
Fruit: capsule splitting open into 5 parts, exposing whitish pulp covered with tiny seeds.
Height: creeper.
Flowering: February–May.
Habitat: Sandy or rocky woods, especially on acid soil.
Range: Quebec and Nova Scotia; south from New England and New York to Florida; west to Mississippi and Ohio.
Comments: For this favorite wildflower with an exquisite fragrance, one must search among the fallen leaves in early spring. It favors exposed sites where the plants are not smothered by leaf litter. It appears to be sensitive to abrupt environmental disturbances, such as lumbering and grazing, which may account for its present scarcity. It is difficult to cultivate.

229 Teaberry; Wintergreen
(*Gaultheria procumbens*)
Heath Family (Ericaceae)

Description: The creeping stem of this low, evergreen shrub has upright branches with *white, bell-shaped, nodding flowers,* solitary or in groups of 2 or 3 in the leaf axils.
Flowers: about ⅓″ (8 mm) long; corolla lobes 5.
Leaves: 1–2″ (2.5–5 cm) long; oval, slightly toothed, with a *wintergreen flavor.*
Fruit: edible, bright red, pulpy, berry-like capsules with a spicy taste.
Height: creeper, with branches 2–6″ (5–15 cm) high.
Flowering: April–May.
Habitat: Oak woods or under evergreens, especially on sandy sites.
Range: Eastern Canada south to Georgia; west to Alabama; north to Michigan, Wisconsin, and Minnesota.
Comments: This leathery, semi-woody, aromatic perennial has creeping underground stems, thus forming small colonies of plants. Showy red fruits may persist through the winter. The genus was named for Dr. Gaultier, a Canadian physician of the mid-18th century. Teaberry extract is used to flavor teas, candies, medicines, and chewing gum.

585 Sheep Laurel
(*Kalmia angustifolia*)
Heath Family (Ericaceae)

Description: An evergreen shrub with small, *deep pink, saucer-shaped flowers in dense clusters around the stem,* mostly below the leaves.
Flowers: ⅓–½″ (8–13 mm) wide; petals 5. The 10 stamens (whose anthers are tucked into pockets of the corolla) pop out when touched.
Leaves: 1½–2″ (3.8–5 cm) long; *in*

whorls of 3, oblong, dark green above,
pale beneath when mature.
Fruit: globular capsule, persisting
through winter.
Height: 1–3′ (30–90 cm).

Flowering: May–August.

Habitat: Dry or wet sandy or sterile soil, old
fields, bogs.

Range: Manitoba to Newfoundland and Nova
Scotia; south to Virginia and the
mountains of Georgia; northwest to
Michigan.

Comments: Sometimes called Lambkill, this small
shrub is poisonous to livestock. Because
of its clonal habit it can form sizable
stands. The flowers are miniatures of
the larger Mountain Laurel
(*K. latifolia*). Pale or Bog Laurel
(*K. polifolia*) has pink flowers in
terminal clusters, two-edged twigs, and
opposite leaves with rolled margins,
very white beneath. It is a northern bog
plant and occurs only as far south as
northern New Jersey and Pennsylvania.
Two other species are found in the
South. The genus is named for Peter
Kalm, a student of Linnaeus, who
traveled and collected plants in America
in the 18th century.

212, 586 Mountain Laurel
(*Kalmia latifolia*)
Heath Family (Ericaceae)

Description: A large evergreen shrub with showy
clusters of *deep pink buds and pinkish-
white flowers on sticky stalks.*
Flowers: ¾–1″ (2–2.5 cm) wide;
corolla with 5 united lobes, each having
2 pockets with 1 stamen tucked into
each.
Leaves: 2–4″ (5–10 cm) long; mostly
alternate, ovate-lanceolate or elliptic,
pointed at each end, shiny green with
yellow-green petiole, leathery.
Fruit: dry, brown capsule.
Height: 3–15′ (90–450 cm).

Flowering: Late May—mid-July.

Habitat: Open hardwood forests.

Range: New England and New York south to Florida; west to Louisiana; north to Indiana.

Comments: As the flowers mature, the stamens may pop out of the petal pouches or they may be dislodged as an insect enters the flower, spraying the pollen onto its back. Mountain laurel is frequently used in ornamental plantings. Somewhat shade-tolerant, it can be planted in open woods, where it lends an evergreen touch in winter and showy flowers in early summer. It is relatively tolerant of fire; when stem-killed to the ground, it grows back vigorously. It is long-lived, and over 100 tree rings have been reported on large plants.

209 Labrador Tea
(*Ledum groenlandicum*)
Heath Family (Ericaceae)

Description: A low, *evergreen* shrub with *densely hairy twigs* and rounded terminal clusters of white flowers.
Flowers: ⅓–½" (8–13 mm) wide; petals 5, spreading.
Leaves: 1–2" (2.5–5 cm) long; evergreen, narrow, oblong, *rusty-woolly beneath,* with rolled margins, slightly fragrant when crushed.
Fruit: 5-valved capsule on a recurved stalk.
Height: 1–4' (30–120 cm).

Flowering: June—August.

Habitat: Peaty soils, especially bogs.

Range: Across Canada to Newfoundland; south to New England and northern New Jersey; west to Ohio; north to Michigan, Wisconsin, and Minnesota.

Comments: This boreal shrub, typical of acidic boggy areas, can easily be recognized by the woolly brown undersurfaces of its leaves. A pleasant tea can be made from them, and they were used for this purpose during the American Revolution. In northern Canada the plant is known as Hudson's Bay Tea.

456   Sand Myrtle
(*Leiophyllum buxifolium*)
Heath Family (Ericaceae)

Description: A low, upright, widely branching evergreen shrub with crowded, leathery leaves and small pink or pinkish-white flowers in dense, bracted clusters.
Flowers: about ¼" (6 mm) wide; sepals and petals 5; stamens 10.
Leaves: ⅓–1" (8–25 mm) long; opposite or alternate, oval to oblong, *smooth, shining.*
Height: 4–20" (10–50 cm).
Flowering: April–June.
Habitat: Rocky or sandy woods and bluffs.
Range: New Jersey, North and South Carolina, eastern Kentucky.
Comments: The genus name is from the Greek *leios* ("smooth") and *phyllon* ("leaf"). The species name also refers to the leaves, similar to those of Box (*Buxus*).

454   Alpine Azalea
(*Loiseleuria procumbens*)
Heath Family (Ericaceae)

Description: A creeping, much-branched, mat-forming, dwarf shrub with terminal clusters of 2–5 pink, bell-shaped flowers and *evergreen leaves with rolled margins.*
Flowers: about ¼" (6 mm) long and ⅕" (5 mm) wide; petals 5, spreading.
Leaves: about ⅓" (8 mm) long; leathery, elliptic, mostly opposite, on short stalks.
Height: creeper.
Flowering: June–August.
Habitat: Peaty or rocky exposed areas and mountain summits.

Range: Across Canada to Greenland; south to Maine and New Hampshire.

Comments: In the Northeast this showy, prostrate shrub is especially common above the treeline on Mt. Washington, New Hampshire. It is frequently associated with Lapland Rosebay (*Rhododendron lapponicum*) or Diapensia (*Diapensia lapponica*).

228 Maleberry
(*Lyonia ligustrina*)
Heath Family (Ericaceae)

Description: A much-branched, deciduous shrub with terminal clusters of globular white or pale rose flowers, constricted at the tip.
Flowers: about ⅛″ (3 mm) wide.
Leaves: 1–3″ (2.5–7.5 cm) long; alternate, oblong-oval, finely toothed.
Fruit: brown, rounded, 5-angled capsule, persisting through winter.
Height: 3–12′ (90–360 cm).

Flowering: May–July.

Habitat: Wet thickets, swamps.

Range: New England south to Florida; west to Texas; north to Kentucky and Oklahoma.

Comments: These blueberry-like shrubs are frequently associated with shrubby or wooded swamps. At least 3 more species occur in our range: Staggerbush (*L. mariana*) has urn- or bell-shaped capsules; a southern evergreen species, Fetterbush (*L. lucida*), occurs from Virginia to Florida and Louisiana and has white to pale pink flowers, 3-angled branches, and dark green lustrous leaves with a conspicuous vein next to the rolled margin; another species (*L. ferruginea*) is evergreen, with white flowers and dull green leaves. The genus name honors the early American botanist and explorer John Lyon, who died in 1818.

380 Flame Azalea
(*Rhododendron calendulaceum*)
Heath Family (Ericaceae)

Description: A deciduous shrub with terminal
clusters of tubular, vase-shaped, *orange,
red, or yellow flowers.*
Flowers: 1½–2″ (3.8–5 cm) wide, with
5 corolla lobes exceeded by 5 long
stamens and style; *corolla tube glandular
and sticky;* flowers not fragrant.
Leaves: 2–4″ (5–10 cm) long, ovate.
Fruit: hairy capsule.
Height: to 15′ (4.5 m).

Flowering: May–June.

Habitat: Dry open woods and mountain balds.

Range: Southwest Pennsylvania south through
mountains to Georgia and Alabama;
west to West Virginia and southeastern
Ohio.

Comments: This beautiful southern Azalea forms
striking displays on some of the grassy
balds of the southern Appalachians.
A wide variation of color forms occurs,
from all shades of yellow to orange-
yellow and scarlet. The flowers appear
before or with the new leaves. This
species is extensively planted as an
ornamental. Like most members of the
heath family, it does best in acid soil.

589 Rhodora
(*Rhododendron canadense*)
Heath Family (Ericaceae)

Description: A deciduous shrub with *few-flowered
terminal clusters* of lavender flowers.
Flowers: ½–¾″ (1.3–2 cm) long; short
corolla tube, 3-lobed upper lip, lower
lip divided into 2 narrow segments;
stamens 10.
Leaves: ¾–1½″ (2–3.8 cm) long;
oblong, with hairy and rolled margins,
gray-green beneath.
Height: 1–3′ (30–90 cm).

Flowering: March–July.

Habitat: Bogs, wet slopes, rocky summits.

Range: Eastern Quebec to Newfoundland and Nova Scotia; south through New England to northern New York, northern New Jersey, and northeastern Pennsylvania.

Comments: This small northern shrub has very showy flowers that open before or with its leaves.

---

587 Mountain Rosebay; Catawba Rhododendron
(*Rhododendron catawbiense*)
Heath Family (Ericaceae)

Description: An evergreen shrub with clusters of large, rose or purple-lilac, *funnel-shaped flowers*.
Flowers: 2–2½″ (5–6.3 cm) wide; corolla lobes 5.
Leaves: 2–6″ (5–15 cm) long; thick, leathery, oblong, dark green above but lighter beneath, with smooth margins and *blunt base and tip*.
Fruit: hairy, rusty capsule.
Height: 3–20′ (90–600 cm).

Flowering: May–June.

Habitat: Rocky summits and slopes, woods, stream banks.

Range: Virginia south to Georgia; west to Alabama; north to Kentucky and West Virginia.

Comments: This attractive flowering shrub with southern affinities forms dense thickets on mountain slopes. Frequently used as an ornamental, it has been hybridized with the less hardy Himalayan species, and from these crosses have been produced some of our most spectacular showy rhododendrons.

590 **Lapland Rosebay**
(*Rhododendron lapponicum*)
Heath Family (Ericaceae)

Description: A *low, aromatic, mat-forming evergreen*
with scaly twigs and few-flowered
clusters of bell-shaped, pink to lavender
flowers.
Flowers: ⅔″ (1.6 cm) wide; corolla
deeply 5-lobed.
Leaves: about ⅔″ (1.6 cm) long;
leathery, elliptic to oblong, yellow-
green, scaly beneath.
Fruit: dry, erect capsule.
Height: 4–12″ (10–30 cm).

Flowering: May–June.

Habitat: Mountain summits, sandstone cliffs.

Range: Arctic and subarctic areas of North
America: Quebec to Newfoundland;
south to Maine, New Hampshire, and
New York; also Wisconsin.

Comments: This mat-forming little shrub is one of
the first showy alpine species to flower.
It is found on the peaks of higher New
England mountains such as Mt.
Washington, New Hampshire, and the
Adirondack peaks of New York. It is
also found in alpine dells of Wisconsin.

210 **Great Laurel**
(*Rhododendron maximum*)
Heath Family (Ericaceae)

Description: A large evergreen shrub with clusters of
pinkish-white, cup-shaped flowers on
glandular and sticky stalks.
Flowers: 1½–2″ (3.8–5 cm) wide, with
5 blunt corolla lobes.
Leaves: 4–8″ (10–20 cm) long;
leathery, smooth, elliptic-oblong,
pointed at base and tip, dark green above,
often paler and closely hairy below.
Fruit: smooth brown capsule.
Height: 5–35′ (1.5–10.5 m).

Flowering: June–July.

Habitat: Damp woods and forested wetlands.

Range: Maine south to Georgia and Alabama;

north to Ohio and southern Pennsylvania; most common from Pennsylvania southward.

Comments: This tall, straggly shrub often forms impenetrable thickets on moist slopes or in swamps. It is frequently used as an ornamental for its showy flowers and handsome foliage. The leaves droop in frost and may curl under lengthwise; the colder the temperature, the tighter the roll. The hard wood may be used for making tools and ornaments. *R. minus* has thinner leaves, 2–5″ (5–12.5 cm) long and heavily dotted with brown beneath, and occurs in the mountains of the Southeast.

588 Pinxter Flower; Pink Azalea
(*Rhododendron nudiflorum*)
Heath Family (Ericaceae)

Description: A deciduous shrub, with terminal clusters of *pink, tubular, vase-shaped, slightly fragrant flowers.*
Flowers: 1½–2″ (3.8–5 cm) wide; 5 corolla lobes exceeded by 5 long, curved stamens and 1 style.
Leaves: 2–4″ (5–10 cm) long; thin, oblong, pointed at both ends, *clustered in pseudo-whorls* near ends of twigs; *hairy only on midrib beneath.*
Fruit: slender, erect, hairy capsule.
Height: 2–6′ (60–180 cm).

Flowering: May–June.

Habitat: Upland woods and thickets; borders of swamps and bogs.

Range: Massachusetts south to South Carolina; west to Tennessee and southern Ohio.

Comments: This much-branched shrub is especially showy in flower. It is relatively tolerant of dry sites and can be transplanted into wild shrub gardens. The species name, Latin for "naked-flowered," refers to the fact that the flowers often appear before its leaves are fully expanded. Mountain Azalea (*R. canescens*) and Woolly Azalea (*R. roseum*) are also found in our range.

208   Swamp Honeysuckle
(*Rhododendron viscosum*)
Heath Family (Ericaceae)

Description: A deciduous shrub with *hairy twigs* and
clusters of fragrant, white, vase-shaped
flowers.
Flowers: 1½–2″ (3.8–5 cm) long;
corolla 5-lobed, with *reddish, sticky
hairs;* stamens 5, long, curved,
projecting beyond corolla; style 1,
longer than stamens.
Leaves: 1–2½″ (2.5–6.3 cm) long;
obovate, *glossy above, often whitish
beneath,* with hairs on midrib.
Height: 3–9′ (90–270 cm).

Flowering: June–August.

Habitat: Swamps.

Range: Maine south to Georgia; west to Texas.

Comments: This typical wetland shrub is
sometimes called the Clammy Azalea
because of its very sticky corolla. The
species name means "sticky" in Latin.
The flowers appear after the leaves.
Another white wetland species of more
southern distribution, the Smooth
Azalea (*R. arborescens*), has smooth
twigs, leaves without hairs, and red
stamens. Dwarf Azalea (*R. atlanticum*),
with white or pink fragrant flowers on a
shrub 3–4′ (90–120 cm) tall, is
common in deep sand along the coastal
plain from southern New Jersey to
South Carolina.

232, 657   Highbush Blueberry
(*Vaccinium corymbosum*)
Heath Family (Ericaceae)

Description: A multi-stemmed shrub with *green, or
often red, twigs* and terminal clusters of
small, urn-shaped white flowers.
Flowers: ¼–½″ (6–13 mm) long;
corolla 5-toothed.
Leaves: 1½–3″ (3.8–7.5 cm) long;
elliptic, entire, smooth above but
usually somewhat hairy beneath.

Fruit: *blue berry* with whitish bloom.
Height: 5–15′ (1.5–4.5 m).

Flowering: Flowers, May–June; fruit, June–
August.

Habitat: Swamps or dry upland woods.

Range: Quebec to Nova Scotia; south to
Georgia; west to Alabama; north to
Wisconsin.

Comments: Our cultivated blueberries have been
derived from this tall-growing shrub. It
is often found in wet areas, but closely
related growths occur in dry sites.
These plants are very important to
wildlife: their berries are relished by
songbirds, game birds, bear, and small
mammals; the twigs and foliage are
eaten by deer and rabbits. Because of
their food value and spectacular red fall
foliage, these shrubs are excellent for
naturalized landscaping.

78, 452 Cranberry
(*Vaccinium macrocarpon*)
Heath Family (Ericaceae)

Description: The ascending branches of this
evergreen, trailing shrub have nodding,
pinkish-white flowers with *4 backward-
pointing petals* in clusters arising in the
leaf axils.
Flowers: about ½″ (1.3 cm) long;
stamens 8–10, with *anthers united into a
long, pointed cone projecting upward.*
Leaves: ⅛–⅔″ (5–16 mm) long;
alternate, oval, blunt, shiny above but
slightly whitish beneath.
Fruit: *dark red, globose berry.*
Height: creeper, with branches to 8″
(20 cm) high.

Flowering: June–August.

Habitat: Open bogs, swamps, and lake shores.

Range: Newfoundland to Nova Scotia; south to
North Carolina; west to Illinois; north
to Minnesota.

Comments: Cultivated varieties of cranberry
developed from this native species are
grown extensively on Cape Cod and in

the pine barrens of New Jersey. The Small Cranberry (*V. oxycoccus*), a native of North America and Eurasia that occurs in the same range, has smaller leaves that are whiter beneath and have rolled edges. Wild cranberries often form low, dense masses over sphagnum dominated, boggy areas, where they can be picked in the fall. They were originally known as Craneberries because of the resemblance of their petals and anther "beak" to the head of those wading birds. Two more related species occur in the East.

567 Mountain Cranberry
(*Vaccinium vitis-idaea*)
Heath Family (Ericaceae)

Description: A *low evergreen shrub* with creeping stems and upright branches having small, terminal clusters of *pink, nodding, bell-shaped flowers.*
Flowers: about ¼" (6 mm) long; corolla 4-lobed; stamens 8.
Leaves: about ⅔" (1.6 cm) long, elliptic to oblong, leathery, rounded at both ends, *with black dots beneath.*
Fruit: dark red berries almost ½" (1.3 cm) across.
Height: creeper, with branches 3–8" (7.5–20 cm) high.
Flowering: June–July.
Habitat: Rocky places and bogs.
Range: Northern Canada south to Maine (and the higher mountains of New England); west to Minnesota.
Comments: The acid fruits are somewhat bitter but can be used as a substitute for regular cranberries when cooked. They often overwinter on the plant and become sweeter by the time the snow melts.

PIPEWORT FAMILY
(Eriocaulaceae)

Bog or aquatic herbs with a crowded head of tiny flowers on a long, leafless stalk.

Flowers: usually radially symmetrical; unisexual; nestled in a bract; sepals 2–3 and petals 2 or 3, much alike; stamens as many as or fewer than petals. All these parts attached at base of ovary; entire flower head has conspicuous bracts at base.

Leaves: basal, tufted, grass-like.

Fruit: capsule.

The family includes more than 9 genera and 360 species, widely distributed in warm tropical zones and extending into temperate regions.

108 Common Pipewort; Hatpins
(*Eriocaulon septangulare*)
Pipewort Family (Eriocaulaceae)

Description: The *7-sided, leafless floral stalk* with a grayish-white, *knob-like flower head* at its summit emerges from the water above a submerged tuft of grass-like basal leaves.
Flowers: about $\frac{1}{12}''$ (2 mm) long, in a head up to $\frac{1}{2}''$ (1.3 cm) wide; petals 2; flowers interspersed with bracts; bracts also present beneath heads.
Leaves: 1–4″ (2.5–10 cm) long.
Height: 1½–9″ (3.8–22.5 cm).
Flowering: July–September.
Habitat: Still water, edges of ponds and lakes.
Range: Ontario to Nova Scotia; south from New England to Delaware and central Virginia; west to Indiana; north to Wisconsin and Minnesota.
Comments: This striking wetland plant with cottony, button-like flower heads is the most common and widespread of several species of Pipeworts. The common name Hatpins is especially appropriate to its overall aspect.

SPURGE FAMILY (Euphorbiaceae)

Commonly herbs, with milky sap; in the tropics also includes shrubs or trees
Flowers: unisexual; radially symmetrical; calyx and corolla each with 5 separate parts, or corolla absent, or both calyx and corolla absent; stamens 1—10 or more. All these parts attached at base of ovary.
Leaves: simple or compound, alternate or opposite.
Fruit: round, 3-lobed, dividing into 3 one-seeded sections.
There are about 290 genera and 7,500 species, mostly of warm or hot regions. Among the valuable products of the family are rubber, castor and tung oils, and tapioca. Most members of the family are poisonous, and their milky sap will irritate the membranes of the eyes and mouth.

---

165 **Tread-softly; Spurge Nettle**
   (*Cnidoscolus stimulosus*)
   Spurge Family (Euphorbiaceae)

Description: White, trumpet-shaped flowers are in a few-flowered, terminal cluster on a *plant covered with stinging hairs.*
Flowers: male, about 1″ (2.5 cm) wide, usually in upper forks of cluster, calyx showy, with 5 spreading lobes, petals lacking; female flowers in lower forks of cluster, lacking petals and showy calyx.
Leaves: 2–9″ (5–22.5 cm) long, roundish in outline, *deeply palmately lobed* into 3–5 segments, long-stalked, with fewer stinging hairs than the stem.
Fruit: oblong capsule.
Height: 6–36″ (15–90 cm).
Flowering: March–September.
Habitat: Sandy woods and fields along the coastal plain.
Range: Virginia south to Florida; west to Texas.

Comments: The stinging hairs which cover this
southern plant can produce a painful
rash on contact and cause a severe
reaction in some people. The sting is
similar to that of the northern Nettles.

198 Flowering Spurge
(*Euphorbia corollata*)
Spurge Family (Euphorbiaceae)

Description: Flowers are in an umbellate cluster,
with each flower having 5 *round, white,
petal-like structures* (bracts) surrounding
a group of minute true flowers; stem
juice is milky.
Flowers: bracted groups ⅜″ (9 mm)
wide.
Leaves: about 1½″ (3.8 cm) long, linear
to oblong, mostly alternate but whorled
just below flower cluster.
Height: 10–36″ (25–90 cm).

Flowering: June–October.

Habitat: Dry open woods, fields, and roadsides.

Range: Ontario; New York south to Florida;
west to Texas; north to Michigan,
Wisconsin, and Minnesota.

Comments: The petal-like bracts, which are often
colored, are typical of the spurges, as is
the milky juice. The Christmas
Poinsettia (*E. pulcherrima*) is a relative,
with showy red bracts surrounding the
true flowers. The common name of this
group comes from the Latin *expurgare*
("to purge"). This plant has been used
as a laxative, but an overdose may be
poisonous. Snow-on-the-mountain
(*E. marginata*), native to the Midwest,
has upper leaves with white margins.

350 Cypress Spurge
(*Euphorbia cyparissias*)
Spurge Family (Euphorbiaceae)

Description: A *flat-topped cluster* of yellow flowers is
at the summit of a stem covered with

needle-like, light green leaves; stem juice is milky.

Flowers: ⅜" (9 mm) wide, each actually consisting of a group of tiny, inconspicuous true flowers with crescent-shaped glands, surrounded by 2 yellow, *petal-like bracts* that turn orange or red with age.

Leaves: ½–1½" (1.3–3.8 cm) long, linear; alternate, but the uppermost whorled.

Height: 6–12" (15–30 cm).

Flowering: March–June (sporadically to September).

Habitat: Roadsides, cemeteries, disturbed areas.

Range: Throughout.

Comments: This plant, introduced from Europe, forms colonies by spreading from horizontal rootstalks; it frequently escapes cultivation. Although purgatives have sometimes been made from its roots, an overdose can cause poisoning, and animals can be poisoned by repeated feeding on hay containing this and other spurges. Contact with the milky sap can cause dermatitis. Many other similar, closely related species occur—all with wider leaves.

435 Wild Poinsettia
(*Euphorbia heterophylla*)
Spurge Family (Euphorbiaceae)

Description: Surrounded by blotched red or white (rarely all green) leaf-like bracts are unisexual, petal-less flowers occurring in clusters at the tip of a slender stalk with milky juice.

Flowers: about ⅙" (4 mm) wide; female flowers, stalked and conspicuous as ball-shaped structures.

Leaves: about 3" (7.5 cm) long, highly variable, from narrow to ovate to fiddle-shaped.

Height: 2–3' (60–90 cm).

Flowering: August–September.

Habitat: Open or wooded disturbed areas, usually in sandy soil.

Range: Virginia south to Florida; west to Texas; north to Minnesota and South Dakota.

Comments: The common Christmas Poinsettia (*E. pulcherrima*), with large leaf-like bracts completely red, pink, or white, is a closely related species. Another species, *E. dentata,* which occurs in the Midwest but is spreading east to New England, has hairier stems, opposite leaves, and leafy bracts, usually green or white at the base.

PEA OR BEAN FAMILY
(Fabaceae or Leguminosae)

Trees, shrubs, herbs, or vines with compound leaves and flowers in clusters.

Flowers: 3 distinct kinds. The most commonly described in this book, the "pea-like flower," has a broad upper petal (banner or standard), 2 lateral petals (wings), and 2 bottom petals (keel) joined and shaped like the prow of a boat; usually has 9 stamens joined and 1 free, surrounding the ovary and hidden inside the keel. The two other kinds of flowers are those of Acacias, radially symmetrical and with conspicuous stamens, and those of Sennas, bilaterally symmetrical, but without a distinct banner and keel.
Leaves: pinnately or palmately compound; or sometimes simple by evolutionary loss of leaflets.
Fruit: 1-chambered pod that usually opens along one or two seams.
This enormous family includes such products as peas, beans, soybeans, peanuts, and lentils. Alfalfa and Clover provide forage for domestic livestock, but many other species are poisonous range weeds. Exotic hardwoods and gum arabic are provided by tropical trees belonging to this family, and numerous members are cultivated as handsome ornamentals.

449 **Crab's-eye**
(*Abrus precatorius*)
Pea Family (Fabaceae)

Description: A woody, somewhat hairy vine with axillary clusters of pink or lavender flowers.
Flowers: ⅔" (1.6 cm) long; pea-like.
Leaves: pinnately compound with oblong untoothed leaflets ½" (1.3 cm) long.

Fruit: rectangular or oblong pod
1–1½″ (2.5–3.8 cm) long, with 3–5
*striking shiny red seeds, each with a black
spot.*
Height: vine, to 10′ (3 m) long.

Flowering: May–September.
Habitat: Roadsides, thickets.
Range: Florida.
Comments: The seeds of this plant are very
poisonous. If one is swallowed without
first being chewed, it is apparently less
toxic, but if the seedcoat is crushed,
one seed can cause death. Because of
their attractive scarlet color the seeds
are sometimes strung for necklaces
or rosaries; but since children might be
tempted to put these items in their
mouths, such use is not recommended.

118 Prairie Acacia
(*Acacia angustissima*)
Pea Family (Fabaceae)

Description: A shrub with *round masses of creamy
white or salmon-colored flowers* resembling
shaving brushes, rising on slender
stalks from the axils of the compound
leaves.
Flowers: florets minute, in clusters up
to ¾″ (2 cm) wide; stamens numerous,
protruding beyond sepals.
Leaves: about 2½″ (6.3 cm) long;
twice-compound, with 10–50 pairs of
narrow leaflets.
Fruit: oblong to linear seedpod.
Height: 1–5′ (30–150 cm).

Flowering: June–October.
Habitat: Dry bluffs, prairies, rocky woodlands.
Range: Missouri, Arkansas, and Texas.
Comments: This attractive native legume has seeds
that are rich in protein; the plant is
readily eaten by livestock and decreases
in abundance with heavy grazing. The
species name, meaning "most narrow"
in Latin, refers to the nature of the
leaflets. This species resembles the
taller Prairie Mimosa (*Desmanthus*

illinoensis), also a native perennial with doubly pinnately compound leaves, which is not a woody shrub, however.

632 Leadplant; False Indigo
(*Amorpha canescens*)
Pea Family (Fabaceae)

Description: A *gray-colored shrub* with white-hairy stems, pinnately compound leaves, and many small, blue flowers in spike-like clusters.
Flowers: about ⅛″ (4 mm) long; only 1 petal (the standard); stamens 10, bright orange.
Leaves: 2–4″ (5–10 cm) long; covered with dense short hairs giving a grayish appearance, divided into 15–45 leaflets, each about ½″ (1.3 cm) long.
Height: 1–3′ (30–90 cm).

Flowering: May–August.

Habitat: Dry prairies, hills.

Range: Indiana to Arkansas, Texas, and New Mexico; north to Saskatchewan and Michigan.

Comments: This is one of the most conspicuous and characteristic shrubs of the upland prairies. It is also called Prairie Shoestring, probably because of the laced-shoestring look of the leaves and roots. It has very deep roots, 4′ (1.2 m) or more, and thus avoids competition from the associated grasses. Indians used the leaves for tobacco and for making a tea. The genus name, from the Greek *amorphos* ("formless" or "deformed"), alludes to the fact that the flower, with only a single petal, is unlike the typical pea-like flowers of the family.

631 Indigobush; False Indigo
(*Amorpha fruticosa*)
Pea Family (Fabaceae)

Description: Shrub with groups of erect elongated clusters (racemes) of purple flowers.
Flowers: ¼–⅓" (6–8 mm) long; 1 petal (the standard) wraps around 10 orange stamens and the style; other petals missing.
Leaves: 4–12" (10–30 cm) long, long-petioled, pinnately compound, with 13–25 dull green *leaflets marked with resinous dots*.
Fruit: oblong, compressed, rough pod.
Height: 5–17' (150–510 cm).

Flowering: May–June.

Habitat: Alluvial soils, riverbanks, and moist thickets.

Range: Throughout.

Comments: This shrub, which often forms thickets on riverbanks and islands, is occasionally cultivated in the northeast. Another False Indigo (*A. herbacea*) has whitish to blue-violet flowers in fan-like masses on top of the plant and gray-downy foliage with up to 40 leaflets.

575 Hog Peanut
(*Amphicarpa bracteata*)
Pea Family (Fabaceae)

Description: A *twining vine* with *2 kinds of flowers*.
Flowers: those on upper branches ½" (1.3 cm) long, pale purple or lilac, 2-lipped, in clusters hanging from the leaf axils; those on lower or creeping branches inconspicuous, without petals.
Leaves: pinnately divided into *3 leaflets* ¾–3" (2–7.5 cm) long, ovate, pointed.
Fruit: those of the upper flowers flattened, oblong-linear, ⅔–1½" (1.6–3.8 cm) long, 3–4 seeded; those of the lower flowers fleshy, ovate or pear-shaped, often subterranean, 1-seeded.

Height: vine, to 4' (120 cm) long.
Flowering: August–September.
Habitat: Damp woodlands.
Range: Quebec and Nova Scotia south to
Florida; west to Texas and Nebraska;
north to Montana and Manitoba.
Comments: The genus name is from the Greek
amphi ("of both kinds") and *carpos*
("fruit") and refers to the two kinds of
fruits. The seeds of the aerial fruits are
inedible, but those from the
underground pods can be eaten boiled.
Birds feed on the seeds of both kinds of
fruit and hogs eat those below ground.

412 Groundnut
(*Apios americana*)
Pea Family (Fabaceae)

Description: Climbing vine with maroon or reddish-
brown pea-like flowers in compact
racemes arising from the
leaf axils.
Flowers: ½" (1.3 cm) long; keel (two
fused lower petals) *scythe-shaped,
upturned.*
Leaves: 4–8" (10–20 cm) long,
pinnately compound, with 5–7 ovate to
lanceolate leaflets.
Height: vine, to 10' (3 m) long.
Flowering: July–September.
Habitat: Moist, low sites and thickets.
Range: New Brunswick and Nova Scotia; New
England south to Florida; west to
Louisiana and Texas; north to
Minnesota, particularly Great Lakes
area.
Comments: This legume has a cord-like rootstalk
with edible tubers the Indians gathered
for food. The Pilgrims relied on them
as a food source during their initial
years in Massachusetts. The tubers can
be used in soups and stews or fried like
potatoes; the cooked seeds can also be
eaten. The flowers are sufficiently
beautiful to warrant cultivation, but
the plant tends to take over. The

generic name, from Greek for "pear,"
alludes to the shape of the tubers.
Price's Groundnut (*A. priceana*), a rare
species with greenish-white flowers and
purple tips, occurs in Kentucky,
Tennessee, and southern Illinois.

---

531 **Woolly Locoweed**
(*Astragalus mollissimus*)
Pea Family (Fabaceae)

Description: Low-growing, hairy, bushy plant with
compound woolly leaves and dense spikes
of violet, pea-like flowers.
Flowers: 1" (2.5 cm) long; 2 united
lower petals of flower form a *blunt keel*.
Leaves: about 6" (15 cm) long;
pinnately compound, with 8–12 pairs
of narrow leaflets.
Fruit: roundish pod with shallow
depressions on each side.
Height: 8–18" (20–45 cm).

Flowering: June.

Habitat: Prairies and sandy soil.

Range: Across southwestern Canada; South
Dakota and Minnesota south to Texas,
and beyond.

Comments: It is similar to Locoweeds in the genus
Oxytropis, whose flowers have a pointed,
rather than blunt, keel and leaves
arising directly from the ground. Some
members of both genera are called
"locoweeds" and are poisonous plants of
the American western grasslands. They
contain a toxic substance that affects an
animal's muscular control and may
impair its vision (so a horse may seem
to behave oddly, jumping high over
small depressions or knocking into
objects); hence the name "loco." The
toxicity appears to vary with soil
conditions, but the decaying plants are
believed to pass on their toxicity to
other forage crops. Some members of
this group are known as "Poison
Vetches"; others as "Milk Vetches."

146 Prairie False Indigo; White Wild Indigo
(*Baptisia leucantha*)
Pea Family (Fabaceae)

Description: Bushy perennial with smooth leaves and white or cream-colored, pea-like flowers held in *stiffly erect clusters*. Stem covered with whitish bloom.
Flowers: to 1″ (2.5 cm) long; in clusters to 12″ (30 cm) long.
Leaves: palmately divided into 3 oblong segments, each 1–2½″ (2.5–6.3 cm) long.
Fruit: black, drooping, oblong, beaked pod, about 1″ (2.5 cm) long.
Height: 2–5′ (60–150 cm).

Flowering: May–July.
Habitat: Prairies, waste places, and open woods.
Range: Ontario; Ohio south to Mississippi; west to Texas; north to Nebraska and Minnesota.

Comments: This showy legume often stands out above surrounding prairie grasses. Many species of this genus contain a blue dye that resembles indigo, which becomes noticeable in autumn as the plants blacken on drying. Large-bracted Wild Indigo (*B. leucophaea*) has 2 large stipules at the base of 3-part leaves, giving the effect of 5 leaflets rather than 3.

328 Wild Indigo
(*Baptisia tinctoria*)
Pea Family (Fabaceae)

Description: Smooth, bushy perennial with numerous few-flowered, elongated terminal clusters of *yellow pea-like flowers.*
Flowers: ½″ (1.3 cm) long.
Leaves: *palmately compound,* with 3 ovate to wedge-shaped leaflets, ½–1½″ (1.3–3.8 cm) long.
Fruit: short, round pod, tipped with a style.

Height: 3' (90 cm).
Flowering: May–September.
Habitat: Dry fields.
Range: Across southeastern Canada; from New England south to Florida; west to Louisiana; north to Minnesota.
Comments: Widely distributed, Wild Indigo often increases in burnt fields. Some 15 other species are found in our range, including numerous yellow species farther south and some white or creamy ones. Blue False Indigo (*B. australis*), which has upright racemes of blue flowers and sap that turns purple when exposed to air, has escaped from cultivation northward to New York and Vermont. The genus name, from Greek *baptizein* ("to dye"), refers to the fact that some species are used as an inferior substitute for true indigo dye.

---

330 Wild Senna
(*Cassia hebecarpa*)
Pea Family (Fabaceae)

Description: Clusters of light yellow flowers top this sparingly branched perennial or are in the axils of the compound leaves.
Flowers: ¾" (2 cm) wide, with 5 slightly unequal petals; stamens 10, prominent and of unequal length, with conspicuous brown anthers opening by two pores.
Leaves: 6–8" (15–20 cm) long, pinnately compound, with 5–9 pairs of oblong, blunt leaflets about 1" (2.5 cm) long; conspicuous *club-shaped gland* present near base of leafstalk.
Fruit: flat, narrow, curved, segmented, *very hairy pod,* with *joints as long as broad.*
Height: 3–6' (90–180 cm).
Flowering: July–August.
Habitat: Moist open woods and disturbed areas.
Range: New England south to North Carolina; west to Tennessee; north to Illinois and Wisconsin.

Comments: The flowers of this large plant are showy but not typically pea-like. Partridge Pea (*C. fasciculata*) is similar but has larger flowers to 1½" (3.8 cm) wide, growing only in the leaf axils. Another Wild Senna (*C. marilandica*), more southern species, has fewer flowers and bigger leaflets. Two other species, Sicklepod (*C. obtusifolia*) and Coffee Senna (*C. occidentalis*), are found in our range.

574 Spurred Butterfly Pea
(*Centrosema virginianum*)
Pea Family (Fabaceae)

Description: Trailing or twining vine with violet flowers, single or in clusters of 2–4 in the axils of compound leaves.
Flowers: ¾–1½" (2–3.8 cm) long; corolla parts reversed from usual position of pea family; *broad standard toward ground, keel upward,* with *small spur* at base.
Leaves: alternate, divided into 3 leaflets, ovate to lanceolate, each 1–2½" (2.5–6.3 cm) long.
Fruit: pod that coils into 2 spirals after splitting at maturity.
Height: vine, 2–4' (60–120 cm) long.
Flowering: July–August.
Habitat: Acid soils, sandy woodlands, and fields.
Range: New Jersey south to Florida; west to Texas; north to Arkansas.
Comments: The flowers of this delicate showy vine are recognized by their "upside-down" position. Sand Butterfly Pea (*C. arenicola*) has ovate leaflets indented at the base; Florida Butterfly Pea (*C. floridana*), with oval to lanceolate leaflets up to 3" (7.5 cm) long, occurs in the pinewoods of Florida.

509 Butterfly Pea
(*Clitoria mariana*)
Pea Family (Fabaceae)

Description: Twining vine, occasionally erect, with *large, showy, lavender-pink, pea-like flowers,* usually solitary but occasionally up to 3, in the axils of compound leaves.
Flowers: 2″ (5 cm) long.
Leaves: compound, divided into 3 ovate leaflets, each 1–2½″ (2.5–6.3 cm) long.
Fruit: few-seeded, flattened pod, about 2″ (5 cm) long, which splits into 2 twisted valves at maturity.
Height: 1–3′ (30–90 cm).
Flowering: June–August.
Habitat: Dry soil, open woods, and thickets.
Range: New York south to Florida; west to Texas and beyond; north to Missouri and Iowa.
Comments: This plant is often confused with Spurred Butterfly Pea (*Centrosema virginianum*), which has upside-down flowers, the banner pointing downward, while that of *Clitoria* stands erect.

572 Crown Vetch; Axseed
(*Coronilla varia*)
Pea Family (Fabaceae)

Description: Pink-and-white pea-like flowers in *head-like clusters* that arise from the leaf axils on a sprawling or upward-curving stem.
Flowers: upper dilated petals (standard) pink; side petals (wings) often whitish; in clusters to 1″ (2.5 cm) wide.
Leaves: 2–4″ (5–10 cm) long, compound, pinnately divided into 15–25 ovate leaflets, each ½–¾″ (1.3–2 cm) long.
Fruit: 4-angled linear pod, 1–2″ (2.5–5 cm) long.
Height: 1–2′ (30–60 cm).

Flowering: June–August.
Habitat: Waste places, roadsides, and fields.
Range: New England south to Virginia; west to Missouri; north to South Dakota.
Comments: This European introduction is often planted along roadsides as a stabilizing perennial. It is now naturalized in many areas, and when in masses, as it often occurs, it makes a striking ground cover. In addition, it adds nitrogen to the soil, as do all members of this family.

327   **Showy Rattlebox**
(*Crotalaria spectabilis*)
Pea Family (Fabaceae)

Description: Yellow, pea-like flowers are in elongated clusters near the top of an *erect plant* with dark, *purplish stems*.
Flowers: about 1″ (2.5 cm) long; calyx bell-shaped, purplish.
Leaves: 2–8″ (5–20 cm) long; *simple, ovate*.
Fruit: inflated pod up to 2″ (5 cm) long.
Height: 2–3′ (60–90 cm).
Flowering: August–October.
Habitat: Fields, roadsides, waste places.
Range: Virginia south to Florida; west to Missouri.
Comments: The rattling of the dry seeds in the pod accounts for both the common and the genus names, from the Greek *crotalon* ("a rattle"). Rattlebox (*C. sagittalis*), which occurs as far north as New England and west to Texas and Minnesota, has smaller flowers and narrower leaves. Two other similar species are Pursh's Rattlebox (*C. purshii*) and Prostrate Rattlebox (*C. angulata*). There are at least 4 species in our range with larger flowers in elongated clusters or leaves with 3 leaflets.

119 Prairie Mimosa; Prairie Desmanthus
(*Desmanthus illinoensis*)
Pea Family (Fabaceae)

Description: Erect plant with *ball-like flower clusters* of small whitish or greenish flowers, on tall stalks arising in the axils of compound leaves.
Flowers: cluster about ½″ (1.3 cm) wide; 5 petals, each less than ¹⁄₁₂″ (2 mm) long, and 5 projecting stamens.
Leaves: 2–4″ (5–10 cm) long, doubly pinnately divided into numerous small leaflets.
Fruit: 20–30 curved or twisted pods, each up to 1″ (2.5 cm) long, forming dense spherical structure.
Height: 2–4′ (60–120 cm).
Flowering: June–August.
Habitat: Plains, prairies, and riverbanks.
Range: South Carolina to Florida; west to Texas and beyond; north to North Dakota and Minnesota; also Illinois and Ohio.
Comments: Distinguished from Prairie Acacia (*Acacia angustissima*) by its fruit, this is a nutritious range plant, high in protein. It is considered by some to be our most important native range legume.

533 Showy Tick Trefoil
(*Desmodium canadense*)
Pea Family (Fabaceae)

Description: Erect, *bushy, hairy plant* with crowded, elongated terminal clusters of pink or rose-purple pea-like flowers.
Flowers: ½″ (1.3 cm) long, on pedicels to ⅓″ (8 mm) long.
Leaves: pinnately compound, with 3 oblong untoothed leaflets, each to 3″ (7.5 cm) long; *stipules at base of leafstalks lanceolate.*
Fruit: hairy, *segmented pod,* with 3–5 joints.
Height: 2–6′ (60–180 cm).
Flowering: July–August.

Habitat: Moist open woods and edges of fields.
Range: Across southern Canada to Nova Scotia;
           New England south to Virginia; west
           to Missouri and Oklahoma; north to
           Canada.
Comments: This most showy of the Tick Trefoils is
           one of some two dozen species
           distinguished by their leaf and fruit
           shape. The distinctively jointed fruits,
           known as loments, break into 1-seeded
           segments that stick to clothes and
           animal fur, thus facilitating seed
           dispersal.

148 Illinois Tick Trefoil
(*Desmodium illinoense*)
Pea Family (Fabaceae)

Description: Tall, *spindly, hairy stem* topped with a
              slender elongated cluster of many
              white, purple, or pinkish-lavender
              pea-like flowers.
              Flowers: up to ½" (1.3 cm) long, on
              stalks to ¾" (2 cm) long.
              Leaves: divided into 3 segments, with
              terminal one 2–3½" (5–8.8 cm) long,
              strongly veined beneath; *ovate stipules* at
              base of leafstalks.
              Fruit: *flattened, jointed pod* with
              3–7 segments.
              Height: 2–5' (60–150 cm).
Flowering: July–August.
Habitat: Dry prairies.
Range: Ontario; south from Ohio and Missouri
              to Texas and Oklahoma; north to
              Nebraska and Iowa.
Comments: A showy plant when in flower, Illinois
              Tick Trefoil develops long fruits with
              segments that separate and attach
              themselves to clothing, thereby
              promoting seed dispersal.

432 Coral Bean
(*Erythrina herbacea*)
Pea Family (Fabaceae)

Description: Erect plant with *prickly stems* and *bright red elongated flower clusters.*
Flowers: standard 2″ (5 cm) long; heart-shaped wing petal ½″ (1.3 cm) long.
Leaves: compound, divided into three arrowhead-shaped leaflets, 1½–3″ (3.8–7.5 cm) long.
Fruit: pod ½″ (1.3 cm) long, with bright red seeds.
Height: 2–5′ (60–150 cm).

Flowering: March–July.

Habitat: Pinewoods, hummocks, and thickets.

Range: Along the coastal plain, southeast North Carolina south to Florida; west to Texas.

Comments: This is a showy member of a large tropical genus with over 100 species. The distinctive flame-like flower clusters appear before or with the leaves. Its hard red seeds are used as beads. The species is a woody shrub in Florida but an herb in the rest of its mainly coastal range.

510 Beach Pea
(*Lathyrus japonicus*)
Pea Family (Fabaceae)

Description: *Trailing vine* with a stout, *angled stem* and pink-lavender pea-like flowers in long-stalked clusters.
Flowers: ¾″ (2 cm) long.
Leaves: pinnately compound, with 6–12 thick, fleshy, oval leaflets to 2½″ (6.3 cm) long, with bristle tips; uppermost leaflets modified into tendrils; *stipules large, arrowhead-shaped,* about 1¼″ (3.1 cm) long.
Fruit: elongated, veiny pod, 2″ (5 cm) long.
Height: vine, 1–2′ (30–60 cm) long.

Flowering: June–August.

Habitat: Beaches and gravelly areas.

Range: Coastal Labrador to New England;
south to New Jersey; along the Great
Lakes.

Comments: In addition to our range, this widely
distributed Sweetpea-like flower is also
found along the Pacific coast from
Alaska to California, and also in Chile
and Japan. Marsh Pea (*L. palustris*), a
similar species with purple flowers and
lanceolate stipules, is found in wet
meadows and marshes in the Northeast
and Midwest. At least 10 species occur
within our range.

573 Creeping Bush Clover
(*Lespedeza repens*)
Pea Family (Fabaceae)

Description: A *trailing plant* with stems bearing
loose clusters of pink to purple, pea-
like flowers and *clover-like leaves*.
Flowers: ¼" (6 mm) long.
Leaves: 3-parted, leaflets about ½"
(1.3 cm) long, ovate.
Fruit: elliptic, *1-seeded pod*.
Height: creeper, with trailing stem
6–24" (15–60 cm) long.

Flowering: May–September.

Habitat: Open woods, clearings, thickets.

Range: Connecticut south to Florida; west to
Texas, Kansas, and Iowa; north to
Wisconsin.

Comments: The Lespedezas are a large, somewhat
cloverlike group in which considerable
hybridizing has made for much
variation in the 18 or more species
found in our region. They are useful
plants for improving the fertility of dry
sites and their seeds are a very
important food source for bobwhite
quail, although they are apparently not
much used by songbirds.

538 Slender Bush Clover
(*Lespedeza virginica*)
Pea Family (Fabaceae)

Description: Upright stem with compound leaves
and *small crowded clusters* of lavender
pea-like flowers in upper leaf axils.
Flowers: ¼" (6 mm) long.
Leaves: divided into *3 narrow blunt
leaflets,* each about 1" (2.5 cm) long.
Fruit: *short, roundish, 1-seeded pod.*
Height: 1–3' (30–90 cm).
Flowering: July–September.
Habitat: Dry open woods, thickets, and
clearings.
Range: Southern Ontario; southern New
Hampshire south to Florida; west to
Texas; north to Wisconsin and
Michigan.
Comments: This is a large, somewhat clover-like
group where considerable hybridizing
has resulted in much variation in the 18
or more species found within our range.
Useful plants for improving the fertility
of dry sites, their seeds are a very
important food for bobwhite quail.
Some cultivated species, such as
Japanese Clover (*L. striata*) and Korean
Clover (*L. stipulacea*), frequently escape
cultivation and occur wild from
Pennsylvania to Kansas and southward.
Other native species include Round-
headed Bush Clover (*L. capitata*), with
dense globose flower clusters in the leaf
axils, a white and magenta-spotted
corolla concealed by long sepals, and
nearly stalkless hairy leaves, each with
3 oblong leaflets.

356 Birdsfoot Trefoil
(*Lotus corniculatus*)
Pea Family (Fabaceae)

Description: Low plant, often with a reclining stem,
with *clover-like leaves* and yellow pea-
like flowers in *flat-topped terminal
clusters.*

Flowers: ½″ (1.3 cm) long.
Leaves: compound, with 3 ovate leaflets
about ½″ (1.3 cm) long, and 2 leaflet-
like stipules at base of stalk.
Fruit: slender pod about 1″ (2.5 cm)
long.
Height: 6–24″ (15–60 cm).

Flowering: June–September.

Habitat: Fields and roadsides.

Range: Newfoundland; New England south to
North Carolina; northwest through
Ohio to Minnesota.

Comments: This showy plant was introduced from
Europe. The pod arrangement suggests
a bird's foot; hence the common name.
The western Prairie Trefoil
(*L. americanus*) has pink and yellowish
flowers, as does the southeastern
Heller's Birdsfoot Trefoil (*L. helleri*).

---

640 **Wild Lupine**
(*Lupinus perennis*)
Pea Family (Fabaceae)

Description: Blue, pea-like flowers are in an upright,
elongated, terminal cluster on an erect
stem with *palmately compound leaves*.
Flowers: up to ⅔″ (1.6 cm) long.
Leaves: the 7–11 lanceolate leaflets, up
to 2″ (5 cm) long, radiate from a central
point.
Fruit: hairy pod, up to 2″ (5 cm)
long.
Height: 8–24″ (20–60 cm).

Flowering: April–July.

Habitat: Dry open woods and fields.

Range: Maine south to Florida; west to
Louisiana and Minnesota.

Comments: The plant was once thought to deplete
or "wolf" the mineral content of the
soil; hence the genus name derived
from the Latin *lupus* ("wolf"). Actually,
the plant and all the family enhances
soil fertility by fixing atmospheric
nitrogen into a useful form. In the
south this flower has narrower leaflets
and is often recognized as a separate

species, Nuttal's Lupine (*L. nuttallii*). Two southern species with undivided elliptic leaves are Spreading Lupine (*L. diffusa*), with blue flowers and a whitish spot on the standard (upper petal), and Hairy Lupine (*L. villosus*), a hairy plant with lavender-blue flowers and a red-purple spot on the standard. They are found from North Carolina to Florida and west to Louisiana. A species found in Nebraska, Wyoming and Colorado, Nebraska Lupine (*L. plattensis*), has blue flowers with a dark spot on the standard and paddle-shaped leaflets. *L. polyphyllus* is becoming extremely abundant in the Northeast, particularly Maine and adjacent Canada; it was introduced from the Northwest.

639 Texas Bluebonnet
(*Lupinus subcarnosus*)
Pea Family (Fabaceae)

Description: Small, deep-blue flowers in a tall, dense, terminal cluster above palmately compound leaves.
Flowers: ½″ (1.3 cm) long; banner (upper petal) of flower bears *central white or yellowish spot* that turns red with age.
Leaves: 4–7 blunt segments, each about 1″ (2.5 cm) long, radiating from a central point.
Height: 12–15″ (30–37.5 cm).
Flowering: April–May.
Habitat: Grasslands.
Range: Texas.
Comments: Although there are four species of Lupines in Texas, this one has been designated the official state flower. It is restricted to the eastern and southern part of the state. A most showy and important prairie species, *L. texensis* grows up to 2′ (60 cm) tall and has a reddish or yellow blotch at the center of its purple or lavender flowers.

135 White Sweet Clover
(*Melilotus alba*)
Pea Family (Fabaceae)

Description: Small, somewhat pea-like flowers,
fragrant when crushed, are in *long,
slender, cylindrical, spike-like clusters*
rising in the leaf axils on a bushy plant.
Flowers: ¼″ (6 mm) long, in clusters
up to 8″ (20 cm) long.
Leaves: pinnately divided into 3
lanceolate, toothed leaflets, each
½–1″ (1.3–2.5 cm) long.
Fruit: small, ovoid pod.
Height: 3–8′ (90–240 cm).
Flowering: May–October.
Habitat: Roadsides and fields.
Range: Throughout.
Comments: This tall, introduced legume has the
fragrance of new-mown hay when
crushed. Both this plant and yellow
Sweet Clover (*M. officinalis*) are widely
used as pasture crops for nitrogen
enrichment of the soil. They are also
highly valued as honey plants as
suggested by the genus name from *meli*
a Greek word meaning "honey."

326 Yellow Sweet Clover
(*Melilotus officinalis*)
Pea Family (Fabaceae)

Description: A smooth, loosely branched plant with
small yellow, pea-like flowers in *slender,
cylindrical, spike-like clusters* rising in the
axils of 3-parted leaves.
Flowers: ¼″ (6 mm) long, in clusters to
6″ (15 cm) long.
Leaves: each leaflet ½–1″ (1.3–2.5 cm)
long; lanceolate to ovate, toothed.
Fruit: small, ovoid, wrinkled pod.
Height: 2–5′ (60–150 cm).
Flowering: May–October.
Habitat: Waste places, fields.
Range: Throughout.
Comments: The leaves of this plant, like those of
the White Sweet Clover (*M. alba*), have

a vanilla-like fragrance when crushed and can be used as a flavoring. The seeds are eaten by upland gamebirds such as grouse.

540 Crazyweed; Stemless Loco
(*Oxytropis lambertii*)
Pea Family (Fabaceae)

Description: Hairy, deep-rooted plant sending its compound leaves directly up through the soil from the plant crown, with clusters of sweet-scented, pink to lavender, pea-like flowers on leafless stalks that rise above the leaves.
Flowers: about ¾″ (2 cm) long; *keel produced into a point.*
Leaves: pinnately divided into 9–19 linear to oblong, hairy leaflets, each up to 1″ (2.5 cm) long.
Fruit: erect, hairy, beaked pod.
Height: 8–12″ (20–30 cm).

Flowering: May–July.

Habitat: Dry prairies and limestone sites.

Range: Southwest Canada; Minnesota south to Missouri, Oklahoma, and Texas.

Comments: This is one of the most dangerous of the poisonous locoweeds that are widely distributed in mixed prairies. Its huge taproot can penetrate to a depth of 8′ (2.4 m). Fortunately, it is unpalatable to livestock and is seldom eaten unless other forage is scarce. This genus is distinguished from *Astragalus* by its pointed keel petal.

526 Locoweed; Showy Oxytropis
(*Oxytropis splendens*)
Pea Family (Fabaceae)

Description: Tufted plant with *silvery, silky-hairy, leafless stems,* topped by dense spikes of rich lavender flowers, rising from among pinnately compound basal leaves.

Flowers: about ¾" (2 cm) long; in clusters 1½–7" (3.8–17.5 cm) long; pea-like, *keel pointed.*
Leaves: to 9½" (23.8 cm) long, pinnately divided into numerous lanceolate leaflets, often in groups of 3–4.
Fruit: ovoid, *hairy, short-beaked capsule,* up to ⅔" (1.6 cm) long.
Height: 4–12" (10–30 cm).

Flowering: June–July.

Habitat: Prairies and plains.

Range: Southern Manitoba; North Dakota and Minnesota (also occurs beyond our range in the Southwest and farther west).

Comments: This is one of the poisonous Locoweeds similar to the members of the genus *Astragalus* (whose flowers have a blunt keel) also known as Locoweeds or Poison Vetches. There are nonpoisonous members of both genera as well—those of *Oxytropis* being known as Point Vetches.

515 Purple Prairie Clover
(*Petalostemum purpureum*)
Pea Family (Fabaceae)

Description: Tiny rose-purple *flowers in cylindrical, head-like masses* at the ends of upright wiry stems.
Flowers: about ⅛" (4 mm) long, in clusters up to 2" (5 cm) long; corolla not pea-like, with *1 main heart-shaped petal* (the standard) and 4 narrow petal-like structures (modified stamens); calyx 5-part, hairy; 5 true stamens.
Leaves: pinnately divided into 3–7 (usually 5) narrow segments, each ½–¾" (1.3–2 cm) long.
Height: 1–3' (30–90 cm).

Flowering: June–September.

Habitat: Prairies and dry hills.

Range: Indiana and western Tennessee southwest to Arkansas, Texas, and beyond; north to southern Canada.

Comments: This is one of the most widespread of the perennial Prairie Clovers, identifiable by their cone-like flower heads. An excellent range species, with high protein content, Purple Prairie Clover decreases in abundance with overgrazing. A midwestern white-flowering species, White Prairie Clover (*P. candidum*), has elongated flower heads and is only 2′ (60 cm) tall. A white-flowering southeastern coastal plain species, *P. albidum,* has conspicuous green bracts within the heads.

637 Silverleaf Scurf Pea
(*Psoralea argophylla*)
Pea Family (Fabaceae)

Description: Small, *very dark blue, pea-like flowers* in groups of 2–4 at tops of branches with *silvery foliage.*
Flowers: ⅓″ (8 mm) long, stalkless.
Leaves: compound, palmately divided into 3–5 elliptic leaflets, each ¾–2″ (2–5 cm) long, covered with soft whitish hairs.
Fruit: ovate, 1-seeded, silky pod.
Height: 1–2′ (30–60 cm).
Flowering: Late June–August.
Habitat: Prairies and moist, level land.
Range: Wisconsin south to Missouri; west to Oklahoma and beyond; north to southwest Canada.
Comments: This legume is often associated with Little Bluestem (*Andropogon scoparius*) in grasslands. It is reported to be poisonous to cattle. The common name "scurf pea" alludes to small scale-like glands covering the plant parts. Its pods have only one seed, whereas most legumes have numerous seeds. Several species of these rather delicate plants occur. Many-flowered Psoralea (*P. tenuifolia*) is a widely branching plant with small blue flowers that appear in early June.

576 Kudzu Vine
(*Pueraria lobata*)
Pea Family (Fabaceae)

Description: *High-climbing vine* with a *hairy stem* and violet-purple, pea-like flowers in dense clusters in the leaf axils, blooming from base of the cluster upward.
Flowers: 1" (2.5 cm) long; upper ovate petal (standard) with a conspicuous yellow patch at the base.
Leaves: compound, pinnately divided into 3 broadly ovate or rounded leaflets, 4–6" (10–15 cm) long, sometimes lobed.
Fruit: linear-oblong, flattened, brownish, *hairy pod,* up to 2" (5 cm) long.
Height: vine, to 60' (18 m).
Flowering: Late summer.
Habitat: Borders of woods and fields.
Range: Pennsylvania to Tennessee and farther south (rarely flowering north of Virginia).
Comments: This exceedingly aggressive vine, which can grow to 50–60' (15–18 m), forms a continuous blanket of foliage over trees, resulting in grotesque forms. Although considered a pest for this reason, it is also planted to shade and feed livestock and for erosion control. The common name Kudzu is vernacular from Japan, where its starchy tuberous root is eaten.

513 Sensitive Brier
(*Schrankia nuttalii*)
Pea Family (Fabaceae)

Description: Branching, trailing *plant armed with curved spines* and bearing round balls of pink flowers on long stalks arising in the axils of compound leaves.
Flowers: tiny, in clusters about 1" (2.5 cm) wide; corolla funnelform, 5-lobed.
Leaves: up to 6" (15 cm) long, twice

pinnately divided; leaflets elliptic, about ⅓″ (8 mm) long; leafstalks prickly.
Fruit: spiny, narrow, beaked pod, about 2½″ (6.3 cm) long.
Height: creeper, 2–4′ (60–120 cm) long.

Flowering: June–September.
Habitat: Sandy grasslands and woods.
Range: Illinois south to Alabama; west to Texas; north to Nebraska.
Comments: The filaments of the purplish-pink stamens contribute to the powderpuff effect of the flowers. Numerous species of these spiny plants occur. Narrow-leaved Sensitive Brier (*S. microphylla*), found from Virginia to Florida and Texas, has smaller leaves and flower heads less than 1″ (2.5 cm) in diameter; its pods are both spiny and downy.

524 Goat's Rue; Devil's Shoestrings
(*Tephrosia virginiana*)
Pea Family (Fabaceae)

Description: *Bicolored, pea-like flowers,* with pink wings and a yellow standard, crowded into clusters atop a hairy stem.
Flowers: ¾″ (2 cm) long; in clusters up to 3″ (7.5 cm) long.
Leaves: compound, pinnately divided into elliptic to linear-oblong, *hoary leaflets,* each ½–1½″ (1.3–3.8 cm) long.
Fruit: narrow, whitish hairy pod to 2″ (5 cm) long.
Height: 1–2′ (30–60 cm).

Flowering: May–August.
Habitat: Dry, sandy woods and clearings.
Range: New Hampshire south to Florida; west to Texas; north to Missouri and Wisconsin.
Comments: A distinctively silvery plant, Goat's Rue has long stringy roots, to which the common name Devil's Shoestrings refers. It was at one time fed to goats to increase their milk production, but

since it contains rotenone (now used as an insecticide and fish poison), this practice has been discontinued. In the South, several white-flowering species occur (*T. spicata, T. chrysophylla,* etc.), with fewer flowers per cluster on the tips of long stalks. These flowers eventually turn pink, and the foliage is often distinctive because of brownish or golden hairs.

316 Hop Clover
(*Trifolium agrarium*)
Pea Family (Fabaceae)

Description: Small, yellow, pea-like flowers clustered in roundish-oblong heads above leaves divided into 3 *wedge-shaped leaflets;* stems mostly smooth and erect.
Flowers: ¼″ (6 mm) long, in heads ½–1″ (1.3–2.5 cm) wide, with 20–40 flowers turning brown with age.
Leaves: leaflets ½–¾″ (1.3–2 cm) long, lanceolate to oblong, stalkless.
Height: 6–18″ (15–45 cm).
Flowering: June–September.
Habitat: Fields, roadsides, and waste places.
Range: Throughout, but most common in northeastern U.S.
Comments: This species, also known as *T. aureum,* is one of 3 annual yellow clovers in the United States, all introduced from Europe. They are primarily low plants, often found in lawns and gardens. Low Hop Clover (*T. campestre*) has sprawling hairy stems, and its terminal leaflet is stalked and notched. Least Hop Clover (*T. dubium*) is similar but has a very small flower head with only 3–15 flowers. A very similar yellow group, the Medicks (*Medicago* spp.), are prostrate plants with distinctive spiral-coiled fruits.

518 Rabbit-foot Clover
(*Trifolium arvense*)
Pea Family (Fabaceae)

Description: Tiny flowers in *fuzzy, soft pink or gray-pink cylindrical heads* at top of erect, silky-hairy stems, above leaves divided into *3 narrow, elliptic leaflets.*
Flowers: ⅕" (5 mm) long, in heads about ¾" (2 cm) long; pea-like; sepals covered with long hairs that obscure the small corolla.
Leaves: leaflets ½–¾" (1.3–2 cm) long, toothed only at the tips.
Height: 6–18" (15–45 cm).

Flowering: May–October.

Habitat: Dry, sandy or gravelly areas.

Range: Throughout.

Comments: This attractive annual is well named, since its flower head is as furry as a rabbit's foot. It is frequently found in dry open sites, where it is especially showy in masses. The flowers make an interesting dried bouquet.

516 Red Clover
(*Trifolium pratense*)
Pea Family (Fabaceae)

Description: Dense, rounded, head-like masses of magenta pea-like flowers on an erect, hairy stem, with leaves divided into *3 oval leaflets.*
Flowers: ½" (1.3 cm) long, in heads about 1" (2.5 cm) long and ½–1" (1.3–2.5 cm) wide; upper petal (standard) folded over 2 fused lower petals (keel) and lateral petals (wings).
Leaves: leaflets ½–2" (1.3–5 cm) long, each with a *lighter, V-shaped pattern near the middle.*
Height: 6–24" (15–60 cm).

Flowering: May–September.

Habitat: Old fields, lawns, and roadsides.

Range: Throughout.

Comments: Introduced from Europe and extensively planted here as a hay and pasture crop, this is one of our most common perennial clovers. It stores nitrogen in its root nodules and is used in crop rotation to improve soil fertility. Zigzag Clover (*T. medium*), a very similar but rarer species, has narrower leaflets, and its flower head is raised above the top leaves on the stem. Alsike Clover (*T. hybridum*) has white-pink flower heads and lacks the chevron pattern on the leaves.

120 White Clover
(*Trifolium repens*)
Pea Family (Fabaceae)

Description: White or pinkish, head-like flower clusters and 3-part leaves rise on *separate stalks from a creeping stem.*
Flowers: ¼–½″ (6–13 mm) long, pea-like, in long-stalked clusters about ¾″ (2 cm) wide; turning brown with age.
Leaves: on long stalks, leaflets ¾–1″ (2–2.5 cm) long, ovate.
Height: creeper, with stem 4–10″ (10–25 cm) long.

Flowering: May–October.

Habitat: Lawns, roadsides, and fields.

Range: Throughout.

Comments: This introduced perennial is common in lawns, where one may sometimes find a "4-leaf" clover. A similar, but more western, species is Buffalo Clover (*T. stoloniferum*), with heart-shaped, often notched leaflets. It is found in West Virginia and Kentucky, west to Missouri and eastern Kansas, and north to South Dakota.

534 Cow Vetch; Blue Vetch
(*Vicia cracca*)
Pea Family (Fabaceae)

Description: Climbing plant with gray-green leaves and long, *one-sided, crowded spikes* of

pea-like tubular lavender to blue flowers,
directed downward on a long stalk.
Flowers: ½″ (1.3 cm) long.
Leaves: pinnately compound, with
8–12 pairs of narrow *bristle-tipped
leaflets,* each 1″ (2.5 cm) long; pair of
tendrils at end of each leafstalk.
Fruit: narrow, lanceolate pod.
Height: vine, to 4′ (1.2 m) long.

Flowering: May–August.

Habitat: Roadsides and fields.

Range: Across southern Canada to
Newfoundland and Nova Scotia; south
from New England to North Carolina;
west to Illinois.

Comments: This is one of 17 Vetches in our range.
They are mostly climbing plants with
compound leaves ending in tendrils.
Used as cover crops, they frequently
escape from cultivation. Another
species is American Vetch
(*V. americana*), a native species with
blue-purple flowers in loose axillary
clusters and toothed stipules.

532 Hairy Vetch
(*Vicia villosa*)
Pea Family (Fabaceae)

Description: A climbing plant with *spreading hairs on
the stem* and long-stalked, one-sided
clusters of many violet and white, pea-
like flowers.
Flowers: about ⅔″ (1.6 cm) long.
Leaves: pinnately compound, with
5–10 pairs of narrowly oblong to linear
leaflets ½–1″ (1.3–2.5 cm) long.
Tendrils present at ends of leaves.
Height: vine, to 3′ (90 cm) long.

Flowering: May–October.

Habitat: Fields, thickets.

Range: Throughout.

Comments: This plant is widely cultivated for
fodder and often escapes from
cultivation. It differs from the similar
Cow Vetch (*V. cracca*) in the hairiness
of the stem and in its larger flowers.

GENTIAN FAMILY (Gentianaceae)

Leafy herbs commonly with showy bell or trumpet-shaped flowers blooming in a branched cluster.

Flowers: radially symmetrical; sepals 4 or 5, free or united; petals 5, united; stamens as many as petals. All these parts attached at base of ovary.

Leaves: simple, opposite.

Fruit: usually a capsule, rarely a berry. There are about 70 genera and 1,100 species, found in many different habitats in temperate and subtropical regions. Some gentians are cultivated as ornamentals.

---

522 Seaside Gentian: Catchfly Gentian
(*Eustoma exaltatum*)
Gentian Family (Gentianaceae)

Description: Conspicuous lavender or purple, cup-shaped flowers are solitary or in few-flowered terminal clusters.
Flowers: about 1½" (3.8 cm) across; petals united at the base into a short tube and flare out into 5 long, wide lobes.
Leaves: up to 3" (7.5 cm) long; opposite, oblong, covered with a whitish bloom, stalkless, clasp the stem.
Height: 1–3' (30–90 cm).

Flowering: Throughout the year, principally in May–October.

Habitat: Sandy coastal areas, saline to fresh marshes.

Range: Florida west to Louisiana and Texas.

Comments: The generic name is from the Greek *eu* ("good") and *stoma* ("mouth") and refers to the wide opening into the corolla tube.

617 Fringed Gentian
(*Gentiana crinita*)
Gentian Family (Gentianaceae)

Description: A single, *blue, fringed flower,* opening in the sun and closing at night, is at the end of each erect stem of a branching plant.
Flowers: 2″ (5 cm) long; tubular, with *4 flaring petals;* calyx 4-sided, the lobes unequal and pointed, united below.
Leaves: 1–2″ (2.5–5 cm) long; opposite, ovate to lanceolate, rounded at base, pointed at tip.
Height: 1–3′ (30–90 cm), the shorter height more common.

Flowering: Late August–November.

Habitat: Wet thickets and meadows; seepage banks.

Range: Central Maine; south to Georgia; north to Ohio, Indiana, northern Iowa, and Manitoba.

Comments: One of the most beautiful of the gentians, with its delicately fringed petals and striking blue color, it is becoming rare and *must not be picked.* It is a biennial, and along with the other gentians, is among the last wildflowers to bloom in the late summer and fall. The Smaller Fringed Gentian (*G. procera*) is similar but has narrow leaves, a shorter fringe, and is only 6–18″ (15–45 cm) high. It occurs in midwestern, boggy prairies and limy areas. Both the common and generic names of this group come from that of King Gentius of Illyria, who, according to the Ancient Roman naturalist Pliny, discovered the medicinal qualities of the roots for use as an emetic, cathartic, and tonic.

650 Closed Gentian; Bottle Gentian
(*Gentiana andrewsii*)
Gentian Family (Gentianaceae)

Description: Dark blue, *bottle-like, cylindrical flowers nearly closed at the tips,* are in tight clusters at the top of the stem and sometimes in the axils of the upper leaves.
Flowers: 1–1½" (2.5–3.8 cm) long; whitish plaits (or bands) between the 5 corolla lobes are slightly longer than petals and fringed; corolla whitish at base.
Leaves: up to 4" (10 cm) long; ovate or lanceolate, in a whorl below flower cluster, opposite below.
Height: 1–2' (30–60 cm).
Flowering: August–October.
Habitat: Moist thickets and meadows.
Range: Vermont, Massachusetts; south to Georgia; west to Arkansas; north to Saskatchewan and Ontario.
Comments: This is one of our most common perennial gentians and the easiest to grow in a moist wildflower garden. Other bottle gentians include a very similar species, Blind Gentian (*G. clausa*), in which the plaits are not longer than the petal lobes. The Narrow-leaved Gentian (*G. linearis*), which occurs chiefly in the North and in the mountains as far south as West Virginia, has very narrow leaves and opened flowers. The flowers of Soapwort Gentian (*G. saponaria*) are light blue and slightly open at the tip. This midwestern species has soapy juice. The Stiff Gentian (*G. quinquefolia*), an annual, has light blue or lilac opened flowers with bristle-pointed lobes and a four-sided stem. It occurs from southwest Maine south to Florida and from southern Ontario to southern Tennessee, Louisiana, and Missouri.

81 Floating Hearts
(*Nymphoides aquatica*)
Gentian Family (Gentianaceae)

Description: A water-lily-like plant with *floating, heart-shaped leaves* on long stalks, with a flat-topped cluster of small, white flowers rising just below the leaf blade.
Flowers: ½–¾″ (1.3–2 cm) wide; 5 nearly separate petals.
Leaves: 2–8″ (5–20 cm) long; thick, green above, very veiny beneath.
Height: aquatic.

Flowering: July–September.

Habitat: Ponds and slow streams, in the coastal plain.

Range: Southern New Jersey to Florida; west to Texas.

Comments: The genus name refers to the plant's resemblance to the Water-lily genus *Nymphaea*. However, its clusters of small, white flowers with only 5 petals make it quite different from the single, many-petalled Water-lilies. Another Floating Hearts (*N. cordata*), with smaller, green leaves mottled with purple above and smooth beneath, occurs from Newfoundland to Florida, west to Louisiana, and north to Ontario. An introduced, yellow-flowered species is established in the South. It has also been found in the Hudson River Valley of New York, in Missouri, and Rhode Island.

172 Pennywort
(*Obolaria virginica*)
Gentian Family (Gentianaceae)

Description: A low, fleshy plant with dull white or purplish flowers, usually in groups of 3 in the axils of *purplish, bract-like upper leaves* and at the top of the stem.
Flowers: about ½″ (1.3 cm) long; petals 4, united to the middle; sepals 2, spatulate.
Leaves: those under the flowers ½″

(1.3 cm) long, opposite, thick, round or wedge-shaped; lower leaves reduced to small scales.
Height: 3–6″ (8–15 cm).

Flowering: March–May.

Habitat: Moist hardwoods and thickets.

Range: New Jersey and Pennsylvania south to Florida; west to Texas; north to Illinois, Indiana, Ohio, and West Virginia.

Comments: The genus name comes from the Greek *obolos* (a small coin) and relates to the paired, roundish leaves of this low, southern woodland perennial. The common name also reflects the coin-like appearance.

473   Salt-marsh Pink
(Sabatia stellaris)
Gentian Family (Gentianaceae)

Description: Wheel-shaped, *pink flowers with yellowish, star-shaped centers* edged with red are at the ends of the branching stems.
Flowers: ¾–1½″ (2–3.8 cm) wide; sepals long and narrow, edged with red, *shorter than the petals;* stamens yellow; style twisted and divided to below the middle.
Leaves: 1½″ (3.8 cm) long; light green, opposite, linear to narrowly lanceolate.
Fruit: small capsule.
Height: 6–18″ (15–45 cm).

Flowering: July–October.

Habitat: Saline or brackish marshes and meadows.

Range: Coastal; southeastern Massachusetts south to Florida; west to Alabama and Louisiana.

Comments: This showy, annual or biennial salt marsh species is easily recognized by its yellow center. Two other marsh species are the Slender Marsh Pink (*S. campanulata*), found on damp sands and peat in the coastal plain from Massachusetts south to Florida and Louisiana and in the southern

Appalachians, with linear leaves and sepals, the latter as long as the petals; and the Large Marsh Pink (*S. dodecandra*), which grows from 1–2′ (30–60 cm) high and has flowers 1½–2½″ (3.8–6.3 cm) wide. It occurs along the coast from Connecticut to Florida and Louisiana. A more southern and midwestern species, Rose Pink (*S. angularis*), has a 4-angled stem and numerous, opposite, flowering branches.

GERANIUM FAMILY
(Geraniaceae)

Leafy herbs with showy white, pink, or
purple flowers in clusters.
Flowers: usually radially symmetrical;
sepals 5, free or slightly united at base;
petals 5, free; stamens 5, 10, or 15,
with stalks sometimes united at base.
Leaves: alternate or opposite, simple,
pinnately or palmately lobed, or
compound.
Fruit: develops from a long-beaked
pistil with 5 united chambers at its
base, each chamber with a long style
attached to the central core and coiling
away from it at maturity, thus lifting
the chambers of the ovary upward and
aiding in the dispersal of seeds.
There are about 11 genera and nearly
800 species, many frequent in the north
temperate zone. The cultivated
geranium is *Pelargonium,* a tropical
genus especially well developed in
South Africa.

---

462 Storksbill; Alfilaria
(*Erodium cicutarium*)
Geranium Family (Geraniaceae)

Description: *Umbel-like clusters* of 6–9 small, rose-
purple flowers are on long stalks rising
from the axil of *fern-like leaves.*
Flowers: about ½" (1.3 cm) wide;
petals 5; fertile stamens 5; and sterile
stamens 5.
Leaves: mostly in a basal, overwintering
rosette, doubly pinnately cut into ovate
or oblong leaflets up to 1" (2.5 cm)
long.
Fruit: 5-parted, *beaked capsule,* the parts
of the beak separated from each other
and twisted when dry.
Height: 6–12" (15–30 cm).
Flowering: April–October.
Habitat: Disturbed areas, roadsides, fields.
Range: Quebec, Nova Scotia, and New

England; south to Georgia; west to Arkansas and Texas; north to Michigan, and Illinois.

Comments: This plant was introduced from the Mediterranean region. It is quite different from the Cranesbill Geraniums with palmately-lobed leaves; the only similarity is the long, bill-like capsules, hence the common name. The rarer Musk Storksbill (*E. moschatum*), has also been introduced from Europe. It has much coarser foliage.

---

466 **Wild Geranium**
(*Geranium maculatum*)
Geranium Family (Geraniaceae)

Description: Lavender flowers are in loose clusters of 2–5 at the ends of branches above a pair of *deeply 5-lobed leaves.*
Flowers: 1–1½″ (2.5–3.8 cm) wide; sepals 5, pointed; petals 5, rounded, separate; stamens 10; pistil 1.
Leaves: 4–5″ (10–12.5 cm) wide; gray-green, cut into deeply toothed lobes, the basal leaves long-stalked.
Fruit: *elongated, beaked capsule,* splitting up from the base and producing 5 upward-curving strips still united at the base.
Height: 1–2′ (30–60 cm).

Flowering: April–June.
Habitat: Woods, thickets, and meadows.
Range: Maine south to New England and Georgia; west to Tennessee, Missouri, and Kansas; north to Manitoba.
Comments: Geraniums are recognized by their palmately-lobed leaves and distinctive capsules. Bicknell's Cranesbill (*G. bicknellii*) has much smaller flowers, notched petals, and more finely cut leaves. It too is found in the Northeast and Midwest. A more southern species, the closely related Carolina Geranium (*G. carolinianum*), occurs from Florida to New England and westward to Kansas and Wyoming. It has a more

compact flower cluster. The common name Cranesbill, as well as the genus name, from the Greek *geranos* ("a crane"), relate to the bill-like capsule. A number of species are naturalized from Europe.

461 Herb Robert
(*Geranium robertianum*)
Geranium Family (Geraniaceae)

Description: *Paired, pink to lavender flowers* on stalks arising in the axils of *ornamentally cut leaves* on hairy, reddish, branching stems.
Flowers: ½" (1.3 cm) wide; petals 5.
Leaves: up to 3" (7.5 cm) wide; palmately divided into 3–5 lobed or toothed segments, dark green or with a ruddy tinge; a strong odor when crushed.
Fruit: long-beaked capsule.
Height: 1–2' (30–60 cm).
Flowering: May–October.
Habitat: Rocky woods, ravines.
Range: Newfoundland and Nova Scotia; south from New England to Maryland; west to West Virginia, Ohio, Indiana, and Illinois; north to Manitoba.
Comments: This European and native North American species is an especially attractive member of the Geranium family, but it has a disagreeable odor. It is variously reported to have been named for St. Robert of Molesme, whose festival date in April occurs at about the time the flowers bloom in Europe, or for Robert Goodfellow known as Robin Hood.

WITCH HAZEL FAMILY
(Hamamelidaceae)

Shrubs and trees with small flowers in
head-like or spike-like clusters.
Flowers: radially or bilaterally
symmetrical; bisexual or unisexual;
with a tubular base bearing 4–5 sepals,
4–5 petals, and 4 to many stamens;
ovary imbedded in the base.
Leaves: usually alternate, simple or
palmately lobed, often toothed.
Fruit: woody capsule.
There are about 23 genera and 100
species, found in subtropical and warm
temperate regions of North America,
Asia, and South Africa. They are often
planted as ornamentals.

359 Witch Hazel
(*Hamamelis virginiana*)
Witch Hazel Family (Hamamelidaceae)

Description: Tall, autumn-flowering shrub with
clusters of *spidery, yellow flowers* in the
leaf axils or on naked branches from
which the leaves have fallen. Twigs
smooth, zigzag; buds hairy.
Flowers: about ¾″ (2 cm) long; petals
4, very narrow and elongated,
crumpled.
Leaves: 3–6″ (7.5–15 cm) long;
unequal at base, with wavy margins.
Fruit: 2-chambered, ovoid capsule
about ½″ (1.3 cm) long.
Height: 10–15′ (3–4.5 m).

Flowering: September–November.

Habitat: Dry or moist woods.

Range: Nova Scotia and New England south to
Georgia; west to Tennessee, Missouri,
and Minnesota.

Comments: The appearance of the yellow flowers in
autumn makes this shrub unique. The
petals have the ability to curl back into
a bud when the temperature drops and
to expand again when it gets warmer.
When the fruit capsule opens, the seeds

are expelled explosively for a distance of 15–20' (4.5–6 m). The bark and the leaves have long been used as a topical astringent, and the branches are sometimes used by dowsers for locating water. A similar species, Vernal Witch Hazel (*H. vernalis*), flowers in the late winter or early spring, from January to April. It has densely hairy twigs and coppery, fragrant flowers and is found on wet shores in the south-central United States.

WATERLEAF FAMILY
(Hydrophyllaceae)

Usually herbs, rarely shrubs, often bristly or glandular, with flowers often arranged along one side of the branches or at the tip of the stem in coils like fiddlenecks.

Flowers: radially symmetrical; sepals 5, united; corolla has 5 united petals, varying from nearly flat to bell- or funnel-shaped; stamens 5, often protruding. All these parts attached at base of ovary.

Leaves: simple or pinnately compound, alternate or opposite, often in basal rosettes.

Fruit: capsule.

There are about 20 genera and 270 species, nearly worldwide; the western United States is the main center of diversity.

---

166 Virginia Waterleaf
(*Hydrophyllum virginianum*)
Waterleaf Family (Hydrophyllaceae)

Description: Clusters of white or dark violet flowers are on long stalks arising in the leaf axils and extending above the leaves.
Flowers: ¼–½" (6–13 mm) long; corolla 5 parted, *bell-shaped;* stamens 5, with *hairy filaments extending beyond the petals.*
Leaves: 2–5" (5–12.5 cm) long; often *mottled, pinnately divided,* with 5–7 lanceolate or ovate, *sharply toothed leaflets.*
Height: 1–2½' (30–75 cm).

Flowering: May–August.

Habitat: Moist woods, clearings.

Range: Manitoba to Quebec and western New England; south to North Carolina; west to Tennessee, northern Arkansas, and eastern Kansas.

Comments: This woodland perennial with the water-stained appearance of the leaves (suggesting its common name) is one of several in this genus with tubular flowers and protruding stamens. Large-leaved Waterleaf (*H. macrophyllum*), a southern and midwestern species, is rough and hairy. Broad-leaved Waterleaf (*H. canadense*) has flower stalks shorter than its maple-like leaves and occurs from western New England to northern Alabama and Missouri. The flowers of both these species are white, but the Appendaged Waterleaf (*H. appendiculatum*) has showier lavender flowers and leaves that are lobed but not as deeply cut as those of Virginia Waterleaf. Its range is from Ontario and Minnesota south to Pennsylvania, Tennessee, Missouri, and Eastern Kansas.

---

643 Fringed Phacelia
(*Phacelia fimbriata*)
Waterleaf Family (Hydrophyllaceae)

Description: A branching plant with *one-sided, coiled clusters* of light blue, lavender, or white flowers with *deeply fringed petals.*
Flowers: ½" (1.3 cm) wide; corolla somewhat bell-shaped, with 5 *spreading, fringed lobes.*
Leaves: about 2" (5 cm) long; pinnately cut into 5–11 triangular-to-oblong lobes; the upper leaves unstalked, lower ones stalked.
Height: 8–16" (20–40 cm).
Flowering: May–June.
Habitat: Upland woods.
Range: Virginia to Alabama.
Comments: The strikingly fringed petals, especially beautiful under a hand lens, characterize this spring wildflower of the Great Smoky Mountains, where it can occur in abundance.

ST. JOHNSWORT FAMILY
(Hypericaceae)

Leafy herbs or shrubs, usually with
yellow or orange flowers in branched
clusters.
Flowers: radially symmetrical; sepals 5,
separate; petals 5, separate; stamens
numerous, usually united into several
bunches by the bases of the stalks. All
these parts attached at base of ovary.
Leaves: simple, opposite or whorled,
with numerous, often black or
translucent dots.
Fruit: usually a capsule, sometimes a
berry.
There are 8 genera and about 400
species, distributed in temperate and
tropical regions. Some are grown as
ornamentals.

361 Kalm's St. Johnswort
(*Hypericum kalmianum*)
St. Johnswort Family (Hypericaceae)

Description: A *low shrub* with bright yellow flowers
in small clusters at the ends of 4-sided
branches. The bark is papery and peels
when older.
Flowers: ¾–1½″ (2–3.8 cm) wide;
sepals 5; petals 5; stamens numerous;
styles 5.
Leaves: about 2″ (5 cm) long; opposite,
linear to oblong, with translucent dots
beneath, visible when held up to light.
*Clusters of tiny leaves present in axils of
larger leaves.*
Fruit: narrowly ovoid, brown capsule.
Height: 2–3′ (60–90 cm).

Flowering: July–August.

Habitat: Rocky or sandy soil.

Range: Western Ontario and Quebec south to
western New York, Ohio, Indiana, and
Illinois; shores of Great Lakes.

Comments: This is one of several shrubby St.
Johnsworts with yellow flowers and

small axillary clusters of leaves. The species and common names honor Peter Kalm, a student of Linnaeus, who discovered the plant in America around 1750. The range of the other shrubby species extends farther south. The Shrubby St. Johnswort (*H. prolificum*), a coarse plant reaching 4' (1.2 m) in height, is found from Ontario, south to Georgia and west to Alabama, Arkansas, and Minnesota. Golden St. Johnswort (*H. frondosum*) occurs on limestone sites from South Carolina to Alabama and west to Texas, Kentucky, and Indiana. Dense St. Johnswort (*H. densiflorum*) has narrow leaves and is found on acid soils from New Jersey south to Florida and west to Texas, Missouri, Indiana, and West Virginia. Naked St. Johnswort (*H. nudiflorum*) is a southern species, occurring from Virginia and Tennessee to Florida and Texas, and has no leaves on the flower stalk and no axillary clusters of leaves. Still other species are found in the South.

352 Common St. Johnswort
(*Hypericum perforatum*)
St. Johnswort Family (Hypericaceae)

Description: An herb with bright yellow flowers in broad, branched, terminal clusters.
Flowers: ¾–1" (2–2.5 cm) wide; *petals* 5, with *black dots on margins*; stamens numerous, in 3 sets; styles 3.
Leaves: 1–2" (2.5–5 cm) long; opposite, elliptic, numerous, and small, with *translucent dots*.
Fruit: ovoid, brown capsule.
Height: 1–2½' (30–75 cm).
Flowering: June–September.
Habitat: Fields, roadsides, waste places.
Range: Throughout.
Comments: The common name derives from the fact that the flowers are said to bloom on St. John's Eve, June 24. Introduced

from Europe, this highly branched perennial is the most common St. Johnswort and is easily recognized by the tiny translucent dots that can be seen when the leaves are held up to the light. A large-flowered member of this group is the Great St. Johnswort (*H. pyramidatum*), with showy flowers 1–2″ (2.5–5 cm) across, 5 styles, and elliptic leaves. It is 2–6′ (60–180 cm) in height and is found in wet meadows and thickets from New England south to Maryland and west to Kansas. Several smaller-flowered wetland species include Dwarf St. Johnswort (*H. mutilum*), a diffusely branched plant with flowers ⅕″ (5 mm) wide and oblong leaves; and Canada St. Johnswort (*H. canadense*), with flowers ⅕″ (5 mm) wide and linear leaves. Both of these species are found throughout our range. Pale St. Johnswort (*H. ellipticum*) is a more northern species and occurs from southern Canada as far south as Maryland and west to North Dakota. Its flowers are ½″ (1.3 cm) wide, borne on an unbranched stem, and the leaves are oval-elliptic.

268 Pineweed

(*Hypericum gentianoides*)
St. Johnswort Family (Hypericaceae)

Description: Small, yellow, nearly stemless flowers are on the *wiry, ascending branches* of this bushy plant.
Flowers: ⅛–¼″ (3–6 mm) wide; sepals 5; petals 5.
Leaves: up to ⅕″ (5 mm) long; *scale-like,* appressed to stems.
Fruit: lance- or awl-shaped capsule, usually red.
Height: 4–20″ (10–50 cm).

Flowering: July–October.
Habitat: Sandy or rocky, sunny areas.
Range: Southern Ontario, Maine, New

Hampshire, and Vermont; south to
Florida; west to Texas; north to
Wisconsin and Indiana.

Comments: With its tiny flowers and scaly leaves
on erect, wiry branches, this annual is
unlike most St. Johnsworts. It is
typical of sterile, bare, open sites,
where its flowers open only in the sun.
The similar Nits-and-Lice
(*H. drumondii*) has fewer branches,
a broad oval capsule, and larger leaves
½–1″ (1.3–2.5 cm) in length. It
occurs from Maryland to Florida, west
to Texas, north to Iowa, southern
Illinois, and West Virginia.

351 St. Peterswort
(*Hypericum stans*)
St. Johnswort Family (Hypericaceae)

Description: An *erect shrub* with lemon-yellow
flowers at the tips of the branches.
Flowers: 1″ (2.5 cm) wide; *petals 4;
sepals 4 and unequal,* the 2 outer, larger
ones enclosing the 2 much narrower
ones; styles 3 or 4; stamens numerous.
Leaves: ⅔–1½″ (1.6–3.8 cm) long;
opposite, elliptic, partly clasping stem.
Height: 1–3′ (30–90 cm).
Flowering: July–September.
Habitat: Sandy sites, pine barrens.
Range: New York south to Florida; west to
Texas; north to Kansas and Kentucky.
Comments: This shrubby member of the St.
Johnswort family has only 4 petals
instead of the usual 5, and the sepals
are of very unequal sizes. St. Andrew's
Cross (*H. hypericoides*) is similar, with
2 styles, the inner sepals minute or
absent, and narrower leaves. It is found
on sandy sites from Massachusetts south
to Florida. In the north it may form a
mat on the ground. Low St. Andrew's
Cross (*H. suffruticosum*) is a plant only
2½–6″ (6.3–15 cm) tall, with the
calyx on short stalks, nodding after
flowering. It is found in the Coastal

Plain sands from southern South
Carolina to Florida and Mississippi.

472 Marsh St. Johnswort
(*Hypericum virginicum*)
St. Johnswort Family (Hypericaceae)

Description: A *marsh herb* with *pink flowers* clustered
at the top of the leafy stem and in the
axils of the paired leaves.
Flowers: ½–¾" (1.3–2 cm) wide;
sepals 5, often purple-red; petals 5;
3 groups of 3 stamens, alternate, with
3 large, orange glands.
Leaves: 1–2½" (2.5–6.3 cm) long;
opposite, ovate, light green, stalkless,
heart-shaped at base, dotted with
translucent glands.
Height: 8–24" (20–60 cm).

Flowering: July–August.

Habitat: Wet sandy areas, swamps, and bogs.

Range: Coastal, from Nova Scotia to southern
New England and New York; south to
Florida; local in Ohio, Indiana, and
Illinois, along Great Lakes.

Comments: This wetland perennial differs in flower
color from most of the St. Johnsworts,
which are yellow. It and other St.
Johnsworts with similar stamen
arrangments are placed by some in the
genus *Triadenum*. The name derives
from *tri* ("three") and *aden* ("gland")
and refers to the three central glands.
The related Marsh St. Johnswort
(*H. tubulosum*), found only as far north
as southeast Virginia, southern Indiana,
and Missouri, has the base of the leaves
rounded or tapered, not heart-shaped.

IRIS FAMILY (Iridaceae)

Herbs growing from rhizomes, bulbs, or corms, with narrow basal leaves and showy clusters at the tips of long stalks.
Flowers: usually radially symmetrical; calyx has 3 petal-like sepals; corolla has 3 petals; stamens 3. All these parts attached at top of ovary.
Leaves: simple, alternate, folded and overlapping one another at the base and aligned in two rows.
Fruit: capsule.
There are about 60 genera and 1,500 species, distributed in temperate and tropical regions. Among them, Iris, Freesia, Gladiolus, Bugle Lily, and Montbretia are popular ornamentals. Saffron dye is obtained from Crocus, and "essence of violets," used in perfumes, is extracted from the rhizomes of Iris.

369 Blackberry Lily
(*Belamcanda chinensis*)
Iris Family (Iridaceae)

Description: Leafless flower stalks with several red-spotted, orange, *lily-like flowers* that grow from among *narrow, flat, sword-like leaves.*
Flowers: 1½–2″ (3.8–5 cm) wide; 6 widely spreading petaloid parts, lasting only 1 day.
Leaves: 12–18″ (30–45 cm) long, about 1″ (2.5 cm) wide.
Fruit: capsule that splits open to reveal a shiny, black, berry-like seed mass.
Height: 1½–4′ (45–120 cm).
Flowering: June–July.
Habitat: Roadsides, open woods.
Range: Connecticut south to Georgia; west to Texas; north to Nebraska.
Comments: This handsome Chinese introduction has escaped from cultivation. Several flowers usually bloom at one time. The blackberry-like seed cluster, which is

seen when the capsule breaks open, accounts for the common name.

619 Crested Dwarf Iris
(Iris cristata)
Iris Family (Iridaceae)

Description: *A single, violet-blue flower* (occasionally 2), with 6 spreading petaloid parts, is at the top of a short, slender stalk.
Flowers: about 2½″ (6.3 cm) wide; 3 broad, down-curved petal-like sepals and 3 narrower, arching petals. *Sepals "bearded"*—crested with yellow or white ridges, streaked with purple; styles 3, curving over the sepals, 2-lobed; stamens 3, hidden under the styles.
Leaves: 4–7″ (10–17.5 cm) at flowering time, longer later, ½–1″ (1.3–2.5 cm) wide; flat, lanceolate, sheath the stem.
Fruit: sharply 3-sided capsule.
Height: 4–9″ (10–22.5 cm).
Flowering: April–May.
Habitat: Wooded hillsides and ravines.
Range: Maryland south to Georgia; west to Mississippi, Arkansas, Oklahoma, Missouri, and Indiana.
Comments: This is a low, bearded Iris of southern and midwestern wooded uplands. The Dwarf Iris (*I. verna*) is very fragrant, has non-bearded sepals, narrower leaves less than ½″ (1.3 cm) wide, and occurs on peaty soils and pine barrens from Maryland southward.

385 Red Iris
(Iris fulva)
Iris Family (Iridaceae)

Description: Showy, *reddish-brown flowers with 6 widely spreading petaloid parts,* are on a slender stalk taller than the sword-like leaves.
Flowers: about 3″ (7.5 cm) wide; sepals

3, recurved, non-bearded, petal-like; petals 3, narrower, recurved; stamens 3, hidden under 3 petal-like, arching styles.

Leaves: to 3' (90 cm) long, about ½" (1.3 cm) wide; form a basal cluster.

Fruit: 6-sided capsule about 2" (5 cm) long.

Height: 2–5' (60–150 cm).

Flowering: May–June.

Habitat: Wet grasslands or swamp margins.

Range: Southwest Illinois south to Alabama and Louisiana; north to Missouri.

Comments: This beautiful southern Iris of wet sloughs and swampy woods is distinctively flat-topped compared to other Irises. It can be cultivated in moist wildflower gardens.

314 Yellow Flag

(*Iris pseudacorus*)
Iris Family (Iridaceae)

Description: *One to several yellow flowers,* on a robust stalk, often overtopped by the long, stiff, sword-like leaves; often found in clumps.

Flowers: 3" (7.5 cm) wide; sepals 3, backward-curving, non-bearded; petals 3, smaller, narrow, upright; styles 3, arching over sepals, with 3 stamens beneath.

Leaves: to 3' (90 cm) tall; arising from a basal cluster and often taller than the stem.

Fruit: 6-angled, oblong capsule, about 2" (5 cm) long.

Height: 2–3' (60–90 cm).

Flowering: June–August.

Habitat: Marshes, stream margins.

Range: Newfoundland and Minnesota southward, widely established.

Comments: This is a showy species. It was introduced from Europe and escaped from cultivation.

620 Blue Flag
(*Iris versicolor*)
Iris Family (Iridaceae)

Description: Several violet-blue flowers with attractively veined and *yellow-based sepals* are on a sturdy stalk among tall sword-like leaves that rise from a basal cluster.
Flowers: 2½–4" (6.3–10 cm) wide; sepals 3, non-bearded; petals 3, narrower, erect; styles 3, 2-lobed, arching over sepals; stamens 3, hidden under styles.
Leaves: 8–32" (20–80 cm) long, ½–1" (1.3–2.5 cm) wide; pale green to grayish.
Fruit: bluntly 3-lobed, erect capsule.
Height: 2–3' (60–90 cm).

Flowering: May–August.

Habitat: Swamps, marshes, wet shores.

Range: Manitoba to Nova Scotia; south through New England to Virginia; west to western Pennsylvania, Ohio, Michigan, Wisconsin, and Minnesota.

Comments: This is a showy native Iris of northeastern wetlands. Insects attracted to the sepals must crawl under the tip of a style and brush past a stigma and stamen, thus facilitating pollination. The rhizome is extremely poisonous, but it was dried and used in small amounts as a cathartic and diuretic by Indians and colonists. A similar southern wetland species, occurring from Virginia to Florida and Texas, is Southern Blue Flag (*I. virginica*). It is a smaller plant, to 2' (60 cm) tall, with bright green leaves that often lie on the ground or water. A coastal, brackish-water species, Slender Blue Flag (*I. prismatica*) has extremely narrow, grass-like leaves that are less than ¼" (6 mm) wide; it occurs from Maine to Georgia and Tennessee. The name "Flag" is from the middle English *flagge*, "rush" or "reed."

615 **Pinewoods Lily**
(*Nemastylis purpurea*)
Iris Family (Iridaceae)

Description: From a black, scaly bulb rise long,
narrow leaves and a tall floral stalk wit
light to deep purplish-blue, flat or cup
shaped flowers.
Flowers: 1–2″ (2.5–5 cm) wide; 6
colored parts, the outer ones (sepals)
purplish, the inner parts (petals)
smaller, cupped or crimped, and
mottled with brown; *style divided into
6 long branches,* projecting in pairs
sideways between the stamens.
Leaves: 1–2′ (30–60 cm) long; linear
to lanceolate.
Height: 1–2½′ (30–75 cm).
Flowering: May–June.
Habitat: Pinewoods.
Range: Louisiana, Texas.
Comments: A new flower opens each day and
remains open for only a few hours in
the morning. The pairs of thread-like
styles are reflected in the generic name,
from the Greek for "thread."

594 **Pointed Blue-eyed Grass**
(*Sisyrinchium angustifolium*)
Iris Family (Iridaceae)

Description: Small blue or violet-blue flowers with
yellow centers are at the top of a long,
flat, *twisted stalk* that is usually
branched.
Flowers: ½″ (1.3 cm) wide; petals 3;
sepals 3, petal-like, each tipped with
a thorn-like point.
Leaves: 4–20″ (10–50 cm) long, less
than ¼″ (6 mm) wide; basal, linear and
grass-like, may be shorter or longer than
the floral stalk.
Height: 4–20″ (10–50 cm).
Flowering: May–July.
Habitat: Meadows, low woods, shores.
Range: Throughout.
Comments: Although the plant is small and has

grass-like leaves, the flowers have all the features of the Iris family. The various species are all much alike and separation is based on such characteristics as branching pattern and leaf length. Common Blue-eyed Grass (*S. montanum*) is also a widespread species, with slightly wider leaves, over ¼″ (6 mm), and unbranched stalks.

RUSH FAMILY (Juncaceae)

Herbs, rarely shrubs, with mostly grass-like leaves, usually in a basal tuft and small greenish or brownish flowers in dense spikes or heads or sometimes in loose clusters or even solitary.
Flowers: 3 sepals like the 3 petals, scale-like; stamens 3 or 6. All these parts attached at base of ovary.
Leaves: narrow, cylindric to flat, with bases sheathing the stem; in some, blades absent.
Fruit: capsule.
There are 8 genera and about 300 species, in temperate and cold regions but most abundant in the mountains of South America. Their floral structure closely resembles that of the Lilies.

395 Soft Rush
(*Juncus effusus*)
Rush Family (Juncaceae)

Description:	The soft, grass-like stems of this strict wetland plant are in clumps and each bears clusters of very small, greenish-brown, scaly flowers, the clusters diverging from one point on the side of the stalk near the top.

Flowers: about ⅛" (4 mm) long; sepals 3; petals 3; and stamens 3.
Leaves: lacking or represented only by spear-like basal sheaths up to 6" (15 cm) long.
Height: 1½–4' (45–120 cm).

Flowering: July–September.
Habitat: Swamps, damp open ground.
Range: Throughout.
Comments: This common marsh plant is one of many rushes, most of which are found in wet soil or water. Muskrats feed on the rootstalks, and birds find shelter among the stems.

397 Wood Rush
(*Luzula multiflora*)
Rush Family (Juncaceae)

Description: At the top of *densely tufted stems* are
4–12 spike-like or head-like clusters of
many tiny, brownish flowers enclosed
in shiny bractlets, the whole cluster
also subtended by leaf-like bracts.
Flowers: about ⅛" (3 mm) long;
clusters about ⅓" (8 mm) long; sepals
3; petals 3; stamens 6; pistil 1, with
3 stigmas.
Leaves: 3–5" (7.5–12.5 cm) long;
mostly basal, grass-like, pale green,
fringed with web-like, marginal hairs.
Height: 6–16" (15–40 cm).

Flowering: April–July.

Habitat: Fields, open woods.

Range: Across Canada; south to Virginia; west
to Kentucky; north to Wisconsin and
Minnesota.

Comments: In spite of the resemblance of rushes to
grasses or sedges, they have the same
number and arrangement of floral parts
as the Lilies.

MINT FAMILY (Lamiaceae)

Aromatic herbs or shrubs, rarely trees
or vines, usually with stems square in
cross-section, and flowers in long
clusters, heads, or interrupted whorls
on the stem.
Flowers: bilaterally symmetrical; 5
united sepals; 5 united petals, usually
arranged so as to form an upper and
often lower lip; stamens 2 or 4. All
these parts attached at base of ovary.
Leaves: usually simple, opposite, or
whorled.
Fruit: lobes 4, each forming a hard,
single-seeded nutlet; rarely stone-fruit.
There are about 180 genera and 3,500
species nearly worldwide. The
Mediterranean region, the chief area of
diversity, has produced many spices an
flavorings; various mints, oregano,
marjoram, thyme, sage, and basil.
Catnip and lavender are in the family.
Several genera, including *Coleus,* are
popular ornamentals.

329 Horse Balm
(*Collinsonia canadensis*)
Mint Family (Lamiaceae)

Description: The stout, square stem has *loose,*
branching clusters of *lemon-scented,*
yellow flowers.
Flowers: ⅓–½" (8–13 mm) long;
corolla with 5 petals fused into 2 lips,
the lower lip long and *fringed; fertile*
stamens 2, protruding with the pistil
beyond corolla tube.
Leaves: blades 4–8" (10–20 cm) long;
opposite, ovate, sharply toothed.
Height: 2–4' (60–120 cm).
Flowering: July–September.
Habitat: Rich woods.
Range: Vermont and New York south to
Florida; west to Arkansas; north to
Wisconsin and Ontario.
Comments: A tall wildflower, typical of moist

woodlands, its foliage as well as its flowers have a citronella-like odor. Tea can be brewed from the leaves, and the underground stem (rhizome) was formerly used as a diuretic, tonic, and astringent.

648 Ground Ivy; Gill-over-the-ground
(*Glechoma hederacea*)
Mint Family (Lamiaceae)

Description: Ascending branches from a *creeping stem* have 3–7 small, blue-violet flowers whorled in the axils of *scalloped leaves*.
Flowers: ½–¾″ (1.3–2 cm) long; corolla 2-lipped, the lower lip with 3 lobes; stamens 4, not protruding or only slightly protruding.
Leaves: blades ½–1½″ (1.3–3.8 cm) long; roundish, wavy-margined, opposite.
Height: creeper, with flowering stems to 8″ (20 cm) high.

Flowering: March–July.

Habitat: Moist shaded or sunny areas, roadsides, yards.

Range: Ontario to Newfoundland; south to New England, Georgia, and Alabama; west to Missouri and Kansas.

Comments: This European introduction is considered a weed by some since it roots readily at the nodes and spreads rapidly. The name "Gill" comes from the French *guiller,* ("to ferment") because the leaves were once used to help ferment, or flavor, beer. This species is sometimes classified with the Catnip genus (*Nepeta*) but differs in having the flowers in the axils of the leaves rather than at the ends of the stems and branches.

571 Henbit
(*Lamium amplexicaule*)
Mint Family (Lamiaceae)

Description: Lavender flowers are whorled around
the square stem in the axils of
horizontally-held, scalloped leaves.
Flowers: ½–⅔″ (1.3–1.6 cm) long;
hairy, 2-lipped, upper lip concave;
stamens 4, protruding.
Leaves: ½–1½″ (1.3–3.8 cm) long;
roundish to ovate, opposite, stalkless at
the top but long-stalked below.
Height: 4–16″ (10–40 cm).

Flowering: March–November.

Habitat: Waste places, fields, roadsides.

Range: Throughout.

Comments: The genus name, from the Greek *lamios*
("thread"), refers to the straight corolla
tube between the 2 lips. The species
name is from the Latin for "clasping" or
"embracing" and describes the leaves,
while the common name implies that
the seeds of the plant are eaten by
chickens.

559 Motherwort
(*Leonurus cardiaca*)
Mint Family (Lamiaceae)

Description: Small, pale lavender *flowers are
clustered around square stem* in axils of
horizontally-held, paired, *lobed leaves.*
The several clusters together form a
long, interrupted, terminal spike.
Flowers: ½″ (1.3 cm) long and ⅓″
(8 mm) wide; sepals 5, tipped with
sharp spines; corolla 2-lipped, the
upper lip 2-lobed, *bearded,* arching over
the spreading 3-lobed lower lip;
stamens 4; leafy bracts present beneath
clusters.
Leaves: lower ones 2–4″ (5–10 cm)
long, *palmately cut into 3 lobes;* upper
ones smaller and less deeply cut.
Height: 2–4′ (60–120 cm).

Flowering: June–August.

Habitat: Waste places, roadsides, disturbed
areas.
Range: Throughout.
Comments: This introduced perennial with the
distinctly 3-lobed leaves had been used
by herb doctors as a stimulant (the
species name means "for the heart") and
traditionally for menstrual disorders,
hence the common name referring to
"mother." Horehound Motherwort
(*L. marrubiastrum*) and Siberian
Motherwort (*L. sibiricus*) are also
naturalized from Europe and found in
our range.

184 Water Horehound
(*Lycopus americanus*)
Mint Family (Lamiaceae)

Description: Tiny, white, *tubular flowers* are clustered
in dense groups around a square stem in
the axils of the paired, *deeply toothed
leaves.*
Flowers: about $\frac{1}{12}$" (2 mm) long; calyx
with 5 sharply bristle-tipped lobes;
corolla 4-lobed; stamens 2.
Leaves: 1–3" (2.5–7.5 cm) long;
lanceolate, coarsely toothed or lobed,
the lower teeth larger.
Height: 6–24" (15–60 cm).
Flowering: June–September.
Habitat: Moist sites, wetlands.
Range: Throughout.
Comments: The members of this group are non-
aromatic mints and are typical of wet
sites. The various species are
distinguished on the basis of technical
details. One of the most common is
Virginia Bugleweed (*L. virginicus*), with
blunt calyx lobes and toothed leaves;
the common name emphasizes the
flower's resemblance to a bugle. Other
species have less coarsely toothed leaves.
The generic name is from the Greek
lycos ("a wolf") and *pous* ("foot") and
refers to the fancied likeness of some
species' leaves to a wolf's footprint.

About 10 species occur in our area; most are very similar and confusing.

186, 561 Wild Mint
(Mentha arvensis)
Mint Family (Lamiaceae)

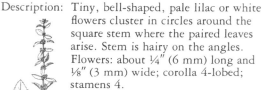

Description: Tiny, bell-shaped, pale lilac or white flowers cluster in circles around the square stem where the paired leaves arise. Stem is hairy on the angles.
Flowers: about ¼″ (6 mm) long and ⅛″ (3 mm) wide; corolla 4-lobed; stamens 4.
Leaves: 2″ (5 cm) long; smaller toward the top, ovate to lanceolate, tapering at both ends, *strongly aromatic*.
Height: 6–24″ (15–60 cm).
Flowering: July–September.
Habitat: Damp and wet places.
Range: Throughout.
Comments: One of the few native mints, these aromatic perennials have glands containing essential oils, and the leaves are used as flavorings in sauces, jellies, and beverages. The flowers of this genus, the so-called "true mints," are 4-lobed and nearly symmetrical. At least 10 mint species occur in our range, but only Wild Mint is native.

560 Peppermint
(Mentha piperita)
Mint Family (Lamiaceae)

Description: Small, lavender, whorled *flowers* are in terminal clusters, *at first crowded and ovoid, but eventually becoming cylindrical and looser*.
Flowers: about ⅕″ (5 mm) long, in clusters ½–¾″ (1.3–2 cm) wide; 4-lobed.
Leaves: 1–2½″ (2.5–6.3 cm) long; opposite, lanceolate to oblong, soft, sharply toothed.

Height: 1–3' (30–90 cm).
Flowering: June–October.
Habitat: Marshes, ditches, brooksides, wet meadows, around homes.
Range: Throughout.
Comments: This introduced Mint, considered by some taxonomists to be a hybrid of Spearmint, (*M. spicata*) and Water Mint (*M. aquatica*), both introduced from Europe. Peppermint has stalked leaves; those of Spearmint are sessile. Peppermint, with its strong odor and hot taste, is used as a tea and as a flavoring.

434 Bee Balm; Oswego Tea
(*Monarda didyma*)
Mint Family (Lamiaceae)

Description: A dense, rounded, terminal, *head-like cluster of bright red, tubular flowers* is at the summit of a square stem.
Flowers: about 1½" (3.8 cm) long; corolla 2-lipped, 5-lobed; stamens 2, projecting; stigma 2-parted. *Reddish bracts* present beneath flower cluster.
Leaves: 3–6" (7.5–15 cm) long; opposite, dark green, ovate to lanceolate, coarsely toothed.
Height: 2–5' (60–150 cm).
Flowering: June–August.
Habitat: Moist woods and thickets, especially along streams.
Range: New York south in uplands to Georgia and Tennessee; west to Michigan.
Comments: This species escaped from cultivation in the Northeast from New England to New Jersey. It is coarser than the "true mints" (*Mentha* spp.), but is very showy and frequently re-introduced to gardens. Hummingbirds are especially attracted to the red flowers. The name "Oswego Tea" comes from the fact that the leaves were used for a tea by the Oswego Indians of New York. Early settlers also used the plant for this purpose when regular tea was scarce.

511   **Wild Bergamot**
(*Monarda fistulosa*)
Mint Family (Lamiaceae)

Description: A dense, *rounded cluster* of lavender
tubular flowers is at the top of a square
stem.
Flowers: 1″ (2.5 cm) long; corolla
with hairy 2-lobed upper lip, broader
3-lobed lower lip, stamens 2,
projecting; bracts under flower cluster
often pink-tinged.
Leaves: about 2½″ (6.3 cm) long; gray-
green, opposite, lanceolate, coarsely
toothed.
Height: 2–4′ (60–120 cm).

Flowering: June–September.

Habitat: Dry fields, thickets, borders, usually
common in calcareous regions.

Range: Quebec and western New England;
south to Maryland and upland to
Georgia and Alabama; west to
Louisiana, eastern Texas, and beyond
our range.

Comments: A showy perennial, frequently in
cultivation, its aromatic leaves can be
used to make mint tea. Long ago, oil
from the leaves was used to treat
respiratory ailments. Basal Balm
(*M. clinopodia*) is also found in our
range.

537   **Plains Bee Balm**
(*Monarda pectinata*)
Mint Family (Lamiaceae)

Description: *Pink-lavender flowers* are in clusters at
the end of a square stem and also
around the stem in the axils of the
opposite leaves.
Flowers: up to ¾″ (2 cm) long;
2-lipped, with the lower lip 3-lobed
and larger than the upper; stamens 2,
not protruding. *Sharp-tipped bracts*
surround the flowers.
Leaves: 1–2½″ (2.5–6.3 cm) long;
lanceolate, toothed.

Height: 6–12″ (15–30 cm).
Flowering: June–July.
Habitat: Dry plains.
Range: Nebraska south to Texas, New Mexico, and Arizona; west to Colorado and Utah.
Comments: This attractive, western grassland species increases on disturbed ranges that are overgrazed. Several other species occur in our range, including Lemon-mint (*M. citriodora*), with pink or white flowers spotted with purple, and Spotted Horsemint (*M. punctata*), with pale yellow flowers with purple spots.

183 Catnip
(*Nepeta cataria*)
Mint Family (Lamiaceae)

Description: A hairy plant with clusters of pale white or whitish-lavender *flowers* with purplish spots, *borne terminally* on the main stem and branches.
Flowers: ½″ (1.3 cm) long; calyx hairy; corolla 2-lipped, tubular; stamens 4.
Leaves: to 2½″ (6.3 cm) long; opposite, triangular, coarsely toothed. *Stem and leaves covered with grayish down.*
Height: 1–3′ (30–90 cm).
Flowering: June–September.
Habitat: Roadsides, waste places, pastures, and barnyards.
Range: Throughout.
Comments: This well-known plant is often grown in gardens for the pleasure it gives cats. It contains a terpene-like chemical, nepeta lactone, which tends to repel insects and can therefore be used to protect other plants. It may be this chemical that affects the behavior of cats. Although introduced here from Europe, the plant may have come originally from Asia. It is easily recognized by its soft, white, downy hairs.

536 Obedient Plant; False Dragonhead
(*Physostegia virginiana*)
Mint Family (Lamiaceae)

Description: *Paired, pinkish flowers* are in a *spike-like*
cluster along the upper part of the
square stem.
Flowers: ¾–1" (2–2.5 cm) long, in
clusters 4–8" (10–20 cm) long; calyx
with 5 pointed teeth; *corolla tubular,*
2-lipped, *spotted with purple, enlarging
outward;* stamens 4.
Leaves: about 4" (10 cm) long;
opposite, smaller toward top, narrow,
lanceolate, pointed, with sharp,
incurved teeth.
Height: 1–4' (30–120 cm).
Flowering: June–September.
Habitat: Damp thickets, swamps, and prairies.
Range: New Brunswick and Quebec south to
Florida; west to Mississippi; north to
Missouri and Minnesota.
Comments: This is an attractive, snapdragon-like
plant, but its square stem is typical of
the mint family. If the flowers are bent
they tend to stay in the new position
for a while, hence the common name
"Obedient Plant." Several garden forms
occasionally escape to the wild.

646 Heal-all; Selfheal
(*Prunella vulgaris*)
Mint Family (Lamiaceae)

Description: The square stem has *dense, cylindrical,*
terminal spikes of purple flowers; the
spikes elongate after flowering.
Flowers: ½" (1.3 cm) long; corolla
2-lipped, the upper lip arched, the
lower lip drooping and fringed; stamens
4; greenish, hairy bracts present under
flowers.
Leaves: 1–3" (2.5–7.5 cm) long;
variable, lanceolate to ovate, smooth or
obscurely toothed, opposite.
Height: 6–12" (15–30 cm), sometimes
sprawling.

Flowering: May–September.
Habitat: Gardens, fields, roadsides.
Range: Throughout.
Comments: This low, introduced perennial is easily
recognized by its erect, many-flowered
spikes and associated, overlapping,
hairy bracts. It is often considered a
weed of lawns and moist shady spots. A
form that flowers when only 2″ (5 cm)
tall has become common in lawns. Its
common name derives from wide use as
a herbal remedy for throat ailments.

185 Hoary Mountain Mint
(*Pycnanthemum incanum*)
Mint Family (Lamiaceae)

Description: The small, white to lavender flowers are
in dense, rounded clusters in the leaf
axils or terminal on the hairy, square
stem and branches; *hoary bracts* are
underneath the flowers.
Flowers: about ⅓″ (8 mm) long, in
clusters up to 1½″ (3.8 cm) wide;
2-lipped, the lower lip spotted with
purple; calyx hairy.
Leaves: 1½–4″ (3.8–10 cm) long;
opposite, lanceolate-ovate, toothed,
stalked, white beneath.
Height: 1–3′ (30–90 cm).
Flowering: July–September.
Habitat: Woods and thickets.
Range: Maine south to northern Florida; west
to Tennessee, Louisiana, and eastern
Texas; north to Michigan.
Comments: The genus name derives from the Greek
for "dense" and "flower" and aptly
describes the crowded flower heads. The
many species are closely related and
difficult to distinguish from one
another. A similar species, Hoary
Mountain Mint (*P. muticum*), has denser
heads of flowers only about ½″ (1.3 cm)
wide. The upper bracts are not
especially whitened. The plants,
particularly the heads, have a very
strong spearmint odor when crushed.

635 Blue Salvia
(*Salvia azurea*)
Mint Family (Lamiaceae)

Description: A tall, delicate plant with *large,*
2-lipped, blue flowers whorled around the
square stem and forming a terminal
spike-like cluster.
Flowers: ⅔–1" (1.6–2.5 cm) long;
corolla glandular and hairy on the
outside, lower lip much larger than
upper lip; stamens 2.
Leaves: up to 4" (10 cm) long; linear to
lanceolate, opposite; basal leaves
absent.
Height: 2–5' (60–150 cm).
Flowering: July–October.
Habitat: Dry prairies and pastures, open or
shaded; open pinelands.
Range: North Carolina south to Florida; west
to Texas; north to Nebraska and
Minnesota.
Comments: A widespread perennial of the
grasslands, it also extends east to the
Carolinas. It begins to flower early and
may continue until fall, or into early
winter in Florida.

429 Salvia; Scarlet Sage
(*Salvia coccinea*)
Mint Family (Lamiaceae)

Description: Several whorls of *red flowers* form an
interrupted spike on a square stem.
Flowers: 1" (2.5 cm) long; corolla
2-lipped, the lower lip 3-lobed, larger
than the 2-lobed upper lip; stamens 2.
Leaves: about 2" (5 cm) long; opposite,
ovate, blunt, and scalloped.
Height: 1–2' (30–60 cm).
Flowering: May–frost.
Habitat: Sandy soil and hummocks.
Range: Coastal; South Carolina to Florida; west
to Texas.
Comments: This showy southern native is
characterized by the loose, widely
spaced nature of the flowering spike. It

is found in the hot sands of the South.
The flamboyant, cultivated member of
this group, Scarlet Sage (*S. splendens*),
was introduced from Brazil.

628 Lyre-leaved Sage
(*Salvia lyrata*)
Mint Family (Lamiaceae)

Description: Whorls of 3–10 *lavender-blue flowers*
surround the square stem in an
interrupted spike-like cluster.
Flowers: about 1″ (2.5 cm) long;
2-lipped, the lower lip longer than
the upper; stamens 2.
Leaves: mostly in basal rosette, up to 8″
(20 cm) long, *deeply lobed* into rounded
segments, stalked; stem leaves few,
much smaller, short-stalked or
unstalked.
Height: 1–2′ (30–60 cm).

Flowering: April–June.

Habitat: Sandy, open woods and thickets.

Range: Connecticut and New York; south to
Florida; west to Texas; north to
Oklahoma, Missouri, Illinois, and
Ohio.

Comments: The exposed lower lip of these flowers
provides an excellent landing platform
for bees. When a bee lands the
2 stamens are tipped, and the insect is
doused with pollen. Salvias can be
grown easily in wildflower gardens.

558 Wild Basil
(*Satureja vulgaris*)
Mint Family (Lamiaceae)

Description: Rose-purple flowers, mingled with
hairy bracts that give them a *woolly
appearance,* are in a dense, rounded
cluster at the top of the square, hairy
stem and in smaller clusters in the
upper leaf axils.
Flowers: about ½″ (1.3 cm) long;

2-lipped; sepals hairy; stamens 4.
Leaves: ¾–1½″ (2–3.8 cm) long;
opposite, ovate, mostly untoothed.
Height: 8–20″ (20–50 cm).

Flowering: June–September.

Habitat: Roadsides, pastures, thickets.

Range: Manitoba to Nova Scotia; south to
upland North Carolina; west to
Tennessee and Kansas; north to
Minnesota.

Comments: This plant is native in the northern part
of its range but was probably
introduced from Europe, where it is
widespread, in the southern part. The
dried leaves can be used as a seasoning
although they are milder than those of
the commercial Basil, another member
of the Mint family.

638 Hyssop Skullcap; Rough Skullcap
(*Scutellaria integrifolia*)
Mint Family (Lamiaceae)

Description: The *bluish-lavender, 2-lipped flowers* are
clustered or solitary in the axils of
bract-like upper leaves, together
forming an elongated cluster along the
finely hairy square stem.
Flowers: about 1″ (2.5 cm) long; *calyx
with prominent hump* on upper side;
corolla lips about equal; stamens 4.
Leaves: ¾–2½″ (2–6.3 cm) long;
opposite, the upper ones elliptic to
lanceolate and untoothed, the lower
ones broader and toothed, often falling
early.
Height: 1–2½′ (30–75 cm).

Flowering: May–July.

Habitat: Clearings, open woods.

Range: New England and New York south to
Florida; west to Alabama and Missouri;
north to Kentucky and Ohio.

Comments: The many different Skullcaps are
recognized by the tiny projection, or
hump, on the top of the calyx
surrounding the base of the flower.

535 Wood Sage; Germander
(*Teucrium canadense*)
Mint Family (Lamiaceae)

Description: A *terminal, spike-like cluster* of lavender-
pink flowers on a downy, square stem.
Flowers: ¾" (2 cm) long; corolla
appears 1-lipped (actually 2) with 5
lobes, the lower lobe long and
flattened, the lateral and upper lobes
short; projecting stamens 4.
Leaves: 2–4" (5–10 cm) long; opposite,
lanceolate, toothed, with undersurfaces
densely hairy.
Height: 1–3' (30–90 cm).
Flowering: June–September.
Habitat: Thickets, woods, shores.
Range: Eastern New Brunswick and Nova
Scotia south along the coast to Florida
and Texas; up Mississippi River and
west to Oklahoma.
Comments: The name "Germander" was originally
altered from a Greek name for ground
oak, *chamaidrys*. Two smaller, bushier
species have been introduced from
Europe into our range: Wood Sage
(*T. scorodonia*), with yellow flowers, and
Cut-leaved Germander (*T. botrys*), an
annual with purplish flowers.

612 Blue Curls
(*Trichostema dichotomum*)
Mint Family (Lamiaceae)

Description: A small plant with 2 or 3 blue,
2-lipped flowers at the tips of short
branches arising from the leaf axils.
Plant sticky.
Flowers: ½–¾" (1.3–2 cm) long;
upper lip 4-lobed, lower lip with
1 recurved lobe; 4 stamens, *protruding
from corolla, long, distinctly curled.*
Leaves: ¾–2½" (2–6.3 cm) long;
opposite, narrow, oblong to lanceolate,
untoothed.
Fruit: 4 nutlets, conspicuous within
calyx.

Height: 6–30″ (15–75 cm).
Flowering: August–October.
Habitat: Dry, open, sandy, or sterile sites.
Range: Southern Maine south to Florida; west to Texas; north to Missouri and Michigan.
Comments: The long, curled stamens characterize this dainty little plant. Perennial Blue Curls (*T. suffrutescens*), southern, has tiny oblong leaves and may not be a distinct species. False Pennyroyal (*T. brachiatum*) has short stamens not protruding from the flowers. It ranges from Quebec to Georgia, west to Texas, and north to Minnesota.

LAUREL FAMILY (Lauraceae)

Aromatic plants, mainly trees and shrubs, with inconspicuous yellow or green flowers.
Flowers: bisexual or unisexual; radially symmetrical; sepals 6; no petals; stamens in 3 or 4 whorls of 3 each. All these parts usually attached at base of ovary.
Leaves: alternate, simple, leathery and evergreen or thin and deciduous.
Fruit: stone-fruit or berry.
There are about 40 genera and 1,000 species, occurring mostly in tropical zones. Some are ornamentals and some provide avocados, bay leaves and cinnamon.

365 Spicebush
(*Lindera benzoin*)
Laurel Family (Lauraceae)

Description: A deciduous shrub with dense clusters of tiny, *pale yellow flowers that bloom before the leaves* from globose buds along the twigs.
Flowers: ⅛″ (3 mm) wide; sepals and petals all alike, 6. Male and female flowers occur on separate plants.
Leaves: 2–5½″ (5–13.8 cm) long; dark green, oblong, smooth, untoothed, and have an *aromatic, spicy, fragrance* when crushed.
Fruit: ovoid, shiny, red, berry-like drupes.
Height: 6–17′ (1.8–5.1 m).

Flowering: March–April.
Habitat: Swamps, wet woods.
Range: Maine south to Florida; west to Texas; north to Missouri, Iowa, and Ontario.
Comments: In the North this plant is thought of as the "forsythia of the wilds" because its early spring flowering gives a subtle yellow tinge to many lowland woods where it is common. A tea can be made from the aromatic leaves and twigs, and

the dried and powdered fruit can be used as a spice. Hairy Spicebush (*L. melissaefolium*), with hairy twigs, is the only other species in our range. The fruit is eaten by birds and is particularly relished by wood thrushes and veerys.

BLADDERWORT FAMILY
(Lentibulariaceae)

Herbs of moist or aquatic habitats, usually carnivorous, with flowers solitary or in racemes.

Flowers: bilaterally symmetrical; 2–5 united sepals; 5 united petals form an upper and lower lip, the lower with a spur projecting backward; stamens 2. All these parts attached at base of ovary.

Leaves: alternate or in rosettes, simple or highly divided.

Fruit: capsule with one chamber and a central column to which seeds attach.

There are about 4 genera and possibly 200–300 species distributed throughout the world.

272 Yellow Butterwort
(*Pinguicula lutea*)
Bladderwort Family (Lentibulariaceae)

Description: A solitary, yellow flower blooms at the end of a leafless, glandular stalk rising from a *basal rosette of yellow-green, sticky leaves.*

Flowers: 1" (2.5 cm) wide; tubular, with 5 flattish lobes, the lower lobe tongue-like and spurred.

Leaves: to 2½" (6.3 cm) long, lying flat against the ground; ovate to oblong, with *rolled edges.*

Height: 5–18" (12.5–45 cm).

Flowering: February–May.

Habitat: Moist sandy sites.

Range: Coastal northeastern North Carolina south to southern Georgia and Florida; west to southeastern Louisiana.

Comments: Insects trapped by the sticky leaves of this plant are digested by enzymes secreted by the leaves, which then absorb the nutrients. The genus name derives from the Latin *pinguis* ("somewhat fat") and alludes to the greasy-feeling upper leaf surface.

596 Common Butterwort
(*Pinguicula vulgaris*)
Bladderwort Family (Lentibulariaceae)

Description: A solitary violet flower tops a leafless stalk that rises from a *basal rosette of sticky leaves.*
Flowers: ⅓" (8 mm) wide; corolla tubular, with 5 flattish lobes, the lower lobe spurred.
Leaves: to 2" (5 cm) long, lying flat against the ground; yellow-green, with *uprolled edges,* strap-like, shiny, sticky.
Height: 2–6" (5–15 cm).

Flowering: June–August.

Habitat: Wet rocks, open soils in limestone areas.

Range: Across Canada to northern Vermont, central New York, Michigan, and Minnesota.

Comments: This carnivorous plant has greasy leaves on whose surface insects are caught and digested by enzymes. The very similar Violet Butterwort (*P. caerulea*) is found in sandy, moist pinelands, bogs, and ditches from North Carolina to Florida and Louisiana. Dwarf Butterwort (*P. pumila*), found from North Carolina to Florida and Texas, is smaller with a pale lavender flower less than ½" (1.3 cm) long on a stalk usually less than 4" (10 cm) high. Primrose-leaved Butterwort, (*P. primulifolia*), found from Georgia and western Florida to Mississippi, usually in running water, has a violet flower with a white ring in the center and a yellow beard inside the lower lip.

313 Horned Bladderwort
(*Utricularia cornuta*)
Bladderwort Family (Lentibulariaceae)

Description: The brownish stalk of this *terrestrial, carnivorous plant* has a few scale-like bracts and 1–5 yellowish, 2-lipped flowers near the summit.

Flowers: about ¾" (2 cm) long; lower
lip large, helmet-shaped, with a
pendant *spur.*
Leaves: minute, threadlike,
subterranean, seldom seen, occasionally
on the surface, bearing minute
bladders.
Height: 2–12" (5–30 cm).

Flowering: June–September.

Habitat: Wet, sandy, muddy, or peaty shores;
bogs.

Range: Ontario to Nova Scotia; south to
Pennsylvania; west to Illinois,
Wisconsin, and Minnesota. Also North
Carolina south to Florida, and in
eastern Texas.

Comments: This species differs from many other
bladderworts in being terrestrial rather
than aquatic, although it may
occasionally be submerged. It is able to
suck very small organisms in through
the bladders and digest them.

271 Swollen Bladderwort
(*Utricularia inflata*)
Bladderwort Family (Lentibulariaceae)

Description: A carnivorous, *aquatic plant* with
several yellow flowers on a stem that
rises above the water over a *wheel-like
float of inflated leaf stalks.*
Flowers: ⅔" (1.6 cm) wide; 2-lipped.
Leaves: floating ones to 3" (8 cm) long;
repeatedly divided into thread-like
segments; submerged leaves with small,
ovoid bladders on some segments.
Height: aquatic, with flower stalks
1½–8" (3.8–20 cm).

Flowering: May–November.

Habitat: Ponds and ditches.

Range: Nova Scotia and New England south to
Florida; west to Texas; north to
Tennessee; northwest to Indiana.

Comments: When swimming prey, such as minute
crustaceans, touch the trigger hairs
surrounding the mouth of one of the
bladders, a trapdoor-like flap of tissue

swings open and the bladder quickly expands, sucking the organisms inside. Enzymes are secreted to dissolve the prey into nutritional elements for the plant. Among the fifteen species that occur in our area, only this one has floats. Reversed Bladderwort (*U. resupinata*) and Purple Bladderwort (*U. purpurea*) have purple flowers. *U. olivacea* is the most delicate. The entire plant is no longer than a dime, with a yellowish-white flower less than $\frac{1}{10}''$ (2.5 mm) long borne on a stalk $\frac{1}{10}-\frac{1}{3}''$ (2.5–8 mm) tall. Greater Bladderwort (*U. vulgaris*) is a common yellow-flowering form that lacks the inflated leaf stalks.

LILY FAMILY (Liliaceae)

Mostly perennial herbs from rhizomes, bulbs, or corms, some rather woody and treelike, and often showy flowers in racemes or branched racemes.

Flowers: usually bisexual and radially symmetrical; calyx has 3 free sepals which commonly resemble petals; corolla has 3 free petals, or petals and sepals may be united into a tube; stamens 6, or rarely 3. All these parts attach at base of ovary.

Leaves: alternate or basal, simple, usually narrow.

Fruit: 3-chambered capsule or berry.

The family is extremely complex and botanists estimate 250 genera and 4,000–6,000 species. Many, including tulips and day lilies, are handsome ornamentals. Asparagus, Sarsaparilla, onions, and the medicinally useful Aloë are from the family. A few species are poisonous.

---

127 **Colicroot; Stargrass**
(*Aletris farinosa*)
Lily Family (Liliaceae)

Description: At the top of a sturdy, round stem is a *spike-like cluster* of small, white, *urn-shaped flowers*.
Flowers: ¼–½" (6–13 mm) long; sepals 3 and petals 3, fused to form a swollen-based, 6-lobed tube, *granular* on outside, with small bracts beneath; stamens 6, showy orange.
Leaves: 2–7" (5–17.5 cm) long; pale green, lanceolate, long-pointed, arranged in basal cluster. Stem leaves very small, bract-like.
Fruit: capsule enclosed by persisting petals and sepals (perianth).
Height: 1–3′ (30–90 cm).
Flowering: May–August.
Habitat: Dry or wet meadows, peaty bog edges,

open woods in acid soils.

Range: Southern Ontario, southwestern Maine, southern New Hampshire, central Massachusetts, and southeastern New York; south to Florida; west to Texas; north to Michigan and Wisconsin.

Comments: Until the 19th century the roots were collected and used medicinally to treat colic. In the South, Blunt-leaved Colicroot (*A. obovata*) has globose white flowers. Yellow Colicroot (*A. aurea*) has globose yellow flowers ¼″ (6 mm) wide. Flowers of this group resemble Ladies' Tresses (*Spiranthes*), members of the Orchid Family.

---

553 Wild Garlic
(*Allium canadense*)
Lily Family (Liliaceae)

Description: From between narrow, grass-like leaves, which originate near its base, rises a stem topped by a *dome-like cluster* of star-shaped, pink or whitish flowers; plant has *strong, onion-like odor*.
Flowers: about ½″ (1.3 cm) wide; sepals 3, petal-like; petals 3; flowers often replaced by ovoid bulblets, with or without long "tails;" 3-parted spathe present beneath cluster.
Leaves: 6–18″ (15–45 cm) long; linear, flat.
Height: 8–24″ (20–60 cm).

Flowering: May–July.

Habitat: Low woods, thickets, meadows.

Range: Ontario, Quebec, and New Brunswick; south to Florida; west to Texas; north to Minnesota and Wisconsin.

Comments: This native perennial has a brown, fibrous skin on an edible bulb that tastes like onion. Field Garlic (*A. vineale*) is similar but has a strong garlic taste. It has greenish or purplish flowers, long-tailed bulblets, a single-parted spathe, and hollow cylindrical leaves. Introduced from Europe, it has become a problem weed occurring from

New England south to Georgia and west to Arkansas, Kansas, and Minnesota. If these plants are too abundant in pastures or wheat fields they add an undesirable flavor to such products as milk, butter, or flour. Wild Leek (*A. ampeloprasum*), naturalized from Europe, is 3–4½' (90–135 cm) tall with long flat leaves 1–2' (30–60 cm) long and a lavender flower cluster 2–2½" (5–6.3 cm) wide; it is found from Virginia to Florida.

554 Nodding Wild Onion
(*Allium cernuum*)
Lily Family (Liliaceae)

Description: Rose or white, bell-shaped flowers are clustered in a *nodding umbel* at the top of a leafless stem.
Flowers: ¼" (6 mm) long; petals 3; petal-like sepals 3.
Leaves: 4–16" (10–40 cm) long; basal, flat, linear.
Fruit: 3-lobed, crusted capsule.
Height: 8–24" (20–60 cm).
Flowering: July–August.
Habitat: Open woods, rocky soil.
Range: Throughout.
Comments: This plant is closely related to the Autumn Wild Onion (*A. stellatum*) but differs in its nodding flower cluster and earlier flowering.

551 Autumn Wild Onion
(*Allium stellatum*)
Lily Family (Liliaceae)

Description: A *dome-like cluster* of lavender flowers at the top of a leafless stem rises above flat, grass-like basal leaves.
Flowers: ¼" (6 mm) long, in clusters about 2½" (6.3 cm) wide; 6-pointed, petals 3 and sepals 3, all the same color; stamens 6.

Leaves: 6–18″ (15–45 cm) long, ½–¾″
(1.3–2 cm) wide; rise from bulb,
potent onion scent and flavor.
Fruit: 3-lobed, crested capsule.
Height: 1–2′ (30–60 cm).
Flowering: July–September.
Habitat: Rocky slopes, prairies, and shore.
Range: Saskatchewan and Ontario south to
Illinois, Missouri, Kansas, and Texas.
Comments: The bulbs of Wild Onions are very
strong but can be eaten raw or
parboiled. Early explorers ate them,
and they were also used by the
American settlers to treat colds,
coughs, and asthma, and to repel
insects. Chives (*A. schoenoprasum*) has
hollow leaves and long, narrow, sharply
pointed lavender petals. It is found in
the northern United States and Canada.

157 **Wild Leek; Ramp**
(*Allium tricoccum*)
Lily Family (Liliaceae)

Description: Tall leaves rise from an *onion-like bulb*
and wither before the flowers appear,
leaving a naked stem topped by a
domed cluster of creamy-white flowers;
entire plant has a mild onion taste.
Flowers: ¼″ (6 mm) long, in clusters
about 1½″ (3.8 cm) wide; cup-like,
petals 3 and sepals 3, all the same
color.
Leaves: 8–12″ (20–30 cm) long, ¾–2″
(2–5 cm) wide; lanceolate-elliptic.
Fruit: 3-lobed capsule.
Height: 6–20″ (15–50 cm).
Flowering: June–July.
Habitat: Rich, moist woods.
Range: New Brunswick, Nova Scotia, Quebec,
and New England; south to Delaware
and Maryland, in uplands to Georgia
and Tennessee; west to Illinois, Iowa,
and Minnesota.
Comments: In late April, before flowering, the
people of the Great Smoky Mountains
gather these plants for their annual

Ramp Festival. The foliage and bulbs can be used in salads and soups. Indians treated insect stings with juice from the crushed bulbs.

138 Fly Poison
(*Amianthium muscaetoxicum*)
Lily Family (Liliaceae)

Description: At the top of a mostly leafless stem is a *cylindrical cluster* of small, white flowers that turn greenish-purple with age.
Flowers: ½" (1.3 cm) wide; petals 3 and petal-like sepals 3; both persist as fruit matures.
Leaves: basal ones 12" (30 cm) or longer, ¾" (2 cm) wide, *grass-like,* blunt-tipped; stem leaves much reduced, bract-like.
Fruit: 3-beaked capsule.
Height: 1–4' (30–120 cm).

Flowering: June–July.

Habitat: Bogs, open woods, and low, sandy sites.

Range: Coastal plain from New York to Florida and in mountains from Pennsylvania to West Virginia; west to Missouri and Oklahoma

Comments: This plant contains a very poisonous alkaloid that can kill livestock. Pulp from a crushed bulb, mixed with sugar, is used to poison flies; hence the species name, from the Latin *muscae* ("flies") and *toxicum* ("poison"). A somewhat similar white flower is Bunchflower (*Melanthium virginicum*). Its 3 petals and 3 sepals have narrow, stalk-like bases with 2 dark glands on each; there are several spikes in a cluster.

621   Wild Hyacinth
(*Camassia scilloides*)
Lily Family (Liliaceae)

Description: A leafless stem with lavender-blue
flowers in an elongated, *loose-flowered
cluster* rises from an underground bulb.
Flowers: 1″ (2.5 cm) wide; 6-pointed,
with petals 3 and similarly-colored
sepals 3; long, *green bracts* flare out from
under the flowers.
Leaves: 8–16″ (20–40 cm) long; basal,
flabby, linear, *keeled.*
Fruit: triangular-globular capsule.
Height: 6–24″ (15–60 cm).

Flowering: May–June.

Habitat: Moist meadows and open woods.

Range: Pennsylvania south to South Carolina,
Georgia, and Alabama; west to Texas
and eastern Kansas; north to Iowa,
Wisconsin, Michigan, and southern
Ontario.

Comments: The bulbs were used by Indians and
early explorers for food. The flower
somewhat resembles the cultivated
Easter Hyacinth which belongs to this
family but is in the genus *Hyacinthus.*
Grape Hyacinth (*Muscari botryoides*),
which occasionally escapes from
cultivation, has blue ball- or grape-like
flowers.

124   Devil's Bit; Fairy Wand
(*Chamaelirium luteum*)
Lily Family (Liliaceae)

Description: A wand-like stem, often *drooping* at the
tip, arises from a basal cluster of leaves
and has a *densely packed, elongated
terminal cluster* of tiny white flowers.
Flowers: about ⅛″ (3 mm) long, with
very narrow segments (petals 3 and
sepals 3); male and female flowers on
separate plants, with female cluster
shorter, more slender.
Leaves: basal ones 3–8″ (8–20 cm)
long, spatulate to ovate; stem

leaves smaller, narrower,
Fruit: 3-valved, dry, elliptic capsule.
Height: 1–4' (30–120 cm); male plant
shorter.

Flowering: May–July.

Habitat: Wet meadows, rich woods and
thickets.

Range: Southern Ontario, Massachusetts, and
New York; south to Florida; west to
Arkansas; north to Illinois, Michigan,
and Ohio.

Comments: Fairy Wand is a most descriptive name
for this interesting plant. On the plants
with all-male flowers, the yellow
stamens create the more creamy color of
the male flower spike. The plant can be
readily cultivated.

6, 658 Bluebead Lily; Yellow Clintonia
(*Clintonia borealis*)
Lily Family (Liliaceae)

Description: The stalk rises from a basal set of shiny,
bright green, oblong leaves and has at
its summit 3–6 *yellowish-green, drooping,
bell-like flowers.*
Flowers: ¾–1" (2–2.5 cm) long; sepals
3, petal-like; petals 3; stamens 6.
Leaves: 5–8" (12.5–20 cm).
Fruit: *shiny, oval, pure-blue berry* ½"
(1.3 cm) in diameter.
Height: 6–15" (15–38 cm).

Flowering: May–August.

Habitat: Moist woods, acid soils.

Range: Labrador to northern New England;
south to mountains of Georgia and
Tennessee; north to Michigan,
Wisconsin, and Minnesota.

Comments: The cluster of beautiful fruits are noted
for their extraordinary true-blue color.
The berries are somewhat poisonous.
The plant was named in honor of the
former governor of New York, DeWitt
Clinton (1769–1828). A less common
species, White Clintonia
(*C. umbellulata*), has numerous, erect,
white flowers and black berries.

106 Nodding Mandarin
(*Disporum maculatum*)
Lily Family (Liliaceae)

Description: Hanging singly or in pairs from the
ends of the usually forked stems,
directly opposite the last leaf, are
creamy white or yellowish flowers,
spotted with purple.
Flowers: 1″ (2.5 cm) long; 6-parted,
with stamens projecting beyond the
separate sepals and petals.
Leaves: 2–4″ (5–10 cm) long, elliptic,
hairy beneath, with pronounced parallel
veins; stalkless.
Fruit: red, *hairy berry.*
Height: 8–24″ (20–60 cm).

Flowering: April–May.

Habitat: Moist wooded slopes.

Range: North Carolina to Georgia and
Alabama; west to Ohio and southern
Michigan.

Comments: A similar yellow-flowering species,
Yellow Mandarin (*D. lanuginosum*),
found from New York to Georgia, has
yellow unspotted flowers and smooth
red fruit. These plants resemble the
Bellworts (*Uvularia* spp.).

278 Trout Lily; Dogtooth Violet
(*Erythronium americanum*)
Lily Family (Liliaceae)

Description: A pair of *brownish-mottled leaves* sheath
the base of a stalk that bears a solitary,
nodding flower, yellow inside, bronzy
outside.
Flowers: 1″ (2.5 cm) wide; petals 3 and
petal-like sepals 3, all *curved backwards;*
stamens 6, with brownish or yellow
anthers.
Leaves: 2–8″ (5–20 cm) long, elliptic.
Fruit: ovoid capsule.
Height: 4–10″ (10–25 cm).

Flowering: March–June.

Habitat: Rich woods and meadows.

Range: Ontario to New Brunswick and Nova

Scotia; south through New England to Georgia; west to Tennessee, Arkansas, Oklahoma; north to Minnesota.

Comments: Recognized by its brown-mottled leaves, this is one of our most common spring wildflowers, and it is found in sizable colonies. The common name ("Dogtooth Violet") refers to the toothlike shape of the white underground bulb. The name "Trout Lily" (a more suitable name since the flower is not a Violet) refers to the similarity between the leaf markings and those of the brown or brook trout. The White Dogtooth Violet (*E. albidum*) has narrow, mottled leaves and white, bell-shaped flowers, often tinged with lavender on the outside. It is found from southern Ontario to Georgia, west to Kentucky, Missouri, and Oklahoma, and north to Minnesota. Minnesota Adder's Tongue (*E. propullans*), found only in Minnesota, has pink flowers and produces a small bulb midway up the stem.

514 Swamp Pink
(*Helonias bullata*)
Lily Family (Liliaceae)

Description: A mostly leafless stem with a *dense cluster* of small, pink flowers at its top rises from a rosette of evergreen basal leaves.
Flowers: about ½" (1.3 cm) wide, in a cluster 1–3" (2.5–7.5 cm) long; each with 6 pink segments (sepals 3 and petals 3) and 6 *blue-tipped stamens.*
Leaves: basal ones 3–10" (7.5–25 cm) long; lanceolate; stem leaves reduced to bracts.
Height: 1–3' (30–90 cm).
Flowering: April–May.
Habitat: Swamps, bogs.
Range: New York south to Virginia and the mountains of northwestern Georgia.

Comments: This is a handsome and relatively rare
wetlands species. Its flowers should not
be picked nor should the plants be
removed from their natural habitat.

---

370 **Day Lily**
(*Hemerocallis fulva*)
Lily Family (Liliaceae)

Description: Rising from *sword-like basal leaves* is a
leafless stalk bearing several orange
funnel-shaped flowers.
Flowers: 3½″ (8.8 cm) wide; 3 net-
veined, petal-like, *erect sepals* and 3 net-
veined, *erect petals with wavy margins;*
stamens 6.
Leaves: 1–3′ (60–90 cm) long; narrow,
channeled, shorter than the floral stem.
Height: 2–4′ (60–120 cm).
Flowering: May–July.
Habitat: Roadsides, meadows, and borders.
Range: Throughout.
Comments: This native of Eurasia was introduced to
our gardens and has escaped from
cultivation. Apparently a hybrid, it
does not set fertile seed but reproduces
vegetatively from the roots. Each flower
lasts only one day. Every part of the
plant is mild and edible, but the flower
buds taste like green beans when
cooked and served with butter. A
smaller, yellow species, the Yellow Day
Lily (*H. flava*), has also escaped from
cultivation. It, too, is edible.

277, 368 **Canada Lily; Meadow Lily; Wild Yellow Lily**
(*Lilium canadense*)
Lily Family (Liliaceae)

Description: From 1 to several *nodding flowers,* each
on a long stalk and ranging in color
from yellow to orange-red with dark
spots, are at the top of a stem that also
bears *whorled leaves.*

Flowers: 2–3″ (5–7.5 cm) wide; 3 petals and 3 *petal-like sepals arch outward* but not backward; stamens 6, with brown anthers.
Leaves: to 6″ (15 cm) long; lanceolate, in whorls of 4–10, with veins beneath bearing minute prickles.
Fruit: erect capsule 1–2″ (2.5–5 cm) long.
Height: 2–5′ (60–150 cm).

Flowering: June–August.

Habitat: Wet meadows, woodlands, and borders.

Range: Ontario, Quebec, and Nova Scotia; south to New England, eastern Maryland, Pennsylvania, and, in the mountains, to South Carolina; Florida west to Alabama; north to southern Indiana.

Comments: As many as 16–20 of these beautiful, stalked, nodding flowers may be borne on one plant, either rising from the axils of leafy bracts or in a group at the end of the flowering stalk. The flower buds and roots were gathered and eaten by Indians. A similar Midwestern species, Michigan Lily (*L. michiganense*), has sepals and petals which curve backward until they touch the flower tube.

371 Wood Lily
(*Lilium philadelphicum*)
Lily Family (Liliaceae)

Description: An erect stem bears whorled leaves and 1–5 *upward-opening, orange flowers* with purplish-brown spots.
Flowers: 2″ (5 cm) wide; 6-segmented, with 3 petals and 3 petal-like sepals, each tapering to a stalked base with spaces between the stalks; stamens 6.
Leaves: 1–4″ (2.5–10 cm) long; lanceolate, usually in whorls of 3–8.
Fruit: an oblong capsule, 1–2″ (2.5–5 cm) long.

Height: 1–3′ (30–90 cm).
Flowering: June–August.
Habitat: Dry woods and thickets.
Range: Southern Ontario and Quebec; south to Maine, southern New England, Delaware, Maryland, West Virginia, and, in the mountains, to North Carolina and Kentucky.
Comments: This bulbous Lily, one of our truly showy woodland species, is usually found in relatively dry sites. The bulbs were gathered for food by Indians. A variety of this species, found in the Midwest, has leaves scattered along the stem. Among several southern species, the Southern Red Lily (*L. catesbaei*) has alternate, lanceolate leaves pressed against the stem, and the Orange Lily (*L. bulbiferum*), a European native, has sepals and petals downy within and bulblets in the axils of the upper leaves.

367 Turk's-cap Lily
(*Lilium superbum*)
Lily Family (Liliaceae)

Description: The tall, flowering stem bears several somewhat drooping, orange flowers, spotted reddish-brown, with *strongly recurved petals* and petal-like sepals; a green streak at the base of each flower segment forms a *green "star."*
Flowers: 2½″ (6.3 cm) long, with stamens exposed, bearing dangling brown anthers.
Leaves: 2–6″ (5–15 cm) long; lanceolate, alternate or whorled.
Fruit: a capsule.
Height: 3–7′ (90–210 cm).
Flowering: July–September.
Habitat: Wet meadows, swamps, and woods.
Range: Southern New Hampshire, Massachusetts, and New York; south to Georgia and Alabama.
Comments: The largest and most spectacular of the native Lilies; up to 40 flowers have been recorded on a single plant. The

recurved sepals and petals, which presumably resemble a type of cap worn by early Turks, and the showy extruded stamens, are distinctive features. Indians used the bulbs for soup. A somewhat smaller southern species, Carolina Lily (*L. michauxii*), also has its floral parts bent strongly backwards but lacks the green central star. Its whorled leaves are thick, whitish, and broadest toward the tip.

125 Canada Mayflower
(*Maianthemum canadense*)
Lily Family (Liliaceae)

Description: The short, often zigzag stem has a small, dense, cluster of tiny, white, *star-shaped flowers* at its top and 1–3 ovate leaves.
Flowers: about ⅙″ (4 mm) long; petals 2; petal-like sepals 2; stamens 4.
Leaves: 1–3″ (2.5–7.5 cm) long; *heart-shaped at base*.
Fruit: berries, initially green, but turning a speckled, dull red in late summer and red in fall.
Height: 2–6″ (5–15 cm).

Flowering: May–June.

Habitat: Upland woods, clearings.

Range: Manitoba to Labrador, Newfoundland, and Nova Scotia; south to New England, Pennsylvania, Delaware, and, in the mountains, to Georgia and Tennessee; west to Iowa.

Comments: This common forest herb spreads by rhizomes and frequently forms carpet-like colonies. An unusual member of the Lily Family, it has only 2 petals, 2 sepals, and 4 stamens instead of the usual 3-3-6 pattern. A somewhat similar plant, Three-leaved Solomon's Seal (*Smilacina trifolia*), usually has 3 elliptic leaves which taper at the base and white floral parts in a 6-pointed, star-like pattern. It is found in wet, boggy, or mossy areas from New Jersey west to Minnesota and north into Canada.

---

3   Indian Cucumber Root
(*Medeola virginiana*)
Lily Family (Liliaceae)

Description: Several *nodding, yellowish-green flowers* emerge from the center of a *whorl of 3 leaves* at the top of a slender, woolly, unbranched stem, on stalks that sometimes bend down below the leaves.
Flowers: ½" (1.3 cm) long; 3 recurved petals and 3 recurved petal-like sepals; stamens 6, reddish; ovary with *3 long, brownish, recurved stigmas.*
Leaves: in 2 whorls: those atop stem are 1–3" (2.5–7.5 cm) long; midway down the stem is another whorl of 6–10 leaves, 2½–5" (6.3–12.5 cm) long. All ovate to lanceolate.
Fruit: dark bluish-purple berry.
Height: 1–2½' (30–75 cm).
Flowering: May–June.
Habitat: Moist woodlands.
Range: Ontario, Quebec, and Nova Scotia; south to Florida; west to Alabama and Louisiana; north to Minnesota.
Comments: The root, 2–3" (5–7.5 cm) long and ½–1" (1.3–2.5 cm) wide is white, has a brittle texture, and tastes and smells somewhat like a cucumber. It was used by Indians for food, but digging it for such purposes today is not recommended because the plant is scarce. Birds are attracted to the fruit. At the time the berries turn bluish-purple, the cluster of leaves below them turns red at the lower half.

4, 115 **Smooth Solomon's Seal**
(*Polygonatum biflorum*)
Lily Family (Liliaceae)

Description: *Hanging from the leaf axils on an arching
stem* are a few (often 2) greenish-white,
bell-like flowers.
Flowers: ½–⅔" (1.3–1.6 cm) long;
6-lobed; stamens 6.
Leaves: 2–6" (5–15 cm) long; stalkless,
lanceolate to ovate, untoothed, light
green, *smooth on both sides*, conspicuously
parallel-veined.
Fruit: blue-black berry.
Height: 8–36" (20–90 cm).

Flowering: May–June.

Habitat: Dry to moist woods and thickets.

Range: Connecticut and New York; south to
Florida, west to Texas; north to
Nebraska and southern Ontario.

Comments: The graceful arching stem and
pendulous flowers (often hidden)
characterize this common plant.
Another, almost identical, species,
Hairy Solomon's Seal (*P. pubescens*), is
distinguished by minute hairs along
veins on undersides of leaves. A much
larger form, Great Solomon's Seal
(*P. canaliculatum*), has larger flowers,
2–10 per cluster, and may be 7'
(2.1 m) tall. The rootstalk, or rhizome,
of the Solomon's Seals is jointed; the
leaf stalk breaks away from it, leaving a
distinctive scar said to resemble the
official seal of King Solomon. Indians
and colonists used the starchy rhizomes
as food.

122 **False Solomon's Seal**
(*Smilacina racemosa*)
Lily Family (Liliaceae)

Description: An arching *stem bears at its tip a
pyramidal cluster* of many small white
flowers.
Flowers: ⅛" (3 mm) long; petals 3;
sepals 3, petal-like; stamens 6.

Leaves: 3–6″ (7.5–15 cm) long; alternate, elliptic, hairy beneath and along margins, conspicuously parallel-veined.
Fruit: berry; at first green speckled with red, finally translucent, ruby-red.
Height: 1–3′ (30–90 cm).

Flowering: May–July.
Habitat: Woods and clearings.
Range: Quebec and Nova Scotia; south through New England to Virginia, Georgia, and Missouri.

Comments: The feathery, creamy-white masses of flowers borne at the end of the stem distinguish this species from the true Solomon's Seals (*Polygonatum* spp.), which have pendulous, axillary, bell-like flowers. The rhizome lacks the seal-like pattern of the true Solomon's Seals, but exhibits circular stem scars. A smaller species, Star-flowered Solomon's Seal (*S. stellata*), has larger star-shaped flowers, ¼″ (6 mm) long, leaves clasping stem, and larger berries, at first with blackish-red stripes, eventually completely blackish-red.

40, 655　**Carrion Flower**
(*Smilax herbacea*)
Lily Family (Liliaceae)

Description: *Vine with broad leaves and stalked, round, axillary clusters of small green putrid-smelling flowers.*
Flowers: about ½″ (1.3 cm) across; petals 3, greenish; sepals 3, petal-like; stamens 6. Male and female flowers borne on separate plants.
Leaves: to 5″ (12.5 cm) long; pale green, ovate, parallel-veined.
Fruit: blue berry.
Height: vine, with stem 3–9′ (90–270 cm) long.

Flowering: May–June.
Habitat: Moist woods, thickets, and meadows.
Range: Manitoba to Quebec and New Brunswick; south to New England,

Virginia, and Georgia; west to
Alabama, Tennessee, and Missouri.

Comments: This attractive vine climbs over other
vegetation by means of tendrils. The
bad-smelling flowers attract insects,
especially carrion flies, which serve as
pollinators. Within this genus are at
least 6 Catbriers: thorny, green-
stemmed, often evergreen vines that
form tangled thickets. The most
common are Greenbrier (*S. rotundifolia*),
with heart-shaped leaves and stout
thorns; Sawbrier (*S. glauca*), with heart-
shaped leaves, a whitish bloom
beneath, and weak spines; and Bullbrier
(*S. bona-nox*), a southern and
midwestern species with triangular
leaves, stout thorns, and 4-angled
stem.

142 Featherbells
(*Stenanthium gramineum*)
Lily Family (Liliaceae)

Description: A large, narrow, pyramidal cluster of
small, white, *nodding flowers* blooms on
a stem rising from a basal rosette of
folded, grass-like leaves.
Flowers: about ½" (1.3 cm) wide; 6
sharp-pointed perianth parts (petals and
petal-like sepals).
Leaves: 8–16" (20–40 cm) long and
only up to ⅔" (1.6 cm) wide.
Fruit: erect capsule.
Height: 3–5' (90–150 cm).
Flowering: June–September.
Habitat: Open, rocky woods, sandy bogs, acid
soils.
Range: Pennsylvania south to Virginia and
upland to northwestern Florida; west to
Alabama and eastern Texas; north to
Missouri and Indiana.
Comments: The genus name, from the Greek *stenos*
("narrow") and *anthos* ("flower") refers
to the narrow pointed sepals and petals,
and to the shape of the panicle.

505 Rose Twisted-stalk
(*Streptopus roseus*)
Lily Family (Liliaceae)

Description: A branching plant with *zig-zag stems* and nodding, pink, bell-shaped flowers on short *twisted stalks* rising near leaf axils.
Flowers: ⅓″ (8 mm) long; corolla 6-pointed.
Leaves: 2½–6″ (6.3–15 cm) long; lanceolate, slightly clasping the stem, with distinct parallel veins, and margins fringed with hair or minute teeth.
Fruit: red berry.
Height: 1–3′ (30–90 cm).
Flowering: April–July.
Habitat: Moist woods and thickets.
Range: Canada south to New England, northern New Jersey, Pennsylvania, and along the mountains to North Carolina, Georgia, and Kentucky; west to Michigan, Wisconsin, and Minnesota.
Comments: This plant is easily recognized by its branching habit and distinctly twisted flower stalks, reflected in the genus name, from the Greek *streptos* ("twisted") and *pous* ("foot" or "stalk"). A similar species, White Mandarin (*S. amplexifolius*), has greenish-white flowers and clasping leaves. South of northern New England it is found only locally in the mountains.

478 Catesby's Trillium
(*Trillium catesbaei*)
Lily Family (Liliaceae)

Description: The somewhat nodding, *stalked, pink or white flowers* have their flower parts and leaves in 3's.
Flowers: 2–3″ (5–7.5 cm) wide; sepals 3, *narrow;* petals 3; stamens 6, with yellow anthers.
Leaves: 1½–3″ (3.8–7.5 cm) long;

elliptic, in a whorl of 3, usually with
5 main veins.
Height: 8–20″ (20–50 cm).

Flowering: April–June.
Habitat: Woodlands.
Range: North Carolina south to Georgia; west
to Alabama and Tennessee.
Comments: This beautiful pink Trillium of the
southeast Piedmont and the adjacent
Appalachian slopes may be confused
with the Large-flowered Trillium
(*T. grandiflorum*) that turns pink with
age. The flowers of Catesby's Trillium,
however, turn downward and the sepals
are narrower and more sickle-shaped
than those of the Large-flowered
Trillium. The species is named for
Mark Catesby (1679–1749), an English
naturalist.

75 Nodding Trillium
(*Trillium cernuum*)
Lily Family (Liliaceae)

Description: The short stalk of this *nodding, white
flower* is curved so that the *flower hangs
beneath the whorled leaves.*
Flowers: about 1½″ (3.8 cm) wide;
petals 3, white (rarely pink), recurved;
sepals 3, green; stamens 6, with pink
anthers.
Leaves: 2½–4″ (6.3–10 cm) long; in a
whorl of 3, diamond-shaped, barely
stalked.
Fruit: reddish-purple berry.
Height: 6–24″ (15–60 cm).

Flowering: April–July.
Habitat: Moist, acid woods and swamps.
Range: Newfoundland, Nova Scotia and
Quebec; south to New England,
Maryland, and Delaware, and, in
mountains, to Georgia and West
Virginia.
Comments: The species name, from the Latin
cernuus ("drooping" or "nodding") refers
to the dangling flowers.

384 Purple Trillium
(*Trillium erectum*)
Lily Family (Liliaceae)

Description: The solitary, nodding flower, with an
unpleasant odor, rises *on a stalk* above a
whorl of 3 broadly ovate, diamond-
shaped leaves.
Flowers: about 2½" (6.3 cm) wide;
petals 3, maroon or reddish-brown;
sepals 3, green; stamens 6.
Leaves: to 7" (17.5 cm) long; dark
green, *net-veined* not parallel-veined as is
typical of most members of this family.
Fruit: oval reddish berry.
Height: 8—16" (20—40 cm).

Flowering: April—June.

Habitat: Rich woods.

Range: Ontario, Quebec, and Nova Scotia;
south to New England, Delaware,
Pennsylvania, West Virginia, and, in
the mountains, to Georgia; west to
Tennessee; north to Michigan.

Comments: This is one of the most common eastern
Trilliums. Its foul smell attracts carrion
flies that act as pollinators. Early
herbalists used this ill-scented plant to
treat gangrene, since, according to the
Doctrine of Signatures, plants were
used to cure the ailments they
resembled. As the genus name
suggests, the floral parts and leaves of
these perennials are arranged in 3's or
multiples of 3, typical of the Lily
family. Vasey's Wake-robin (*T. vaseyi*),
of the southern Appalachians, is larger
in all respects and has pleasant-smelling
flowers.

77 Large-flowered Trillium
(*Trillium grandiflorum*)
Lily Family (Liliaceae)

Description: The large, solitary, *waxy-white flower*
(turning pink with age) is on an *erect
stalk* above a whorl of 3 broad leaves.
Flowers: 2—4" (5—10 cm) wide; petals

3, large, wavy-edged; sepals 3, green;
stamens 6, with yellow anthers.
Leaves: 3–6″ (7.5–15 cm) long;
broadly ovate to diamond-shaped,
pointed.
Fruit: red berry.
Height: 8–18″ (20–45 cm).

Flowering: April–June.

Habitat: Rich woods, thickets, usually basic or
neutral soils.

Range: Ontario, Quebec, western Maine, and
New Hampshire; south to Georgia;
west to Arkansas; north to Minnesota.

Comments: This largest and most showy Trillium
is frequently cultivated in wildflower
gardens. The underground rootstalks
were gathered and chewed by Indians
for a variety of medicinal purposes. The
plants have also been picked and eaten
as cooked greens. This practice may be
fatal to the plant, since these Trilliums
arise from the rootstalks, which often
die if the leaves are removed.

383 Toadshade; Red Trillium
(*Trillium sessile*)
Lily Family (Liliaceae)

Description: The *stalkless flower* is directly above the
3 whorled leaves and *appears closed*, an
impression created by its narrow, erect
petals.
Flowers: about 1½″ (3.8 cm) long;
petals 3, reddish-brown or maroon;
sepals 3, green, spreading; stamens 6.
Leaves: 1½–6″ (3.8–15 cm) long;
unstalked, ovate, *mottled with light and
dark green areas.*
Fruit: red berry.
Height: 4–12″ (10–30 cm).

Flowering: April–June.

Habitat: Rich woods.

Range: Western New York; south to Virginia
and Georgia; west to Mississippi,
Arkansas, and Missouri; north to
Indiana.

Comments: This flower somewhat resembles Purple

Trillium (*T. erectum*) but is
distinguished by its lack of stalk and
closed appearance. Several other
stalkless species that appear closed are
Little Sweet Betsy (*T. cuneatum*), an ill-
scented southeastern species with large
flowers up to 3″ (7.5 cm) long and
weakly mottled leaves; Yellow Trillium
(*T. luteum*), in southern and midwestern
areas, with yellow, lemon-scented
flowers and mottled leaves; Green
Wake-Robin (*T. viride*), also in
southern and midwestern areas, with
narrow, greenish, clawed petals up to
2″ (5 cm) long; and Prairie Trillium
(*T. recurvatum*), a midwestern plant
with erect, clawed, maroon petals,
drooping sepals, and mottled leaves.

76 Painted Trillium
(*Trillium undulatum*)
Lily Family (Liliaceae)

Description: The *erect, stalked flower* has an *inverted, pink V* at the base of each white, wavy-edged petal.
Flowers: 2–2½″ (5–6.3 cm) wide; sepals 3, green; petals 3, white and pink; stamens 6, pink-tipped.
Leaves: 2½–5″ (6.3–12.5 cm) long, in a whorl of 3, stalked, ovate, tapering to a point, bluish-green, waxy.
Fruit: shiny red berry.
Height: 8–20″ (20–50 cm).

Flowering: April–June.

Habitat: Moist, acid woods and swamps.

Range: Manitoba to Nova Scotia and Quebec; south to New England, New Jersey, Pennsylvania, West Virginia, and, in the mountains, to Georgia and Tennessee; west to Michigan and Wisconsin.

Comments: This is one of the most attractive woodland Trilliums. It is easily recognized by the splash of pink in the center of the white flower.

318 Wild Oats; Sessile Bellwort
(*Uvularia sessilifolia*)
Lily Family (Liliaceae)

Description: The 1 or 2 creamy-yellow, *drooping flowers* are at the top of an angled stem having *unstalked leaves.*
Flowers: about 1" (2.5 cm) long; narrowly bell-shaped; sepals 3, petal-like; petals 3; stamens 6.
Leaves: 1¾–3" (4.5–7.5 cm) long; oblong, light green above, whitish below.
Fruit: *3-angled capsule* similar to a beechnut.
Height: 6–12" (15–30 cm).

Flowering: April–June.

Habitat: Woods, thickets.

Range: New Brunswick, Nova Scotia, and New England; south to Georgia; west to Alabama, Missouri, and North Dakota.

Comments: This common woodland wildflower has a near relative, Perfoliate Bellwort (*U. perfoliata*), whose stem appears to pierce the leaves. The interior surface of the flowers is roughened with small glands. A bigger version, Large-flowered Bellwort (*U. grandiflora*), has bright yellow flowers and perfoliate leaves which are downy beneath. It reaches a height of 20" (50 cm). Mountain Bellwort (*U. pudica*) has shiny leaves and stems in clumps, and is similar to Sessile Bellwort, as is Florida Bellwort (*U. floridana*), which has a small, leaf-like bract on the flower stalk. At one time these plants were thought to be good for treating throat diseases because the drooping flowers resembled the uvula, the soft lobe hanging into the throat from the soft palate.

27 False Hellebore; Indian Poke
(*Veratrum viride*)
Lily Family (Liliaceae)

Description: A stout plant with *large leaves* clasping a stem that bears a branching cluster of greenish, *star-shaped, hairy flowers.*
Flowers: about ½" (1.3 cm) wide; sepals 3, petal-like; petals 3; stamens 6, curved.
Leaves: 6–12" (15–30 cm) long, 3–6" (8–15 cm) wide; large, *plaited, parallel veined.*
Fruit: 3-lobed capsule.
Height: 2–7' (60–210 cm).

Flowering: May–July.
Habitat: Swamps, wet woods, and meadows.
Range: New Brunswick, Quebec, and New England; south to Maryland and, in uplands, to Georgia and Tennessee; west to Minnesota.
Comments: The ribbed, yellow-green leaves of this wetland plant are conspicuous in spring; the plant withers away before summer. The rootstock is poisonous, as is the foliage. Although the latter has a burning taste and is usually avoided by animals, it can be lethal. It is said that some Indian chiefs were selected only if they survived eating this plant. Small-flowered Veratrum (*V. parviflorum*), with leaves stalked and mostly basal, occurs in drier woods from Virginia to Georgia, eastern Tennessee, and West Virginia. Wood's False Hellebore, (*V. woodii*), with greenish-purple to blackish-purple flowers, is found in dry woods from Ohio to Missouri and Oklahoma, and in Iowa.

139 Turkey Beard
(*Xerophyllum asphodeloides*)
Lily Family (Liliaceae)

Description: Small, white flowers are in a dense, elongated cluster on a stem that has short, bristle-like leaves toward the top

and *long, grass-like leaves at the base.*
Flowers: about ½" (1.3 cm) wide; 6
widely-spreading segments (3 petals
and 3 petal-like sepals).
Leaves: basal ones to 1½' (45 cm) long
and $\frac{1}{12}$" (2 mm) wide, toothed; stem
leaves gradually reduced to bracts.
Height: 2–4' (60–120 cm).

Flowering: May–July.
Habitat: Dry, sandy pinelands, mountain woods,
strongly acid soils.
Range: Coastal New Jersey and Delaware;
mountains of western North Carolina;
south to Georgia; west to Tennessee.
Comments: The genus name, from the Greek *xeros*
("dry") and *phyllon* ("leaf"), refers to
the dry, wiry basal leaves of this showy
Lily. It is difficult to cultivate and
seldom blooms in gardens.

140 Yucca; Bear-grass
(*Yucca filamentosa*)
Lily Family (Liliaceae)

Description: A tall, stout stem rises from a rosette of
rigid, sword-like leaves and bears a loose
cluster of white, nodding, bell-shaped
flowers.
Flowers: 1½" (3.8 cm) wide; petals 3;
sepals 3, petal-like; stamens 6.
Leaves: to 30" (75 cm) long and 2½"
(6.3 cm) wide; spoon-shaped, tapering,
loose threads along margins.
Fruit: oblong capsule, often constricted
near middle.
Height: 2–10' (60–300 cm).

Flowering: June–September.
Habitat: Sandy beaches, dunes, old fields.
Range: Coastal; New Jersey south to Florida;
west to Alabama.
Comments: Although Yuccas are more typical of
southwestern deserts, some are native in
our range. This species escapes from
cultivation northward to New England.
Spanish Bayonet (*Y. aloifolia*), found
from North Carolina to Florida and
Alabama, has toothed, hairless leaf

margins. Soapweed (*Y. glauca*) is a typical western plains species found eastward to Iowa and Missouri. The rigid bayonet-like leaves have marginal hairs, and the flowering stalk reaches 4' (1.2 m). The fruits of the Yuccas can be cooked and eaten with the seeds removed; the large petals are used in salads.

136 Camas
(*Zigadenus leimanthoides*)
Lily Family (Liliaceae)

Description: The tall, smooth, stem bears an elongated, branching cluster of small creamy or yellow, *star-like flowers*.
Flowers: about ⅓" (8 mm) wide; sepals 3 and petals 3, all of the same color and each with 2 small glands at the base.
Leaves: *grass-like basal leaves* to 2' (60 cm) long, about 3" (7.5 cm) wide; upper ones much shorter, sharp-pointed.
Height: 1–4' (30–120 cm).
Flowering: June–August.
Habitat: Sandy pinelands, bogs.
Range: Along Coastal Plain; Long Island to Delaware; in the mountains of Virginia to West Virginia and Alabama.
Comments: Several species occur, mostly in the South and Midwest. The leaves, stems, flowers, and seeds of most species are poisonous and, particularly in the West, endanger livestock. Large-flowered Zygadenus (*Z. glaberrimus*), 3–5' (90–150 cm) high, has whitish-yellow flowers with purple spots in the centers, and is found in wet pinelands and bogs from Virginia south to Florida and west to Louisiana.

137 Death Camas
(*Zigadenus nuttalii*)
Lily Family (Liliaceae)

Description:  From an onion-like bulb arise *grass-like basal leaves* and a leafless stem with a branching cluster of numerous greenish-white, star-like flowers.
Flowers: about ½" wide; 6 similar parts (sepals 3 and petals 3) each with 1 gland at base.
Leaves: 8–24" (20–60 cm).
Height: 1–2½' (30–75 cm).

Flowering: April–May.

Habitat: Prairies, open woodlands.

Range: Tennessee west to Texas and Kansas.

Comments: Grazing livestock can be poisoned by this plant, or by hay containing any part of it. The toxic substance, also present in the bulb, is an alkaloid which causes vomiting, breathing difficulties, and coma in humans. This species is similar to the preceding Camas (*Z. leimanthoides*) but has a papery coat on the bulbous base.

FLAX FAMILY (Linaceae)

Herbs, rarely shrubs or trees, with flowers borne in a forked cluster.

Flowers: radially symmetrical; sepals 5, separate; petals 5, separate, each with a narrow base and readily dropping off the flower; stamens 10, joined by bases of their stalks. All these parts attached at base of ovary.

Leaves: alternate or opposite, simple.

Fruit: 5-chambered capsule, rarely drupe.

There are about 12 genera and almost 300 species distributed nearly throughout the world. Linen and linseed soil are obtained from the family.

600 Wild Flax
(*Linum perenne*)
Flax Family (Linaceae)

Description: A *tufted plant with leafy stems* that bear loose, much-branched clusters of blue flowers.
Flowers: 1–1½″ (2.5–3.8 cm) wide; petals 5; sepals 5, much shorter than the petals.
Leaves: numerous, *linear,* ½–¾″ (1.3–2 cm) long.
Height: 1–2′ (30–60 cm).

Flowering: May–July.

Habitat: Prairies and plains.

Range: Manitoba, South Dakota, and Wisconsin; south to Texas and Arkansas; west to Utah; north to Alaska.

Comments: This perennial is related to the common Flax, (*L. usitatissimum,*) source of the flax from which linen is made and of linseed oil, a plant which often escapes from cultivation. It is an annual with solitary stems and few flowers.

LOGANIA FAMILY (Loganiaceae)

Herbs, shrubs, or trees with flowers
often clustered in spikes.
Flowers: radially symmetrical; calyx
with 4–5 lobes; corolla tubular or bell-
shaped with 4–5 lobes; stamens 4–5.
All these parts usually attached at base
of ovary.
Leaves: opposite, simple, margins
smooth or toothed.
Fruit: berry, capsule or drupe.
There are more than 30 genera and 400
species, widely distributed in warm and
tropical regions. Some are cultivated as
ornamentals.

357 Yellow Jessamine
(*Gelsemium sempervirens*)
Logania Family (Loganiaceae)

Description: A *woody vine* with short, axillary
clusters of very *fragrant, yellow, trumpet-
shaped flowers.*
Flowers: about 1″ (2.5 cm) wide at the
flaring mouth and 1½″ (3.8 cm) long;
corolla 5 lobed.
Leaves: 1–4″ (2.5–10 cm) long;
evergreen, opposite, untoothed,
lanceolate, margins rolled.
Fruit: oblong capsule.
Height: vine, with stem to 17′ (5.1 m)
long.
Flowering: January–April.
Habitat: Thickets, dry woods, sandy areas.
Range: Southeastern Virginia; south to Florida;
west to Texas and Arkansas.
Comments: This high-climbing vine is very
common in parts of the South,
frequently found in abandoned fields.
The flowers, leaves, and roots are
poisonous and may be lethal to
livestock. Rankin's Yellow Jessamine
(*G. rankinii*), with odorless flowers,
occurs in swamps from North Carolina
to Florida.

425 Indian Pink
(*Spigelia marilandica*)
Logania Family (Loganiaceae)

Description: *Trumpet-shaped flowers, red outside and yellow inside,* are in a narrow, one-sided curving terminal cluster.
Flowers: 1″ (2.5 cm) wide, with a narrow tube and 5 sharp-pointed lobes stamens 5, protruding.
Leaves: 2–4″ (5–10 cm) long, opposite ovate to lanceolate-ovate, stalkless.
Height: 1–2′ (30–60 cm).

Flowering: March–June.

Habitat: Moist woods.

Range: Maryland south to Florida; west to Texas, Missouri, and Oklahoma.

Comments: This plant does very well in gardens. It blooms from the bottom upward and the flowering season can be prolonged by removing the flowers as they wither.

MISTLETOE FAMILY
(Loranthaceae)

Mostly evergreen shrubs that lack roots but have chlorophyll and are attached to and half-parasitic on trees. Flowers solitary or in clusters in leaf axils or at ends of branches.

Flowers: usually radially symmetrical, bisexual or unisexual; sepals 2–3, sometimes barely developed; petals 2–3, free or united; stamens 2–3. All these parts attached at top of ovary.

Leaves: opposite or whorled, simple, entire, mostly leathery, or reduced to scales.

Fruit: berry or drupe.

There are about 21 genera and 500 species, widely distributed, most abundant in tropical regions; in temperate areas, found on chestnuts, oaks, poplars, pines and other trees.

239 Mistletoe
(*Phoradendron serotinum*)
Mistletoe Family (Loranthaceae)

Description: *Semi-parasitic shrub* with short, interrupted, axillary clusters of *tiny yellow flowers* on smooth, *green, jointed stems.*
Flowers: about ⅛″ (3 mm) wide; petals lacking; calyx 3-lobed; male and female flowers on different plants.
Leaves: ¾ to 5″ (2–12.5 cm) long, opposite, ovate to lanceolate, thick, leathery.
Fruit: white, berry-like, less than ¼″ (6 mm) in diameter.
Height: 1′ (30 cm).

Flowering: September–October.

Habitat: Parasitic on branches of deciduous trees exposed to sun.

Range: New Jersey and Pennsylvania south to Florida and west to West Virginia, Ohio, Indiana, Illinois, Missouri, Kansas, and eastern Texas.

Comments: This is the common Mistletoe hung at Christmastime. The genus name derive from the Greek *phor* "a thief," and "*dendron*" "tree," and refers to their getting at least some nourishment from the trees on which they grow. The fruits are covered with a sticky substance poisonous to man, but relished by such birds as cedar waxwings and bluebirds. The birds spread the seeds through their droppings and by wiping their beaks on branches, where a new plant may become established. The small, northern Dwarf Mistletoe (*Arceuthobium pusillum*), has short yellow-green stems 1″ (2.5 cm) long, with leaves reduced to thin brown scales. This plant occurs only on evergreens, especially spruce, and is found in northern bogs south to New Jersey and Pennsylvania, and west to Michigan.

LOOSESTRIFE FAMILY
(Lythraceae)

Herbs, shrubs, or trees with flowers borne in racemes or branched clusters. Flowers: radially or bilaterally symmetrical; sepals 4–6, joined at the base to form a tube to which petals and stamens attach; as many separate petals as there are sepals, or petals may be absent, often crumpled like crepe paper; usually twice as many stamens as sepals, in 2 series of different lengths; tube attached at base of ovary. Leaves: simple, usually opposite or whorled. Fruit: capsule with 2–6 chambers. There are about 25 genera and 550 species distributed throughout the world, except for very cold regions. A few species yield dyes; some are grown as ornamentals.

562 Swamp Loosestrife; Water Willow
(*Decodon verticillatus*)
Loosestrife Family (Lythraceae)

Description: *Arching stems* have showy, deep pink flowers in tufts in the axils of the upper, opposite or whorled, *willow-like leaves.*
Flowers: about ½" (1.3 cm) long; bell-shaped; petals 5, wedge-shaped; stamens 10, 5 long and protruding, 5 short.
Leaves: 2–6" (5–15 cm) long; lanceolate.
Fruit: round capsule.
Height: stem arching, to 8' (2.4 m) long.
Flowering: July–August.
Habitat: Swamps, bogs, edges of shallow water, wet soils.
Range: Ontario, central Maine, and southern New Hampshire; south to Florida; west to Louisiana; north to southern Illinois.
Comments: The many intertwining, arching stems

of this herb- to shrub-like plant may form sizable patches at the edges of lakes and sluggish streams or on floating bog mats. Wherever a stem touches the water, air-filled, spongy tissue may develop. This tissue buoys the stem so that it may root and form a new arching stem. Despite the common name and its willow-like leaves, the plant is not related to the willows.

542 Purple Loosestrife
(*Lythrum salicaria*)
Loosestrife Family (Lythraceae)

Description: An *erect stem* has a spike of purple-pink flowers above *opposite or whorled, unstalked leaves.*
Flowers: ½–¾" (1.3–2 cm) wide; *petals 4–6, wrinkled;* stamens as many or twice as many as petals; flowers of 3 types, each with different stamen and pistil lengths.
Leaves: 1½–4" (3.8–10 cm) long; lanceolate to linear, the lower ones downy, clasping the stem.
Height: 2–4' (60–120 cm).
Flowering: June–September.
Habitat: Wet meadows, flood plains, and roadside ditches.
Range: Newfoundland, Quebec, Nova Scotia, and New England; south to North Carolina; west to West Virginia, Ohio, Indiana, Missouri, and Minnesota.
Comments: This showy, magenta-flowered perennial, a European introduction, covers acres of wetlands, providing a truly spectacular sight. It is an aggressive species and tends to crowd out native aquatics valuable to waterfowl and other wildlife.

MALLOW FAMILY (Malvaceae)

Herbs, shrubs, or rarely small trees, often velvety with starlike or branched hairs, the flowers borne singly or in branched clusters.

Flowers: usually bisexual, radially symmetrical; 3–5 partly united sepals; 5 separate petals; many stamens are joined by their stalks into a tube; all these parts attached at the base of the ovary.

Leaves: alternate, simple, often palmately veined and lobed or deeply divided.

Fruit: 5 to many chambers that separate from one another, or form a capsule or berry.

There are about 85 genera and 1,500 species, many in tropical America. Rose-of-Sharon and other *Hibiscus,* and Hollyhocks are grown as ornamentals. Okra is the edible fruit of one species of *Hibiscus,* and the hairs of seeds of *Gossypium* provide the fiber cotton.

256 Velvetleaf; Pie-maker
(*Abutilon theophrasti*)
Mallow Family (Malvaceae)

Description: A tall plant with large, *heart-shaped, velvety leaves* and stalked, yellow flowers in the leaf axils.
Flowers: 1″ (2.5 cm) wide; corolla 5-petalled, stamens numerous, forming a tube.
Leaves: to 8″ (20 cm) long.
Fruit: dry, capsule-like structure of 12–17 hairy, united parts (carpels) *ending in beaks.*
Height: 1–6′ (30–180 cm).
Flowering: July–October.
Habitat: Open disturbed areas, roadsides.
Range: Throughout; rare in extreme southeastern United States.
Comments: A native of India, this tall plant has distinctively beaked fruit, the sides of

which resemble the crimped edges of a piecrust.

---

420   Hibiscus; Rose Mallow
(*Hibiscus coccineus*)
Mallow Family (Malvaceae)

Description: A large plant with *big, showy, crimson flowers* in the upper leaf axils.
Flowers: 6–8″ (15–20 cm) wide; petals 5; many yellow stamens forming a tube around the style and its red, disc-like stigmas; anthers of stamens outside tube; very narrow bracts beneath calyx.
Leaves: *palmately divided into narrow, pointed, toothed segments,* 2–10″ (5–25 cm) long.
Fruit: ovoid capsule about 1″ (2.5 cm) long.
Height: 3–10′ (90–300 cm).
Flowering: June–September.
Habitat: Fresh and brackish marshes, swamps.
Range: Georgia, Florida, and Alabama.
Comments: This very showy species, typical of the Mallow Family, is sometimes cultivated. It is certainly one of the loveliest of our native flowers.

---

470   Swamp Rose Mallow
(*Hibiscus palustris*)
Mallow Family (Malvaceae)

Description: This tall, coarse plant has *large, pink, 5-lobed, musky-smelling flowers,* usually borne singly on short stalks from leaf axils.
Flowers: 4–7″ (10–17.5 cm) wide; stamens numerous, forming column around style, with anthers outside; 5 style branches and stigmas protrude from end of column. Narrow, green, leaf-like bracts present beneath calyx.
Leaves: 4″ (10 cm) long; yellow-green, ovate, toothed, pointed; white down beneath.

Fruit: 5-parted capsule.

Height: 3–8' (90–240 cm).

Flowering: July–September.

Habitat: Tidal marshes and inland freshwater marshes.

Range: Coastal; from Massachusetts to Florida; Great Lakes region from New York to Indiana, Illinois, and Michigan.

Comments: This strikingly showy species is often found along edges of salt marshes but is more common in upper-valley wetlands. Some botanists recognize a very similar plant, *H. moscheutos* (also called Swamp Rose Mallow), as a separate species; others regard it as a variety of *H. palustris*.
The flowers of *H. moscheutos* are usually creamy-white (sometimes pink) with red or purple centers and lower leaves palmately veined, sometimes lobed.
The very lovely Flower-of-an-hour (*H. trionum*) is an annual 12–24" (30–60 cm) tall with palmately divided leaves and a flower 2" (5 cm) wide, pale yellow with a purple band running up 1 side of each petal.

521 Seashore Mallow
(*Kosteletzkya virginica*)
Mallow Family (Malvaceae)

Description: A large plant with *pink, terminal or axillary, stalked flowers* with yellow stamens.
Flowers: 1½–2½" (3.8–6.3 cm) wide; petals 5, numerous; stamens form a tubular column around style, with anthers outside.
Leaves: 2–5" (5–12.5 cm) long; gray-green, ovate, slightly hairy or rough, with *divergent basal lobes*.
Fruit: *flat ring of 1-seeded segments*.
Height: 1–3' (30–90 cm).

Flowering: May–October.

Habitat: Brackish to nearly freshwater marshes.

Range: Long Island south to Florida; west to Louisiana.

Comments: This Mallow is especially abundant in
southern Louisiana. It is distinguished
from *Hibiscus* by the flat ring of fruit
segments. *K. altheaeifolia,* found on eas
coast of Texas, is recognized by some
botanists as separate species; others
regard is as a variety of *K. virginica.* It
has very velvety, downy leaves.

467 Musk Mallow
(*Malva moschata*)
Mallow Family (Malvaceae)

Description: Pink (sometimes white or lavender),
musk-scented flowers are in scattered
groups at ends of branches.
Flowers: 1½″ (3.8 cm) wide. Petals 5,
notched, wedge-shaped; stamens many,
fused into column around style with
anthers protruding along column.
Leaves: 3–4″ (7.5–10 cm) wide;
*palmately dissected into very narrow toothed
lobes.*
Fruit: *circular, hairy, doughnut-like
cluster of segments.*
Height: 8–24″ (20–60 cm).
Flowering: June–October.
Habitat: Disturbed areas.
Range: Newfoundland and northern New
England south to Maryland and
Delaware; mountains of North
Carolina; west to Tennessee and
Nebraska.
Comments: A native of Europe, this beautiful
perennial is now widely naturalized
here in fields, old gardens, and along
roadsides. The highly dissected leaves
and the hairy ring of fruit segments are
distinctive. European Mallow (*M. alcea*)
differs only in having little star-like
clusters of hairs on the stems.

72 Cheeses
(*Malva neglecta*)
Mallow Family (Malvaceae)

Description: A *low, trailing plant,* with small,
axillary, whitish-lavender flowers.
Flowers: ½–¾" (1.3–2 cm) wide;
petals 5, notched at tips; stamens
united in a column around style.
Leaves: about 1½" (3.8 cm) wide;
round, scallop-edged, prominently
veined.
Fruit: *ring of segments,* separating at
maturity.
Height: creeper, with stem to 2'
(60 cm) long.

Flowering: April–October.

Habitat: Disturbed areas.

Range: Throughout.

Comments: This low-growing Mallow is considered
a weed of barnyards and waste places,
but the foliage and flowers are
attractive. The flowers are somewhat
like Hollyhocks but much smaller. The
fruit is distinctive, consisting of many
round, flattish segments forming a ring
which, as the common name implies,
resembles a wheel of cheese. The related
Low Mallow (*M. rotundifolia*) has white
flowers about ¼" (6 mm) wide;
otherwise it is very similar to *M.
neglecta.*

372 Carolina Mallow
(*Modiola caroliniana*)
Mallow Family (Malvaceae)

Description: A *low, creeping perennial* with reddish-
orange to purple-red flowers on slender
stalks in the leaf axils.
Flowers: to ½" (1.3 cm) wide; petals 5;
stamens united to form tube around
style; 3 bracts beneath calyx.
Leaves: ¾–2¾" (2–7 cm) long;
palmately divided into 6–7 coarsely
toothed lobes.
Fruit: *ring of black, 1-seeded, 2-spined,*

nut-like segments, separating at maturity
Height: creeper.

Flowering: February–June.

Habitat: Lawns, gardens, disturbed sites, wet areas.

Range: Virginia south to Florida; west to Louisiana, Texas, Arkansas, and Mississippi.

Comments: This widely distributed species, abundant in the South, is often a lawn weed. It has many branches, and roots at the nodes.

MEADOW BEAUTY FAMILY
(Melastomaceae)

Herbs, trees or shrubs in tropical regions, with flowers generally in clusters.

Flowers: radially symmetrical; calyx tube usually 4–5 lobed; petals 4–5; stamens twice as many as petals. All these parts usually attached at top of ovary.

Leaves: usually opposite, the margins smooth or toothed with opposite veins; simple.

Fruit: capsule or berry.

There are about 175 genera and 3,000 species mostly in tropical regions, particularly South America, but *Rhexia* is native to the United States and Cuba.

---

477 Virginia Meadow Beauty
(*Rhexia virginica*)
Meadow Beauty Family
(Melastomataceae)

Description: Several pink flowers are in broad, terminal clusters on a sturdy *4-sided, slightly winged stem.*
Flowers: 1–1½″ (2.5–3.8 cm) wide; petals 4; 8 *prominent stamens,* anthers opening by pores.
Leaves: ¾–2½″ (2–6.3 cm) long; paired, ovate to elliptic, toothed, rounded at base; 3–5 prominent veins.
Fruit: *urn-shaped* capsule with 4 points.
Height: 1–2′ (30–60 cm).
Flowering: July–September.
Habitat: Wet sands and peats.
Range: Nova Scotia to Ontario; south to Florida; west to Mississippi, Tennessee, and Missouri.
Comments: Members of this genus have a distinctive urn-shaped fruit that Thoreau once compared to a little cream pitcher. Although the family is mostly tropical, we have at least 10

native species. Awn-petalled Meadow
Beauty (*R. aristosa*) is similar but has
very narrow, 3-ribbed, unstalked leaves
and sharp-pointed petals. It is found in
pine barrens from New Jersey
southward. Maryland Meadow Beauty
(*R. mariana*) has 4 lop-sided, pink to
white petals and is found in sandy
swamps from Massachusetts south to
Florida, west to Kentucky and Texas.

MOONSEED FAMILY
(Menispermaceae)

These are woody vines, occasionally herbaceous, with inconspicuous flowers.
Flowers: unisexual, radially symmetrical, clustered; petals commonly 6, separate; sepals petal-like, larger than petals, those in staminate flowers in 2–4 whorls; stamens 6 or 3, or indefinite. All these parts attached at base of ovary.
Leaves: usually simple, but sometimes alternate, lobed, or 3-parted.
Fruit: berry-like drupe.
These vines are mostly tropical, with a few extending into temperate zones. Some are grown as ornamentals. In North America there are 4 genera and 5 species.

204 Common Moonseed
(*Menispermum canadense*)
Moonseed Family (Menispermaceae)

Description: A *climbing vine* with small, greenish-white flowers in small, loose clusters in the axils of *large leaves*.
Flowers: about ⅙″ (4 mm) wide; sepals 4–8; petals 4–8, shorter than sepals; stamens 12–24, longer than sepals.
Leaves: 4–7″ (10–17.5 cm) wide; ovate to shield-shaped, entire or shallowly lobed.
Fruit: black, 1-seeded, berry-like drupe.
Height: vine, stem to 12′ (3.6 m) long.

Flowering: June–July.

Habitat: Rich thickets, streambanks.

Range: Manitoba to Quebec and New England; south to Georgia; west to Arkansas and Oklahoma.

Comments: The fruits of this plant ripen in September and resemble whitish-powdered grapes, but are poisonous if eaten in large enough quantities.

INDIAN PIPE FAMILY
(Monotropaceae)

Saprophytic fleshy herbs devoid of
chlorophyll, and therefore not green.
Flowers: radially symmetrical, borne
singly or in racemes or heads; sepals
2–6, separate; 3–6 separate or united
petals; stamens 6–12, often united by
the stalks. All these parts attached at
base of ovary.
Leaves: simple, alternate, scale-like.
Fruit: capsule.
There are about 12 genera and 30
species in north temperate regions.
Roots of the plants grow in a close,
apparently mutually beneficial,
association with fungi. This family is
often considered to be part of the larger
Heath family, Ericaceae.

421 Pinesap; False Beech-drops
(*Monotropa hypopitys*)
Indian Pipe Family (Monotropaceae)

Description: A saprophytic, red, pink, lavender, or
yellow plant with *several vase-like,
nodding flowers* on a downy, scaly stem;
stem and flower same color.
Flowers: about ½" (1.3 cm) long; petals
4 on lateral flowers, 5 on terminal one.
Leaves: reduced to scales up to ½"
(1 cm) long; clasp the stem, more
numerous toward base of plant.
Fruit: erect, ovoid capsule.
Height: 4–16" (10–40 cm).
Flowering: June–November.
Habitat: Upland woods, usually in acid soil.
Range: Throughout.
Comments: The plant pictured here is an autumn-
flowering one, characterized by the red
color. Early-flowering plants are
genetically different forms and are
yellow. Like its single-flowered relative,
Indian Pipe (*M. uniflora*), this plant
does not carry on photosynthesis but
obtains its nourishment from fungi

associated with roots, often those of oaks or pines. Sweet Pinesap (*Monotropsis odorata*), closely related and similar, occurs in the southern mountains and Piedmont. It has 2 flowering periods: February to April, when the flowers produced are old rose-colored and very fragrant, and September and October, when the flowers are lavender and odorless.

112 Indian Pipe
(*Monotropa uniflora*)
Indian Pipe Family (Monotropaceae)

Description: A white, saprophytic plant with a thick, *translucent stem* covered with scaly bracts and terminated by a *solitary nodding flower.*
Flowers: ½–1″ (1.3–2.5 cm) long; white or salmon-pink; petals 4–5; stamens 10–12; single pistil.
Leaves: reduced to scales.
Fruit: ovoid capsule, becoming enlarged and erect as seeds mature.
Height: 3–9″ (7.5–22.5 cm).
Flowering: June–September.
Habitat: Woodland humus.
Range: Throughout.
Comments: This non-green, waxy plant gets its nourishment from decayed organic material through a fungal relationship (mycorrhiza) associated with the roots. The plant turns black as the fruit ripens or when it is picked and dried.

WATER LILY FAMILY
(Nymphaeaceae)

Perennial aquatic herbs, usually with
floating orbicular or heart-shaped leaf
blades, and large flowers either floating
or held above the water surface on long
stalks.
Flowers: radially symmetrical; sepals 3
to many, often intergrading into many
petals; stamens 3 to many; pistils 3 to
numerous, sometimes held together in
a common fleshy base.
Leaves: simple, with very long stalks.
Fruit: each pistil may open on one side,
or each may form a little nut, or all
may be grown together as a leathery
berry.
There are about 7 genera and nearly 70
species in aquatic habitats throughout
temperate and tropical regions. Several
are cultivated as pond ornamentals.

---

245 American Lotus; Water Chinaquin
(Nelumbo lutea)
Water Lily Family (Nymphaeaceae)

Description: An aquatic plant with fragrant, pale
yellow flowers and *bowl-shaped leaves
borne on stalks above the water.*
Flowers: 6–10" (15–25 cm) wide;
numerous petals and petal-like sepals
intergrade into one another; stamens
many. Center of flower has large,
convex receptacle, 3–4" (7.5–10 cm)
long, with *numerous cavities,* each
containing a pistil.
Leaves: 1–2' (30–60 cm) wide; petiole
attached in middle.
Height: aquatic, with leaves to 3'
(90 cm) above water.
Flowering: July–September.
Habitat: Ponds, quiet streams.
Range: Southern Ontario to southern New
England and New York; south to
Florida; west to Texas; north to Iowa
and Minnesota.

Comments: This member of the Water Lily group is recognized by large, umbrella-like leaves and the inverted, cone-like structure in the middle of the flowers. It covers extensive areas along the Mississippi River from Iowa to Wisconsin and southward. Introduced from Asia, the pink Sacred Lotus (*N. nucifera*), which escaped from cultivation, has leaves that rise 3–5′ (90–150 cm) from rhizomes buried in the muck. The seed-like fruits can be shaken from the receptable and are edible.

244 Yellow Pond Lily; Bullhead Lily
(*Nuphar variegatum*)
Water Lily Family (Nymphaeaceae)

Description: A floating aquatic plant with yellow, *cup-like flowers.*
Flowers: 1½–2½″ (3.8–6.3 cm) wide; corolla composed of 6 showy, petal-like sepals and numerous small, yellow, stamen-like petals; stamens numerous, in several rows; carpels numerous, united into a greenish, disc-like compound pistil with 7–25 radiating stigmatic surfaces.
Leaves: 3–15″ (7.5–37.5 cm) long; mostly *floating on water,* heart-shaped, with V-shaped notch at base.
Height: aquatic.

Flowering: May–September.

Habitat: Pond margins, quiet streams.

Range: Across Canada; south to New England, Delaware, and Maryland; west to Ohio, Indiana, Illinois, Iowa, Nebraska, South Dakota, and beyond.

Comments: This is the most familiar yellow Pond Lily in the Northeast. Common Spatterdock (*N. advena*) is very similar, but its leaves are frequently raised above the water. It occurs in the southern United States and as far north as New England, New York, Ohio, Michigan, and Wisconsin. A smaller species, Small Pond Lily (*N. microphyllum*) has leaves only 2–4″ (5–10 cm) long, flowers 1″ (2.5 cm) wide, and a stigmatic disc with 6–10 rays. It occurs in Canada and only as far south as New Jersey. Arrow-leaf Pond Lily (*N. sagittifolium*), found from Virginia to northeast South Carolina, has leaves 3 times as long as they are wide. The leaves and long, stem-like petioles of the Water Lilies and Pond Lilies die back each year and contribute to the organic buildup in lakes and marshes.

246 Yellow Water Lily
(*Nymphaea mexicana*)
Water Lily Family (Nymphaeaceae)

Description: An aquatic plant with bright yellow flowers and *floating leaves*.
Flowers: 4–5″ (10–12.5 cm) wide, rising about 4″ (10 cm) above the water; sepals 4, green; petals and stamens numerous.
Leaves: 3–5″ (7.5–12.5 cm) wide; ovate, dark green with brown blotches on top, reddish-brown with dark dots below.
Height: aquatic.
Flowering: Spring–summer.
Habitat: Quiet water, ponds, ditches.
Range: South Carolina, Florida, Mexico.
Comments: The lovely flowers are open from midday to late afternoon. When the plants are crowded, the leaves may rise above the water. The plant was first discovered in Mexico, which accounts for the species name. It is also known as the Sun-lotus or Banana Water Lily.

82 Fragrant Water Lily
(*Nymphaea odorata*)
Water Lily Family (Nymphaeaceae)

Description: A floating aquatic plant with fragrant white or pink flowers and flat, *floating leaves.*
Flowers: 3–5" (7.5–12.5 cm) wide; petals many, narrowing in width toward the center and intergrading with numerous yellow stamens; sepals 4, green; pistil compound, with several united parts (carpels).
Leaves: 4–12" (10–30 cm) in diameter; shiny green above, purplish-red beneath.
Fruit: *fleshy, ripens beneath the water on coiled stalk.*
Height: aquatic.
Flowering: June–September.
Habitat: Ponds, quiet waters.
Range: Throughout.
Comments: One of the most common white Water Lilies, this plant's flowers and leaves float on the water. It usually flowers only from early morning until noon. The stomata, tiny openings on the leaf surface through which carbon dioxide and other gases pass into the plant, are on the upper, shiny leaf surface rather than on the lower surface as is the case for most dry-land plants. The leaf stalk, which is soft and spongy, has 4 main air channels for the movement of gases, especially oxygen, from the leaves to the large stems (rhizomes) buried in the muck, which are frequently eaten by muskrats. The Small White Water Lily (*N. tetragona*), has white flowers 1½" (3.8 cm) wide, that open in the afternoons. It is found in Canada, south to northwest Maine, and west to northern Michigan and Minnesota.

EVENING PRIMROSE FAMILY
(Onagraceae)

Usually herbs, rarely shrubs or trees
with often showy flowers borne singly,
in racemes or spikes, or in branched
clusters.

Flowers: usually radially symmetrical,
sepals usually 4, mostly separate; petals
4, mostly separate, both series united
into a long, short, or barely discernible
tube at the base; stamens usually 4 or
8. All these parts attached at top of
ovary.

Leaves: simple, alternate or opposite.

Fruit: commonly 4-chambered capsule,
less commonly berry or hard nut-like
structure.

The family of about 20 genera and 650
species is found worldwide, but is
especially abundant in temperate
regions of the New World. Evening
primroses, *Fuschsia* and *Lopezia* are
popular ornamentals. "Primrose"
ultimately derives from a Latin word
meaning "first" and the true primroses
(Primulaceae), unrelated to evening
primroses, are among the first flowers
to bloom in the spring. Apparently in
the early 1600's when an eastern
United States species of *Oenothera* was
being described, its sweet scent
reminded the botanist of wild primroses
of Europe. He gave the name to these
plants and it stuck.

170 Enchanter's Nightshade
(*Circaea quadrisulcata*)
Evening Primrose Family (Onagraceae)

Description: Small white flowers in elongated
terminal clusters.
Flowers: less than ¼" (6 mm) wide, in
clusters to 8" (20 cm) long; *2 deeply-cleft
petals* (that look like 4) and *2 recurved
sepals*.
Leaves: 2½–5" (6.3–12.5 cm) long,

dark green, opposite, thin, ovate, pointed, and slightly toothed; decrease in size as they reach flower cluster.
Fruit: nut-like, *bristle-covered,* oblong to ovoid, bending downward at maturity.
Height: 1–3′ (30–90 cm).

Flowering: June–August.

Habitat: Damp, shady, rich woods.

Range: Ontario, New Brunswick and Nova Scotia; south to Georgia; west to Tennessee, Missouri, and Oklahoma; north to North Dakota.

Comments: This is one of the few 2-petalled flowers. A smaller species of more northern distribution, Smaller Enchanter's Nightshade (*C. alpina*), has smaller leaves that are more coarsely toothed. Both the generic and common names derive from the mythological enchantress, Circe, who is said to have used a poisonous member of this genus in her sorcery.

541 Fireweed
(*Epilobium angustifolium*)
Evening Primrose Family (Onagraceae)

Description: A terminal, spike-like cluster of deep pink flowers and narrow *willow-like leaves* on a tall stem.
Flowers: 1″ (2.5 cm) wide; petals 4, spreading; stamens 8; and a 4-parted stigma at the end of the style.
Leaves: up to 8″ (20 cm) long, lanceolate to linear.
Fruit: capsule up to 3″ (7.5 cm) long; splits open to reveal white, silky down aiding in seed dispersal.
Height: 2–6′ (60–180 cm).

Flowering: July–September.

Habitat: Recently cleared woodlands, especially burned over areas.

Range: Throughout Canada; south to Maryland and in the mountains of North Carolina and Tennessee; west to northern Ohio, central Indiana, and South Dakota; southwest beyond our range.

Comments: This is a showy, post-fire invader and a spectacular sight in mass. The seeds are dispersed far and wide by long, white, silky hairs. The plant spreads rapidly in wildflower gardens. Bees value it as a source of nectar, and the very young shoots and leaves can be eaten as cooked greens. Nine other much smaller-flowered, native species occur in the East.

465 Hairy Willow Herb
(*Epilobium hirsutum*)
Evening Primrose Family (Onagraceae)

Description: Branching, *hairy stems* with rose-purple flowers at the top and in the axils of the upper leaves.
Flowers: about 1″ (2.5 cm) wide; petals 4, *notched;* stigma 4-cleft, forming a cross in center of flower.
Leaves: 1½–4″ (3.8–10 cm) long; mostly opposite, lanceolate or oblong, sharply toothed, hairy on both sides, unstalked.
Fruit: 2–3″ (5–7.5 cm) long, a narrow elongated, erect capsule.
Height: 2–5′ (60–150 cm).
Flowering: July–September.
Habitat: Waste places, roadsides, meadows.
Range: Ontario and Quebec south to New England, New York, Ohio, Michigan, and Illinois.
Comments: This plant is similar to Fireweed (*E. angustifolium*), but differs in the hairiness of the leaves, reflected in the species name, and in having notched petals.

569 Morning Honeysuckle; Southern Gaura
(*Gaura angustifolia*)
Evening Primrose Family (Onagraceae)

Description: Small pink or white flowers in *wand-like clusters* at the ends of rather straggly branches.
Flowers: ¼" (6 mm) wide; calyx cylindrical, 3–4 lobed; petals 3–4; stamens 6–8, protruding; style with 4-cleft stigma.
Leaves: 1½–3" (3.8–7.5 cm) long, narrowly lanceolate, sharply toothed, progressively smaller toward the top, frequently clustered.
Fruit: nut-like, *4-angled.*
Height: 2–5' (60–150 cm).
Flowering: May–September.
Habitat: Open woods, sandy fields, roadsides, dunes.
Range: North Carolina south to Florida.
Comments: The rather inconspicuous flowers, which open near sunset and fade the next day, are at first white but soon turn pink. The fruit is distinctive in that it does not split open when mature.

257, 413 Seedbox
(*Ludwigia alternifolia*)
Evening Primrose Family (Onagraceae)

Description: A many-branched, smooth-stemmed plant with solitary, *yellow flowers on short stalks* in the upper-leaf axils.
Flowers: about ½" (1.3 cm) wide; petals 4, framed by *4 broad, green sepals of unequal length.*
Leaves: 2–4" (5–10 cm) long, lanceolate, pointed at both ends, toothless.
Fruit: smooth, slightly *winged capsule,* opening first by an apical pore but eventually splitting open.
Height: 2–3' (60–90 cm).
Flowering: June–September.

Habitat: Swamps and wet soil.
Range: Southern Ontario to Massachusetts and New York; south to Florida; west to Texas; north to Kansas and Iowa.
Comments: The Seedboxes, which are mostly wetland plants, bear a distinctive, box-like fruit, square on top and filled with many seeds. Other members of this genus do not have these distinctive fruits.

354 Evening Primrose
(*Oenothera biennis*)
Evening Primrose Family (Onagraceae)

Description: At the top of a leafy stalk bloom *lemon-scented, large yellow flowers*. Stem hairy, often purple-tinged.
Flowers: 1–2″ (2.5–5 cm) wide; petals 4; sepals 4, reflexed, arising from top of *long, floral tube;* stamens 8, prominent; stigma cross-shaped.
Leaves: 4–8″ (10–20 cm), slightly toothed, lanceolate.
Fruit: *oblong capsule,* about 1″ (2.5 cm) long, often persisting.
Height: 2–5′ (60–150 cm).
Flowering: June–September.
Habitat: Fields, roadsides.
Range: Throughout.
Comments: The flowers of this night-flowering biennial open in the evening and close by noon. The plant takes 2 years to complete its life cycle, with basal leaves becoming established the first year, and flowering occurring the second. The roots are edible, and the seeds are important as bird feed. Of the 18 species occurring in our area, all but 2 have yellow flowers. Showy Evening Primrose (*O. speciosa*) has pink or white flowers; Tooth-leaved Primrose (*O. serrulata*) has white flowers.

468 Showy Evening Primrose
(*Oenothera speciosa*)
Evening Primrose Family (Onagraceae)

Description: *Nodding buds,* opening into pink or white flowers, are in the upper leaf axils on slender, downy stems.
Flowers: 3″ (7.5 cm) wide; petals 4, broad, sometimes white with pink lines.
Leaves: 2–3″ (5–7.5 cm) long, wavy-margined or pinnately cleft, linear to lanceolate.
Fruit: club-shaped, 8-ribbed capsule up to 2″ (5 cm) long.
Height: 8–24″ (20–60 cm).

Flowering: May–July.

Habitat: Prairies, plains, roadsides.

Range: Virginia south to Florida, west to Louisiana, north to Illinois.

Comments: A hardy and drought resistant species that can form colonies of considerable size. The flowers may be as small as 1″ (2.5 cm) wide under drought conditions. The plant is frequently grown in gardens and escapes from cultivation. The flowers of some members of the genus open in the evening so rapidly that the movement can almost be observed.

ORCHID FAMILY (Orchidaceae)

Perennial herbs with complicated, unusual and often beautiful flowers borne singly or in spikes, racemes, or branched clusters.

Flowers: usually bisexual, bilaterally symmetrical, twisting one-half turn during development, the top of the flower originally the bottom; sepals 3, separate, often resembling petals; petals 3, separate, the lower usually different from the other two and modified into an elaborate lip, often bearing a backward projecting spur or sac; stamens 1 or 2, united with the style and stigma, forming a complex structure called the column. All these parts attached at top of ovary.

Leaves: simple, usually alternate.

Fruit: 3-chambered capsule.

This is the largest family of flowering plants in number of species, but rarely, if ever, is it dominant. The 600–700 genera and 20,000 species are most abundant in the tropics, where they most frequently grow upon other vegetation. Elsewhere they are usually terrestrial. Vanilla is obtained from the fruits of the tropical genus *Vanilla,* and many species are grown as beautiful greenhouse novelties. Certain species and hybrids, once very rare and difficult to acquire, are now reproduced in great numbers by cloning. The elaborate flower has highly specialized relationships with pollinators. Pollen is usually held together in masses and in many cases must be properly positioned on the insect for pollination of another flower to occur.

492 Swamp Pink; Dragon's Mouth
(*Arethusa bulbosa*)
Orchid Family (Orchidaceae)

Description: The smooth stalk, with 1–3
ensheathing, scale-like bracts, has a
single, bright pink, scented flower at its
summit.
Flowers: about 2″ (5 cm) long; *showy lip
petal spotted with darker pink and crested*
with 3 rows of yellow or whitish hairs;
side petals 2, arch over lip; sepals 3,
erect.
Leaves: absent when plant is in flower,
grow to 9″ (22.5 cm) as fruit matures.
Fruit: 6-ribbed, elliptical capsule,
about 1″ (2.5 cm) long.
Height: 5–10″ (12.5–25 cm).
Flowering: May (south)–August (north).
Habitat: Bogs, swamps, wet meadows.
Range: Ontario and Newfoundland to Quebec;
south through New England to the
mountains of North Carolina;
northwest through the Central and Lake
states to Minnesota.
Comments: Named for the fountain nymph
Arethusa, the flower suggests an
animal's open mouth. Its unusual lip
petal serves as a platform for insects,
especially bumblebees, that enter the
flower for nectar and pick up the
powdery pollen masses as they leave.

498 Grass Pink
(*Calopogon pulchellus*)
Orchid Family (Orchidaceae)

Description: Fragrant, *pink flowers in a spike-like
cluster of 2–10,* open sequentially up
the leafless stalk.
Flowers: 1½″ (3.8 cm) long; *yellow-
bearded lip petal stands erect* over 5
similar floral parts (sepals 3 and side
petals 2) that spread forward and
laterally; column incurved, somewhat
petal-like.
Leaves: to 12″ (30 cm) long, single,

basal, grass-like.
Height: 6–20" (15–50 cm).

Flowering: Principally March–August; throughout year in Florida.

Habitat: Bogs and bog meadows; acid, sandy or gravelly sites.

Range: Ontario to Nova Scotia and Newfoundland; south through New England and the Atlantic states to Florida; west to Texas; through Central and Lake states to Minnesota, Iowa, Missouri, Arkansas, and Oklahoma.

Comments: This delicate, sweet-smelling Orchid often springs from sphagnum moss and is easily recognized by the bearded, uppermost lip petal and single, grass-like leaf. Its genus name is from the Greek, "beautiful beard," and the species name is Latin for "little beauty." The Bearded Grass Pink (*C. barbatus*), found from North Carolina south, also has pink flowers and all open together, whereas the flowers of Grass Pink open successively. Another pink, Pale Grass Pink (*C. pallidus*), found from Virginia to Florida and Louisiana, has pale pink to whitish flowers and is smaller in all respects than *C. pulchellus*.

491 Calypso; Fairy Slipper
(*Calypso bulbosa*)
Orchid Family (Orchidaceae)

Description: A single, showy pendant flower with an *inflated, slipper-like lip petal.*
Flowers: 1½–2" (3.8–5 cm) long; lip petal white blotched with purple, bearded with yellow hairs, and with 2 horn-like points at the toe; 5 purplish-pink, narrow parts (sepals and petals) are above the lip.
Leaves: about 3" (7.5 cm) long, solitary, basal, ovate, margin wavy; it withers after plant flowers and is replaced by an overwintering leaf.
Height: 3–8" (7.5–20 cm).

Flowering: May—July.
Habitat: Cool, damp, mossy woods, mainly coniferous.
Range: Across Canada; south to New England and northern New York; west to Michigan and Minnesota.
Comments: This short perennial rises from a small tuber and is the only species in this genus found in the northern latitudes. Its name is that of the nymph in Homer's *Odyssey*.

497 Rosebud Orchid
(*Cleistes divaricata*)
Orchid Family (Orchidaceae)

Description: A pink, tubular flower, with 3 very *long, narrow, spreading, brownish or purplish-green sepals* tops a long stalk.
Flowers: about 2″ (5 cm) long; petals and lip united to form cylindrical tube.
Leaves: up to 8″ (20 cm) long, solitary, basal, oblong-lanceolate, inserted above middle of stem; narrow, leaf-like bract present behind flower, up to 4″ (10 cm) long.
Height: 1–2′ (30–60 cm).
Flowering: April—July.
Habitat: Wet to dry grasslands, pine barrens, and thickets.
Range: North Carolina (rarely southern New Jersey) south to Florida; west to Texas.
Comments: This orchid, the only species in this genus, is related to the genus *Pogonia*. Although it can occupy either wet or dry sites, it apparently requires a habitat with very acid soil.

392 Spotted Coralroot
(*Corallorhiza maculata*)
Orchid Family (Orchidaceae)

Description: A saprophytic Orchid with 10–30 purplish-brown to yellowish flowers along a *yellowish or brownish, leafless floral stalk* that has several sheaths toward the base.

Flowers: about ¾" (2 cm) long; 3 short petal-like sepals above and 2 longer side petals embracing the upper part of lip petal; lip white, squarish, spotted with crimson.

Leaves: absent, represented by tubular sheaths to 3" (7.5 cm) long.

Fruit: ovoid, nodding capsule up to 1" (2.5 cm) long.

Height: 6–20" (15–50 cm).

Flowering: July–September.

Habitat: Moist, upland, deciduous or coniferous forests, occasionally dry forests.

Range: Newfoundland south to New Jersey and in the mountains to North Carolina; west to Minnesota.

Comments: This northern Orchid is the most common and largest Coralroot. It lacks chlorophyll and gets its nourishment from fungi in its coral-like underground stem. Several smaller species differ in color and in the nature of the lip. Five species occur in our area, among them: Wister's Coralroot (*C. Wisteriana*), which flowers from March to May, before any of the others, and Late or Autumn Coralroot (*C. odontorhiza*), with flowers less than ⅛" (5 mm) long, the last to flower, appearing from late August to October.

---

422 **Striped Coralroot**
(*Corallorhiza striata*)
Orchid Family (Orchidaceae)

Description: A saprophytic Orchid with *10–20 purplish-red flowers in an elongated cluster* along a purplish, leafless floral stalk.

Flowers: about 1¼" (3.1 cm) long; 5 flower parts (sepals and petals) curving around the upper part of the white, tongue-shaped lip petal, striped with reddish purple, or all purple.

Leaves: reduced to sheathing scales near the base.
Fruit: elliptic capsule, bent backward, about ⅔" (16 mm) long.
Height: 8–20" (20–50 cm).
Flowering: May–August.
Habitat: Rich or calcareous woods.
Range: Ontario and Quebec; south to New York; west to Michigan, Wisconsin, and Minnesota. Also British Columbia and Alberta south to Wyoming, Idaho, and California.
Comments: The most attractive of several Coralroot species, it can withstand cold but not heat and cannot be successfully cultivated south of its natural range. These Orchids lack chlorophyll and get their nourishment from organic material absorbed from the "coral root," a much-branched ground stem.

493 Pink Lady's Slipper; Pink Mocassin-flower
(*Cypripedium acaule*)
Orchid Family (Orchidaceae)

Description: A leafless stalk bears 1 flower (rarely 2) with a *distinctive pink, inflated, slipper-like lip petal,* veined with red and with a fissure down the front.
Flowers: lip about 2½" (6.3 cm) long; sepals and side petals greenish-brown, spreading; petals lanceolate, narrower than sepals.
Leaves: to 8" (20 cm) long, in twos, basal, oval, ribbed, dark green above, silvery-hairy beneath.
Fruit: erect capsule, to 1¾" (4.5 cm) long.
Height: 6–15" (15–37.5 cm).
Flowering: April–July.
Habitat: Dry forests, especially pine woods; often in humus mats covering rock outcrops; occasionally in moist woods.
Range: Saskatchewan to Newfoundland and Nova Scotia; south to South Carolina and Georgia; west to Alabama and

Comments: This is one of the largest native Orchids
and is found both in low, sandy woods
and in higher, rocky woods of
mountains. At times several hundred of
these striking flowers can be counted
within a small area. Nevertheless, like
other woodland wildflowers it should
not be picked. These Orchids propagate
poorly and are very difficult to grow in
wildflower gardens. The genus name
derives from the Latin for "Venus'
slipper."

---

320 Yellow Lady's Slipper
(*Cypripedium calceolus*)
Orchid Family (Orchidaceae)

Description: Borne terminally on a *leafy stalk* are 1
or 2 fragrant flowers with an *inflated,
yellow, pouch-shaped lip petal.*
Flowers: lip about 2" (5 cm) long; side
petals 2, spirally twisted, greenish-
yellow to brownish-purple; sepals 2,
greenish-yellow, lanceolate, 1 above
and 1 below lip.
Leaves: up to 8" (20 cm) long, usually
3–5, oval to elliptic, with pronounced
parallel veins.
Height: 4–28" (10–70 cm).

Flowering: April–August.

Habitat: Bogs and swamps, rich woods.

Range: Newfoundland, south to mountains of
Georgia; west to Texas, Arkansas,
Kansas, and northwest beyond our
range.

Comments: These plants form a highly variable
population. Other varieties are
recognized, among them Small Yellow
Lady's Slipper (var. *parviflorum*), once
considered a separate species, which has
very fragrant flowers, a lip petal only
¾–1½" (2–3.8 cm) long, brownish
lateral petals, and a height of about 22"
(55 cm). It is found mostly in
limestone wetlands, only rarely as far
south as the Appalachian mountains.

The species name derives from Latin and means "a little shoe." Cherokee Indians made a preparation from the roots that was drunk as a treatment for worms.

494 Showy Lady's Slipper
(*Cypripedium reginae*)
Orchid Family (Orchidaceae)

Description: A stout, hairy, often twisted, *leafy stalk* bears 1–3 large flowers with a *white and pink, pouch-like lip petal.*
Flowers: lip 1–2″ (2.5–5 cm) long, white, rose-pink in front, often veined with purple or deep pink, with many shallow, vertical furrows; sepals and side petals waxy-white, ovate-lanceolate, spreading.
Leaves: up to 10″ (25 cm) long, usually 3–7, ribbed, elliptic.
Fruit: elliptic capsule to 1¾″ (4.5 cm) long.
Height: 1–3′ (30–90 cm).

Flowering: May–August.

Habitat: Swamps, moist woods, especially limestone sites.

Range: Saskatchewan to Newfoundland; south through New England to the mountains of North Carolina and Tennessee; northwest to North Dakota.

Comments: This flower, the tallest and most beautiful of our northern native Orchids, is especially common in the lake states. It has been overpicked and should be protected from further exploitation. The glandular hairs of the foliage may cause a rash similar to that caused by Poison Ivy. Small White Lady's Slipper (*C. candidum*), is a smaller plant, and has a little flower with a white lip; it occurs in limestone soils and boggy places from western New York to northern New Jersey, eastern Pennsylvania, and Kentucky, west to Missouri, and north to North Dakota.

7 Greenfly Orchid
(*Epidendrum conopseum*)
Orchid Family (Orchidaceae)

Description: An *epiphytic Orchid,* with numerous
grayish-green flowers, sometimes
tinged with purple, in a terminal
cluster.
Flowers: about ⅓" (8 mm) wide; sepals
3 and lateral petals 2, narrow, blunt,
colored alike; lip petal spreading,
3-lobed.
Leaves: 1–3" (2.5–7.5 cm) long, 1–3,
elliptic, smooth, often purplish.
Fruit: pendulous, ellipsoid capsule.
Height: 2½–16" (6.3–40 cm).

Flowering: Throughout year, mainly January–
August.

Habitat: On live oak, magnolia, and other trees
in cypress swamps and hammocks.

Range: North Carolina south along Atlantic
Coast to Florida; west along Gulf Coast
to Louisiana.

Comments: This Orchid is often found in
association with, and hidden by, the
epiphytic Resurrection Fern (*Polypodium
polypodioides*). It is one of the most
widespread and hardiest of the
epiphytic Orchids and the only one
found north of Florida. Its common and
species names (the latter from a Greek
term meaning "gnat-like") reflect the
resemblance of the rather inconspicuous
flowers to an insect.

128 Rattlesnake Plantain; Rattlesnake Orchid
(*Goodyera pubescens*)
Orchid Family (Orchidaceae)

Description: A cylindrical cluster of many small,
white, globose flowers tops a leafless,
woolly stalk which rises from a rosette of
dark blue-green, white-veined leaves.
Flowers: ¼" (6 mm) long; upper sepal
and 2 united petals form a hood over
cupped lip petal; side sepals ovate,

concave; sepals and petals colored alike.
Leaves: 1–3½" (2.5–8.8 cm) long,
ovate to oblong; short, scale-like bracts
present on stalk.
Height: to 18" (45 cm).

Flowering: May–September.

Habitat: Dry or moist deciduous (oak) and
coniferous woods; well-drained wooded
slopes.

Range: Ontario, Quebec, and New England
south to Florida; west to Arkansas and
Tennessee; north to Minnesota and the
lake states.

Comments: The highly decorative leaves are most
unusual and often collected for terraria,
a practice to be discouraged. A smaller
species, Dwarf Rattlesnake Plantain
(*G. repens*) has flowers less than ¼"
(6 mm) long on only 1 side of the
flowering stalk. Two species found in
Canada and the northern states are
Checkered Rattlesnake Plantain
(*G. tesselata*), which has dull green
leaves mottled with paler lines, and
Green-leaved Rattlesnake Plantain
(*G. oblongifolia*), whose leaves usually
have only 1 main, white vein. The
common name refers to the mottled
leaves, which resemble a snake's skin, a
similarity that once suggested their use
as a snakebite remedy.

---

151 **White Fringed Orchid**
(*Habenaria blephariglottis*)
Orchid Family (Orchidaceae)

Description: At the top of a leafy stalk is an
elongated, dense or sparse cluster
of pure white flowers with *deeply
fringed lip petals*.
Flowers: about 1½" (3.8 cm) long;
upper sepal and 2 narrow petals form
hood over lip; lateral sepals oblong-
elliptic; long, narrow spur projects
behind flower; sepals and petals colored
alike.
Leaves: lower ones to 14" (35 cm) long,

ovate-lanceolate to linear-lanceolate;
upper leaves reduced to bracts.
Height: 1–2′ (30–60 cm).

Flowering: June–September.

Habitat: Wet meadows, marshes, bogs.

Range: Newfoundland south through New
England to Florida, west along Gulf
Coast to Mississippi, and inland to
Wisconsin and southern Quebec.

Comments: The appropriate species name derives
from Greek and means "fringe-
tongued." Other white species include
the Small Woodland Orchid
(*H. clavellata*), found throughout our
range, with a short blunt lip and a
single clasping leaf on the floral stalk;
the Round-leaved Orchid
(*H. orbiculata*), with greenish-white
flowers and 2 roundish basal leaves,
found in Canada and the northern
United States and in the mountains of
the South; the Prairie White Fringed
Orchid (*H. leucophaea*), with a 3-parted,
deeply fringed lip, found on wet
prairies of the Midwest; and Snowy
Orchid (*H. nivea*), which has white
flowers and no fringe on the lip.

378 Yellow Fringed Orchid
(*Habenaria ciliaris*)
Orchid Family (Orchidaceae)

Description: Terminating a leafy stem is a large,
many-flowered cluster of deep orange to
bright yellow flowers with *drooping,
deeply fringed lip petals.*
Flowers: lip ¾″ (2 cm) long, with spur
to 1½″ (3.8 cm); upper sepal and 2
lateral petals erect; lateral sepals
broadly ovate, spreading; long, slender
spur projects downward and backward.
Leaves: lower ones 3–10″ (7.5–25 cm)
long, lanceolate, sheathing the stem;
upper leaves smaller.
Height: 1–2½′ (30–75 cm).

Flowering: July–September.

Habitat: Peaty or wet, sandy woods and

thickets, dry meadows and slopes.

Range: Southern New England (rare) and New York; south to Florida; west to Texas; north to Missouri, southern Michigan, and Wisconsin.

Comments: This is a very showy Orchid of meadows and open woods. A more southern species, Orange Fringed Orchid (*H. cristata*), has a flower ⅜″ (9 mm) wide and a spur ½″ (1.3 cm) long, shorter than the fringed lip. Yellow Fringeless Orchid (*H. integra*), found in southern New Jersey and eastern North Carolina south to Florida and Texas and north to Tennessee, has orange-yellow flowers with a fringeless lip. Yellow Fringed Orchid and White Fringed Orchid frequently hybridize when growing together; similarly, *H. ciliaris* crosses with Orange Fringed Orchid.

525 Large Purple Fringed Orchid
(*Habenaria fimbriata*)
Orchid Family (Orchidaceae)

Description: The *deeply fringed, fragrant, lavender flowers* are in a many flowered, elongated cluster on a leafy stem. Flowers: 1″ (2.5 cm) long; upper sepal and 2 lateral petals, erect; lateral sepals ovate, spreading; lip petal with 3 fan-shaped, fringed lobes and backward-pointing spur; sepal and petals similarly colored.
Leaves: lower ones to 8″ (20 cm) long, ovate to lanceolate, sheathing the stem; upper ones small, lanceolate.
Height: 2–4′ (60–120 cm).

Flowering: June–August.

Habitat: Cool moist woods, wet meadows, swamp margins.

Range: Newfoundland to New England; south to Maryland and West Virginia; in the mountains to North Carolina and Tennessee; northwest to Wisconsin and Ontario.

Comments: A close-up of the individual flowers reveals the striking beauty of these Fringed Orchids. The method of pollination by moths is interesting. The pollen masses (pollinia) bear a sticky disc that protrudes below the anther. As the moth extends its tongue into the spur of the lip petal and then out again, it pulls the pollen mass from the anther and carries it to another flower where cross-pollination occurs. The Small Purple Fringed Orchid (*H. psycodes*), has smaller flowers. The Purple Fringeless Orchid (*H. peramoena*), has a fringeless lip.

---

8 **Ragged Fringed Orchid**
(*Habenaria lacera*)
Orchid Family (Orchidaceae)

Description: Whitish-green or creamy-yellow flowers with *highly-lacerated, 3-parted lip petals* are in spike-like clusters.
Flowers: ½″ (1.3 cm) long; sepals and petals colored alike; upper sepal and 2 narrow petals erect; lateral sepals ovate, spreading; lip petal deeply 3-parted, the lateral divisions deeply cut, the middle division coarsely fringed; spur curved, slender, ½″ (1.3 cm) long.
Leaves: lower ones to 8″ (20 cm) long, lanceolate, sheathing the stem; upper ones smaller.
Height: 1–2′ (30–60 cm).
Flowering: June–September.
Habitat: Bogs, wet woods, dry to wet meadows and fields.
Range: Nova Scotia and New England; south to Florida; west to Texas; north to Tennessee, Minnesota, and Ontario.
Comments: This Orchid is one of the more common and widespread members of the genus. The genus name is from the Latin *habena* ("rein") and refers to the long spur at the base of the lip, present in all members of this group. In the Nova Scotia area this species crosses freely

with the Large Purple Fringed Orchid
(*H. fimbriata*). At least 10 other
greenish-flowered species occur in our
range, but none with the lip so fringed.

---

319 Small Whorled Pogonia
(*Isotria medeoloides*)
Orchid Family (Orchidaceae)

Description: The 1 or 2 greenish-yellow flowers are
at the top of a greenish stem just above
a *whorl of 5–6 leaves.*
Flowers: about ¾" (2 cm) long; sepals
greenish-yellow, the lateral ones shorter
than the arching dorsal one; lateral
petals greenish-yellow; lip petal white,
3-lobed, crested with pale green.
Leaves: to 3" (7.5 cm) long, pale dusty
green, elliptic, drooping.
Height: 4–10" (10–25 cm).

Flowering: May–July.

Habitat: Dry woodlands.

Range: New Hampshire and Vermont south to
North Carolina; west to Missouri.

Comments: This is an extremely rare Orchid with a
very long resting period of at least 10
years between bloomings, during which
time it remains dormant underground.
The species name apparently refers to
the similarity of the leaf structure to
that of Indian Cucumber Root (*Medeola
virginiana*).

---

394 Large Twayblade
(*Liparis lilifolia*)
Orchid Family (Orchidaceae)

Description: An angled flower stalk bearing several
brownish-maroon-greenish flowers rises
from between 2 large, oval, *shiny basal
leaves.*
Flowers: lip ½" (1.3 cm) long; sepals
narrow, green; *lateral petals threadlike,
spreading; lip petal translucent, brown
with purple veins,* rounded with point

at bottom center.
Leaves: 2–7" (5–17.5 cm) long; sheathe stem below.
Height: 4–10" (10–25 cm).

Flowering: May–July.

Habitat: Rich or sandy woods and clearings, on moss along streambanks.

Range: New England south to Georgia; west to Alabama; north to Tennessee, Missouri, and Minnesota.

Comments: Three features characterize this little woodland Orchid: its brownish-purple flowers, filamentous petals, and greasy-looking leaves from which comes its generic name (derived from the Greek, *liparos,* for "fat" or "shining"). An inconspicuous flower, it may be easily overlooked. Twayblades are mostly Orchids of tropical Asia. The Fen Orchid (*L. loeselii*) has a small green lip and occurs through southern Canada to New York and south in the mountains to Alabama.

105, 504 **Showy Orchis**
(*Orchis spectabilis*)
Orchid Family (Orchidaceae)

Description: A short floral stalk with 2–15 *white and deep lavender flowers* at the top rises from between *2 large, glossy green leaves.*
Flowers: 1" (2.5 cm) long; 2 lateral petals and 3 sepals fused together, forming a *purple or pink hood over a white spurred lower lip petal;* flowers borne in axils of bracts.
Leaves: 2½–8" (6.3–20 cm) long, ovate or elliptic, sheathe the stem.
Height: 5–12" (12.5–30 cm).

Flowering: April–June.

Habitat: Rich, damp woods, swamp margins.

Range: New Brunswick to New England; south to Georgia; west to Alabama; north to Tennessee, Missouri, northeastern Kansas, Nebraska, Minnesota, and Ontario.

Comments: The long spur of this beautiful, fragrant

Orchid of rich woods provides a syrup very rich in sugar. A rare northern species, Small Round-leaved Orchis (*O. rotundifolia*), has a single leaf and purple spots on a white lip. It occurs mostly in the moss of limestone swamps. The genus name, from the Greek *orchis* ("testicle"), refers to the shape of the roundish, fleshy root.

---

495 **Rose Pogonia**
(*Pogonia ophioglossoides*)
Orchid Family (Orchidaceae)

Description: A slender, greenish stem has a *single leaf about midway up* and is terminated by a single, rose-pink flower.
Flowers: about 1¾" (4.5 cm) long; subtended by a leaf-like bract up to 1" (2.5 cm) long. Sepals and petals colored alike: sepals linear-lanceolate, the dorsal one erect; lateral petals ovate, arching over lip petal; lip spatulate, fringed, and bearded in the center with short, yellowish bristles.
Leaves: to 4¾" (12 cm) long, solitary, ovate to broadly lanceolate.
Height: 3–24" (7.5–60 cm).
Flowering: May–August.
Habitat: Wet open woods, meadows, swamps, sphagnum bogs.
Range: Ontario to Newfoundland and Nova Scotia; south on Coastal Plain to Florida; west to Texas; inland to Pennsylvania, Tennessee, Indiana, Illinois, and Minnesota.
Comments: This Orchid is found in places in the eastern United States, where soil conditions rather than temperature are the controlling factors.

131 Nodding Ladies' Tresses
(*Spiranthes cernua*)
Orchid Family (Orchidaceae)

Description: Small, cream-white, fragrant, *nodding flowers* are arranged on a floral spike in 3–4 *spiral-like rows*.
Flowers: ½" (1.3 cm) long; side petals and upper sepal unite to form a hood over the wavy-edged lower lip petal.
Leaves: basal ones to 10" (25 cm) long, lanceolate; upper stem leaves reduced to scales.
Height: 6–24" (15–60 cm).

Flowering: August (north)–November (south).

Habitat: Fields, damp meadows, moist thickets, and grassy swamps.

Range: Ontario to Nova Scotia and northern New England; south to Florida; west to Texas; north to South Dakota.

Comments: A dozen or more species of Ladies' Tresses are known in the eastern United States. Among those with pronounced spirals are Slender Ladies' Tresses (*S. lacera*), with ovate leaves and a green spot on the lip; Short-lipped Ladies' Tresses (*S. brevilabris*), with a downy floral spike; and Little Ladies' Tresses (*S. grayi*), with tiny flowers. In southern marshes and swamps Fragrant Ladies' Tresses (*S. odorata*), grows to 2–3' (60–90 cm) and has spirally arranged clusters of fragrant flowers.

503 Three-birds Orchid; Little Bird Orchid
(*Triphora trianthophora*)
Orchid Family (Orchidaceae)

Description: Along a fragile stem are scattered small, ovate, *clasping leaves* with a pink or white flower rising singly from each axil of the uppermost 1–6 (usually 3) leaves.
Flowers: about ¾" (2 cm) long; sepals and petals similar; 2 upper petals form hood over lip petal; *lip rounded, with*

crinkled margin and purplish-green crest.

Leaves: to ¾" (2 cm) long.

Height: 3–12" (7.5–30 cm).

Flowering: July–October.

Habitat: Rich woods, swamp edges, floodplains.

Range: New England south to Florida; west to Texas; north to Wisconsin.

Comments: This is the only species of this genus known in the United States. As the common name implies, the flowers resemble a small bird in flight. The plant may remain dormant for long periods, with the underground tuber giving rise to a new stem after several years.

---

111 Lawn Orchid
(*Zeuxine strateumatica*)
Orchid Family (Orchidaceae)

Description: A slender, leafy plant with *small, white or yellowish flowers in dense spikes.*

Flowers: about ¼" (6 mm) long; upper sepal joined to 2 side petals, all forming a hood over column; 2 side sepals ovate-oblong; lip petal yellow, fleshy, broadest near end.

Leaves: ¾–3½" (2–8.8 cm) long, *grass-like, overlapping,* tinged with purplish-brown.

Height: 2–7" (5–17.5 cm).

Flowering: Throughout year, mainly January–February.

Habitat: Lawns, wet fields, hummock edges, roadside ditches.

Range: Central and southern Florida.

Comments: Native of Asia and Africa, this species was introduced to Florida, probably around 1917, and has spread rapidly. It is usually found in lawns and waste places.

BROOMRAPE FAMILY
(Orobanchaceae)

Annual or perennial, usually somewhat fleshy, herbaceous root parasites that lack chlorophyll, are some shade of yellow, brown, violet, or red; and have flowers in racemes, spikes, or borne singly at the top of a slender stem.
Flowers: bilaterally symmetrical; sepals 2–5, united; petals 5, united, forming an upper and lower lip; stamens 4. All these parts attached at base of ovary.
Leaves: simple, scale-like, alternate.
Fruit: 1-chambered capsule.
There are about 13 genera and 180 species of primarily north temperate regions, especially warm parts of the Old World. These parasitic plants are usually not so numerous as to be of economic importance.

307 **Squawroot**
(*Conopholis americana*)
Broomrape Family (Orobanchaceae)

Description: This non-green, parasitic plant has yellowish flowers emerging from beneath lanceolate or ovate, pointed *yellow-tan scales* on the upper part of a fleshy stalk.
Flowers: ½″ (1.3 cm) long, 2-lipped; upper lip forms narrow hood over the 3-lobed, spreading, lower lip; stamens 4.
Leaves: lacking, represented by scales.
Height: 3–10″ (7.5–25 cm).
Flowering: May–June.
Habitat: Woods, often under oaks.
Range: Nova Scotia and New England; south to Florida; west to Alabama; north to Wisconsin.
Comments: This plant has a pine cone-like, scaly stalk that becomes dry and brown with age. As a parasite, it gets its nourishment from the roots of trees, primarily oaks.

393 Beechdrops
(*Epifagus virginiana*)
Broomrape Family (Orobanchaceae)

Description: A parasitic plant with *many-branched, brownish-tan stems* and buff-brown or dull magenta flowers in the axils of scattered, dry scales.
Flowers: upper flowers ½″ (1.3 cm) long, tubular; lower flowers only ⅕ (5 mm) long and bud-like, never open, are self-fertilized, and produce seeds abundantly.
Leaves: none, represented by scales.
Fruit: small brown capsule ¼″ (6 mm) long.
Height: 6–18″ (15–45 cm).

Flowering: August–October.

Habitat: Woods, under beech trees.

Range: Nova Scotia to New England; south to Florida; west to Louisiana; north to Ontario.

Comments: As the generic name, from the Greek *epi* ("upon") and *phagos* ("the Beech") implies, this plant is found under beech trees, where it grows upon and receives nourishment from the roots. The flowers are delicately marked and worth a close-up look with a hand lens. Dried stalks often persist under the trees.

68 One-flowered Cancer Root
(*Orobanche uniflora*)
Broomrape Family (Orobanchaceae)

Description: A parasitic plant with 1–3 erect, slender, leafless stalks rising from an underground stem, each stalk topped by a *single, white to whitish-lavender, fragrant flower* with a yellow center.
Flowers: ¾″ (2 cm) long; corolla finely hairy, with fused petals flaring out into 5 lobes, the lower 3 with yellow stripes.
Leaves: represented by overlapping brown scales near base.
Height: 3–10″ (7.5–25 cm).

Flowering: April–June.

Habitat: Damp woods and thickets.

Range: Quebec, New Brunswick, and Nova Scotia; south from New England to northern Florida; west to Mississippi and Texas; north to Montana.

Comments: This parasitic plant obtains its nourishment from the roots of various other plants. Clustered or Yellow Cancer Root (*O. fasciculata*), has long, slender stalks rising from a short, trunk-like stem; it occurs in the midwestern states. Louisiana Broomrape (*O. ludoviciana*), also found in the Midwest, has flowers in dense, spike-like clusters. Both of these species are parasitic, especially on members of the Sunflower Family. Lesser Broomrape (*O. minor*), with purple-tinged flowers in dense spikes, is parasitic on clover roots; it was naturalized from Europe, and occurs from New Jersey to North Carolina.

WOOD SORREL FAMILY
(Oxalidaceae)

Herbs with alternate or basal leaves that are usually compound, the plants varying to shrubs or rarely trees. Flowers usually borne singly or in an umbel; sap often sour.

Flowers: radially symmetrical; sepals 5, separate; petals 5, separate or united at base; stamens 10, joined by their stalks. All these parts attached at base of ovary; ovary has 5 styles.

Leaves: usually palmately compound and resembling 3-leaved clovers; sometimes leaves with more leaflets, or only 1 by evolutionary reduction, or pinnately compound.

Fruit: 5-chambered capsule, rarely berry.

There are about 8 genera and 1,000 species, primarily of tropical and subtropical regions. Several are cultivated as ornamentals, and one tree-like tropical species produces gooseberry-like, edible fruits.

---

265 **Yellow Wood Sorrel; Sour Grass**
(*Oxalis europaea*)
Wood Sorrel Family (Oxalidaceae)

Description: This low spreading plant has *clover-like, sour-tasting leaves* and one to several yellow flowers.
Flowers: ½" (1.3 cm) wide; petals 5; stamens 10; pistil erect, pencil-like.
Leaves: palmately divided into 3 heart-shaped leaflets, each ½–¾" (1.3–2 cm) wide; leaves close at dusk and open in the morning.
Fruit: capsule on a straight or ascending stalk.
Height: 6–15" (15–37.5 cm).
Flowering: May–October.
Habitat: Waste places, roadsides, fields.
Range: Throughout.
Comments: With their clover-like leaves, the Wood

Sorrels are easy to recognize. The sour taste of the leaves is distinctive and they may be used in salads, but sparingly, because of the oxalic acid content. The genus name comes from the Greek *oxys* ("sour"). This European introduction is especially common as a garden weed. The very similar Upright Yellow Wood Sorrel (*O. stricta*), has its seed pod distinctly reflexed on bent stalks. Especially common southward is the Large Yellow Wood Sorrel (*O. grandis*), with bigger flowers, up to 1″ (2.5 cm) across; the leaves often have purple margins.

---

460   **Common Wood Sorrel**
(*Oxalis montana*)
Wood Sorrel Family (Oxalidaceae)

Description: A low-growing plant with *Clover-like foliage* and several white or pink flowers, with *only 1 flower per stalk.*
Flowers: ¾″ (2 cm) wide; petals 5, notched, with *deep pink veins;* stamens 10; pistil 1.
Leaves: basal, divided into 3 heart-shaped leaflets, each about ½″ (1.3 cm) wide; slightly sour taste, close at night.
Height: 3–6″ (7.5–15 cm).
Flowering: May–July.
Habitat: Rich, damp woods.
Range: Newfoundland and Nova Scotia; south to central and western New England; west to Pennsylvania and in the mountains to North Carolina and Tennessee; west to Ohio, Michigan, Wisconsin, Minnesota, and Manitoba.
Comments: This dainty flower of the mountains and cool, moist woodland glens is especially common in New England and westward to the lake states. It is difficult to grow in gardens. Flowers that fail to open are produced at the base of the plant on curved stems.

463 **Violet Wood Sorrel**
(*Oxalis violacea*)
Wood Sorrel Family (Oxalidaceae)

Description: This fragile plant with *Clover-like foliage*
has several rose-purple flowers on each
stalk, rising above the leaves.
Flowers: ¾″ (2 cm) wide; petals 5,
flaring; stamens 10; sepals green, with
orange tips.
Leaves: palmately divided, leaflets 3,
about ¾″ (2 cm) wide, inversely heart-
shaped, reddish or purple beneath.
Height: 4–8″ (10–20 cm).
Flowering: April–June.
Habitat: Open woods, banks, rocky ground,
prairies.
Range: Massachusetts and New York; south to
Florida; west to Ohio, Indiana,
Wisconsin, Minnesota, North Dakota,
and beyond our range.
Comments: This is a very common woodland and
moist prairie species, which is
cultivated occasionally in the North.
It spreads rapidly by runners from its
bulbs, and often flowers again in
autumn after the leaves have died.

POPPY FAMILY (Papaveraceae)

Annual or perennial herbs, occasionally shrubs, rarely trees, often with white or colored sap; flowers mostly borne singly.

Flowers: radially symmetrical, sepals 2 or 3, separate or united, that quickly drop off; 4–6 separate showy petals, often crumpled in the bud; stamens numerous. All these parts attached at base of ovary.

Leaves: alternate, simple or deeply divided.

Fruit: usually capsule, often oddly shaped, and opening by pores.

There are about 26 genera and 200 species, mostly of temperate and subtropical regions, that are well developed in western North America. Several species are grown as ornamentals and opium is extracted from one.

84 White Prickly Poppy
(*Argemone albiflora*)
Poppy Family (Papaveraceae)

Description: The cupped, white flower is at the top of a tall, *bristly stem;* plant has *white juice* that turns yellow after it has dried.
Flowers: about 3″ (7.5 cm) wide; petals 4–6; stamens numerous, yellow, surrounding the 4- to 6-lobed stigma.
Leaves: 3–8″ (7.5–20 cm) long, lobed, *spiny-edged,* often mottled.
Fruit: spiny capsule.
Height: 1–3′ (30–90 cm).
Flowering: April–August.
Habitat: Waste places, roadsides.
Range: Virginia south to Florida; west to Texas; north to Missouri.
Comments: A similar thistle-leaved species, a native of tropical America, is the Yellow Prickly Poppy (*A. mexicana*), which has yellow flowers. It occurs from Virginia

and Tennessee to Florida and Texas and
has escaped from cultivation northward.

254 Celandine
(*Chelidonium majus*)
Poppy Family (Papaveraceae)

Description: The deep yellow flowers are in small,
loose clusters; plant has *saffron-colored
juice*.
Flowers: ⅔" (1.6 cm) wide; sepals 2,
falling as corolla opens and appearing to
be lacking; petals 4.
Leaves: 4–8" (10–20 cm) long, light
green, divided into several *ornamentally-
lobed segments*.
Fruit: smooth, slender capsule, up to 2"
(5 cm) long.
Height: 1–2' (30–60 cm).

Flowering: April–August.

Habitat: Moist soil of roadsides and edges of
woods, around dwellings.

Range: Nova Scotia to New England; south to
northern Georgia; west to Tennessee
and Missouri.

Comments: This European introduction is attractive
but aggressive, and poisonous to
chickens. Since its juices resemble bile,
it was at one time used for liver
disorders, and also for removing warts
and freckles.

570 Pale Corydalis
(*Corydalis sempervirens*)
Poppy Family (Papaveraceae)

Description: The drooping, sac-like, tubular, *pink
and yellow flowers* are in clusters at the
ends of branched stems bearing
ornamentally divided leaves.
Flowers: ½" (1.3 cm) long; sepals 2;
petals 4 (2 inner and 2 outer); stamens
6. Upper petal has a rounded spur
which protrudes upward; mouth and
bottom of flower are golden yellow.

Leaves: 1–4″ (2.5–10 cm) long, pale bluish-green, pinnately compound, cut into mostly 3-lobed leaflets about ½″ (1.3 cm) long.
Height: 5–24″ (12.5–60 cm).

Flowering: May–September.

Habitat: Rocky clearings.

Range: Across Canada to Newfoundland; south to New England and northern Georgia; west to Tennessee, Illinois, Minnesota, and Montana.

Comments: The delicate, dangling flowers and bluish-green foliage distinguish this Corydalis. Five yellow-flowered species occur in our area. Golden Corydalis (*C. micrantha*), a winter annual or biennial, is found in fields or along roadsides, and has flowers about ½″ (1.3 cm) long, is long spurred, with highly divided leaves. A smaller species, Yellow Harlequin (*C. flavula*), has flowers less than ½″ (1.3 cm) long and a very short spur. Climbing Fumitory (*Adlumia fungosa*), is a closely related vine that climbs to 10′ (3 m). It has similar foliage and pink flowers very like those of Pale Corydalis. It occurs most frequently in the Allegheny Mountains, and is often called Allegheny Vine.

---

114 Dutchman's Breeches
(*Dicentra cucullaria*)
Poppy Family (Papaveraceae)

Description: Clusters of fragrant, *white, pantaloon-shaped flowers* are on a leafless stalk and overtop the much-divided, *feathery basal leaves*.
Flowers: ¾″ (2 cm) long; petals 4, the 2 outer ones with inflated *spurs forming a V* that results in the unique floral shape.
Leaves: 3–6″ (7.5–15 cm) long, compound, long-stalked, *grayish green* above, paler beneath, with *deeply cut leaflets*.

Fruit: oblong to linear capsule, opening
to base into 2 parts when mature.
Height: 4–12″ (10–30 cm).

Flowering: April–May.

Habitat: Rich woods.

Range: Nova Scotia and Quebec; south through
the mountains from New England to
Georgia; west to Alabama, Missouri,
eastern Kansas, North Dakota, and
beyond our range.

Comments: The generic name of this delicate spring
flower derives from the Greek for "two-
spurred." The flowers are pollinated by
early bumblebees, whose proboscis is
long enough to tap the nectar.
Honeybees, with a shorter proboscis,
can gather only the pollen with their
front feet. Squirrel Corn (*D. canadensis*),
closely related to Dutchman's Breeches,
is often found in the same habitats. Its
flowers, however, are heart-shaped. The
root tubers' resemblance to corn kernels
accounts for its common name.

501 Wild Bleeding Heart
(*Dicentra eximia*)
Poppy Family (Papaveraceae)

Description: Several deep pink to red, *drooping,*
heart-shaped flowers are strung along a
leafless stem.
Flowers: ¾″ (2 cm) long; petals 4, in 2
pairs; rounded outer petals form "heart"
while inner petals form "drop of
blood."
Leaves: to 10″ (25 cm) long, all basal,
pinnately compound, finely cut.
Height: 10–18″ (25–45 cm).

Flowering: May–August.

Habitat: Rocky woods, cliffs.

Range: New York south to Georgia; west to
West Virginia and Tennessee.

Comments: This native perennial resembles the
more showy Asian species of Bleeding
Heart (*D. spectabilis*), which is often
cultivated in eastern gardens. Typical of
rocky woods and ledges, this species is

common southward along the
mountains.

53 Bloodroot
(*Sanguinaria canadensis*)
Poppy Family (Papaveraceae)

Description: On a smooth stalk a solitary white
flower, with a golden-orange center,
grows beside a lobed basal leaf that
often curls around the stalk. *Roots and
stem with acrid red-orange juice.*
Flowers: to 1½″ (3.8 cm) wide; petals
8–10, separate, the alternate ones
slightly narrower; sepals 2, falling as
flower opens; *stamens golden,* numerous,
surrounding single pistil.
Leaves: 4–7″ (10–17.5 cm) long,
bluish-green, *palmately scalloped into
5–9 lobes.*
Fruit: 2-parted capsule, pointed at both
ends.
Height: to 10″ (25 cm).
Flowering: March–May.
Habitat: Rich woodlands, along streams.
Range: Across Canada to Nova Scotia; south
from New England to Florida; west to
eastern Texas; north to Manitoba.
Comments: This fragile spring flower develops and
rises from the center of its curled leaf,
opening in full sun, and closing at night.
Like most members of the Poppy
Family, it lasts for a relatively short
time. The red juice from the
underground stem was used by Indians
as a dye for baskets, clothing, and war
paint, as well as for insect repellent.
The generic name, from the Latin
sanguinarius, means "bleeding."

253 Wood Poppy; Celandine Poppy
(*Stylophorum diphyllum*)
Poppy Family (Papaveraceae)

Description: Plant with *yellow juice* and yellow
flowers, solitary or in small clusters at
top of a stem that has a *single pair of
deeply-lobed leaves;* other leaves, basal.
Flowers: 1½–2″ (3.8–5 cm) wide;
petals 4, stamens numerous; pistil 1.
Leaves: 4–10″ (10–25 cm) long;
opposite or basal, pinnately divided
into lobed or toothed segments.
Height: 1–1½′ (30–45 cm).

Flowering: March–May.

Habitat: Rich woods, bluffs.

Range: Western Pennsylvania south to
Virginia; west to Tennessee and
Missouri; north to Wisconsin.

Comments: This midwestern species is typically
found in damp woods. The pair of
opposite leaves below the flower is
emphasized by the Greek species name
("two-leaved").

PASSIONFLOWER FAMILY
(Passifloraceae)

Herbaceous vines climbing by tendrils borne opposite the leaves, or, in tropical regions, woody vines, shrubs, or trees with bizarre, elaborate flowers.
Flowers: radially symmetrical, usually in pairs in leaf axils; sepals usually 5, often petal-like, usually separate but sometimes united at the base; petals 5, separate or none; at the base of the corolla are numerous thread-like structures forming a corona; stamens 3–5, or 10; ovary bears 3–5 styles, often raised on a stalk, which also bears stamens.
Leaves: alternate, simple, often deeply lobed.
Fruit: capsule or berry.
There are about 12 genera and 600 species in this mostly tropical American family. Some are grown for the unusual and often gaudy flowers; a few produce edible fruit.

---

652 Passionflower
(*Passiflora incarnata*)
Passionflower Family (Passifloraceae)

Description: A climbing or trailing vine with large, *strikingly fringed flowers.*
Flowers: 1½–2½" (3.8–6.3 cm) wide; 5 outer sepals and 5 petals form a whitish or bluish, wheel-like backdrop, upon which rests a fringe of 2–3 circles of purple and pinkish, thread-like segments; stamens 5, drooping, suspended around 3-styled pistil.
Leaves: 3–5" (7.5–12.5 cm) wide, palmately 3-lobed; 2 conspicuous glands on petiole near blade; tendrils present.
Fruit: yellow berry, 2–3" (5–7.5 cm) long.
Height: vine.
Flowering: June–September.

Habitat: Sandy thickets, open areas.

Range: Southwestern Pennsylvania to Maryland; south to Florida; west to Texas; north to Oklahoma, Missouri, Illinois, Indiana, and Ohio.

Comments: This unusual flower is widely distributed in the South, especially from Florida to Texas. The name relates to the resemblance of the floral parts to aspects of the crucifixion story. The 10 petal-like parts represent the disciples, excluding Peter and Judas; the 5 stamens the wounds Jesus received; the knob-like stigmas the nails; the fringe the crown of thorns. Yellow Passion Flower (*P. lutea*), a small yellow-flowered species, occurs from southeast Pennsylvania to Florida, west to Louisiana, and north to Missouri, Illinois, and West Virginia.

LOPSEED FAMILY (Phrymaceae)

This family has only one species, which is described below.

145 Lopseed
(*Phryma leptostachya*)
Lopseed Family (Phrymaceae)

Description: Small, white or pinkish-lavender flowers are in pairs in *slender, elongated spike-like clusters* along the top of a main stem and its diverging branches.
Flowers: about ¼" (6 mm) long, in clusters to 6" (15 cm) long; corolla 2-lipped, the lower lip much longer than the upper; stamens 4.
Leaves: 2–6" (5–15 cm) long; opposite, coarsely toothed; the upper ones short-stalked.
Fruit: dry, seed-like; enclosed in calyx, *which hangs down against the stem.*
Height: 1–3' (30–90 cm).
Flowering: July–September.
Habitat: Moist woods, thickets.
Range: New Brunswick south to Florida; west to Alabama, Louisiana, and eastern Texas; north to Manitoba.
Comments: This family, in which there is only one genus and species, also occurs in Asia. It is closely related to the Snapdragon Family. The downward-hanging fruit, which accounts for the common name, makes the plant easily recognizable.

POKEWEED FAMILY
(Phytolaccaceae)

Herbs, shrubs or trees, mostly in tropical or subtropical regions, with flowers in axillary or terminal racemes. Flowers: bisexual or unisexual, radially symmetrical; sepals 4–5, separate; no petals; stamens as many as sepals. All these parts attached at base of ovary.
Leaves: alternate, entire.
Fruit: berry, capsule, or winged seed-like segments.
There are about 17 genera and 110 species, mostly in tropical regions; infrequently cultivated.

143, 656 Pokeweed
(*Phytolacca americana*)
Pokeweed Family (Phytolaccaceae)

Description: A tall, large-leaved, branching plant with *reddish stems* and long clusters of small, white flowers.
Flowers: about ¼" (6 mm) wide; sepals 5, white, petal-like; petals absent.
Leaves: 5–12" (12.5–30 cm) long, elliptic-lanceolate, tapering at both ends.
Fruit: *dark purple-black berry,* ¼" (6 mm) wide, in drooping clusters.
Height: to 10' (3 m).

Flowering: July–September.

Habitat: Open woods, damp thickets, clearings, roadsides.

Range: Ontario to southern Quebec, New England, and New York; south to Florida; west to Texas and Mexico; north to Minnesota.

Comments: This is frequently a troublesome weed with poisonous berries and roots, although emerging shoots can be gathered before the pink color appears, cooked, and eaten as greens. The berry juice was used as a dye by the early colonists and to improve cheap wine.

PLANTAIN FAMILY
(Plantaginaceae)

Herbs with basal leaves and small flowers borne in spikes or heads.
Flowers: radially symmetrical; calyx and corolla each have 4 united membranous or papery sepals or petals; stamens 4, protruding from flower. All these parts attached at base of ovary.
Leaves: alternate, basal, simple, with predominantly parallel veins.
Fruit: capsule, with top lifting free, or small nut.
There are 3 genera and about 270 species, most inconspicuous, a few weedy, found nearly throughout the world. Seeds often become mucilaginous when wet, and those of one species are used in making a bulk-producing laxative.

107 English Plantain
(*Plantago lanceolata*)
Plantain Family (Plantaginaceae)

Description: From a basal rosette of long, *narrow, strongly ribbed leaves* rises a floral stalk with a dense, *globose to cylindrical head* of tiny, spirally-arranged, greenish-white flowers.
Flowers: about ⅛" (3 mm) long; corolla 4-lobed; stamens 4, white, protruding; bracts present under flowers.
Leaves: 4–16" (10–40 cm) long, about ⅙ as wide; narrowly elliptic or lanceolate.
Fruit: small, 2-seeded capsule, opening around the middle.
Height: 6–20" (15–50 cm).
Flowering: May–October.
Habitat: Waste places.
Range: Throughout.
Comments: This introduced, narrow-leaved Plantain, is often a troublesome weed in lawns and gardens. The seeds are often eaten by songbirds and are used for feeding

caged birds. The leaves are a favorite
food of rabbits. The somewhat similar
Hoary Plantain (*P. media*), is much less
frequent and has elliptical leaves. At
least 5 other narrow-leaved Plantains
occur in our range, but they have
elongated flower spikes.

33 Common Plantain
(*Plantago major*)
Plantain Family (Plantaginaceae)

Description: Small flowers are massed in a *narrow,
cylindrical, greenish-white spike,* rising
from a set of *broad, strongly ribbed basal
leaves.*
Flowers: $\frac{1}{12}''$ (2 mm) long; with
4-lobed corolla; stamens 4; pistil 1;
bracts present beneath flowers.
Leaves: to 6″ (15 cm) long and 4″
(10 cm) wide, ovate to elliptic.
Fruit: small, 12–18-seeded capsule,
splitting open around the middle.
Height: 6–18″ (15–45 cm).
Flowering: June–October.
Habitat: Waste places, fields, roadsides.
Range: Throughout.
Comments: This broad-leaved Plantain is
considered a weed in lawns and
gardens. The equally common Pale
Plantain (*P. rugelii*), can usually be
distinguished by the purple bases of its
leaf stalks. Heart-leaved or Water
Plaintain (*P. cordata*), another broad-
leafed species, occurs in streams from
New York south to North Carolina,
west to Alabama and Louisiana, and
north to Wisconsin and Ontario. It can
be distinguished from other species by
its hollow stem.

LEADWORT FAMILY
(Plumbaginaceae)

Herbs or shrubs with leaves often in
basal rosettes, and small flowers borne
in heads, modified racemes, or
branched clusters.
Flowers: radially symmetrical; sepals 5,
united, often plaited, showy, stiff and
membranous; petals 5, united, but
corolla often deeply lobed and seeming
to have separate petals; stamens 5, each
positioned opposite a lobe of the
corolla. All these parts attached at base
of ovary.
Leaves: alternate.
Fruit: 1-chambered; often leathery and
does not open, or opens very late, with
one seed.
There are about 10 genera and 300
species found predominantly in dry
parts of the Mediterranean region and
in central Asia. Statice, Thrift, and
Leadworts are cultivated as
ornamentals.

---

651 **Sea Lavender**
(*Limonium carolinianum*)
Leadwort Family (Plumbaginaceae)

Description: A smooth, salt-marsh plant with *small,
pale purple flowers along 1 side of the stems,*
forming a diffuse branching cluster.
Flowers: about ⅛" (3 mm wide); calyx
5-toothed with 10 faint ribs, persistent;
corolla funnel-form with 5 spatulate
lobes.
Leaves: 2–10" (5–25 cm) long, basal,
lanceolate with broadest part toward
apex, margins smooth or slightly wavy.
Height: 1–2' (30–60 cm).
Flowering: July–October.
Habitat: Salt marshes.
Range: Newfoundland and Quebec south to
Florida; west to Mississippi and Texas.
Comments: A strikingly showy perennial in late
summer on the tidal marshes, it is often

associated with other broad-leaved
marsh plants that occur in masses
or scattered among the marsh grasses.
Specimens may vary greatly in size
and vigor depending upon growing
conditions.

GRASS FAMILY (Poaceae)

Herbs, rarely woody, with cylindrical, jointed flowering stems (culms), hollow between the joints, leaves often mostly basal and tiny flowers aggregated into highly modified clusters.

Flowers: bisexual or unisexual, very small; sepals rudimentary; no petals; stamens 3, or rarely 6. All these parts attached at base of ovary; pistil with 2 feathery styles. Individual flowers associated with scale-like bracts, and arranged into a spikelet. Spikelets held in a conspicuous flower cluster, a spike, head, tassel, or openly branched panicle.

Leaves: alternate, oriented on opposite sides of the stem, in 2 ranks, the base forming sheath around the stem, with a hairy or membranous ring (ligule) at the junction of sheath and blade.

Fruit: grain.

This very important family, consisting of about 525 genera and 5,000 species, provides much of the food used by humans, as well as fodder for livestock. Grasses occur throughout the world in almost every habitat, with the greatest diversity of species found in the tropical zone, and the greatest abundance in the temperate regions.

---

403 Redtop
(*Agrostis alba*)
Grass Family (Poaceae)

Description: A delicate grass with many small, 1-flowered spikelets on branches toward the top of the stem, together forming a *reddish-brown, pyramidal, open cluster.*
Flowers: tiny, lacking petals; stamens 3; styles 2. Flower enclosed by scales, the scales grouped in a spikelet $\frac{1}{12}$″ (2 mm) long on branches up to 3″ (7.5 cm) long; entire cluster up to 9″ (22.5 cm) long.

Leaves: blades 2–8″ (5–20 cm) long,
½″ (6 mm) wide, tapering to a point,
hairy on upper surface, smooth on
lower surface; sheathe stem at base.
Fruit: reddish grain.
Height: 8–30″ (20–75 cm).

Flowering: June–September.

Habitat: Fields, roadsides, low places.

Range: Throughout.

Comments: The fine, pinkish-tinged, cone-shaped
flowering panicles are especially
beautiful in open fields. In flower the
tiny stamens, with conspicuous yellow
anthers, hang out of the scales. This
perennial is widely cultivated as a
pasture and lawn grass. It spreads by
underground rhizomes or stems,
forming colonies. Grasses used for golf
courses belong to this genus.

400 **Little Bluestem Grass**
(*Andropogon scoparius*)
Grass Family (Poaceae)

Description: An erect, *yellowish-tan, tufted grass*
(reddish-tan in fall) with spikelets in
narrow terminal clusters on slender
stems that intermingle with the leaves.
Flowers: tiny, lacking petals; stamens
usually 3; styles 2. Flowers enclosed by
scales tipped with long, slender
bristles. Scales grouped in small
spikelets to ⅓″ (8 mm) long; the
spikelets in a spike-like cluster to
2½″ (6.3 cm) long.
Leaves: blades to 10″ (25 cm) long,
1½″ (3.8 cm) wide; slightly folded,
sheathe stem at base.
Fruit: purplish or yellowish grain.
Height: 1½–4½′ (45–135 cm).

Flowering: August–October.

Habitat: Old fields, prairies, open woods.

Range: Throughout the United States, except
California, Washington, Oregon, and
Nevada.

Comments: This mid-prairie species, also known as
Bunchgrass, gets its name from the

bluish color of the stem bases in the
spring, but most striking is the plant's
reddish-tan color in fall, persisting
through winter snows. In winter the
seeds, fuzzy white at maturity, are of
particular value to small birds. A
related species, Big Bluestem or
Turkeyfoot (*A. gerardi*), has finger-like
seed heads that somewhat resemble a
turkey's foot. It reaches a height of 12'
(3.6 m) in favorable bottomland sites
and is also one of our important native
prairie grasses.

399 Sweet Vernal Grass
(*Anthoxanthum odoratum*)
Grass Family (Poaceae)

Description: Tufted, slender stems bear compact,
spike-like clusters of narrow, greenish-
brown spikelets with projecting
bristles.
Flowers: tiny, lacking petals;
stamens 3; styles 2. Flowers enclosed in
scales, the scales grouped in spikelets
⅓" (8 mm) long; spikelets in a cluster
to 3" (7.5 cm) long.
Leaves: blades to 6" (15 cm) long, up to
¼" (6 mm) wide, flat, rough above;
sheathe stem at base; long ligule
(projection at base of blade) present.
Fruit: yellowish grain.
Height: 12–28" (30–70 cm).

Flowering: April–August.

Habitat: Fields, roadsides, waste places.

Range: Newfoundland south to Georgia; west
to Louisiana and Mississippi; north to
Ontario.

Comments: When in flower, the exerted anthers on
their long filaments are most
conspicuous. This grass is very fragrant
when dried. The genus name is from
the Greek *anthos* ("flower") and *xanthos*
("yellow") and refers to the yellowish
flowers of some species.

398 Grama Grass; Mesquite Grass
(*Bouteloua gracilis*)
Grass Family (Poaceae)

Description: The numerous spikelets of this grass are
arranged *along one side of stalks* that rise
above a curly mass of *very thin leaves*.
Flowers: tiny, lacking petals;
stamens 3; styles 2. Flowers enclosed by
scales, the scales grouped into spikelets
about ¼" (6 mm) long; spikelets
clustered in spikes up to 2" (5 cm)
long.
Leaves: 3–6" (7.5–15 cm) long, ½12"
(2 mm) wide; smooth.
Height: 6–20" (15–50 cm).

Flowering: July–September.

Habitat: Prairies.

Range: Manitoba, Wisconsin, and Minnesota;
south to Illinois, Missouri, and Texas;
west beyond our range.

Comments: This is an important, drought-resistant,
short grass in the mixed prairies and
throughout the Great Plains and the
Southwest. It can be confused with
Hairy Grama Grass (*B. hirsuta*), which
is distinguished by a sharp point
extending beyond the florets. A
somewhat similar but shorter species,
Buffalo Grass (*Buchloe dactyloides*), is
usually less than 6" (15 cm) high and is
typical of dry, short-grass plains.

31 Smooth Crabgrass
(*Digitaria ischaemum*)
Grass Family (Poaceae)

Description: A *smooth, non-hairy,* light green, erect
or mat-forming grass with spikelets
inserted along forked, finger-like stalks.
Flowers: tiny, lacking petals;
stamens 3; pistils 2. Flowers enclosed
in scales; scales grouped into spikelets
1" (2.5 cm) long; spikelets in a cluster
up to 4" (10 cm) long.
Leaves: 1–3" (2.5–7.5 cm) long and ⅙"
(4 mm) wide; sharp-pointed.

Height: 6–16″ (15–40 cm).
Flowering: July–October.
Habitat: Cultivated and waste ground.
Range: Prince Edward Island south to Florida; west to Tennessee, Missouri, Kansas, and Texas; north to Oregon.
Comments: This Crabgrass and its relative, Hairy Crabgrass (*D. sanguinalis*), are the bane of lawn owners who insist on only perennial lawn grasses. These two annuals, introduced from Europe, rapidly take over any bare spots and do provide a green cover that is preferable to bare soil. They can be controlled by maintaining dense perennial vegetation. Crabgrasses produce many seeds, a very valuable food source for many ground-feeding songbirds. Goosegrass (*Eleusine indica*), an annual sometimes confused with Crabgrass, has flattened stems and wider, finger-like, projecting floral stalks. A native species, Slender Fingergrass, (*D. filiformis*), occurs less frequently in our range.

402 Barnyard Grass
(*Echinochloa pungens*)
Grass Family (Poaceae)

Description: A coarse grass having ovate, brown, 1-flowered, *prickly spikelets* that are crowded on one side of ascending or divergent branches and aggregated into an open cluster.
Flowers: tiny, lacking petals; stamens 3; styles 2. Flower enclosed by scales, 1 scale tipped with a long, slender bristle, all scales covered with short bristles. Scales grouped into spikelets ⅙″ (4 mm) long; spikelets in a cluster 4–12″ (10–30 cm) long.
Leaves: blades 6–24″ (15–60 cm) long and about ½″ (1.3 cm) wide; sheathe stem at base; margins rough.
Height: 6–48″ (15–120 cm).
Flowering: July–September.
Habitat: Low ground, marshes, wet places.

Range: Throughout.
Comments: There are several very closely related
species of Barnyard Grasses. All are
weeds of moist, fertile places where
they encroach upon gardens and are
serious competitors of more desirable
forage crops.

404 Bottlebrush Grass
(*Hystrix patula*)
Grass Family (Poaceae)

Description: Greenish-brown *spikelets with bristles* are
in groups of 1−3 in a spike at the top
of an erect, smooth stem.
Flowers: tiny, lacking petals; stamens
3; styles 2. Flowers hidden within
scales terminating in a long, slender
bristle; scales grouped in spikelets;
spikelets at first erect against stem,
later divergent, in a cluster to 10″
(25 cm) long.
Leaves: 4−12″ (10−30 cm) long and to
⅔″ (16 mm) wide, rough to the touch,
diverging; sheaths smooth.
Height: 2−5′ (60−150 cm).
Flowering: June−August.
Habitat: Rich or low woods.
Range: Maine south to Georgia; west to
Oklahoma; north to North Dakota.
Comments: The spikelets are arranged in such a
manner as to resemble a bottlebrush.
The genus name, from the Greek
hystrix ("a hedgehog"), aptly describes
this bristly grass.

32 Timothy
(*Phleum pratense*)
Grass Family (Poaceae)

Description: A *narrow, compact, cylindrical cluster* of
several hundred small, green, flattened,
1-flowered spikelets tops an erect, stiff,
unbranched stem with a distinctly
swollen base.

Flowers: tiny, lacking sepals and
petals; stamens 3, styles 2, plumrose.
Flowers enclosed by bristle-tipped
scales about 1/12" (2 mm) long. Scales
grouped into spikelets, the spikelets in
a cluster up to 7" (17.5 cm) long.
Leaves: 4–10" (10–25 cm) long, 1/4"
(6 mm) wide; tapering to a point.
Height: 1½–3' (45–90 cm).

Flowering: June–August.

Habitat: Fields, roadsides, clearings.

Range: Throughout, but particularly in cooler
areas.

Comments: This common old field or pasture grass,
an introduced species, is easily
recognized by the somewhat bristly
spike, especially fuzzy when in flower
with the stamens projecting. It is an
excellent hay plant; songbirds enjoy the
seeds and the cover provided by the
plants growing along roadsides and
fencerows. Native to our mountaintops
is the much smaller Mountain Timothy
or Foxtail (*P. alpinum*), with shorter
clusters and inflated leaf sheaths.

---

406 Giant Reed
(*Phragmites communis*)
Grass Family (Poaceae)

Description: A tall, thick-stemmed grass producing
large, initially reddish, then silver,
plume-like terminal clusters and smooth,
flat, sharp, blue-green leaves; floral
masses become increasingly downy and
purplish-gray as they mature.
Flowers: tiny, lacking petals;
stamens 3; styles 2. Flowers enclosed in
scales about 1/4" (6 mm) long; scales
grouped into spikelets subtended by a
tuft of silky hairs. Cluster of spikelets
to 1' (30 cm) long.
Leaves: blades up to 20" (50 cm) long
and 2" (5 cm) wide, with rough
margins; sheathe stem at base.
Height: 5–15' (1.5–4.5 m).

Flowering: August–September.

Habitat: Fresh and brackish marshes, ditches.

Range: Throughout, but more abundant along the coast.

Comments: This tall and striking plant rarely produces seed but spreads vigorously by underground stems (rhizomes), often running over the surface of the ground for 17–34' (5.1–10.2 m). It can form dense stands that exclude all other wetland species. It is the dominant vegetation of the still extant Hackensack Meadows of New Jersey where it filters pollutants from the greater New York-New Jersey metropolitan area, thus serving a vital role. In New England, tidal gates across estuaries have restricted tidal flow and created heavily brackish conditions on tidal marshes, with the result that Giant Reed has replaced extensive areas of tidal marsh grasses. It is native both to the American and European continents.

29 Kentucky Bluegrass
(*Poa pratensis*)
Grass Family (Poaceae)

Description: A densely tufted grass with smooth, erect stems topped by *pyramidal clusters* of ovoid, green spikelets borne on *thread-like, spreading or ascending branches.*
Flowers: tiny, lacking petals; stamens 6; styles 2. Flowers enclosed in scales; scales grouped into spikelets about ¼" (6 mm) long; spikelets at the ends of branches, together forming a cluster to 6" (15 cm) long.
Leaves: to 8" (20 cm) long and ¼" (6 mm) wide, basal and on lower part of stem.
Fruit: lustrous red, linear-elliptic grain.
Height: 1–3' (30–90 cm).

Flowering: May–August.

Habitat: Moist or dry soil, meadows, fields.

Range: Throughout.

Comments: This grass is often cultivated as a lawn or pasture grass. It gives Kentucky the name Bluegrass State. The Bluegrass region near Lexington is noted for its famous race horses that graze on the limestone-rich grasses.

---

401 Indian Grass
(*Sorghastrum nutans*)
Grass Family (Poaceae)

Description: A loosely tufted grass with *spikelets forming shiny, golden-brown, plume-like masses* on tall stems.
Flowers: tiny, lacking petals; stamens 3, with *prominent, yellow anthers protruding;* styles 2. Flowers enclosed in hairy scales, with a long, slender twisted bristle projecting. Scales grouped into spikelets up to ⅓" (8 mm) long; spikelets in a narrow cluster to 10" (25 cm) long.
Leaves: blades to 2' (60 cm) long, ½" (1.3 cm) wide; projecting from the stem at a 45° angle.
Height: 3–8' (90–240 cm).
Flowering: August–September.
Habitat: Prairies, dry fields.
Range: Southern Ontario and Quebec; south through New England to Florida; west to Texas; north to North Dakota, Wyoming, and Manitoba.
Comments: This is a beautiful grass with a somewhat metallic golden sheen to its flowering parts. It is an important associate in the tall-grass prairies and is relished by livestock. It appears to be favored by occasional flooding and repeated burning and sometimes forms nearly pure stands in the lowlands.

405 **Sea Oats**
(*Uniola paniculata*)
Grass Family (Poaceae)

Description: *Flat, oval, scaly, brownish spikelets* are
crowded into a curving cluster on a tall,
smooth stem.
Flowers: tiny, lacking petals;
stamens 1–3; styles 2. Flowers enclosed
within rough scales up to ½" (1.3 cm)
long; scales grouped into spikelets to
1½" (3.8 cm) long, on ascending
stalks; spikelets in clusters 8–16"
(20–40 cm) long.
Leaves: blades to 16" (40 cm) long, and
under ½" (1.3 cm) wide, smooth.
Fruit: compressed grain.
Height: 3–7' (90–210 cm).
Flowering: June–July.
Habitat: Coastal sands.
Range: Virginia south to Florida; west
to Texas.
Comments: A spectacular grass, often used for
erosion control along beaches. A similar
but smaller and more delicate species,
Wild Oats (*U. latifolia*), has pendulous
spikelets and does not exceed 5'
(1.5 m) in height. It is sometimes
planted as an ornamental and collected
for dried bouquets.

PHLOX FAMILY (Polemoniaceae)

Usually leafy herbs, rarely small shrubs, commonly with showy flowers in open or dense clusters branched in a forked manner.

Flowers: radially symmetrical or slightly bilaterally symmetrical; sepals 5, united; petals 5, united, often forming slender tube with abruptly expanded top or sometimes dish-like; stamens 5. All these parts attached at base of ovary.

Leaves: alternate or opposite, simple or pinnately compound.

Fruit: 3-chambered capsule.

This chiefly North American family is especially well developed in the western United States. About 18 genera and 300 species occur.

---

179 White-flowered Gilia
(*Gilia longiflora*)
Phlox Family (Polemoniaceae)

Description: The smooth, erect, branching stem bears clusters of white, *trumpet-shaped flowers* and stalkless leaves which are divided into *very narrow segments*.
Flowers: about 2" (5 cm) long; *tube of flower 4–5 times as long as the 5 spreading lobes*.
Leaves: up to 2½" (6.3 cm) long; pinnately divided.
Height: 1–2' (30–60 cm).
Flowering: May–September.
Habitat: Sandy soil.
Range: Nebraska and Colorado south to Texas and Arizona.
Comments: This is a common flower of the sand hills of the Midwest. Members of this tubular-flowered group of the Phlox Family interbreed freely in the wilds and have been variously arranged taxonomically. The generic name honors Felipe Gil, an 18th-century Spanish botanist.

428 Scarlet Gilia; Standing Cypress
(*Ipomopsis rubra*)
Phlox Family (Polemoniaceae)

Description: *Red, tubular flowers* are in a long,
slender, branching cluster on a leafy
stem.
Flowers: about 1″ (2.5 cm) long; 5
somewhat spreading corolla lobes;
corolla marked inside with *red spots
against a yellow background.*
Leaves: pinnately divided into
numerous linear or thread-like,
bristle-tipped segments ⅕–1¼″
(5–31 mm) long.
Height: 2–6′ (60–180 cm).

Flowering: May–September.

Habitat: River banks and sandy open places.

Range: North Carolina to Florida; west to
Texas and Oklahoma.

Comments: This southern biennial is often
cultivated in northern gardens. It is
closely related to the showy *Gilia*
genus, a large group of western plants
in the Phlox family. It grows in
Florida's orange groves where it is often
called "Spanish Larkspur."

644 Wild Blue Phlox
(*Phlox divaricata*)
Phlox Family (Polemoniaceae)

Description: A loose cluster of slightly fragrant,
light blue flowers tops a somewhat
sticky stem that produces leafy, *creeping
shoots at the base.*
Flowers: ¾–1½″ (2–3.8 cm) wide;
petals 5, united, form a trumpet-
shaped corolla; stamens 5, short, arise
from inside of corolla tube; pistil 1,
with stigmas 3.
Leaves: 1–2″ (2.5–5 cm) long,
opposite, ovate to lanceolate,
unstalked.
Height: 10–20″ (25–50 cm).

Flowering: April–June.

Habitat: Rich woods, fields.

Range: Quebec and Vermont south to South
Carolina; west to northern Alabama and
eastern Texas; north to Illinois,
Minnesota, Wisconsin, and Michigan.

Comments: This beautiful species is most common
in midwestern woods and fields. It is
sometimes known as "Wild Sweet
William," a name also given to *P.
maculata*. The mature plants in the
eastern part of the range have notched
petals; those in the western do not. The
basal runners of the lovely Creeping
Phlox (*P. stolonifera*) form large
patches; it has fewer stem leaves and
fewer flowers in its clusters; it occurs
from Pennsylvania and Ohio south to
northern Georgia.

---

417 Annual Phlox; Drummond Phlox
(*Phlox drummondi*)
Phlox Family (Polemoniaceae)

Description: A much-branched, *sticky-glandular plant*
with bright rose-red, pink, or white
flowers in tight clusters at the ends of
stems.
Flowers: 1" (2.5 cm) wide; corolla
trumpet-shaped, with 5 spreading
lobes; stamens 5, short.
Leaves: 1–3" (2.5–7.5 cm) long; ovate
to lanceolate, alternate rather than
opposite as in most Phlox.
Height: 8–18" (20–45 cm).

Flowering: April–July.

Habitat: Waste places, fields.

Range: North and South Carolina south to
Florida; west to Texas.

Comments: This southern flower of roadsides and
fields escaped from cultivation. The
species is named for Thomas
Drummond, who sent seeds from Texas
to England in 1835.

549 Garden Phlox; Fall Phlox
(*Phlox paniculata*)
Phlox Family (Polemoniaceae)

Description: A *pyramidal cluster* of pink to lavender
flowers tops a stout, *smooth, erect stem.*
Flowers: 1″ (2.5 cm) wide; petals 5,
united into a trumpet-shaped corolla
with spreading lobes; stamens 5, short;
pistil 1, stigmas 3.
Leaves: 3–5″ (7.5–12.5 cm) long,
opposite, ovate-lanceolate with bristly
margins and *prominent side veins.*
Height: 2–6′ (60–180 cm).

Flowering: July–October.

Habitat: Open woods and thickets.

Range: Central New York south to interior
North Carolina and northwestern
Georgia; west to northern Mississippi,
Arkansas, and Iowa.

Comments: If found in the wilds beyond its natural
range, this flower has probably escaped
from cultivation. The plant has been
widely used as a medicinal herb and the
leaf extract is used as a laxative and
for treating boils. Many color forms
are found in gardens. The very similar
Large-leaved Phlox (*P. amplifolia*), has a
hairy stem and is found in the southern
Appalachian Mountains.

458 Moss Phlox; Moss Pink
(*Phlox subulata*)
Phlox Family (Polemoniaceae)

Description: This low plant forms *moss-like mats* with
pink to lavender (rarely white) flowers
in clusters at the ends of the stems,
collectively forming a continuous carpet
of flowers.
Flowers: ¾″ (2 cm) wide; petals 5,
notched, united into a tubular corolla
with spreading lobes; stamens 5,
slightly protruding.
Leaves: to ½″ (1.3 cm) long, opposite,
closely set, needle-like.
Height: creeper, with flowering

branches 2–5″ (5–12.5 cm) high.
Flowering: April–May.
Habitat: Dry, sandy places; rocky slopes.
Range: New York south to Maryland, and in uplands, to North Carolina and Tennessee, west to Michigan.
Comments: Various color forms of this species are cultivated, especially in rock gardens. Those growing wild in New England have escaped from cultivation. Trailing Phlox (*P. nivalis*), found in sandy pine or oak barrens from Virginia to Florida, and west to Texas, has unnotched petals. Sand Phlox (*P. bifida*), occurs in sandy habitats in the Midwest and has petals with notches ⅛″ (3 mm) or more deep.

641 Greek Valerian
(*Polemonium reptans*)
Phlox Family (Polemoniaceae)

Description: This smooth, weak-stemmed plant has light blue, *bell-shaped flowers* in loose clusters.
Flowers: ½″ (1.3 cm) wide; corolla with 5 spreading lobes as long as the tube; stamens 5, about equal with corolla; stigma 3-lobed, protruding.
Leaves: *pinnately compound,* with 5–15 ovate to lanceolate leaflets, each about 1½″ (3.8 cm) long.
Height: 1–1½′ (30–45 cm).
Flowering: April–June.
Habitat: Rich woods.
Range: New York south to Georgia; west to Oklahoma; north to Missouri and Minnesota.
Comments: This attractive wildflower, with its delicate, compound leaves, is often cultivated in eastern gardens.

626 Jacob's Ladder
(*Polemonium van-bruntiae*)
Phlox Family (Polemoniaceae)

Description: On an erect stem, leafy to the top,
bloom few-flowered clusters of bell-
shaped, bluish-purple flowers with *long
protruding stamens.*
Flowers: ¾" (2 cm) wide; flaring lobes
5; stamens 5, white-tipped.
Leaves: pinnately divided into
numerous ovate to lanceolate, sharp
pointed leaflets, each ½–1½"
(1.3–3.8 cm) long.
Height: 1½–3' (45–90 cm).

Flowering: June–July.

Habitat: Swamps, bogs, mountain glades.

Range: Vermont and New York south to
Maryland and West Virginia, mainly in
mountains.

Comments: The paired leaflets seem to form a
ladder up the stem and account for the
common name, which alludes to the
ladder to heaven seen by Jacob in a
dream.

MILKWORT FAMILY
(Polygalaceae)

Herbs, shrubs, or small trees with odd-shaped flowers borne in spikes, racemes, or branched clusters.
Flowers: bilaterally symmetrical; sepals usually 5, separate, the inner 2 larger and petal-like; petals 3, often fringed; stamens usually 8, united. All these parts attached at base of ovary.
Leaves: alternate, simple.
Fruit: usually 2-chambered capsule.
There are about 13 genera and 800 species nearly throughout the world, although absent from New Zealand and the Arctic. A few are grown as ornamentals. The flower superficially resembles the "pea flower" of the Pea Family (Fabaceae), and is often confused with it by those unfamiliar with Milkworts.

377 **Orange Milkwort**
(*Polygala lutea*)
Milkwort Family (Polygalaceae)

Description: Compact, head-like clusters of *brilliant orange flowers* terminate leafy, simple or branched stems.
Flowers: ¼" (6 mm) long, in clusters about 1" (2.5 cm) long and ¾" (2 cm) wide. Sepals 5, the 2 lateral ones larger and forming petal-like "wings"; petals 3, united and forming a tube-like structure.
Leaves: stem leaves to 1¾" (4.5 cm) long, lanceolate to spatulate; basal leaves broader, in a rosette.
Height: 6–12" (15–30 cm).
Flowering: June–October.
Habitat: Damp sandy or peaty soil.
Range: Coastal Plain; Long Island south to Florida; west to Louisiana.
Comments: This flower is typical of the wet sandy soil and bogs of the pine barrens. The

species name, Latin for "yellow," refers
to the flower's distinctive color when
dried; when fresh, it is bright orange,
differing from most of the Milkworts,
which are pinkish, yellow, or white.
P. cymosa is very similar, but taller,
while *P. nana* has lemon-yellow flowers
on stems only to 6″ (15 cm) tall.

496 Fringed Polygala; Gaywings
(*Polygala paucifolia*)
Milkwort Family (Polygalaceae)

Description: A low plant, flowering from prostrate,
underground stems and rootstocks, with
pink flowers tinged with purple in the
axils of *clustered upper leaves.*
Flowers: ¾″ (2 cm) long; sepals 5, the
2 lateral ones wing-like; petals 3,
forming a tube with a delicate, finely-
fringed yellow or pink crest.
Leaves: upper ones ¾–1½″ (2–3.8 cm)
long; oval, crowded at top of stem;
lower ones reduced, bract-like.
Height: 3–7″ (7.5–17.5 cm).
Flowering: May–June.
Habitat: Rich, moist woods.
Range: Manitoba to New Brunswick; south
through New England, and inland to
Virginia and the mountains of Georgia;
west to Tennessee, northern Illinois,
Minnesota, and Manitoba.
Comments: This exquisite Orchid-like wildflower
resembles a tailless, tiny airplane. It
was thought that, if eaten by nursing
mothers or fed to cows, Milkworts
would increase milk production.

348 Yellow Milkwort
(*Polygala ramosa*)
Milkwort Family (Polygalaceae)

Description: The very small, yellow flowers are in a
branched, *flat-topped cluster.* Roots have
spicy fragrance.

Flowers: about ⅛" (3 mm) long, in clusters 5–6" (12.5–15 cm) wide. Sepals 5, 3 minute, the 2 lateral ones larger and petal-like; petals 3, united into a short tube with tiny lobes; stamens 8, the filaments united into a tube.

Leaves: basal ones about 1" (2.5 cm) long or less, ovate or narrowly elliptic; stem leaves progressively smaller.

Height: 5–16" (12.5–40 cm).

Flowering: June–August.

Habitat: Marshes, pine-barren swamps, low ground.

Range: Coastal plain; New Jersey south to Florida; west to Texas.

Comments: Other species of Milkworts with flat-topped inflorescences include *P. cymosa,* a larger plant to 4' (1.2 m) tall with yellow flowers and narrow, mostly basal leaves. *P. baldwinii* is a southern, white-flowering species.

517 Field Milkwort; Purple Milkwort
(*Polygala sanguinea*)
Milkwort Family (Polygalaceae)

Description: Tiny, pink to rose or greenish flowers in a *dense, cylindrical, head-like cluster,* with floral bracts beneath the flowers that persist on stem when flowers fall. Underground root gives off wintergreen odor when crushed.

Flowers: about ¼" (6 mm) long, in cluster about ½–¾" (1.3–2 cm) long. Sepals 5, green or pink, the 2 lateral ones forming wings; petals 3.

Leaves: ½–1½" (1.3–3.8 cm) long, alternate, narrow, scattered.

Height: 5–15" (13–38 cm).

Flowering: June–October.

Habitat: Damp grasslands.

Range: Ontario to Nova Scotia; south through New England to South Carolina; west to Tennessee and Louisiana; north to Oklahoma and Minnesota.

Comments: At least a dozen species of Milkworts

occur with pink or white flowers. A somewhat similar pink-flowering species, Racemed Milkwort (*P. polygama*), is a perennial with a looser floral cluster. It also produces a different kind of flower, one that does not open, on whitish, subterranean, horizontal branches. The white-flowering Seneca Snakeroot (*P. senega*), has an elongated cluster of tiny, white flowers and lanceolate to ovate leaves. These species are typical of dry, often sandy, or rocky woods.

BUCKWHEAT FAMILY
(Polygonaceae)

Mostly herbs, sometimes shrubs or
vines, rarely trees, with small flowers in
racemes, spike-like clusters, or in
heads. Stems commonly have swollen
nodes. (The family name refers to this,
deriving from Greek words meaning
"many knees".)
Flowers: usually bisexual, radially
symmetrical; sepals 3–6, separate,
petal-like, sometimes in two series of
3 each, the outer series differing
somewhat from the inner; no petals;
stamens 3–9. All these parts attached
at base of ovary.
Leaves: simple, usually alternate, at the
base often forming a membranous
sheath around the stem above the node.
Fruit: small, hard, generally 3-sided or
lens-shaped.
There are about 40 genera and 800
species, chiefly in north temperate
regions. Rhubarb and Buckwheat are
sources of food, and a few species are
grown as ornamentals.

---

530 **Long-bristled Smartweed**
(*Polygonum caespitosum*)
Buckwheat Family (Polygonaceae)

Description: Narrow, spike-like clusters of tiny,
pink flowers terminate stems with *long
bristles radiating from encircling sheaths* at
the leaf axils.
Flowers: about ⅛" (3 mm) long, in
clusters ¾–1½" (2–3.8 cm) long.
Calyx 5-parted; petals absent.
Leaves: up to 3" (7.5 cm) long; elliptic
to lanceolate; bristles of encircling
sheath at leaf axil up to ½" (1.3 cm)
long.
Fruit: seed-like, black, triangular.
Height: 1–3' (30–90 cm).
Flowering: June–October.
Habitat: Waste places, moist soil.

Range: Quebec south through New England to
Georgia; west to Louisiana; north to
Minnesota.

Comments: This slender, loosely branched annual is
distinguished from the many other
Smartweeds by long bristles on the leaf
sheath, equal to, or longer than, the
sheath itself.

527 **Swamp Smartweed**
(*Polygonum coccineum*)
Buckwheat Family (Polygonaceae)

Description: A variable plant having terrestrial and
aquatic forms, both with *tiny, deep pink
flowers in slender, elongated, spike-like
clusters.*
Flowers: about ⅙″ (4 mm) long, in
clusters 1½–7″ (3.8–17.5 cm) long.
Petals lacking; calyx 5-parted, colored.
Leaves: those of terrestrial forms up to
8″ (20 cm) long, lanceolate, tapering at
both ends, with encircling sheath where
leaf stalk joins stem. Leaves of
aquatic forms floating, up to 6″
(15 cm) long, thin, lanceolate-ovate
with rounded or heart-shaped bases.
Fruit: seed-like, dark brown or black.
Height: aquatic, with terrestrial forms
2–3′ (60–90 cm) high.

Flowering: July–September.

Habitat: Shores, wet prairies, swamps, ponds,
quiet streams.

Range: Throughout.

Comments: The genus name of this group is from
the Greek *poly* ("many") and *gonu*
("knee" or "joint"), and refers to the
thickened joints of the stem where a
sheath often surrounds the stem at the
leaf axil. This group includes the
Smartweeds, with tiny flowers in
terminal spikes, and the Knotweeds,
with flower clusters in the leaf axils.

223 Japanese Bamboo; Japanese Knotweed
(*Polygonum cuspidatum*)
Buckwheat Family (Polygonaceae)

Description: A large, bushy plant with spreading, axillary clusters of greenish-white flowers on *large, hollow, jointed and mottled stems;* male and female flowers on separate plants.
Flowers: about ⅛″ (3 mm) long, in clusters 2–3″ (5–7.5 cm) long; sepals mostly 5; petals absent.
Leaves: 4–6″ (10–15 cm) long, rounded or ovate, coming to a point.
Fruit: seed-like, black, smooth, 3-angled.
Height: 3–7′ (90–210 cm).
Flowering: August–September.
Habitat: Waste places and roadsides.
Range: Newfoundland south to North Carolina; west to Minnesota and Ontario.
Comments: An Asiatic introduction recognized by the stout, bushy, branched, jointed stems resembling bamboo. It qualifies more as a weed than as a wildflower, since once established it can rapidly take over a given area and is most difficult to eradicate. Its young shoots can be cooked and eaten like asparagus, and the seeds are eaten by ground-feeding songbirds.

529 Pennsylvania Smartweed; Pink Knotweed
(*Polygonum pensylvanicum*)
Buckwheat Family (Polygonaceae)

Description: Dense, erect, spike-like clusters of small, bright pink flowers are on *sticky-haired stalks.*
Flowers: about ⅛″ (3 mm) long, in clusters ½–2½″ (1.3–6.3 cm) long. Petals absent; petal-like sepals 4–6, showy, colorful; stamens 3–9.

Leaves: 4–6" (10–15 cm) long, narrow, lanceolate; *leaf bases form a distinctive cylindrical sheath* where the petiole joins the stem.
Fruit: 2-sided, concave, smooth.
Height: 1–4' (30–120 cm).

Flowering: May–October.
Habitat: Moist waste places, fields.
Range: Throughout.
Comments: Over 30 species of Smartweeds occur, and are identified by their spikes of numerous flowers and encirling leaf sheaths. A closely related species, Pale Smartweed (*P. lapathifolium*), has white or pale rose, arching flower spikes and usually smooth stems. Both are found in gardens as well as in damp waste places. There are also climbing species of Smartweeds. The seeds of these plants are eaten by songbirds and waterfowl.

528 Lady's Thumb
(*Polygonum persicaria*)
Buckwheat Family (Polygonaceae)

Description: Dense, erect, oblong or cylindrical spikes of small, pink or purplish flowers are at the tops of simple or branching, *pinkish stems.*
Flowers: about ⅛" (4 mm) long, in clusters ⅔–2" (1.6–5 cm) long. Petals absent; sepals 4–6, colored.
Leaves: 2–6" (5–15 cm) long, narrowly or broadly lanceolate, punctate, with a *dark green triangle in the middle.* The *cylindrical sheath* formed by the leaf base where it joins the stem is *fringed with short bristles.*
Fruit: seed-like, glossy black, 3-angled.
Height: 8–32" (20–80 cm).

Flowering: June–October.
Habitat: Roadsides, damp clearings, cultivated ground.
Range: Throughout.
Comments: This is an abundant weed, common in the United States, the British Isles, and

Europe. The dark green splotch in the
center of the leaf was apparently
thought to resemble a lady's
thumbprint.

---

440 **Sheep Sorrel; Common Sorrel**
(*Rumex acetosella*)
Buckwheat Family (Polygonaceae)

Description: A *sour-tasting weed* with distinctive
arrowhead-shaped leaves and long, spike-
like clusters of tiny, reddish or greenish
flowers; male and female flowers are on
separate plants.
Flowers: about $\frac{1}{12}''$ (2 mm) long, in
clusters up to ½ the length of the stem.
Calyx 6-parted; petals absent. Male
flowers nodding on short, jointed
stalks; female flowers with fruit
protruding from deciduous sepals.
Leaves: $\frac{3}{4}-2''$ (2–5 cm) long.
Fruit: seedlike, shiny golden brown.
Height: 6–12" (15–30 cm).
Flowering: June–October.
Habitat: Open sites, especially sour soils.
Range: Throughout.
Comments: This vigorous, perennial weed, with
running rootstalks, is especially favored
by acid soils low in nutrients. In pure
stands the flowers are sufficiently showy
to be attractive, and bees and small
butterflies serve as pollinators. The
seeds are eaten by ground-feeding
songbirds and the leaves, or even whole
plants, by rabbits and deer. Engleman's
Sorrel (*R. hastatulus*), is very similar but
taller. Green Sorrel (*R. acetosa*) is taller
still, with leaves 4–6" (10–15 cm)
long.

439 Curly Dock
(*Rumex crispus*)
Buckwheat Family (Polygonaceae)

Description: A stout plant with small, reddish or
greenish flowers in a long, slender,
branching cluster at the top of a stem
bearing *leaves with very wavy margins.*
Flowers: about ⅛" (4 mm) long; sepals
in 2 cycles of 3; petals absent.
Leaves: 6–10" (15–25 cm) long,
oblong to lanceolate, margins crisped.
Fruit: seed-like, brown, enclosed by
calyx of 3 "wings" with smooth
margins.
Height: 2–4' (60–120 cm).

Flowering: June–September.

Habitat: Old fields, waste places.

Range: Throughout.

Comments: A somewhat similar plant, Bitter Dock
(*P. obtusifolius*), has heart-shaped leaves
with reddish veins and calyx lobes with
toothed margins. These introduced
species are common pasture, meadow,
garden, or roadside weeds. The young
leaves have a rather pleasantly bitter,
lemonish, flavor and can be used with
other greens in salads.

PICKERELWEED FAMILY
(Pontederiaceae)

Erect or floating aquatics with flowers usually clustered in spikes or solitary.
Flowers: more or less bilaterally symmetrical; sepals 6, petal-like, often united at the base; stamens 3 or 6. All these parts attached at base of ovary.
Leaves: alternate, long-stalked, the blades floating or emergent, or sometimes absent in submerged forms.
Fruit: capsule or seed-like.
There are 6 genera and about 20 species in shallow fresh water in the warm and temperate regions of America, Asia, and Africa.

624 Water Hyacinth
(Eichornia crassipes)
Pickerelweed Family (Pontederiaceae)

Description: A *floating aquatic* with a spike of showy, bluish-purple or lavender, funnel-shaped flowers.
Flowers: about 2" (5 cm) wide and long; 6-lobed, the upper lobe larger with a conspicuous yellow spot; sepals similar to the petals; stamens 6.
Leaves: 1–5" (2.5–12.5 cm) broad, roundish or kidney-shaped, bright green, shiny; petioles with *inflated "bulbs"* filled with spongy, air-filled tissue that act as floats.
Height: aquatic, with flower stalk to 16" (40 cm) above water.
Flowering: All year.
Habitat: Swamps, fresh water marshes, streams, lakes, ditches.
Range: Virginia south to Florida; west to Texas and Missouri.
Comments: An introduced tropical plant, it spreads rapidly, clogging waterways in the southern states. It may have some potential for removing excessive nutrients from overly enriched aquatic systems. If the plants are harvested

periodically, the nutrient load in the water can be reduced. This plant can screen heavy metals and other toxins from polluted water.

---

623 Pickerelweed
(*Pontederia cordata*)
Pickerelweed Family (Pontederiaceae)

Description: An aquatic herb with a creeping rhizome beneath the water and *violet-blue flower spikes extending above water.*
Flowers: ⅓″ (8 mm) long; funnel-shaped, with 3-lobed upper lip, the middle one marked with 2 yellow spots; 3 lower flower parts separate; stamens 6, 3 long and 3 short, often abortive; 2 bracts present beneath flower spike, the lower one resembling the basal leaves, the upper one a sheath.
Leaves: 4–10″ (10–25 cm) long, basal, heart-shaped, indented at bases and tapering to a point, *extend above water.*
Fruit: seed-like.
Height: aquatic, with flower stalk 1–2′ (30–60 cm) above water.

Flowering: June–November.

Habitat: Fresh water marshes, edges of ponds, lakes, and streams.

Range: Ontario to Nova Scotia and New England; south to northern Florida; west to Missouri and Oklahoma; north to Minnesota.

Comments: This emergent aquatic, with its leaves and flowers above water and portions of the stem under water, is found typically in shallow, quiet water. The seeds can be eaten like nuts and the young leaf-stalks cooked as greens. Deer also feed on these plants. The common name suggests that this plant, as well as the fish known as pickerel, occupy the same habitat.

PURSLANE FAMILY
(Portulacaceae)

Herbs, often succulent, with delicate flowers borne singly or in branched inflorescences.

Flowers: radially symmetrical; sepals usually 2, united or separate; petals 4–6 or more, separate or united at the base; 1 stamen opposite each petal, or many stamens. All these parts attached at base of ovary.

Leaves: simple, alternate, opposite or in a dense basal rosette.

Fruit: usually capsule, often opening at the top like a lid.

There are about 19 genera and nearly 600 species throughout the world, with many in the Americas. A few are grown as ornamentals and some are eaten as potherbs.

---

459 **Spring Beauty**
(*Claytonia virginica*)
Purslane Family (Portulacaceae)

Description: A low plant with loose clusters of *pink or whitish flowers, striped with dark pink.*
Flowers: ½–¾" (1.3–2 cm) wide; sepals 2; petals 5; stamens 5 with pink anthers.
Leaves: 2–8" (5–20 cm) long, *usually a single pair*, opposite, dark green, linear, tapering at both ends, present midway up stem.
Fruit: small capsule enclosed by the 2 sepals.
Height: 6–12" (15–30 cm).

Flowering: March–May.

Habitat: Moist woods, thickets, clearings.

Range: Ontario to Quebec and southern New England; south to Georgia; west to Louisiana and Texas; north to Minnesota.

Comments: This most attractive spring perennial is spectacular in large patches. It grows from an underground tuber like a small potato; this has a sweet, chestnut-like flavor. Indians and colonists used them for food and they are still enjoyed by those interested in edible wild plants. A similar species, Carolina Spring Beauty (*C. caroliniana*), has broader, oval to oblong leaves. It is found primarily in the moist woods of the eastern mountains and extends westward to Minnesota.

266 Purslane
(*Portulaca oleracea*)
Purslane Family (Portulacaceae)

Description: A *sprawling plant* with *smooth, thick, fleshy, reddish stems* and small, pale yellow flowers, solitary or in small rounded clusters.
Flowers: about ¼″ (6 mm) wide; sepals 2; petals usually 5; stamens 8 or more.
Leaves: ½–1½″ (1.3–3.8 cm) long, alternate and opposite, *fleshy*, flat, spatulate to ovate, rounded at the summit.
Fruit: small, round capsule.
Height: creeper, with prostrate branches to 12″ (30 cm) long.
Flowering: June–November.
Habitat: Cultivated and waste ground.
Range: Throughout.
Comments: This widespread and well-known weed, with flowers that open only in the sun, can become quite a pest in gardens during hot weather, but it has the virtue of being easily pulled out. It was at one time valued as a salad plant and potherb because its iron content is exceptionally high.

453 Rose Moss; Rose Purslane
(*Portulaca pilosa*)
Purslane Family (Portulacaceae)

Description: A *prostrate, fleshy, branching plant* with small, pink or purplish flowers at the end of branches with *tufts of whitish hairs in the leaf axils.*
Flowers: about ⅔" (16 mm) wide; sepals 2; petals large, usually 5; stamens many.
Leaves: about 1" (2.5 cm) long, fleshy, spatulate, linear, or lanceolate.
Fruit: dry capsule with a "lid" that opens near the middle to expose the smooth, red seeds.
Height: 2–8" (5–20 cm).

Flowering: June–October.

Habitat: Dry, sandy soil; disturbed areas.

Range: Coastal plain; North Carolina south to Florida; west to Texas.

Comments: This low, sprawling, native plant is similar to the Garden Portulaca (*P. grandiflora*), which also has tufts of hairs in the leaf axils but larger flowers to 2" (5 cm) wide. Introduced from South America, it is a popular garden annual which often escapes from cultivation. The Latin name, for "little gate," describes the lid on the fruit capsule.

PRIMROSE FAMILY
(Primulaceae)

Leafy herbs usually with showy flowers
blooming singly or in clusters.
Flowers: radially symmetrical; sepals 5,
often united at base; petals 5, united or
separate, or no petals; stamens 5,
opposite the petals or lobes of the
corolla, or alternate with sepals in
flowers lacking petals. All these parts
usually attached at base of ovary.
Leaves: opposite, whorled, or basal;
usually simple.
Fruit: one-chambered capsule.
There are about 28 genera and 800
species mostly in the north temperate
zone. In the United States the family is
most diverse in the eastern region.
Primroses, Cyclamens and several
others are grown as ornamentals.

---

373 Scarlet Pimpernel
(*Anagallis arvensis*)
Primrose Family (Primulaceae)

Description:	The sprawling, low-branched plant has *long-stalked,* nodding, solitary, star-like flowers arising from the leaf axils. Flowers: ¼" (6 mm) wide; corolla 5-lobed; petals commonly orange to scarlet, but also white or blue, *fringed with minute teeth;* stamens 5, the filaments bearded. Leaves: ¼–1¼" (6–31 mm) long, opposite, ovate, unstalked. Height: 4–12" (10–30 cm).
Flowering:	June–August.
Habitat:	Sandy soil, waste places, roadsides.
Range:	Throughout.
Comments:	Introduced from Europe, this attractive little annual often shows up in flower beds or in other open soil sites. Its flowers close in late afternoon; in England it has been called "Poorman's Weatherglass" because it closes its flowers in cloudy or bad weather. It was

at one time used as a cure for
melancholy. The leaves may cause a
severe dermatitis.

---

508 Shooting Star
(*Dodecatheon meadia*)
Primrose Family (Primulaceae)

Description: Nodding flowers with *strongly backward-
pointing petals* are in flat-topped clusters.
Flowers: 1″ (2.5 cm) long; petals 5,
rose, lilac, or white; stamens 5, yellow,
protruding.
Leaves: up to 6″ (15 cm) long, basal,
dark green, lanceolate with reddish
bases.
Height: 8–20″ (20–50 cm).
Flowering: April–June.
Habitat: Open woods, meadows, prairies.
Range: Pennsylvania to Georgia; west to
eastern Texas; north to Wisconsin.
Comments: It is often cultivated. Bees, the chief
pollinators, must force their tongues
between the united stamens to reach
the stigma of the pistil. The plant was
far more abundant during the days of
the prairie settlers, who called it
"Prairie Pointers." Amethyst Shooting
Star (*D. amethystinum*), with reddish-
purple flowers and usually green leaf
bases, occurs along bluffs on such rivers
as the Mississippi, Susquehanna, and
Ohio.

---

110 Featherfoil
(*Hottonia inflata*)
Primrose Family (Primulaceae)

Description: An aquatic plant with several thick,
hollow, inflated, upright stalks emerging
from the water and bearing tiny,
greenish-white flowers in terminal
clusters and in circles at the joints.
Flowers: ⅓″ (8 mm) long; petals 5,
white, inconspicuous compared to the

5 larger, linear, green sepals.

Leaves: ¾–2½″ (2–6.3 cm) long, crowded at base of plant, alternate, opposite, or whorled, pinnately compound, divided into narrow segments.

Height: aquatic, with stem 3–8″ (7.5–20 cm) above water.

Flowering: April–June.

Habitat: Pools, ditches, stagnant ponds, usually in more than 1′ (30 cm) of water.

Range: New England and New York; south to Florida, west to Texas; north to Missouri, Illinois, Indiana, and Ohio.

Comments: The unusual appearance of this floating aquatic plant is due to the ½″ (1.3 cm) thick, inflated, floral stalks that are constricted at the joints and essentially leafless. Plants appear in great abundance for a season and completely vanish for as many as 7 or 8 years before appearing again.

---

353 Fringed Loosestrife
(*Lysimachia ciliata*)
Primrose Family (Primulaceae)

Description: The erect stem, simple or branched, bears yellow flowers rising on stalks in the axils of opposite leaves with *leaf stalks fringed with spreading hairs*.

Flowers: ¾″ (2 cm) wide, usually pointing outward or even downward; petals 5, minutely toothed and coming to a sharp point; stamens 10, 5 fertile and separate, 5 rudimentary.

Leaves: 2½–5″ (6.3–12.5 cm) long, lanceolate to ovate.

Height: 1–4′ (30–120 cm).

Flowering: June–August.

Habitat: Damp woods and thickets, flood plains.

Range: Quebec and Nova Scotia south to Georgia; west to Texas; west and northwest beyond our range.

Comments: The species name emphasizes the hairy leaf stalks of this wetland plant that is sometimes placed in the genus

Steironema. Southern Loosestrife
(*L. tonsa*), with smooth leaf stalks
and only to 3′ (90 cm) tall, occurs from
Virginia to Georgia, west to Arkansas
and Kentucky. Lance-leaved Loosestrife
(*L. lanceolata*) has narrow leaves to the
bases and occurs in a range similar to
that of Fringed Loosestrife, but
northwest only as far as North Dakota
and western Ontario. Trailing
Loosestrife (*L. radicans*) has very weak
stems, virtually trailing on the ground;
it occurs in the south-central United
States.

261 Moneywort
(*Lysimachia nummularia*)
Primrose Family (Primulaceae)

Description: A trailing plant with *paired, nearly
round leaves* and showy, yellow flowers
on slender stalks rising from the leaf
axils.
Flowers: 1″ (2.5 cm) wide; petals
usually 5, dotted with dark red;
stamens 5, erect.
Leaves: ½–1″ (1.3–2.5 cm) long.
Height: creeper, with stem 6–20″
(15–50 cm) long.
Flowering: June–August.
Habitat: Damp roadsides, shores, and
grasslands.
Range: Newfoundland south to New England,
New Jersey, and Georgia; west to
Missouri and Kansas; north to Ontario.
Comments: This introduced species takes well to
cultivation, especially in rock gardens
or in hanging baskets. The species
name is from the Latin *nummus*
("a coin") and refers to the shape of the
leaves.

321 Garden Loosestrife
(*Lysimachia punctata*)
Primrose Family (Primulaceae)

Description: Yellow flowers are crowded into the axils of *whorled leaves on a hairy stem.*
Flowers: ¾" (2 cm) wide; petals 5, minutely hairy.
Leaves: 2–4" (5–10 cm) long, occasionally only opposite, lanceolate.
Height: 2–3' (60–90 cm).
Flowering: June–September.
Habitat: Waste places, roadsides.
Range: Newfoundland and Nova Scotia; south to Pennsylvania.
Comments: This plant, a native of Eurasia, has escaped from gardens and become a weed, especially in the Northeast. Plants in the family Lythraceae are also called Loosestrifes, which demonstrates the confusion often caused by the use of common names.

322 Whorled Loosestrife
(*Lysimachia quadrifolia*)
Primrose Family (Primulaceae)

Description: Delicate, yellow, stalked, *star-like flowers* rise from the axils of *whorled leaves.*
Flowers: about ½" (1.3 cm) wide; *corolla* 5-lobed, *marked with red around the center* and often in streaks extending into the lobes; stamens 5; pistil 1, protruding beyond the stamens.
Leaves: 2–4" (5–10 cm) long, in whorls of 3–6 (usually 4), light green, lanceolate.
Fruit: capsule about as long as sepals.
Height: 1–3' (30–90 cm).
Flowering: June–August.
Habitat: Dry or moist open woods, thickets, and fields.
Range: Southern Ontario to Maine and New England south to Georgia; west to Alabama; north to Tennessee, Illinois, and Wisconsin.

Comments: The whorled leaves and flowers are the
characteristic features of this rapidly
spreading member of the Primrose
Family. The generic name honors
Lysimachus, a king of ancient Sicily
who is said to have used a member of
the genus to pacify a maddened bull.
Colonists also fed the plant to oxen so
that they would work together
peacefully.

324 Swamp Candles
(*Lysimachia terrestris*)
Primrose Family (Primulaceae)

Description: The erect stem bears a *terminal, spike-
like cluster* of yellow flowers with 2 red
spots at the base of each petal.
Flowers: ½″ (1.3 cm) wide; petals 5;
stamens 5.
Leaves: 1½–4″ (3.8–10 cm) long,
lanceolate, opposite, sharp-pointed at
both ends. *Small, reddish bulblets* often
present in axils of leaves after flowering.
Height: 1–3′ (30–90 cm).
Flowering: June–August.
Habitat: Marshes, moist thickets, low grounds.
Range: Newfoundland, Nova Scotia, and
Ontario; south through New England
to Georgia; west to Kentucky and
Arkansas; north to Iowa, Minnesota,
and Manitoba.
Comments: In a wetland garden this showy species
will spread rapidly by underground
stems. Loomis' Loosestrife (*L. loomisii*),
with candle-like clusters of yellow
flowers and whorled, very narrow,
1″ (2.5 cm) long leaves, occurs from
North Carolina to Georgia. Tufted
Loosestrife (*L. thyrsiflora*), looks very
different, with flower clusters borne
from the axils of the lower leaves. It is
found in swamps and bogs in much of
Canada, south to New Jersey, west to
West Virginia, Missouri, Colorado, and
California. Swamp Candles freely
hybridize with Whorled Loosestrife

(*L. quadrifolia*), producing lovely intermediates, and with Tufted Loosestrife, producing plants with both terminal and axillary flower clusters.

---

61 Starflower
(*Trientalis borealis*)
Primrose Family (Primulaceae)

Description: Fragile, white flowers are on delicate stalks arising from a *whorl of 5–9 leaves*.
Flowers: about ½" (1.3 cm) wide; petals usually 7; stamens usually 7, with golden anthers.
Leaves: 1¾–4" (4.5–10 cm) long, lanceolate; small scale leaf present near middle of stem below whorled leaves.
Fruit: 5-valved capsule.
Height: 4–8" (10–20 cm).

Flowering: May–August.

Habitat: Cool woodlands, peaty slopes, ascending to subalpine regions.

Range: Saskatchewan to Labrador, Newfoundland, and Nova Scotia; south through New England to Virginia; west to West Virginia, Ohio, Indiana, Illinois and Minnesota.

Comments: The backgrounds of shiny green leaves against which these pure white, star-like flowers are set accentuates the allusion to a star. The generic name is from a Latin word meaning "⅓ of a foot" and refers to the height of the plant.

WINTERGREEN FAMILY
(Pyrolaceae)

Perennial herbs with or without leaves, flowers often dish-shaped, borne singly, in racemes, or in branched clusters.

Flowers: radially symmetrical; sepals 4 or 5, separate or slightly united; petals 4 or 5, separate; stamens usually 10, the pollen sacs opening by terminal pores. All these parts attached at base of ovary.

Leaves: alternate or nearly whorled, simple.

Fruit: 4- or 5-chambered capsule, more or less spherical.

There are 4 genera and about 40 species. They are found mostly in the northern temperate region, and are sometimes considered a part of the Heath Family (Ericaceae).

67 Spotted Wintergreen; Striped Wintergreen
(*Chimaphila maculata*)
Wintergreen Family (Pyrolaceae)

Description: Nodding, fragrant, waxy, white or pinkish flowers are in small clusters at the top of a stem with *whorled, evergreen leaves, mottled with white.*
Flowers: about ⅔" (16 mm) wide; petals 5; stamens 10; pistil knobby.
Leaves: ¾–2¾" (2–7 cm) long, lanceolate, striped with white along midvein.
Fruit: brown capsule, persisting through the winter.
Height: 3–9" (7.5–22.5 cm).
Flowering: June–August.
Habitat: Dry woods.
Range: Southern Ontario to southern New Hampshire; south to Georgia; west to Alabama, Tennessee, northeastern Illinois, and Michigan.
Comments: This is a conspicuous plant in both

winter and summer because of its white
and green mottled leaves. It appears to
increase both vegetatively and by
seedling reproduction following light
wildfires. A slightly taller relative,
Pipsissewa (*C. umbellata*), has shiny,
dark green leaves that lack the
mottling. The genus name is from the
Greek *cheima* ("winter") and *philein*
("to love").

132 Shinleaf
(*Pyrola elliptica*)
Wintergreen Family (Pyrolaceae)

Description: Greenish-white, *waxy, fragrant flowers*
are in an elongated cluster on a stalk
that rises above evergreen basal
leaves.
Flowers: about ⅔" (16 mm) wide;
petals 5, thin, encircling 10 stamens
with yellow anthers; pistil 1, with
distinctly curved protruding style.
Leaves: up to 2¾" (7 cm) long, dark
olive-green, broadly elliptic or oblong;
stalk red.
Fruit: 5-chambered capsule.
Height: 5–10" (12.5–25 cm).
Flowering: June–August.
Habitat: Dry or moist woods.
Range: Newfoundland, Nova Scotia, and New
England to Pennsylvania; west to West
Virginia, Ohio, Indiana, northern
Illinois, Iowa, South Dakota, and
beyond our range to British Columbia.
Comments: One of the commonest of several species
of *Pyrola*. One-sided Pyrola (*P. secunda*),
has flowers arranged along one side of
the stem. Round-leaved Pyrola
(*P. rotundifolia*), has leathery, roundish
leaves. The Pyrolas contain a drug
closely related to aspirin; the leaves
have been used on bruises and wounds
to reduce pain. Such a leaf plaster has
been referred to as a shin plaster, which
accounts for the common name of this
plant.

BUTTERCUP FAMILY
(Ranunculaceae)

Usually leafy herbs, sometimes woody vines or shrub-like, with flowers borne singly, in racemes, or in branched clusters.

Flowers: usually bisexual, radially or bilaterally symmetrical; sepals and petals variable in number, separate, or petals may be lacking and sepals petal-like; usually many stamens; pistils vary in number from 1 to many.

Leaves: alternate, rarely opposite, commonly palmately lobed or divided, sometimes pinnate or simple and not lobed.

Fruit: pod (follicle), seed-like (achene), or berry.

The family has 35 or more genera and about 2,000 species mostly in cool regions of the Northern Hemisphere. Several are grown as ornamentals, others provide drugs, and some are poisonous. The family is most likely to be confused with the Rosaceae, from which it is distinguished by the absence of an hypanthium.

---

613 Monkshood
(*Aconitum uncinatum*)
Buttercup Family (Ranunculaceae)

Description: Several *hooded, violet-blue flowers* are in loose clusters at the top of a *weak stem.*
Flowers: ¾" (2 cm) long; sepals 5, violet and petal-like, the upper enlarged and helmet-shaped; petals 2–5, inconspicuous; stamens numerous; pistils several.
Leaves: to 6" (15 cm) long and wide, palmately divided into 3–5 lobes, toothed.
Height: 2–4' (60–120 cm), often leaning on other plants.
Flowering: August–October.
Habitat: Low woods and damp slopes.

Range: Pennsylvania south to Georgia; west to Alabama and Indiana.

Comments: The roots and seeds of this plant contain alkaloids which are particularly poisonous just before the plant flowers. A drug made from the plant has been used to treat neuralgia and sciatica. A white-flowering southern Appalachian species, Trailing Wolfsbane (*A. reclinatum*), has a trailing or sometimes erect stem. New York Monkshood (*A. noveboracense*), a very similar violet-blue flowering species, occurs from the Catskill Mountain area of New York to Wisconsin and Iowa.

162, 238 White Baneberry
(*Actaea pachypoda*)
Buttercup Family (Ranunculaceae)

Description: An erect stem bears large, highly divided leaves and, at the top, a dense, *oblong flower cluster* of many small white flowers.
Flowers: about ¼" (6 mm) wide; petals 4–10, narrow, stamens numerous; pistil single.
Leaves: leaflets to 4" (10 cm) long, toothed, ovate.
Fruit: clustered *shiny white berries*, each with a black dot, on *thick red stalks*.
Height: 1–2' (30–60 cm).

Flowering: May–June.
Habitat: Rich woods and thickets.
Range: Manitoba to Nova Scotia; south through New England to Georgia; west to Alabama, Louisiana, and Oklahoma.

Comments: This plant is sometimes called "Doll's Eyes" because the shiny white fruits resemble the china eyes once used in dolls. A red-fruited form of this species is distinguished from the otherwise similar Red Baneberry (*A. rubra*), by its thick floral stalk. The berries of both are very poisonous.

161, 442 Red Baneberry
(*Actaea rubra*)
Buttercup Family (Ranunculaceae)

Description: A bushy plant with large, highly
divided leaves and a *short, thick, rounded
cluster* of small white flowers.
Flowers: about ¼″ (6 mm) wide; petals
fall as flower opens leaving the
numerous stamens.
Leaves: 9—27 ovate, sharply-toothed
leaflets, each about 2½″ (6.3 cm) long.
Fruit: clustered red berries on slender
stalks.
Height: 1—2′ (20—60 cm).

Flowering: May—July.

Habitat: Woods and thickets.

Range: Newfoundland and Nova Scotia; south
through New England to West
Virginia; west beyond our range.

Comments: When in flower the clustered stamens
give this plant a feathery appearance.
The showy red fruits are poisonous, as
are those of the white-fruited species,
White Baneberry (*A. pachypoda*).

83 Carolina Anemone
(*Anemone caroliniana*)
Buttercup Family (Ranunculaceae)

Description: A tuberous underground stem gives rise
to a set of 1—3 *deeply cut basal leaves* and
a slender stalk bearing a single, white
or pale blue flower subtended by a set
of paired or whorled, stalkless leaves.
Flowers: about 1½″ (3.8 cm) wide;
sepals 5—20, petal-like; petals absent;
stamens numerous.
Leaves: basal ones deeply palmately
3-parted, with segments ½—1¼″
(1.3—3.1 cm) long, lobed; stem leaves
3-cleft.
Fruit: seed-like, woolly, cylindrical head.
Height: 4—10″ (10—25 cm).

Flowering: April—May.

Habitat: Prairies, open places, on limestone
soils.

Range: North Carolina south to Florida; North and South Dakota and Indiana.

Comments: This Anemone is distinguished by having a greater number of sepals than other species. A similar species, Canada Anemone (*A. canadensis*), abundant in the prairies, extends east into New England. It has more stem leaves, and its flowers have 5 broad sepals.

---

602 Pasqueflower
(*Anemone patens*)
Buttercup Family (Ranunculaceae)

Description: From a cluster of deeply cut basal leaves rises a *silky-hairy stalk* with a solitary, blue to purple or white flower above a *circle of 3 unstalked leaves* with linear segments.
Flowers: about 2½" (6.3 cm) wide; sepals 5–7, petal-like, about 1" (2.5 cm) long; petals absent; stamens numerous; pistils numerous, with long styles.
Leaves: basal to 3" (7.5 cm) long, hairy, palmately divided into segments cut again into narrow divisions; leaves beneath flowers hairy, divided into linear lobes.
Fruit: seed-like, in *heads with long, feathery styles.*
Height: 6–16" (15–40 cm).

Flowering: April–June.

Habitat: Grasslands.

Range: Northwest Canada east to northern Wisconsin and Michigan; south through Illinois and Missouri to Texas; west beyond our range.

Comments: The feathery, silky fruiting head is the distinctive feature of this western grasslands species. The common name refers to the Eastertime flowering throughout much of its range.

54 Wood Anemone
(*Anemone quinquefolia*)
Buttercup Family (Ranunculaceae)

Description: A low, delicate plant with a whorl of 3
stalked, *deeply cut leaves* and a solitary,
stalked white flower.
Flowers: 1″ (2.5 cm) wide; sepals 4–9,
white, often pink on the reverse side,
petal-like; petals absent; pistils and
stamens numerous.
Leaves: palmately divided into 3, or
more often 5, sharply toothed
segments, each about 1¼″ (3.1 cm)
long; basal leaves similar.
Fruit: seed-like, hairy, in a globose
cluster.
Height: 4–8″ (10–20 cm).
Flowering: April–June.
Habitat: Open woods, clearings, thickets.
Range: Quebec to western New York; south to
North Carolina; locally in Ohio and
Kentucky.
Comments: This is an early spring wildflower which
often forms sizable stands on woodland
borders. Since Anemones are usually
slender-stalked and tremble in the
breeze, they have been called "Wind
Flowers."

66 Thimbleweed
(*Anemone virginiana*)
Buttercup Family (Ranunculaceae)

Description: A *tall, hairy plant* with 3–9 greenish-
white (sometimes pure white) flowers
on a stem with several paired or
whorled, deeply cut leaves.
Flowers: about 1″ (2.5 cm) wide; 4–9,
usually 5, petal-like sepals; petals
absent; stamens and pistils numerous.
Leaves: to 3″ (7.5 cm) long; basal and
stem leaves similar, palmately divided
into pointed, wedge-shaped to oblong,
toothed, lobed segments.
Fruit: *thimble-like cluster* of mature seed-
like pistils; about 1″ (2.5 cm) long.

Height: 2–3′ (60–90 cm).
Flowering: June–August.
Habitat: Dry or rocky open woods and thickets.
Range: Central Maine south to Georgia; west to Tennessee, Arkansas, Kansas, and Minnesota.
Comments: The thimble-shaped group of pistils is the distinctive feature of this flower and accounts for the common name. Long-headed Thimbleweed (*A. cylindrica*), has narrower leaf segments and fruit in a long cylindrical cone, 1½″ (3.8 cm) long. It is found in the Northeast, but is more common westward, and is generally associated with limestone.

55 Rue Anemone
(*Anemonella thalictroides*)
Buttercup Family (Ranunculaceae)

Description: A delicate plant with several stalked, white flowers rising above a pair or whorl of compound leaves with *3 round-lobed leaflets*.
Flowers: 1″ (2.5 cm) wide; sepals 5–10, white or pinkish-tinged, petal-like; petals lacking; stamens and pistils numerous.
Leaves: basal and stem leaflets to 1″ (2.5 cm) wide, ovate, with 3 rounded lobes.
Height: 4–8″ (10–20 cm).
Flowering: April–June.
Habitat: Open woods.
Range: Southwest Maine to northwest Florida; west to Alabama, Mississippi, Arkansas, and Oklahoma; north to Minnesota.
Comments: This slender spring flower is easily cultivated in wildflower gardens. It is similar to Wood Anemone (*Anemone quinquefolia*), except for the numerous flowers and rounded leaflets. The leaves of Rue Anemone are similar to those of the Meadow Rues (*Thalictrum* spp.), which accounts for both the common and species names.

426   Wild Columbine
(*Aquilegia canadensis*)
Buttercup Family (Ranunculaceae)

Description: A nodding, red and yellow flower with *upward spurred petals* alternating with spreading, colored sepals and numerous yellow stamens hanging below the petals.
Flowers: 1–2″ (2.5–5 cm) long; sepals 5, red; petals 5, the blade yellow and the hollow spur red; stamens forming a column.
Leaves: 4–6″ (10–15 cm) wide, compound, long-stalked, divided into 9–27 light green, 3-lobed leaflets.
Fruit: beaked, dry pod, splitting open along inner side.
Height: 1–2′ (30–60 cm).
Flowering: April–July.
Habitat: Rocky, wooded or open slopes.
Range: Ontario to Quebec; south throughout New England to Georgia; west to Tennessee and Wisconsin.
Comments: This beautiful woodland wildflower has showy, drooping, bell-like flowers equipped with distinctly backward-pointing tubes, similar to the garden Columbines. These tubes, or spurs, contain nectar that attracts long-tongued insects especially adapted for reaching the sweet secretion. European Columbine (*A. vulgaris*), with blue, violet, pink, or white short-spurred flowers, was introduced from Europe and has now become well established in many parts of our range.

276   Marsh Marigold; Cowslip
(*Caltha palustris*)
Buttercup Family (Ranunculaceae)

Description: A succulent plant with glossy, heart- or kidney-shaped leaves and a *thick, hollow, branching stem* with bright, *shiny yellow flowers.*
Flowers: 1–1½″ (2.5–3.8 cm) wide;

petal-like sepals 5—9; no petals;
numerous stamens and pistils.
Leaves: basal ones 2—7″ (5—17.5 cm)
wide, stalked, dark green, shallowly
toothed; upper leaves becoming
stalkless.
Fruit: in a whorl, each fruit splitting
open along one side (follicle).
Height: 1—2′ (30—60 cm).

Flowering: April—June.

Habitat: Swamps, marshes, wet meadows, along
streams and brooks.

Range: Across Canada; south through New
England to North Carolina; west to
Tennessee, Iowa, and Nebraska.

Comments: The flowers of this showy spring plant
resemble large Buttercups rather than
the Marigolds. The leaves are
sometimes used as potherbs but require
several short boilings with changes of
water between. They should not be
eaten raw. A smaller species, Floating
Marsh Marigold (*C. natans*), found from
Alaska southeastward to northern
Minnesota, has small white or pinkish
flowers, kidney-shaped leaves, and
stems that often float.

134 Black Cohosh; Bugbane
(*Cimicifuga racemosa*)
Buttercup Family (Ranunculaceae)

Description: A large plant with small white flowers
growing in several long, narrow clusters
on a leafy stalk; plant has an *unpleasant
odor*.

Flowers: ½″ (1.3 cm) wide; sepals 4—5,
frequently falling as flower opens; petals
absent; stamens numerous, in a tuft;
pistil single.
Leaves: large, biternately compound
(twice divided into 3s), sharply
toothed, the leaflets to 4″ (10 cm) long.
Fruit: dry, several seeded pod.
Height: 3—8′ (90—240 cm).

Flowering: June—September.

Habitat: Rich woods.

Range: Southern Ontario; western
Massachusetts; south to Georgia; west
to Tennessee and Missouri.

Comments: The bad odor of this plant is repellent
to bugs, which accounts for the
common and genus names. The root
was used in the 1800s to treat various
conditions, ranging from snakebite and
lung inflammations, to the pains of
childbirth. The American or Mountain
Bugbane (*C. americana*), is slightly
smaller, from 2–6' (60–180 cm) high,
lacks the unpleasant odor, and has
flowers with several pistils. It is found
mostly from Pennsylvania southward in
the Appalachian Mountains to Georgia.

---

507 Pine Hyacinth; Dwarf Clematis
(*Clematis balduinii*)
Buttercup Family (Ranunculaceae)

Description: Long stalks each bear a solitary,
*nodding, pink to bluish-lavender, bell-
shaped flower.*
Flowers: 1–2" (2.5–5 cm) long; sepals
4, petal-like; petals lacking; stamens
and pistils many.
Leaves: 1–4" (2.5–10 cm) long,
opposite, variable in shape, the lower
ones entire, the upper lobed.
Fruit: seed-like, tipped by *long styles* up
to 4" (10 cm) long, and in *feathery
heads.*
Height: 1–2' (30–60 cm).

Flowering: Winter and spring.

Habitat: Wet areas or pinewoods.

Range: Peninsular Florida.

Comments: The vine Leather Flower (*C. crispa*), has
very similar, extremely fragrant flowers,
but occurs in a wider range from
southeast Virginia to Florida and west
to Texas and southern Missouri.

38, 206 Virgin's Bower
(*Clematis virginiana*)
Buttercup Family (Ranunculaceae)

Description: A *climbing vine* with white flowers in
many clusters arising from the leaf
axils.
Flowers: about 1″ (2.5 cm) wide; sepals
4 or 5, petal-like; petals lacking;
stamens or pistils numerous. Male and
female flowers on separate plants;
female flowers with sterile stamens.
Leaves: compound with 3 *sharply-toothed*
(*sometimes lobed*), *ovate leaflets*, each about
2″ (5 cm) long.
Fruit: 1-seeded, with plumy tails, and
in globose heads.
Height: vine, with stem 6–10′
(1.8–3 m) long.

Flowering: July–September.

Habitat: Borders of woods, thickets, moist
places.

Range: Manitoba to Nova Scotia; south from
New England to Georgia; west to
Alabama, Mississippi, and Louisiana;
north to eastern Kansas.

Comments: A beautiful and common Clematis, it
trails over fences and other shrubs along
moist roadsides and riverbanks. The
female flowers, with their feathery tails
or plumes, give a hoary appearance and
are especially showy in late summer.
Lacking tendrils, the vine supports
itself by means of twisted stems, or
petioles, that wrap around other plants.
A few susceptible people may acquire a
dermatitis from handling the leaves of
this plant.

62 Goldthread
(*Coptis groenlandica*)
Buttercup Family (Ranunculaceae)

Description: A small plant with solitary white
flowers and lustrous, *evergreen basal
leaves* rising from a *thread-like, yellow
underground stem*.

Flowers: ½″ (1.3 cm) wide; sepals 5–7, white, petal-like; petals very small, club-like; stamens numerous; pistils several.
Leaves: 1–2″ (2.5–5 cm) wide, all basal, palmately divided into 3 leaflets with scalloped, toothed margins.
Fruit: dry pod, splitting open along one side.
Height: 3–6″ (7.5–15 cm).

Flowering: May–July.

Habitat: Cool woods, swamps, bogs.

Range: Manitoba to Greenland, Labrador, Newfoundland, and Nova Scotia; south through New England and New Jersey to the mountains of North Carolina; west to Tennessee, Ohio, Indiana, and Iowa.

Comments: The common name refers to the golden-yellow underground stem that both Indians and colonists chewed to treat mouth sores. (Hence another common name for the plant, Canker-root.) It was also made into a tea for use as an eyewash.

---

622 Spring Larkspur
(*Delphinium tricorne*)
Buttercup Family (Ranunculaceae)

Description: An open cluster of blue or violet *spurred flowers* is at the top of a simple, fleshy stem which has deeply cleft leaves.
Flowers: ¾″ (2 cm) wide; sepals 5, petal-like, the upper one prolonged into a slightly bent, backward-projecting spur about ½″ (1.3 cm) long; petals 4, very small, the upper ones enclosed in the calyx spur.
Leaves: 2–4″ (5–10 cm) wide; deeply palmately cut into narrow lobes.
Fruit: seedpod which separates into 3 widely-diverging parts, *the dried ends curling upward like horns.*
Height: 4–24″ (10–60 cm).

Flowering: April–May.

Habitat: Rich woods.

Range: Pennsylvania south to Georgia; west to Arkansas, Oklahoma, and Nebraska; north to Minnesota.

Comments: The species name refers to the 3-horned fruits. The flower structure is similar to that of the Rocket Larkspur (*D. ajacis*), which is often cultivated in gardens. Tall Larkspur (*D. exaltatum*), reaches a height of 6' (1.8 m) and is leafier, with more flowers. Larkspurs contain a harmful alkaloid that frequently poisons grazing cattle.

152 Prairie Larkspur
(*Delphinium virescens*)
Buttercup Family (Ranunculaceae)

Description: The white to pale blue *spurred flowers* are borne in a narrow cluster on a finely downy stalk.
Flowers: about 1" (2.5 cm) long; sepals 5, petal-like, the upper prolonged into a spur ½" (1.3 cm) or more long; petals 4, inconspicuous, the upper pair extending into the spur, the lower pair with short claws.
Leaves: palmately divided, with narrow leaf segments, each about ¼" (6 mm) wide.
Fruit: 3 or more seedpods which split open along one side.
Height: 1–3' (30–90 cm).

Flowering: May–July.

Habitat: Prairies and dry, open woods.

Range: Manitoba and northwestern Wisconsin; south to Missouri, Kansas, Oklahoma, and Texas.

Comments: The flowers of this midwestern species can cover acres of prairie before the grasses take over. The showy sepals range from white to pale blue to greenish, which accounts for the species name (Latin for "to become green").

464, 592 Round-lobed Hepatica
(*Hepatica americana*)
Buttercup Family (Ranunculaceae)

Description: A low plant with *round-lobed basal leaves*
and several hairy stalks bearing solitary,
pinkish, lavender-blue, or white
flowers.
Flowers: ½–1″ (1.3–2.5 cm) wide;
sepals 5–9, petal-like; petals lacking;
stamens numerous; pistils several.
Three green *sepal-like, broadly oval to
elliptic bracts* surround flower.
Leaves: 2–2½″ (5–6.3 cm) wide, basal,
with 3 rounded lobes.
Fruit: several, hairy, seed-like.
Height: 4–6″ (10–15 cm).

Flowering: March–June.

Habitat: Dry rocky woods.

Range: Manitoba to Nova Scotia; south to
northern Florida; west to Alabama;
north to Missouri and Minnesota.

Comments: This is an early spring wildflower,
usually with lavender flowers and
3-lobed leaves which persist throughout
the winter. The Sharp-lobed Hepatica
(*H. acutiloba*), has more pointed leaf
lobes and bracts. The genus name refers
to the 3-lobed leaf that supposedly
bears a resemblance to the liver.
Because of this, early herbalists
assumed the plant to be effective in
treating liver ailments.

117 Goldenseal
(*Hydrastis canadensis*)
Buttercup Family (Ranunculaceae)

Description: From a yellow, underground stem rises
a *single, large, wrinkled basal leaf* and a
hairy stalk with a solitary flower above
2 5-lobed stem leaves.
Flowers: ½″ (1.3 cm) wide; sepals 3,
whitish-green, falling early, leaving
many *prominent stamens;* petals lacking;
pistils numerous.
Leaves: up to 4″ (10 cm) wide at

flowering time, up to 10″ (25 cm) wide
later, toothed, prominently veined;
basal leaf similar to stem leaves but
long-stalked.
Fruit: red berry.
Height: 1–1¼′ (30–37.5 cm).

Flowering: April–May.

Habitat: Rich woods.

Range: Vermont south to Georgia; west to
Alabama; northwest to Arkansas,
Minnesota, and Nebraska.

Comments: The plant was used medically by
Indians and colonists. In the early
decades of the 20th-century, it was
used as a tonic, astringent, and insect
repellent, as well as a yellow dye. Its
current rarity may be related to
overcollection of its roots.

56 False Rue Anemone
(*Isopyrum biternatum*)
Buttercup Family (Ranunculaceae)

Description: White, Anemone-like flowers bloom in
small clusters at the ends of the stems
or on stalks rising in the leaf axils.
Flowers: ½″ (1.3 cm) wide; sepals
petal-like; petals lacking; stamens
numerous; pistils several.
Leaves: compound, with 9 broadly
ovate, 3-lobed leaflets, each about
½″ (1.3 cm) long.
Fruit: 2–4 dry, curved pods with
tapering beaks, splitting open along
one side.
Height: 4–16″ (10–40 cm).

Flowering: April–May.

Habitat: Rich or limestone woods and thickets.

Range: Southern Ontario south to North
Carolina and northwest Florida; west to
Texas; north to Missouri, Minnesota,
and eastern South Dakota.

Comments: This is a small, herbaceous perennial
that grows from thick, tuberous,
fibrous roots. It is found mostly in the
southern and the less populated western
part of our range, extending to the

eastern part of the Black Hills of South
Dakota, where it is rare.

---

259   Kidneyleaf Buttercup;
Small-flowered Buttercup
(*Ranunculus abortivus*)
Buttercup Family (Ranunculaceae)

Description: A branching plant with *kidney-shaped
basal leaves* and inconspicuous yellow
flowers with *drooping sepals.*
Flowers: to ¼″ (6 mm) wide; sepals 5,
reflexed; petals shorter and narrower
than sepals; stamens and pistils
numerous.
Leaves: basal ones ½–1½″ (1.3–
3.8 cm) wide, stalked, with scalloped
margins; stem leaves stalkless, divided
into 3–5 lobes.
Fruit: dry, 1-seeded, aggregated into
globose heads.
Height: 6–24″ (15–60 cm).

Flowering: April–August.
Habitat: Shady, moist areas.
Range: Throughout.
Comments: With its small petals it does not look
much like a Buttercup, but its many
separate stamens and pistils are typical
of the genus. The species name refers,
in Latin, to the reduced petals. At least
10 similarly small-flowered species
occur in our range.

---

264   Common Buttercup
(*Ranunculus acris*)
Buttercup Family (Ranunculaceae)

Description: A *tall,* erect, hairy, branching plant
with *glossy yellow flowers.*
Flowers: 1″ (2.5 cm) wide; petals 5,
longer than sepals; sepals 5, spreading,
greenish; stamens and pistils numerous.
Leaves: basal ones, 1–4″ (2.5–10 cm)
wide, long-petioled, *blades deeply and
palmately cut into unstalked segments;*

upper leaves smaller, scattered.
Fruit: dry, seed-like, in a globose cluster.
Height: 2–3' (60–90 cm).

Flowering: May–September.
Habitat: Old fields, meadows, disturbed areas.
Range: Throughout.
Comments: This European introduction is one of our tallest and most common Buttercups. It thrives best in moist sites. The distinctive, shiny, waxy texture of Buttercup petals is caused by a special layer of cells just beneath the surface cells. As the species name implies, the juice from stems and leaves is acrid, discouraging browsing animals, and favoring the spread of the plant.

262 Bulbous Buttercup
(Ranunculus bulbosus)
Buttercup Family (Ranunculaceae)

Description: A hairy plant with golden-yellow flowers and *bulbous roots.*

Flowers: 1" (2.5 cm) wide; *sepals 5, downward-pointing;* petals 5, longer than sepals; stamens and pistils numerous.
Leaves: basal ones 1–4" (2.5–10 cm) wide, stalked, cut into 3 lobed and cleft parts, the *terminal lobe stalked* and about 1" (2.5 cm) long; stem leaves smaller, fewer.
Fruit: dry, seed-like, in globose clusters.
Height: 1–2' (30–60 cm).

Flowering: April–June.
Habitat: Old fields, roadsides, lawns, gardens.
Range: Ontario to Nova Scotia; south through New England to Georgia; west to Louisiana; north to Michigan; also present in western North America.
Comments: At the base of the petal is a distinctive scale under which the nectar is hidden. Most of the common species of Buttercups are somewhat poisonous and will affect animals if eaten fresh, but not when dried and eaten in hay.

However, milk produced by cows that have eaten the plants has an unpleasant flavor or reddish color. A similar species, Hairy Buttercup (*R. sardous*), lacks the bulbous root and is common in the South.

---

260 Yellow Water Buttercup
(*Ranunculus flabellaris*)
Buttercup Family (Ranunculaceae)

Description: An *aquatic plant* with golden-yellow flowers extending above the water on stout, hollow stems.
Flowers: ½–1½" (1.3–3.8 cm) wide; sepals 5; petals 5, longer than sepals; stamens and pistils numerous.
Leaves: submerged ones 1–3" (2.5–7.5 cm) long, divided into hair-like segments; emerged leaves (when present) ½–2" (1.3–5 cm) wide, repeatedly divided and lobed.
Fruit: dry, seed-like, in a globose head.
Height: aquatic, with stem to 2' (60 cm) high.

Flowering: May–June.

Habitat: Quiet waters, muddy shores.

Range: Across Canada; south from Maine to North Carolina; west to Louisiana, Kansas, and beyond our range.

Comments: Usually found in quiet waters, this plant, with the typical Buttercup flower, occasionally grows on wet shores. In a similar habitat we find White Water Buttercup (*R. longirostris*), with 5 white petals and submerged filamentous leaves. Some botanists recognize it and *R. circinatus* as different species, others as the same species.

263 Swamp Buttercup; Marsh Buttercup
(*Ranunculus septentrionalis*)
Buttercup Family (Ranunculaceae)

Description: *Arching or reclining, hollow stems* bear bright, glossy, yellow flowers.
Flowers: 1″ (2.5 cm) wide; sepals 5; petals 5, showy; stamens and pistils numerous.
Leaves: divided into 3-lobed segments, each 1½–4″ (3.8–10 cm) long, on *short stalks*.
Fruit: dry, seed-like, with winged margins and bird-like beaks, in a globose cluster.
Height: 1–3′ (30–90 cm).
Flowering: April–July.
Habitat: Moist woods, thickets, meadows.
Range: Manitoba to Quebec; south through New England to Maryland; west to Kentucky and Missouri.
Comments: A native, weak-stemmed Buttercup, it is typical of swamps and marshes. Between 20 and 30 species of Buttercups are found in a variety of habitats; all are pollinated by flies and bees.

168 Early Meadow Rue
(*Thalictrum dioicum*)
Buttercup Family (Ranunculaceae)

Description: *Drooping, greenish-white flowers* are in long-stalked terminal and axillary clusters on a smooth, leafy stem.
Flowers: about ¼″ (6 mm) long; petals absent. Male and female flowers on separate plants; the male flowers with numerous long, yellow, *showy stamens* protruding from the 4–5 petal-like sepals; female flowers with a few elongated, purplish pistils.
Leaves: *on long stalks,* divided into 3–4 roundish, lobed segments ½–2″ (1.3–5 cm) wide, pale beneath.
Fruit: ovoid, 1-seeded, strongly ribbed.
Height: 8–30″ (20–75 cm).

Flowering: April–May.
Habitat: Rich moist woods, ravines.
Range: Ontario to Quebec; south to Georgia; west to Missouri; north to North Dakota and Minnesota.
Comments: This flower blooms in the early spring, just as the trees are leafing out, which accounts for its common name. The species name alludes to the fact that the male and female flowers are on separate plants, and is derived from a Greek word meaning "two households."

---

200 Tall Meadow Rue
(*Thalictrum polygamum*)
Buttercup Family (Ranunculaceae)

Description: A tall plant with *plumy clusters* of white flowers.
Flowers: about ⅓″ (8 mm) wide; sepals greenish-white, falling early; petals lacking. Flowers with both male and female flowers on the same plant, or partially unisexual, the female with several pistils and usually some stamens, the male with *many erect, thread-like stamens.*
Leaves: compound, bluish to olive-green, divided into roundish, 3-lobed leaflets, each about 1″ (2.5 cm) long.
Fruit: seed-like, in rounded clusters, the lower ones bent backward.
Height: 2–8′ (60–240 cm).
Flowering: June–August.
Habitat: Swamps, meadows, streamsides.
Range: Ontario to Nova Scotia; south through New England to Georgia; west to Tennessee.
Comments: This summer-blooming flower is constantly visited by bees and butterflies. At least 10 other species are found in our range.

255 Globeflower
(Trollius laxus)
Buttercup Family (Ranunculaceae)

Description: A solitary, greenish-yellow flower is at the top of a leafy stem; *the upper leaves are stalkless and surround the stem.*
Flowers: 1–1½" (2.5–3.8 cm) wide; sepals 5–7, petal-like; petals numerous, minute; yellow stamens and pistils numerous.
Leaves: 2–4" (5–10 cm) wide, smooth, palmately divided into 5–7 toothed or cleft lobes.
Fruit: dry pods that open along one side.
Height: 12–20" (30–50 cm).
Flowering: April–June.
Habitat: Moist meadows and swamps.
Range: Western Connecticut south to Pennsylvania; west to Michigan.
Comments: This is a rare or local species and should not be picked or disturbed. It is listed as an endangered species in 8 eastern states.

BUCKTHORN FAMILY
(Rhamnaceae)

Shrubs, trees, or vines with usually
small flowers in clusters.
Flowers: radially symmetrical, sepals 5
or rarely 4, separate; petals often 5,
sometimes 4 or none, separate; stamen 1
opposite each petal or, if petals are
absent, between the sepals, attached
to the flower near the edge of a
conspicuous disk that surrounds
the ovary.
Leaves: simple, unlobed, alternate or
opposite.
Fruit: 2- or 3-chambered berry.
There are nearly 60 genera and 900
species throughout the world. Edible
fruits are obtained from the tropical
Jujube, and Cascara bark was once
collected for its purgative properties.
Several species are grown as
ornamentals.

225 New Jersey Tea
(*Ceanothus americanus*)
Buckthorn Family (Rhamnaceae)

Description: A low shrub with tiny white flowers in
oval clusters rising from the leaf axils
on the current year's shoots.
Flowers: about ⅕″ (5 mm) wide; petals
5, clawed; stamens 5, protruding.
Leaves: 1–3″ (2.5–7.5 cm) long,
3-veined, toothed, ovate, sharp-
pointed.
Fruit: 3-lobed, splitting into 3 parts.
Height: 3–4′ (90–120 cm).

Flowering: May–July.

Habitat: Open woods, roadside clearings.

Range: Manitoba to Quebec and Maine; south
to Florida; west to Alabama.

Comments: The dried leaves of this nitrogen-fixing
shrub make an excellent tea that was
very popular during the Revolutionary
War period. Smaller Red-root
(*C. ovatus*), with flowers in a globose

cluster and narrower leaves, ranges from Manitoba and western Quebec to western Maine, south to western Georgia, west to Alabama, Arkansas, and Texas. Small-leaved Red-root (*C. microphyllus*), has tiny leaves, less than ½" (1.3 cm) long, and occurs in sandy pine or oak woods in the South.

ROSE FAMILY (Rosaceae)

Herbs, shrubs, or trees with mostly prickly stems.
Flowers: usually bisexual, radially symmetrical; sepals 5; petals 5 or sometimes none, separate; stamens usually numerous, attached at edge of cup (hypanthium); pistils 1 or many, with other parts of flower sometimes attached at top of ovary.
Leaves: alternate, simple or compound, usually with stipules at the base of the leaf stalk.
Fruit: dry or fleshy, opening at maturity or remaining closed.
There are about 100 genera and 3,000 species in this worldwide family. Apples, pears, quinces, cherries, plums, peaches, apricots, loquats, blackberries, raspberries, and strawberries are important fruits. Roses, Cotoneaster, Firethorn, Mountain Ash, Spirea, and Hawthorns are common ornamentals.

---

323 Agrimony
(*Agrimonia gryposepala*)
Rose Family (Rosaceae)

Description: An *erect, wand-like cluster* of small, yellow flowers extends above the pinnately compound leaves; *stem has spicy odor when crushed.*
Flowers: about ¼" (6 mm) wide; petals 5; stamens several; pistils 2.
Leaves: leaflets 2–4" (5–10 cm) long, bright green, many veined, coarsely toothed, often with *3 pairs of tiny leaflets* present between larger leaflets.
Fruit: seed-like, *top-shaped, with hooked bristles.*
Height: 1–6' (30–180 cm), usually 4–5' (1.2–1.5 m).
Flowering: July–August.
Habitat: Thickets, borders of woods.
Range: Southern Quebec to Nova Scotia; south

through New England to North Carolina; west to Tennessee, Missouri, and eastern Kansas; north to North Dakota; also west beyond our range.

Comments: The species name means "having hooked sepals." A similar species, Woodland Agrimony (*A. striata*), has a hairy stem that lacks glands. It does not occur south of Pennsylvania and West Virginia, but extends westward to Nebraska and southwestward beyond our range. Five other very similar species occur in our range.

153 Goatsbeard
(*Aruncus dioicus*)
Rose Family (Rosaceae)

Description: The small, whitish-cream flowers are in *narrow, elongated, spike-like clusters* that branch off a tall flower stalk.
Flowers: each about ⅙" (4 mm) wide; petals and sepals 5. Flowers either male or female; the male with numerous stamens, the female usually with 3 pistils.
Leaves: to 15" (37.5 cm) long; alternate, compound, divided 2–3 times into toothed leaflets, 2–5" (5–12.5 cm) long.
Height: 3–6' (90–180 cm).

Flowering: May–July.
Habitat: Rich woods, ravines.
Range: Pennsylvania south to Georgia; west to Alabama and Kentucky.
Comments: The showy, finger-like flower clusters form feathery masses of all male or all female flowers. The common name refers to the shape of the white flower cluster. A very similar Saxifrage, False Goatsbeard (*Astilbe biternata*), has a lobed terminal leaflet on each leaf and 2 pistils.

59 False Violet
(*Dalibarda repens*)
Rose Family (Rosaceae)

Description: A low, creeping plant with white
flowers, each on a separate, reddish,
leafless stalk.
Flowers: about ½" (1.3 cm) wide;
petals 5; stamens numerous. Plant also
produces flowers that fail to open on
short, recurved stalks.
Leaves: 1–2" (2.5–5 cm) long, *dark
green, heart-shaped,* downy, scallop-
toothed, *on separate stalks.*
Height: creeper, with flower stalks
2–5" (5–12.5 cm) high.

Flowering: June–August.

Habitat: Swampy woods.

Range: Ontario to Nova Scotia; south to
Maine, Massachusetts, northwestern
Connecticut, and the mountains of
North Carolina; west to Ohio; north to
Michigan.

Comments: This northern species is found in cool
woods and boggy areas and will grow in
wet bog gardens. Its Violet-like
appearance accounts for the common
name.

251 Indian Strawberry
(*Duchesnea indica*)
Rose Family (Rosaceae)

Description: A strawberry-like, *trailing plant* with
yellow flowers, each rising from the axil
of a *3-parted leaf.*
Flowers: ¾" (2 cm) wide; sepals and
petals 5; stamens numerous. Back of
flower bears 5, 3-toothed, *leaf-like bracts*
that are longer than the sepals and
petals.
Leaves: leaflets ¾–3" (2–7.5 cm) long,
ovate to elliptic, toothed.
Fruit: resembles a strawberry but is
tasteless.
Height: creeper, with flower stalk to
3" (7.5 cm) high.

Flowering: April–June.

Habitat: Waste places, disturbed areas.

Range: Connecticut south to northern Florida; west to Oklahoma.

Comments: This plant is an introduction from India, which accounts for the species and common names. The genus name honors Antoine Nicolas Duchesne, a 17th- and early 18th-century botanist who wrote a study on *Fragaria,* the genus to which the true Strawberry belongs. This plant may be confused with Common Cinquefoil (*Potentilla simplex*), which, however, has 5 leaflets.

58 Common Strawberry
(*Fragaria virginiana*)
Rose Family (Rosaceae)

Description: This low perennial forms runners and produces several small, white flowers and *long-stalked, 3-parted basal leaves.*
Flowers: ¾″ (2 cm) wide; sepals 5; petals 5, roundish; stamens many, numerous; pistils many, on a *dome-like structure.*
Leaves: leaflets 1–1½″ (2.5–3.8 cm) long, toothed, and with hairy stalks.
Fruit: dry, seed-like, *sunken within enlarged, fleshy cone—the "strawberry."*
Height: creeper, with flower stalk 3–6″ (7.5–15 cm) high.

Flowering: April–June.

Habitat: Open fields, edges of woods.

Range: Throughout.

Comments: Found in patches in fields and dry openings, this plant produces the finest, sweetest, wild strawberry. The edible portion of the strawberry is actually the central portion of the flower (receptacle) which enlarges greatly with maturity and is covered with the embedded, dried, seed-like fruit. Cultivated Strawberries are hybrids developed from this native species and the South American one.

The similar Wood Strawberry
(*F. vesca*), has seed-like fruit on the
surface, not embedded, and sepals that
point backwards.

---

566 Queen-of-the-Prairie
(*Filipendula rubra*)
Rose Family (Rosaceae)

Description: This plant bears large, *feathery clusters* of
small, fragrant, pink flowers.
Flowers: ⅓–½" (8–13 mm) wide;
sepals and petals 5; stamens numerous,
protruding; pistils 5–7.
Leaves: pinnately compound, divided
into deeply lobed and toothed leaflets,
the terminal leaflet to 8" (20 cm)
wide and long.
Fruit: dry, 1-seeded.
Height: 3–6′ (90–180 cm).
Flowering: June–August.
Habitat: Prairies, meadows, thickets.
Range: Pennsylvania south to Georgia; west to
Kentucky, Illinois, Iowa, and
Michigan; escaped from cultivation in
New England and New York.
Comments: A showy species, this coarse-leaved
perennial can be grown readily in
wildflower gardens. Meadow-Queen
(*F. ulmaria*), a shorter plant with white
or greenish-white flowers, is also found
in our range.

---

408 Prairie Smoke
(*Geum triflorum*)
Rose Family (Rosaceae)

Description: A softly hairy plant with reddish brown
or pinkish flowers, often in groups of 3,
at the summit of a stalk that rises from
a set of *fern-like basal leaves.*
Flowers: up to ¾" (2 cm) long; calyx
lobes 5; petals 5; narrow bracts
alternate with sepals.
Leaves: 4–9" (10–22.5 cm) long,

pinnately divided into wedge-shaped to oblong, toothed or lobed leaflets; stem leaves few, small.

Fruit: seed-like, with *long, plumy, gray "tails"* 2" (5 cm) long.

Height: 6–16" (15–40 cm).

Flowering: Late April–July.

Habitat: Woods and prairies.

Range: New York west to Minnesota and Iowa and beyond our range; north across Canada.

Comments: One of the earliest flowers to appear on the prairies, it attracts attention when in fruit with its "feather duster" look, especially when it forms colonies. Indians once made a tea from the roots.

89 Bowman's Root; Indian Physic
(*Gillenia trifoliata*)
Rose Family (Rosaceae)

Description: This erect plant has white or pinkish flowers, with *narrow, oblique petals* and almost stalkless, 3-parted leaves.

Flowers: about 1½" (3.8 cm) wide; sepals and petals 5; stamens numerous; pistils 5.

Leaves: leaflets 2–4" (5–10 cm) long, toothed, with tiny stipules (leaf-like appendages at base of leafstalk).

Height: 2–3' (60–90 cm).

Flowering: May–July.

Habitat: Rich woods.

Range: Southern Ontario to New York; south to Georgia; west to Alabama; north to Michigan.

Comments: The 5 petals of this slender-stalked plant project somewhat irregularly. The powdered, dried root was used by Indians as a laxative and emetic, hence the common names. A southern and western relative, American Ipecac (*G. stipulata*), has large, sharply toothed or jagged stipules.

249 Silverweed
(*Potentilla anserina*)
Rose Family (Rosaceae)

Description: A prostrate plant with a solitary, golden-yellow flower on a leafless stalk and compound *basal leaves, with white-silvery hairs underneath,* on separate stalks.
Flowers: ⅔–1″ (1.6–2.5 cm) wide; petals usually 5, blunt; stamens and pistils numerous.
Leaves: to 1′ (30 cm) long, pinnately compound, divided into numerous sharply toothed leaflets, each to 1½″ (3.8 cm) long, with smaller ones interspersed between the larger.
Fruit: dry, seed-like.
Height: creeper, with runners 1–3′ (30–90 cm) long.

Flowering: June–August.

Habitat: Sandy shores, banks, wet meadows.

Range: Across Canada to Nova Scotia; south through northern New England and New York; west to Indiana, Illinois, and Iowa and beyond our range.

Comments: This plant grows as far north as the edge of the Arctic. The roots are especially tasty; boiled, they resemble parsnips. Another species having leaves with silvery undersides is Silvery Cinquefoil (*P. argentea*), an erect perennial, 6–12″ (15–30 cm) high, of dry open fields. It has 5 deeply and palmately cut, wedge-shaped leaflets with edges that are rolled back.

252 Canadian Dwarf Cinquefoil
(*Potentilla canadensis*)
Rose Family (Rosaceae)

Description: A low, spreading plant with *silvery-downy stems* and yellow flowers blooming singly on long stalks rising from the axils of palmately 5-parted leaves.
Flowers: ½–⅔″ (1.3–1.6 cm) wide;

sepals 5; petals 5; stamens and pistils numerous. *First flower arises from axil of first leaf.*
Leaves: leaflets up to 1½″ (3.8 cm) long, toothed at the summit, entirely below the middle.
Height: 2–6″ (5–15 cm), with stem becoming prostrate after flowering.

Flowering: March–June.
Habitat: Dry, open soil.
Range: Ontario to Nova Scotia; south to Georgia; west to Tennessee, Missouri, and Ohio.
Comments: This species is very similar to Common Cinquefoil (*P. simplex*), but the latter has larger leaflets, up to 2½″ (6.3 cm) long, and the first flower arises from the axil of the second leaf. Both species are indicators of impoverished soil.

247 Rough-fruited Cinquefoil
(*Potentilla recta*)
Rose Family (Rosaceae)

Description: Erect, *hairy plant* with flat-topped, sparse clusters of pale yellow flowers with *notched petals.*
Flowers: ¾″ (2 cm) wide; sepals and petals usually 5, the petals large compared to the sepals; stamens and pistils numerous.
Leaves: compound, divided into 5–7 blunt-tipped, toothed leaflets, each 1–3″ (2.5–7.5 cm) long.
Height: 1–2′ (30–60 cm).

Flowering: May–August.
Habitat: Roadsides, dry fields.
Range: Ontario to Nova Scotia; south from New England to Virginia; west to Tennessee, Arkansas, Kansas; north to Minnesota.
Comments: Its forage value is low and it is seldom eaten by livestock, consequently this European introduction is now considered to be one of the most rapidly increasing weeds in Nebraska.

250   Dwarf Cinquefoil; Robbins' Potentilla
(*Potentilla robbinsiana*)
Rose Family (Rosaceae)

Description: A *tufted, dwarf plant* with a fuzzy, hairy
appearance, lacking the runners
characteristic of other Potentillas. It has
deeply toothed, 3-parted leaves and
single yellow flowers (rarely 2) on
thread-like, hairy stems.
Flowers: up to ⅓" (8 mm) wide; sepals
and petals usually 5; stamens and pistils
numerous; green bracts present beneath
the sepals.
Leaves: leaflets ⅕–⅓" (5–8 mm) long,
wedge-shaped to ovate.
Height: ½–2" (1.3–5 cm).

Flowering: June–July.

Habitat: Alpine regions.

Range: Mount Washington, New Hampshire.

Comments: This small plant, found only on Mt.
Washington, and listed as an
endangered species in New Hampshire,
is one of the rarest in the United
States.

218   Red Chokeberry
(*Pyrus arbutifolia*)
Rose Family (Rosaceae)

Description: A spreading shrub with terminal
clusters of white or pink-tinged flowers
on *hairy stalks.*
Flowers: ½" (1.3 cm) wide; petals 5;
stamens numerous with conspicuous,
black or dark red anthers.
Leaves: 1–3" (2.5–7.5 cm) long;
toothed, oval to broadly lanceolate,
with pointed tips, dark green and
smooth above, *densely hairy* and pale
beneath; glands along upper midrib
evident with hand lens.
Fruit: bright or dull red, berry-like, ¼"
(6 mm) in diameter.
Height: 3–12' (90–360 cm).

Flowering: April–July.

Habitat: Thickets and clearings, low woods, swamps.

Range: Southern Ontario to Nova Scotia; south through New England to Florida; west to Texas.

Comments: A native shrub, it forms sizable colonies and is excellent for naturalistic landscaping. The closely related black-fruited species, Black Chokeberry (*P. melanocarpa*), has leaves hairless beneath. Purple chokeberry (*P. floribunda*), has purple fruits. Although Chokeberry fruits persist through much of the winter, they appear to be of little importance to wildlife, but are occasionally eaten by gamebirds and songbirds, and reportedly by bears.

211 Multiflora Rose
(*Rosa multiflora*)
Rose Family (Rosaceae)

Description: On prickly, *arching stems* are clusters of many small, fragrant, white flowers. Flowers: ¾–1½" (2–3.8 cm) wide; sepals 5, lanceolate, sharp-tipped; petals 5; stamens and pistils numerous. Leaves: pinnately divided into 7–9 ovate, toothed leaflets, about 1" (2.5 cm) long; *highly fringed, winged leaf appendages* present at base of leaf stalks. Thorns curved, flattened. Fruit: small, fleshy, many-seeded hip. Height: 6–15' (1.8–4.5 m).

Flowering: May–June.

Habitat: Borders of fields and woods, roadsides.

Range: Southern New England south throughout our range.

Comments: This small-flowered Rose is sold as a living hedge by nurseries. It forms dense impenetrable masses and provides excellent wildlife cover; however, it has also become a pest in many areas, spreading into fields and pastures. In the South, the White Cherokee Rose (*R. laevigata*), an introduction from

China, has flowers 2–3″ (5–7.5 cm)
wide and evergreen leaves with 3
leaflets. It has escaped from cultivation,
especially in Louisiana, Mississippi,
Texas, and Arkansas. Another
introduced white-flowering species, the
Macartney Rose (*R. bracteata*), with
5–9 leaflets, has become a pest in the
South.

582 Rugosa Rose; Wrinkled Rose
(*Rosa rugosa*)
Rose Family (Rosaceae)

Description: The large, rose-lavender or sometimes
white flowers are borne on *very spiny,
hairy stems.*
Flowers: 2–3″ (5–7.5 cm) wide; sepals
and petals 5; stamens and pistils
numerous.
Leaves: 3–6″ (7.5–15 cm) long,
pinnately compound, with toothed,
elliptic to oblong, *dark green leaflets that
appear wrinkled.*
Fruit: fleshy hip, brick red, capped by
long, persistent sepals.
Height: 4–6′ (1.2–1.8 m).
Flowering: June–September.
Habitat: Seashore thickets, sand dunes,
roadsides.
Range: Quebec to Nova Scotia and New
England; south to New Jersey; west to
Illinois, Wisconsin, and Minnesota.
Comments: This large, showy Rose was introduced
from the Orient. It is frequently used as
a plant to stabilize beaches and dunes.
The Sweet-brier (*R. eglanteria*), with
non-hairy, prickly stems, smaller pink
flowers, and highly aromatic leaves, was
introduced from Europe and has spread
in pastures. Dog Rose (*R. canina*), also
a European introduction, is similar but
has non-aromatic leaves.

584 Prairie Rose
(*Rosa suffulta*)
Rose Family (Rosaceae)

Description: Small clusters of deep pink-tinged or white flowers are on densely *prickly stems* of new growth or the short lateral branches from older stems.
Flowers: about 2″ (5 cm) wide; sepals and petals 5; stamens and pistils numerous.
Leaves: pinnately divided into 9–11 toothed, ovate to oblong leaflets to 2″ (5 cm) long, covered with *soft hairs underneath;* size variable according to moisture conditions.
Fruit: a bright red, fleshy hip.
Height: 2′ (60 cm).
Flowering: June.
Habitat: Prairies, roadsides, and ditches.
Range: Manitoba south to Indiana and southwest to Texas.
Comments: The flower buds are a deeper pink than the open flowers, which can range from white to pink. The colorful fruits remain on the plants into the fall and winter.

581 Virginia Rose
(*Rosa virginiana*)
Rose Family (Rosaceae)

Description: The hairy stems of this bushy shrub have *scattered, stout, curved thorns,* pink flowers, and pinnately compound leaves.
Flowers: 2–3″ (5–7.5 cm) wide; sepals 5; petals 5; stamens numerous.
Leaves: divided into 5–9 dark green, smooth, shining, oval, toothed leaflets 1–2½″ (2.5–6.3 cm) long. The leafstalk "wings" (stipules) are narrow and flaring.
Fruit: red, fleshy hip.
Height: 1–6′ (30–180 cm).
Flowering: June–August.
Habitat: Clearings, thickets, and shores.

Range: Southern Ontario to Newfoundland and
Nova Scotia; south to Virginia and
North Carolina; west to Alabama,
Tennessee, and Missouri.

Comments: Numerous species of Roses occur in a
variety of sites, from dry uplands to
wetlands and sand dunes. Their fruit,
the Rose hips, is rich in vitamin C and
can be eaten, made into jams, or
steeped to make Rose hip tea. Another
pink species, this one of wet sites, is
Swamp Rose (*R. palustris*), which grows
to 7' (2.1 m), has flowers 1½–2½"
(3.8–6.3 cm) wide, very narrow
stipules, and stout, hooked thorns.
Pasture Rose (*R. carolina*) is a shorter
shrub, not more than 3' (90 cm) tall,
with pink flowers, dull green leaves,
very narrow stipules, and straight
thorns. It is found in dry pastures and
open woods throughout most of our
range.

57 **Swamp Dewberry; Bristly Dewberry**
(*Rubus hispidus*)
Rose Family (Rosaceae)

Description: The trailing, woody stems have *weak,
backward-directed bristles* and erect
branches, usually with *3-parted, shiny
leaves* and loose terminal or axillary
clusters of white flowers.
Flowers: ¾" (2 cm) wide; sepals and
petals 5; stamens and pistils many.
Leaves: leaflets to 2" (5 cm) long, thick,
ovate, toothed, mostly evergreen.
Fruit: red or blackish, blackberry-like.
Height: creeper, with canes 4–12"
(10–30 cm) high.

Flowering: June–September.

Habitat: Usually moist thickets, open woods,
and clearings.

Range: Ontario, Quebec, and Nova Scotia;
south to Maryland and uplands of
North Carolina; north to Wisconsin.

Comments: A great many species of dewberries
occur, some with bristles and some

with stronger prickles. Among the latter is the Prickly Dewberry (*R. flagellaris*), a prostrate plant of drier sites, with stout, curved prickles and usually 5-parted, thin leaves. Southern Dewberry (*R. trivialus*), is widely distributed in the South. These plants and the related Blackberries are among the most important summer foods for songbirds and gamebirds, as well as for many mammals.

583 Purple-flowering Raspberry
(*Rubus odoratus*)
Rose Family (Rosaceae)

Description: This erect, shrubby, *thornless plant* has rose-lavender flowers in loose clusters; new branches have bristly hairs.
Flowers: 1–2″ (2.5–5 cm) wide; 5 rose-like petals; many stamens and pistils.
Leaves: 4–10″ (10–25 cm) wide, *large, maple-like,* 3–5 lobed, heart-shaped at base.
Fruit: red, broad, shallow, becoming raspberry-like when mature.
Height: 3–6′ (90–180 cm).

Flowering: June–September.

Habitat: Rocky woods, thickets.

Range: Southern Ontario to Nova Scotia; south through New England to Georgia; west to Tennessee; north to Michigan.

Comments: Thimbleberry (*R. parviflorus*), with very similar white flowers and similar but smaller leaves, occurs from Alaska to Mexico and northeast to Ontario. Baked-apple Berry (*R. chamaemorus*), is a dwarf form only 12″ (30 cm) tall, with a solitary white flower, an amber-colored berry, and leaves similar to the above, but smaller. It is found on mountaintops in New England and northward into Canada. All other species in our range have compound leaves and usually spiny stems.

141 Canadian Burnet
(*Sanguisorba canadensis*)
Rose Family (*Rosaceae*)

Description: This plant bears dense, erect, *cylindrical masses* (spikes) of small, white flowers.
Flowers: about ¼" (6 mm) wide, in spikes to 6" (15 cm) long. Sepals 4, petal-like; petals absent; stamens 4, *long;* pistil 1.
Leaves: pinnately compound, with 7–15 *stalked, oblong, toothed leaflets,* each 1–3" (2.5–7.5 cm) long.
Fruit: dry, one-seeded.
Height: 1–5' (30–150 cm).

Flowering: June–October.

Habitat: Swamps, bogs.

Range: Labrador south to Newfoundland, New England, New Jersey, Delaware, and in mountains to Georgia; northwest to Indiana, Illinois, and Michigan.

Comments: The conspicuous stamens give the finger-like flower clusters a fuzzy appearance. The flowers of the European species, European Great Burnet (*S. officinalis*), are red-brown; this accounts for the common name, from an old French word for "brown." It and Garden Burnet (*S. minor*), with greenish flowers, were both introduced from Europe and naturalized in our range. The generic name is from the Latin *sanguis* ("blood") and *sorbere* ("to drink up") and refers to the juice of the plant which was reputed to stop bleeding.

219 Meadowsweet
(*Spiraea latifolia*)
Rose Family (Rosaceae)

Description: A woody shrub with a *dense, pyramidal terminal cluster* of small, white or pale pinkish flowers.
Flowers: about ¼" (6 mm) wide; sepals 5; petals 5; stamens numerous; pistils usually 5.

Leaves: 1½–2¾″ (3.8–7 cm) long, narrowly ovate to broadly lanceolate, smooth, coarsely toothed, pale on underside.
Fruit: dry, splitting open along 1 side and persisting.
Height: 2–5′ (60–150 cm).
Flowering: June–September.
Habitat: Low, moist ground, meadows, old fields.
Range: Newfoundland to Nova Scotia; south from New England to the mountains of North Carolina; west to Michigan.
Comments: The brown fruits, which persist after flowering, are a distinctive feature. Although less spectacular than the showy introduced garden Spiraeas, this native species is most suitable for naturalistic landscaping. Virginia Spiraea (*S. virginiana*), with a rounded flower cluster and thin, oblong leaves, is native to the southern Appalachian Mountains.

539 Steeplebush
(*Spiraea tomentosa*)
Rose Family (Rosaceae)

Description: An erect shrub, with dense, *steeple-shaped, branched clusters* of pink flowers.
Flowers: less than ¼″ (6 mm) wide; sepals 5; petals 5; stamens numerous; pistils 5–8.
Leaves: 1–2″ (2.5–5 cm) long, oblong, toothed, *very woolly on underside.*
Fruit: small, dry, woody follicle in persisting clusters.
Height: 2–4′ (60–120 cm).
Flowering: July–September.
Habitat: Old fields, meadows, sterile low grounds.
Range: Ontario to Nova Scotia; south through New England to Georgia; west to Arkansas; north to Minnesota.
Comments: A similar species, the pink-flowered Japanese Spiraea (*S. japonica*), from Asia, differs from Steeplebush in having flat-

topped clusters of flowers and smooth leaves. It occurs from New England to Georgia, and west to Tennessee and Indiana.

275 **Barren Strawberry**
(*Waldsteinia fragarioides*)
Rose Family (Rosaceae)

Description: A low, strawberry-like plant with *evergreen basal leaves* and several yellow flowers on a leafless flower stalk.
Flowers: about ½" (1.3 cm) wide; sepals 5, united into cup; petals 5; stamens many; pistils 3–6.
Leaves: long-stalked, divided into 3 wedge-shaped, toothed leaflets, each 1–2" (2.5–5 cm) long.
Fruit: dry, 1-seeded, with persistent calyx cup.
Height: 3–8" (7.5–20 cm).

Flowering: April–June.

Habitat: Woods, thickets, clearings.

Range: Quebec to New Brunswick; south through Maine to uplands of Georgia and Tennessee; west to Minnesota; local in Indiana and Missouri.

Comments: Although the plant is Strawberry-like, the flowers are yellow and the fruits are neither fleshy at maturity, nor edible. A southern species, Lobed Strawberry (*W. lobata*), found along river banks in Georgia, has lobed toothed leaves and narrow, yellow petals no longer than the sepals.

BEDSTRAW FAMILY
(Rubiaceae)

Herbs, shrubs, or trees, with flowers borne in a branched cluster.

Flowers: usually radially symmetrical; sepals 4 or 5; petals 4 or 5, united; stamens 4 or 5. All these parts attached at top of ovary.

Leaves: opposite or whorled, the bases often connected by fused stipules that extend across the node, or the stipules large and leaflike.

Fruit: usually 2-chambered capsule or berry.

There are about 500 genera and 6,000 species, primarily of tropical regions. Madder (a dye), coffee, and quinine are obtained from the family. Gardenias are popular ornamentals in mild climates.

---

227 Buttonbush
(*Cephalanthus occidentalis*)
Bedstraw Family (Rubiaceae)

Description: An *aquatic shrub* with small, white, tubular flowers collectively forming globose "balls."
Flowers: about ⅓" (8 mm) long, in clusters about 1½" (3.8 cm) in diameter. Corolla with 4 erect or spreading lobes; stamens 4; style long, protruding.
Leaves: 3–6" (7.5–15 cm) long, opposite or whorled, ovate, untoothed, pointed.
Height: 3–10' (90–300 cm).
Flowering: June–August.
Habitat: Swamps, borders of ponds and streams.
Range: Southern Ontario to Nova Scotia; south through New England to Florida; west to Texas and beyond; north to Minnesota.
Comments: This species is noted for its ability to withstand flood conditions. The distinctive, ball-like flower and fruit heads account for the common name.

The fruits have some appeal to wildlife, especially mallard ducks.

---

171 Cleavers; Goosegrass
(*Galium aparine*)
Bedstraw Family (Rubiaceae)

Description: A weak-stemmed, reclining plant with
*backward-hooked bristles on stems and
leaves,* and clusters of 1–3 (usually 2)
very small white flowers on stalks rising
from *whorled leaf axils.*
Flowers: about ⅛″ (3 mm) wide; sepals
absent; corolla 4-lobed.
Leaves: 1–3″ (2.5–7.5 cm) long,
lanceolate to linear, *in whorls of 6 to 8.*
Fruit: dry, hairy, hooked at the
summit.
Height: creeper, with stems 8–36″
(20–90 cm) long.
Flowering: May–July.
Habitat: Reclining on bushes in woods and
thickets.
Range: Throughout.
Comments: The common name is appropriate since
the bristles cause the stems, leaves, and
fruits to cleave to clothes and the fur of
animals. The fact that geese eat the
plants accounts for the other common
name. The plants are also known as
Bedstraws since the pleasant smelling
foliage of a yellow-flowered species
(*G. verum*), was used to stuff mattresses
in medieval times.

---

182 Northern Snow Bedstraw
(*Galium boreale*)
Bedstraw Family (Rubiaceae)

Description: A simple or branched, *erect, leafy stem*
has compact, branched, terminal
clusters of small, white flowers and
leaves in whorls of 4.
Flowers: ¼″ (6 mm) wide; sepals
absent; corolla 4-lobed.

Leaves: ¾–2″ (2–5 cm) long; lanceolate to linear.
Fruit: dry, smooth or with short, straight hairs.
Height: 8–36″ (20–90 cm).
Flowering: June–August.
Habitat: Rocky soil, shores, streambanks.
Range: Across Canada; south to Delaware; west to Kentucky, Missouri, New Mexico, and California.
Comments: This is a smooth species compared to others in the genus with rough bristly stems. It often forms sizable patches which may smother other, more desirable plants.

181 Wild Madder
(*Galium mollugo*)
Bedstraw Family (Rubiaceae)

Description: A mostly smooth plant with an erect stem arising from a sprawling base; numerous, small, white flowers form a loose, branched, terminal cluster, and *leaves in whorls of* 6–8.
Flowers: about ⅛″ (4 mm) wide; sepals absent; corolla 4-lobed.
Leaves: ½–1¼″ (1.3–3.1 cm) long, linear-oblong to lanceolate, margins rough.
Fruit: dry, dark brown, smooth.
Height: 1–3′ (30–90 cm).
Flowering: June–August.
Habitat: Roadsides, fields.
Range: Ontario to Newfoundland and Nova Scotia; south through New England to Virginia; west to Indiana.
Comments: Introduced from Europe, this weed has now become common over its range. The generic name is from the Greek *gala* ("milk") and refers to an old use of the plant to curdle milk in making cheese. At least 30 species of *Galium* occur in our range.

593 **Bluets**
(*Houstonia caerulea*)
Bedstraw Family (Rubiaceae)

Description: A low plant with erect, slender stems
bearing *pale blue flowers with golden-
yellow centers.*
Flowers: about ½″ (1.3 cm) wide;
corolla tubular, with 4 flattish lobes.
Flowers pistillate (female), with
abortive stamens, or staminate (male),
with abortive pistils.
Leaves: basal ones to ½″ (1.3 cm) long,
oblong, in tufts; stem leaves tiny,
opposite.
Height: 3–6″ (7.5–15 cm).
Flowering: April–June.
Habitat: Grassy slopes and fields, thickets, and
lawns on acid soils.
Range: Ontario to Nova Scotia; south to
Georgia; west to Alabama; north to
Wisconsin.
Comments: This lovely, delicate, flowering plant is
often found in striking patches of light
blue. The Star Violet (*H. minima*), to 4″
(10 cm) high, has a tiny purple flower
and occurs in fields and open woods
westward to Kansas, Arkansas, and
Texas. A tall southern species, 6–16″
(15–40 cm) high, Large Houstonia
(*H. purpurea*), has 3–5, ribbed,
opposite, ovate leaves, and white or
pink flowers.

74, 445 **Partridgeberry**
(*Mitchella repens*)
Bedstraw Family (Rubiaceae)

Description: A trailing, *evergreen herb* with white,
fragrant, *tubular flowers in pairs.*
Flowers: ½–⅔″ (1.3–1.6 cm) long;
corolla funnel-form with 4 spreading
lobes, fringed on the inside. Flowers are
either staminate (male) with abortive
pistil, or pistillate (female) with
abortive stamens.
Leaves: ½–¾″ (1.3–2 cm) long,

opposite, roundish, shiny, green, with white veins.

Fruit: ovaries of the paired flowers fuse to form a red, edible, berry-like fruit.

Height: creeper, with stem 4–12″ (10–30 cm).

Flowering: June–July.

Habitat: Dry or moist woods.

Range: Throughout.

Comments: A most attractive woodland creeper with highly ornamental foliage, it can be used as a groundcover under acid-loving shrubs and in terraria in the winter. The common name implies that the scarlet fruits are relished by partridges, but they do not appear to be of much importance to wildlife. Indian women drank a tea made from the leaves as an aid in childbirth.

WILLOW FAMILY (Salicaceae)

Shrubs or trees with tiny flowers in erect or pendulous plump spikes called catkins.

Flowers: unisexual; no sepals or petals; 2 or more stamens and 1 pistil borne in the axils of bracts.

Leaves: alternate, simple.

Fruit: small capsule.

There are 4 genera and over 300 species, found in cold and temperate climates. Only the Willows and Poplars occur in North America.

---

364 Pussy Willow
(*Salix discolor*)
Willow Family (Salicaceae)

Description: A large shrub or small tree with *furry flower catkins* that appear in the spring before the leaves.
Flowers: catkins with male flowers yellow, up to 2″ (5 cm) long; those with female flowers greenish, approximately 2½″ (6.3 cm) long; both age to yellow-brown.
Leaves: 2–4″ (5–10 cm) long, oblong to lanceolate, bright green above, whitish below, wavy-toothed above the middle.
Height: 2–20′ (60–600 cm).

Flowering: February–May.

Habitat: Damp thickets, swamps, streambanks.

Range: Across Canada; south through New England to Maryland; west to Kentucky, Missouri, South Dakota, and beyond our range.

Comments: For many people the appearance of these flower catkins signals the arrival of spring. The male catkins with their bright yellow stamens are especially showy compared to the more drab female catkins, which appear on separate plants. The willows are represented in our area by about 50 species, not all restricted to wet sites.

SANDALWOOD FAMILY
(Santalaceae)

Trees, shrubs, or herbs, sometimes
parasitic on roots of other species, with
small flowers borne singly in leaf axils
or in clusters.
Flowers: radially symmetrical; sepals
4 or 5, often petal-like; no petals;
1 stamen opposite each sepal. All
these parts attached at top of ovary.
Leaves: commonly opposite, sometimes
alternate.
Fruit: berry-like drupe or small, hard,
seed-like nut.
There are about 26 genera and 600
species common in warm temperate and
tropical areas. In the United States, this
family is best represented in the
Southeast. Tropical, sweet-scented,
attractive Sandalwood is prized for
cabinet work.

180 Bastard Toadflax
(*Comandra umbellata*)
Sandalwood Family (Santalaceae)

Description: A parasitic plant with *compact terminal
clusters* of small, greenish-white, funnel-
like flowers.
Flowers: ⅛″ (4 mm) wide; petals absent;
sepals 5, often connected to anthers
with tufts of hair; stamens 5; pistil 1.
Leaves: ¾–1¼″ (2–3.8 cm) long,
oblong, pale beneath.
Height: 6–16″ (15–40 cm).

Flowering: April–June.

Habitat: Dry fields, thickets.

Range: Maine south to Georgia; west to
Alabama; north to Michigan.

Comments: Although a photosynthetic plant that
manufactures its own food, it is also a
parasite, obtaining some of its nutrients
from the roots of trees and shrubs.
Although usually found in dry fields,
it is also seen in bogs that dry
out periodically. The generic name

derives from the Greek *come* ("hair")
and *andros* ("a male") and refers to the
hairy attachment of the anthers to the
sepals. Northern Comandra (*Geocaulon
lividum*), a related plant common in
Canada, may be seen on some of the
New England mountains. It is smaller
and has purple flowers.

PITCHER PLANT FAMILY
(Sarraceniaceae)

Carnivorous herbs with tubular leaves
and large, nodding flowers borne singly
or in racemes at the end of a long stalk.
Flowers: radially symmetrical; sepals 4
or 5, often petal-like; petals 5; stamens
12 or more. All these parts attached at
base of ovary; ovary topped by an
umbrella-like style.
Leaves: basal, long, commonly with a
decorative opening to the tube.
Fruit: 3- to 6-chambered capsule.
There are 3 genera and 17 species in
North America and northern South
America; in the United States all but
one are in the East. A few species are
grown as curiosities, and collecting for
this purpose threatens the rarest.
Several species are classified as
endangered or threatened in many
states.

312 **Trumpets**
(*Sarracenia flava*)
Pitcher Plant Family (Sarraceniaceae)

Description: A carnivorous plant with showy, bright
yellow, drooping flowers and *erect,
trumpet-shaped, hollow, inflated leaves;*
flower has musty odor.
Flowers: 3–5" (7.5–12.5 cm) wide;
sepals 5; petals 5; stamens numerous;
style large, disk-like.
Leaves: 1–3' (30–90 cm) high; hood,
purple at constricted neck, arches over
opening that collects water.
Height: 1½–3½' (45–105 cm), flower
stalk equal to or taller than leaves.
Flowering: April–May.
Habitat: Wet pinelands, bogs.
Range: Southeastern Virginia south to Florida;
west to Alabama.
Comments: A southern plant with hollow leaves
that fill with water in which insects and
other small organisms drown; their soft

parts are then digested by the plant. A
similar species, Trumpet Pitcher Plant
(*S. alata*), with fiddle-shaped petals and
leaves without the purple constriction
at the base of the hood, is found from
Alabama to eastern Texas. The ranges
of the two species apparently do not
overlap. The Green Pitcher Plant
(*S. oreophila*), known only in
northeastern Alabama, is classified as an
endangered species.

---

424 Crimson Pitcher Plant; Fiddler's Trumpet
(*Sarracenia leucophylla*)
Pitcher Plant Family (Sarraceniaceae)

Description: A carnivorous plant with nodding,
brownish-red flowers and clusters of
erect, hollow, pitcher-like leaves, colored at
the top with *reddish-purple veins on a
white background,* and topped by an
erect, roundish hood with wavy
margin.
Flowers: 2–3″ (5–7.5 cm) wide; petals
5, fiddle-shaped; stigma distinctive,
forming a large, reddish-green,
umbrella-like structure in center of flower.
Leaves: 2–3′ (60–90 cm) tall.
Height: 2–3′ (60–90 cm), flower stalk
as tall as leaves.
Flowering: March–April.
Habitat: Sandy bogs.
Range: Coastal Plain; Georgia to northern
Florida; west to Mississippi.
Comments: Insects and other small organisms are
attracted to the plant by the colorful
leaf opening and by nectar secreted
inside. They fall into the collected
water and are unable to escape. They
are then digested by plant enzymes or
by bacterial action, thereby providing
essential nutrients. Sweet Pitcher Plant
(*S. rubra*), has a slender, erect trumpet,
4–20″ (10–50 cm) tall, green-veined
with red. The flowers are very fragrant,
with the odor of English Violets.

311 Hooded Pitcher Plant
(*Sarracenia minor*)
Pitcher Plant Family (Sarraceniaceae)

Description: Yellow flowers on a leafless stalk amid
clustered, hollow, tubular leaves,
patterned near the top with *reddish veins*
and pale spots and expanding at the
summit into an *overarching hood.*
Flowers: about 2″ (5 cm) wide; petals 5;
sepals 5; stamens numerous; pistil bears
an umbrella-like style.
Leaves: 6–24″ (15–60 cm) long, winged
along one side.
Height: 6–24″ (15–60 cm), leaves
taller than floral stalk.

Flowering: Spring.

Habitat: Low pinelands, marshes, bogs.

Range: Coastal Plain; North Carolina south to
Florida.

Comments: This is the most common of the Florida
Pitcher Plants. Because of the hood-like
dome at the tip of the leaf, rain is not
collected in this species. Instead,
insects and other small organisms are
lured up a nectar path on the wing of
the leaves and into the hood where
there are translucent spots through
which the victims try to escape. Unable
to do so, they eventually exhaust
themselves and drop to the base of the
leaf. The plant secretes a liquid that
digests the organism and the resulting
nutrients are then absorbed by the
plant.

423 Northern Pitcher Plant
(*Sarracenia purpurea*)
Pitcher Plant Family (Sarraceniaceae)

Description: A carnivorous plant with a large,
solitary, purplish-red flower on a
leafless stalk rising above a rosette of
bronzy, reddish-green, *hollow, inflated,
curved leaves.*
Flowers: 2″ (5 cm) wide; petals 5;
stamens numerous; style expanded into

an umbrella-shaped structure.

Leaves: 4–12″ (10–30 cm) long, with a broad flaring terminal lip covered with stiff, downward-pointing hairs.

Fruit: capsule.

Height: 8–24″ (20–60 cm).

Flowering: May–August.

Habitat: Sphagnum bogs.

Range: Saskatchewan to Labrador and Nova Scotia; south through New England to Florida; west to Texas; north to Indiana, Illinois, and Minnesota.

Comments: A striking plant with lipped, pitcher-like leaves that collect water; organisms attracted to the colored lip have difficulty crawling upward because of the recurved hairs and eventually fall into the water and drown. Enzymes secreted by the plant aid in the digestion of the insect but much of the breakdown is passive, a result of bacterial activity. The plant absorbs the nutrients, especially nitrogenous compounds. A southern species, Parrot Pitcher Plant (*S. psittacina*) has many prostrate "pitchers" with hooked lips like a parrot's bill.

LIZARD TAIL FAMILY
(Saururaceae)

Herbs, mostly of moist places, with small flowers in dense spikes or racemes, often associated with colored bracts, with the entire cluster resembling a single large flower.
Flowers: radially symmetrical; calyx and corolla absent; stamens 3, 6, or 8; pistils 3 or 4, sometimes partly joined at the base.
Leaves: alternate, simple.
Fruit: succulent capsule.
There are 5 genera and 7 species, which occur in North America and eastern Asia.

---

121 Lizard's Tail
(*Saururus cernuus*)
Lizard Tail Family (Saururaceae)

Description: Many tiny, fragrant, white flowers are on a slender, tapering, *stalked spike with a drooping tip.*
Flowers: spike to 6″ (15 cm) long; sepals and petals absent; stamens 6–8, showy, about ⅛″ (4 mm) long; pistils 3–4, united.
Leaves: 3–6″ (7.5–15 cm) long, heart-shaped, indented at base.
Fruit: fleshy, wrinkled.
Height: 2–5′ (60–150 cm).

Flowering: June–September.

Habitat: Swamps, shallow water.

Range: Ontario to Rhode Island, Connecticut, and New York; south to Florida; west to Texas, Missouri, and Kansas; north to Illinois and Michigan.

Comments: This is a mostly southern species of shaded marshes and stream margins. The common name and the genus name, from the Greek *sauros* ("lizard") and *oura* ("tail"), depict the shape of the drooping flower cluster.

SAXIFRAGE FAMILY
(Saxifragaceae)

Usually herbs with small flowers borne in raceme-like or openly branched clusters.
Flowers: radially symmetrical; sepals 5; petals 5 or 10, separate; stamens 5 or 10. All these parts attached to edge of cup-like flower base (hypanthium), with ovary in center.
Leaves: usually alternate, and basal.
Fruit: capsule, small pod, or berry.
There are about 30 genera and 580 species, which occur mainly in cooler regions of the Northern Hemisphere. Species of *Saxifraga, Bergenia,* and *Astilbe* are commonly grown as ornamentals.

154 False Goatsbeard
(*Astilbe biternata*)
Saxifrage Family (Saxifragaceae)

Description: Small, white or yellowish flowers are in elongated clusters that branch off the hairy stalk; collectively the clusters form a *large, much-branched terminal cluster*.
Flowers: about ⅙″ (4 mm) long; some perfect (both male and female), others with male and female flowers on separate plants. Petals 4–5, those of female flowers minute or lacking; stamens 10; pistils 2.
Leaves: to 2′ (60 cm) wide, compound, divided into 3 parts which are again divided into 3 toothed or lobed, ovate leaflets; terminal leaflet usually 3-lobed.
Height: 2–6′ (60–180 cm).
Flowering: May–July.
Habitat: Mountain woods.
Range: West Virginia and Virginia south to Georgia; west to Tennessee.
Comments: A southern species, found in mountain forests, the flower masses resemble a goat's beard and are similar to those of

the true Goatsbeard (*Aruncus dioicus*), of the Rose Family. The species name refers to the double subdivision of the leaves.

5 Alumroot
(*Heuchera americana*)
Saxifrage Family (Saxifragaceae)

Description: Yellowish-green, bell-shaped, *drooping flowers* are on a somewhat hairy stalk, in loose, slender, branching clusters, with usually 4–5 flowers on each branch.
Flowers: to ¼" (6 mm) long; calyx 5-lobed, cup-shaped; petals 5, small, greenish; stamens 5, projecting, *with orange anthers;* pistil 1, of 2 united carpels.
Leaves: 3–4" (7.5–10 cm) wide, basal, long-stalked, heart-shaped, lobed, somewhat maple-like.
Height: 2–3' (60–90 cm).

Flowering: April–June.
Habitat: Woods, shaded slopes and rocks.
Range: Connecticut south to Georgia; west to Alabama; north to Oklahoma, Michigan, and Ontario.

Comments: A western species, Midland Alumroot (*H. richardsonii*), has flowers distinctly unequal in shape, and very hairy leaf stalks and leaf undersurfaces. The genus is named for the 18th-century German physician and botanist, Johan von Heucher. Eight other similar species occur in our range.

129 Miterwort
(*Mitella diphylla*)
Saxifrage Family (Saxifragaceae)

Description: A slender, elongated cluster of tiny white flowers with 5 *delicately fringed petals* is above a *single pair of stalkless stem leaves.*
Flowers: about ⅛" (4 mm) wide;

stamens 10; pistil 1.
Leaves: basal ones to 3″ (7.5 cm) long, ovate, lobed, stalked; stem leaves opposite, mostly 3-lobed.
Fruit: *miter-shaped capsule* with black seeds exposed when pod splits open.
Height: 8–18″ (20–45 cm).

Flowering: April–June.

Habitat: Rich woods.

Range: Southwestern Quebec and New Hampshire; south to uplands of Georgia; west to Tennessee, Mississippi, Missouri, and Minnesota.

Comments: The flower is a fantastic bit of geometry when viewed with a hand lens. The distinctive leaves halfway down the stalk are responsible for the species name. The common and genus names allude to the fruit, which has the shape of a small cap or bishop's miter. Naked Miterwort (*M. nuda*), a lovely smaller species, has only basal leaves and fewer, slightly larger, greenish to brownish flowers. It occurs from Labrador and Newfoundland south through New England to Pennsylvania, and west to Ohio, Minnesota, and Montana.

73 Grass-of-Parnassus
(*Parnassia glauca*)
Saxifrage Family (Saxifragaceae)

Description: A solitary white flower, striped with green veins, tops a stalk at the middle of which is a *single, rounded, clasping leaf;* other leaves basal.
Flowers: 1″ (2.5 cm) wide; sepals 5; petals 5; stamens 5, yellow, alternating with the petals; 3-pronged, gland-tipped, sterile stamens at the base of each petal form a circle around the pistil.
Leaves: Basal ones to 2½″ (6.3 cm) wide, heart-shaped, ovate, or round.
Fruit: 4-parted capsule.
Height: 6–20″ (15–50 cm).

Flowering: July–October.

Habitat: Wet soils, usually limestone.

Range: Manitoba to New Brunswick; south through New England to Pennsylvania; west to Ohio, Indiana, Illinois, Iowa, and South Dakota.

Comments: The delicate green veins of the petals are the distinctive feature of this perennial (which does not really resemble a grass). "Parnassus" refers to the Greek mountain, sacred to Apollo, where the ancient naturalist Dioscorides observed similar plants in meadows. Three other very similar species occur in the South.

455 Purple Saxifrage
(*Saxifraga oppositifolia*)
Saxifrage Family (Saxifragaceae)

Description: A low, *densely tufted plant* with solitary, rose-purple flowers topping stems with small, opposite, purplish leaves, overlapping toward the bottom.
Flowers: about ½" (1.3 cm) wide; sepals and petals 5; stamens 10; pistils 2.
Leaves: to ¼" (6 mm) long; ovate to roundish, upper ones fewer than the lower, margins hairy, 1–3 lime-encrusted pores present at tips.
Height: ¾–4" (2–10 cm).

Flowering: May–August.

Habitat: Rocks, ledges, and cliffs.

Range: Arctic regions south to Newfoundland, Quebec, and northern Vermont; also in mountains of Wyoming and Washington.

Comments: There are other species of this family found on New England mountains. Star-like Saxifrage (*S. stellaris*), has thin, green basal leaves and white flowers which appear only on the larger plants. It is found in the United States only on Mt. Katahdin in Maine. White Mountain Saxifrage (*S. aizoon*), has tufted, toothed basal leaves and small, white flowers and is found on ledges and gravels on Mt. Katahdin and mountains in Vermont and New York, and in Michigan and Minnesota. Yellow Mountain Saxifrage (*S. aizoides*), has bright yellow flowers and occurs in Vermont, New York, and northern Michigan.

14 Swamp Saxifrage
(*Saxifraga pensylvanica*)
Saxifrage Family (Saxifragaceae)

Description: A stout, hairy, *sticky flower stalk* has branched clusters (at first compact but later elongated and loose) of small flowers, usually yellowish-green.
Flowers: about ⅙″ (4 mm) wide; petals 5; stamens 10, pistils 2, united.
Leaves: 4–8″ (10–20 cm) long; basal, ovate to lanceolate, nearly toothless.
Height: 1–3′ (30–90 cm).

Flowering: April–June.

Habitat: Wet meadows and prairies, swamps, bogs, banks.

Range: Maine south to North Carolina; west to West Virginia, Missouri, and Illinois.

Comments: This is a large Saxifrage of wet areas; the genus name is from the Latin *saxum* ("a stone") and *frangere* ("to break") and alludes either to the supposed ability of the plant to crack rocks (in the crevices where some members of the genus are found) or to the stone-like bulblets on the roots of a European species. In earlier times, the Saxifrages were assumed to have medicinial value in dissolving kidney or gallbladder stones. The young leaves of this species can be eaten in salads or as cooked greens.

159 Early Saxifrage
(*Saxifraga virginiensis*)
Saxifrage Family (Saxifragaceae)

Description: A hairy floral stalk, rising from a
rosette of basal leaves, has branched
clusters of *fragrant white flowers*.
Flowers: ¼" (6 mm) wide; sepals 5;
petals 5; stamens 10, yellow; pistils 2,
nearly separate.
Leaves: to 3" (7.5 cm) long, broadly
toothed, ovate to oblong.
Fruit: 2-beaked brown capsule.
Height: 4–16" (10–40 cm).

Flowering: April–June.

Habitat: Dry rocky slopes and outcrops.

Range: Ontario to New Brunswick; south
through New England to Georgia; west
to Tennessee, Missouri; north to
Minnesota.

Comments: This early spring wildflower can be
planted in shaded rock gardens. Many
members of this genus occur and they
can be found in both wet and dry
habitats. Mountain Saxifrage
(*S. michauxii*), a southern species that
grows up to 18" (45 cm) tall, has coarse
leaves, and white petals of slightly
different sizes, spotted with yellow.

123 Foamflower
(*Tiarella cordifolia*)
Saxifrage Family (Saxifragaceae)

Description: Small, white flowers are in a *feathery,
somewhat elongated, terminal cluster*.
Flowers: ¼" (6 mm) wide; sepals 5;
petals 5, clawed; stamens 10,
protruding, anthers reddish or yellow;
pistils 2, of unequal size.
Leaves: 2–4" (5–10 cm) long; basal,
stalked, lobed and sharply toothed,
somewhat maple-like, usually hairy.
Fruit: pair of capsules, each of which
splits open along one side.
Height: 6–12" (15–30 cm).

Flowering: April–June.

Habitat: Rich woods.

Range: Ontario to Nova Scotia; south through New England to upland North Carolina; west to Tennessee; north to Michigan.

Comments: This attractive wildflower, which spreads by underground stems, forms colonies, and makes excellent groundcover for shady, wooded sites. The tiny flowers and fine texture of the stamens resemble foam and account for the common name. The genus name is from the Greek *tiara,* designating a turban once worn by the Persians, and refers to the shape of the pistil.

SNAPDRAGON OR FIGWORT FAMILY
(Scrophulariaceae)

Mostly herbs, sometimes shrubs, rarely trees, often with showy flowers.
Flowers: bilaterally symmetrical; sepals 4 or 5, united; petals 4 or 5, united, usually forming a corolla with upper and lower lips; stamens usually 4, sometimes 2 or 5; when 5 the fifth often sterile and different from the rest. All these parts attached at base of ovary.
Leaves: alternate, opposite, or whorled, simple or pinnately divided.
Fruit: 2-chambered capsule or berry.
There are about 220 genera and 3,000 species occurring nearly throughout the world. A cardiac drug is extracted from Fox-Glove, also a handsome ornamental. Snapdragon, Speedwell, Beardtongue, and Slipperflower are others grown for their beauty.

520 Purple Gerardia
(*Agalinis purpurea*)
Snapdragon Family (Scrophulariaceae)

Description: Pink, *bell-shaped flowers* on short stalks bloom in the axils of opposite, linear leaves.
Flowers: about 1″ (2.5 cm) long; corolla of 5 fused petals with unequal and spreading lobes; stamens 4, with yellow anthers, attached to petals and not projecting; pistil 1.
Leaves: 1–1½″ (2.5–3.8 cm) long, and ⅛″ (4 mm) wide.
Fruit: globose capsule.
Height: 1–4′ (30–120 cm).
Flowering: July–September.
Habitat: Moist soil.
Range: Southern New England and southeastern New York to Florida; west to eastern Texas; north to Nebraska and Minnesota.

Comments: The rose-purple corolla of this widely
spreading, smooth-stemmed annual has
dark spots on the inside of the throat.
As a group, the Gerardias are slender,
wiry-branched plants with narrow
leaves. A smaller species, found in salt
marshes, Seaside Gerardia
(*A. maritima*), has rather fleshy linear
leaves and smaller flowers. Over fifteen
species of this genus occur, all with
pink to purplish (or occasionally white)
flowers.

334 Smooth False Foxglove; Entire-leafed False Foxglove
(*Aureolaria laevigata*)
Snapdragon Family (Scrophulariaceae)

Description: At the summit of a *smooth stem* is a
cluster of *yellow, funnel-shaped flowers.*
Flowers: ¾" (2 cm) wide; corolla
with 5 flaring lobes.
Leaves: 1½–4" (3.8–10 cm) long,
opposite, lanceolate to ovate, mostly
untoothed, except for the lowest ones.
Height: 1–5' (30–150 cm).
Flowering: July–October.
Habitat: Woods and thickets, chiefly in
mountains.
Range: Pennsylvania south to Georgia; west to
Tennessee and Ohio.
Comments: The members of this group of plants are
semi-parasitic on the roots of oaks and
usually turn black when dried as
herbarium specimens. Northern False
Foxglove (*A. flava*) is very similar, but
with pinnately lobed leaves, and is
found east of the Mississippi. West of
the river is Large-sepaled False Foxglove
(*A. calycosa*), also similar, as well as
Western False Foxglove (*A. grandiflora*),
with hairy stems.

333 Downy False Foxglove
(Aureolaria virginica)
Snapdragon Family (Scrophulariaceae)

Description: At the top of a *downy stem* is a terminal
cluster of funnel-shaped, yellow
flowers, with each flower solitary in the
axils of opposite bracts.
Flowers: 1″ (2.5 cm) wide; corolla
with 5 flaring lobes, stamens 4.
Leaves: 2½–5 (6.3–12.5 cm) long;
opposite, downy, lanceolate to ovate;
the *lower ones pinnately lobed,* upper
leaves with fewer lobes or none.
Height: 1–5′ (30–150 cm).
Flowering: June–August.
Habitat: Dry open woods.
Range: New Hampshire south to northern
Florida; west to Louisiana; north to
Michigan.
Comments: Like the very similar Smooth False
Foxglove (*A. laevigata*), this plant is
partly parasitic on the roots of oaks.
Some taxonomists put both species in
the genus *Gerardia*.

433 Indian Paintbrush; Painted Cup
(Castilleja coccinea)
Snapdragon Family (Scrophulariaceae)

Description: The actual flowers are hidden in the
axils of *scarlet-tipped, fan-shaped bracts*
and arranged in a dense spike.
Flowers: about 1″ (2.5 cm) long,
greenish-yellow, tubular, with a long,
2-lobed upper lip arching over shorter
3-lobed lower lip; styles protrude
beyond bracts; bracts slightly longer
than corolla.
Leaves: basal ones 1–3″ (2.5–7.5 cm)
long; in rosettes, elliptic, untoothed;
stem leaves stalkless, divided into
narrow segments.
Height: 1–2′ (30–60 cm).
Flowering: May–July.
Habitat: Meadows, prairies, damp sandy soil.
Range: Southern Manitoba to southern New

Hampshire; south to northern Florida; west to Louisiana and Oklahoma.

Comments: The conspicuous, red-tipped, brush-like bracts appear to have been dipped in paint, as is suggested by the common names. This is a very large western genus of over 200 species. Purple Painted Cup (*C. purpurea*), with purple or violet bracts, occurs from southwest Missouri to Texas. Downy Painted Cup (*C. sessiliflora*), found from southeast Wisconsin to Illinois and Missouri, and from Texas westward, has green bracts. Pale Painted Cup (*C. septentrionalis*), has whitish or creamy bracts, often suffused with bronze or dull purple, and ranges west and north from subalpine New England.

113 Turtlehead
(*Chelone glabra*)
Snapdragon Family (Scrophulariaceae)

Description: This smooth plant has tight terminal clusters of white (often lavender-tinged), tubular, 2-lipped *flowers resembling turtle heads.*
Flowers: 1–1½″ (2.5–3.8 cm) long; upper lip arches over hairy lower lip; stamens 4, plus 1 short, sterile stamen.
Leaves: 3–6″ (8–15 cm) long, opposite, lanceolate, sharply toothed.
Height: 1–3′ (30–90 cm).

Flowering: July–September.

Habitat: Wet thickets, streambanks, low ground.

Range: Ontario to Nova Scotia; south through New England to Georgia; west to Missouri; north to Minnesota.

Comments: The distinctive shape of this flower is reflected in the genus name, derived from the Greek *chelone* ("a tortoise").

512 Lyon's Turtlehead
(Chelone lyoni)
Snapdragon Family (Scrophulariaceae)

Description: A tall, erect plant with pink or rose-purple flowers *resembling turtle heads,* borne in compact clusters at the top of the stems or in the axils of opposite leaves.
Flowers: about 1″ (2.5 cm) long; 2-lobed upper lip arches over 3-lobed lower lip; lower lip bearded with yellow hairs inside.
Leaves: 3–7″ (7.5–17.5 cm) long, toothed, ovate, round-based; on stalks often over 1″ (2.5 cm) long.
Height: 1–3′ (30–90 cm).
Flowering: July–September.
Habitat: Rich woods, wet thickets, streambanks.
Range: Mountains of Virginia, North Carolina, South Carolina, Georgia, and Tennessee.
Comments: This species occasionally escapes from cultivation in New England. It was named in honor of John Lyon, an American botanist of the early 19th century.

645 Blue-eyed Mary
(Collinsia verna)
Snapdragon Family (Scrophulariaceae)

Description: On a weak stem, whorls of 4–6 stalked, 2-lipped, *blue and white flowers* arise from the axils of opposite, mostly stalkless leaves.
Flowers: ½″ (1.3 cm) long; upper lip divided into 2 white lobes; lower lip 3-lobed, blue, the middle lobe folded and hidden as it envelops 4 stamens and 1 style.
Leaves: ¾–2″ (2–5 cm) long, ovate.
Height: 6–18″ (15–45 cm).
Flowering: April–June.
Habitat: Damp open woods.
Range: New York south to western Virginia; west to Kentucky, Arkansas, Kansas,

Iowa, and Wisconsin.

Comments: The seeds of this delicate winter annual
should be sown in summer since they
germinate in the fall. The species name
is the Latin word for "spring" and
describes the flowering time.

502 Eyebright
(*Euphrasia americana*)
Snapdragon Family (Scrophulariaceae)

Description: A small plant with short, spike-like
terminal clusters of pale lavender
flowers on a *hairy stem* and its branches.
Flowers: ⅓–½" (8–13 mm) long;
upper lip two-lobed, lower lip
marked with deeper purple, large, *with
3 notched lobes;* bracts under flowers
conspicuous, ovate, coarsely toothed.
Leaves: ¼–¾" (6–20 mm) long;
coarsely toothed.
Height: 4–15" (10–37.5 cm).
Flowering: June–September.
Habitat: Fields, roadsides.
Range: Newfoundland south to Maine and
New Hampshire.
Comments: There are several species of Eyebrights,
native of the colder regions. They are
partly parasitic on the roots of other
plants. The common name refers to the
fact that the plants were at one time
used to treat eye diseases and improve
vision. The species name, from the
Greek word for "cheerfulness," may
allude to the same properties.

627 Blue Toadflax; Old-field Toadflax
(*Linaria canadensis*)
Snapdragon Family (Scrophulariaceae)

Description: Small, light blue-violet, 2-lipped,
spurred flowers are scattered in an
elongated cluster on a slender stem.
Flowers: ¼–½" (6–13 mm) long;
sepals 5; upper lip 2-lobed, lower lip

3-lobed, with 2 small white ridges, and long, thread-like spur projecting at base.

Leaves: stem ones to 1½″ (3.8 cm) long, alternate, linear, smooth and shiny; basal leaves small, opposite, on trailing stems that form a rosette.

Height: 6–24″ (15–60 cm).

Flowering: April–September.

Habitat: Open, dry, shady or rocky sites; abandoned fields, usually sandy.

Range: Throughout.

Comments: This is a delicate, attractive, wide-ranging native Toadflax, found locally even on the West Coast. The resemblance of the leaves to those of Flax accounts for the common and genus names, the latter from the Latin *linum* ("flax").

331 Butter-and-eggs
(*Linaria vulgaris*)
Snapdragon Family (Scrophulariaceae)

Description: Yellow, 2-lipped, *spurred, flowers* bloom in a terminal cluster on a leafy stem.

Flowers: about 1″ (2.5 cm) long; sepals 5; petals 5, united, the upper lip 2-lobed, the lower lip 3-lobed with orange ridges, and a prominent spur at base; stamens 4; pistil 1, with green style.

Leaves: 1–2½″ (2.5–6.3 cm) long, gray-green; the upper alternate, linear, grass-like, the lower ones opposite or whorled.

Height: 1–3′ (30–90 cm).

Flowering: May–October.

Habitat: Dry fields, waste places, roadsides.

Range: Throughout.

Comments: This European introduction grows well in dry sites and forms sizable masses. An orange path on the lower lip leads to nectar contained in the long spur and serves as a "honey guide" for insects. Experiments with hawk moths indicated that the moths will try to

stick their tongues into flowers
pressed between glass; tongue
marks on the glass coincide with the
orange honey guide. Even a honey
guide cut out and placed on other
flowers will attract the moths.
Dalmatian Toadflax (*L. dalmatica*),
resembles a larger version of Butter-
and-eggs, with ovate or lanceolate
leaves and flowers to 1¾″ (4.5 cm)
long. It is increasingly common from
Pennsylvania to Illinois and northward.

116 Cow Wheat
(*Melampyrum lineare*)
Snapdragon Family (Scrophulariaceae)

Description: A low, upward-branching plant with
small, tubular *creamy white, 2-lipped
flowers* on short stalks in the axils of
upper leaves.
Flowers: ½″ (1.3 cm) long; upper lip
white, arched, 2-lobed; lower lip
3-lobed, yellow; stamens 4, 2 long
and 2 short, under upper lip.
Leaves: ¾–2½″ (2–6.3 cm) long,
opposite, linear to lanceolate-ovate,
with often 2–4 bristly teeth at base.
Height: 6–18″ (15–45 cm).
Flowering: June–August.
Habitat: Dry to moist woods, bogs, rocky
barrens.
Range: Across Canada; south through New
England to uplands of Georgia; west to
Tennessee, Michigan, Wisconsin, and
beyond our range.
Comments: This small, native, woodland annual has
flowers that seem to resemble a snake's
head. The genus name is from the
Greek for "black" and "wheat" and
refers to the black seeds found in some
species.

267 Muskflower
(*Mimulus moschatus*)
Snapdragon Family (Scrophulariaceae)

Description: This *sticky, hairy, musk-scented plant* has tubular, yellow, flattish-faced flowers in the leaf axils on a weak ascending stem. Flowers: ¾″ (2 cm) long; with sepals 5; corolla 2-lipped, open in the throat; stamens 4, attached to petals; pistil 1. Leaves: 1–2½″ (2.5–6.3 cm) long; opposite, ovate to lanceolate, entire or toothed, short stalked. Fruit: capsule. Height: 8–16″ (20–40 cm).

Flowering: June–September.

Habitat: Streambanks and margins of ponds.

Range: Ontario to Newfoundland and Nova Scotia; south through Massachusetts to North Carolina; west to West Virginia and Michigan. More common in Rocky Mountain and Pacific Coast States.

Comments: This plant has apparently escaped from cultivation over much of its present range. It can be used in wetland wildflower gardens. Two other species, both known as Yellow Monkeyflower, have smooth stems and yellow flowers. *M. guttatus* has flowers ½–1¾″ (1.3–4.5 cm) long, with the throats essentially closed. This naturalized species occurs in Vermont, Connecticut, and eastern New York. *M. glabratus* also has yellow flowers, ¼–1″ (6–25 mm) long, but with wide-open throats; it is found from Michigan to Ontario and into the West and Southwest.

616 Monkeyflower
(*Mimulus ringens*)
Snapdragon Family (Scrophulariaceae)

Description: Asymmetrical, 2-lipped, blue-purple flowers rise from the axils of opposite leaves that clasp the *square stem.* Flowers: about 1″ (2.5 cm) long; upper

lip 2-lobed, erect; lower lip 3-lobed, with 2 yellow spots on inside; stamens 4; white throat of corolla nearly closed.
Leaves: 2–4″ (5–10 cm) long; unstalked, oblong to lanceolate.
Height: 1–3′ (30–90 cm).

Flowering: June–September.

Habitat: Wet meadows and streambanks.

Range: Saskatchewan to Nova Scotia; south to Georgia; west to Alabama, Louisiana, and northeastern Texas.

Comments: The flower looks something like a monkey's face, hence the common and genus names, the latter from the Latin *mimus* ("a buffoon"). A variety of this plant, *M. ringens,* var. *colpophilus,* found from Quebec to Maine on tidal muds, is classified as an endangered species in Maine. The lavender-flowering Sharp-winged Monkeyflower (*M. alatus*) has stalked leaves and a winged stem. It is more common southward and westward in wet sites.

---

436 **Wood Betony; Lousewort**
(*Pedicularis canadensis*)
Snapdragon Family (Scrophulariaceae)

Description: A hairy plant with tubular, 2-lipped flowers, all red, all yellow, or yellow and red in a *short, dense, terminal cluster.*
Flowers: ¾″ (2 cm) long; petals united, the upper lip arched, with 2 small teeth, the lower lip shorter, 3-lobed, spreading; stamens 4, 2 long and 2 short, attached to upper lip. *Leaf-like bracts present beneath flowers.*
Leaves: 3–5″ (7.5–12.5 cm) long, mostly basal, oblong-lanceolate, deeply divided into toothed lobes.
Height: 6–18″ (15–45 cm).

Flowering: April–June.

Habitat: Woods and clearings.

Range: Manitoba to Quebec; south through central Maine to Florida; west to Mississippi, Louisiana, and Texas;

north to Minnesota.

Comments: These low, semi-parasitic plants get some of their nourishment from the roots of other plants. The flower color and the finely cut foliage are distinctive. The genus name, from the Latin *pediculus* ("a louse"), and the common name Lousewort, refer to the misconception once held by farmers that cattle and sheep became infested with lice when grazing on the plants. Swamp Lousewort (*P. lanceolata*), with many opposite leaves on a stem 12–36″ (30–90 cm) tall, has light yellow flowers and usually occurs in wet meadows with limestone soil. Furbish's Lousewort (*P. furbishiae*), is similar, but with finely cut, alternate leaves; it is found on the banks of the St. John River in New Brunswick and in northern Maine, where it is classified as an endangered species.

556, 647   Gray Beardtongue
(*Penstemon canescens*)
Snapdragon Family (Scrophulariaceae)

Description: At the top of a *downy stem* is a loose cluster of showy, tubular, violet-purple to pinkish flowers with darker violet-purple lines inside the corolla.
Flowers: 1–1½″ (2.5–3.8 cm) long; the 3-parted *lower lobe projecting straight out;* the 2-parted *upper lobe erect;* stamens 5, one of them sterile.
Leaves: middle ones 3–6″ (7.5–15 cm), ovate to ovate-lanceolate; upper ones clasping the stem; basal leaves stalked, broadly ovate, in a rosette.
Height: 1–3′ (30–90 cm).
Flowering: May–July.
Habitat: Dry woods and thickets.
Range: Pennsylvania south to Georgia, west to Alabama and north to Indiana.
Comments: This is one of numerous Beardtongues, more common in the western United

States, named for the tuft of hairs found on the sterile stamen of many species, including this one. Cobaea Beardtongue (*P. cobaea*), found on prairies and rocky bluffs from Missouri to Kansas and Nebraska and southward, grows to 2′ (60 cm) and has downy, clasping leaves and white to deep purple flowers up to 2″ (5 cm) long.

519 Large-flowered Beardtongue
(*Penstemon grandiflorus*)
Snapdragon Family (Scrophulariaceae)

Description: On a *smooth stem* above opposite, blue-green, clasping leaves, and in the axils of similar leafy bracts, are large, lavender, *horizontally arranged, tubular flowers.*
Flowers: to 2″ (5 cm) long; corolla tube flares out abruptly above calyx into 5 lobes; fertile stamens 4; 1 sterile stamen, minutely hairy at tip.
Leaves: 1–2½″ (2.5–6.3 cm) long, opposite, broadly ovate, usually with a whitish bloom.
Height: 2–4′ (60–120 cm).
Flowering: May–June.
Habitat: Woods and thickets.
Range: Wisconsin, Illinois, and Missouri; south to Texas; west to Colorado and Wyoming.
Comments: This is a most handsome plant and is especially spectacular when seen in masses. It occasionally escapes from cultivation in the East. At least 15 species occur in our area, and even more grow in the western United States.

555 Hairy Beardtongue
(*Penstemon hirsutus*)
Snapdragon Family (Scrophulariaceae)

Description: A *woolly-stemmed plant* with open, stalked clusters of lavender, trumpet-

shaped flowers, with white lips.
Flowers: 1″ (2.5 cm) long; petals 5,
united, the upper lip erect, 2-lobed,
the lower lip 3-lobed, projecting; fertile
stamens 4 and 1 *sterile hairy stamen.*
Leaves: 2–5″ (5–12.5 cm) long,
opposite, light green, oblong to
lanceolate, toothed or almost toothless.
Height: 1–3′ (30–90 cm).

Flowering: June–July.

Habitat: Dry or rocky ground.

Range: Southern Ontario and Quebec; south
through southern New England to
Virginia; west to Kentucky, Tennessee,
and Wisconsin.

Comments: The Beardtongues are a very large
group, and taxonomically so complex
that separating the species is often
difficult. This species is readily
distinguished, however, by the downy
nature of the stem. The common and
scientific names refer to the tufted
sterile stamen.

332 Yellow Rattlebox
(*Rhinanthus crista-galli*)
Snapdragon Family (Scrophulariaceae)

Description: Erect stem, simple or branched, bears
stalkless yellow flowers in a leafy,
1-sided spike. *Calyx becomes highly
inflated in fruit.*
Flowers: ½″ (1.3 cm) long; calyx
4-toothed, flattened vertically at first,
later becoming nearly globose. Corolla
2-lipped; *upper lip arched,* with a low
tooth on each side; lower lip 3-lobed.
Bracts with bristle-tipped teeth present
beneath flowers.
Leaves: ¾–2½″ (2–6.3 cm) long,
opposite, stalkless, triangular-lanceolate
to oblong, toothed.
Fruit: flattened, circular capsule.
Height: 4–32″ (10–80 cm).

Flowering: May–September.

Habitat: Fields, thickets.

Range: Alaska to Labrador, south to

Newfoundland, Nova Scotia and
northern New England and New York,
along coast of southern Maine; also
Lake Superior area and south to
Michigan.

Comments: As the name implies, the seeds rattle in
the capsule at maturity. The plant is
parasitic, obtaining its nutrients from
the roots of other plants.

389   Maryland Figwort
(*Scrophularia marilandica*)
Snapdragon Family (Scrophulariaceae)

Description: On a 4-sided, grooved stem is a
branching, somewhat pyramidal
terminal cluster of small, erect, sac-
shaped, greenish-brown flowers with
magenta-brown interiors.
Flowers: about ¼" (6 mm) long; upper
lip 2-lobed, projecting forward; lower
lip with 2 lateral lobes, and 1 central
lobe bent straight downward; fertile
stamens 4 and 1 brownish-purple,
gland-like, sterile stamen, all attached
to petals.
Leaves: 4–16" (10–40 cm) long,
opposite, ovate to lanceolate, toothed,
stalked.
Fruit: ovoid capsule.
Height: 3–8' (90–240 cm).

Flowering: June–October.
Habitat: Rich woods, thickets.
Range: Quebec south from Maine to southern
Georgia, west to Alabama and
Louisiana, north to Oklahoma and
Minnesota.

Comments: The Figworts are tall plants with
brownish or greenish flowers in a large,
branched flowering arrangement. The
common name refers to the early use of
the plant in treating piles, an ailment
once known as "figs." The plant was
also used as a tonic, and an infusion of
the roots was given in the 1800s as a
treatment for insomnia and anxiety. A
similar species, Hare Figwort

(*S. lanceolata*), has shiny flowers and the remnant stamen is greenish-yellow. Figwort (*S. nodosa*), a very similar European species, has become established in our area. It has a brownish-purple sterile stamen and usually finishes flowering in June.

150, 335 Moth Mullein
(*Verbascum blattaria*)
Snapdragon Family (Scrophulariaceae)

Description: Yellow or white flowers with *rounded petals*, marked with brownish-purple on the back, are in a slender, open, spike-like cluster on an erect stem.
Flowers: 1″ (2.5 cm) wide; petals 5; stamens 5, with orange anthers and *violet hairs* on the filaments; pistil 1.
Leaves: 1–5″ (2.5–12.5 cm) long; triangular to oblong or lanceolate, coarsely toothed, clasping the stem.
Height: 2–4′ (60–120 cm).
Flowering: June–September.
Habitat: Old fields, roadsides.
Range: Throughout.
Comments: Its fuzzy stamens resemble the antennae of a moth; hence the common name. It is related to the Common Mullein (*V. virgatum*), also known as Moth Mullein, which bears 2–3 flowers from the same point of attachment on the stalk. It is found locally from Nova Scotia to South Carolina, Texas, and Southern Ontario. White Mullein (*V. lychnitis*), with yellow (rarely white) flowers, only ½–¾″ (1.3–2 cm) wide and with leaves to 12″ (30 cm) long, is found from Ontario to New Hampshire, and south to Virginia and West Virginia.

336 Common Mullein
(*Verbascum thapsus*)
Snapdragon Family (Scrophulariaceae)

Description: An erect, woolly stem has a *tightly packed, spike-like cluster* of yellow flowers and white-woolly stem leaves, and rises from a rosette of *thick, velvety* basal leaves.
Flowers: ¾−1″ (2−2.5 cm) wide; petals 5, nearly regular; stamens 5; pistil 1.
Leaves: basal ones to 12″ (30 cm) oblong, stalked; upper leaves smaller, stalkless.
Height: 2−6′ (60−180 cm).
Flowering: June−September.
Habitat: Fields, roadsides, waste places.
Range: Throughout.
Comments: An introduced biennial with very velvety leaves, it has long been used for many purposes. Roman soldiers are said to have dipped the stalks in grease for use as torches. The leaves are still used as wicks in some areas. Indians lined their mocassins with the leaves to keep out the cold, and colonists used them in their stockings for the same purpose. A tea made from the leaves was used to treat colds, and the flowers and roots were employed to treat various ailments from earaches to croup. The leaves are sometimes applied to the skin to sooth sunburn and other inflammations. Clasping-leaved Mullein (*V. phlomoides*), with larger flowers in a more interrupted spike, occurs from Maine to North Carolina, west to Kentucky, Iowa, and Minnesota.

591 Corn Speedwell
(*Veronica arvensis*)
Snapdragon Family (Scrophulariaceae)

Description: A low, hairy, much-branched plant with a *minute violet-blue flower* on each upper leaf axil.
Flowers: less than ⅕″ (5 mm) wide;

sepals 4, very unequal; petals 4, the lower one narrower; stamens 2.
Leaves: lower ones up to ½″ (1.3 cm) long, opposite, rounded, or oval, with low teeth; upper leaves alternate, unstalked, lanceolate.
Height: 2–16″ (5–40 cm).

Flowering: March–August.

Habitat: Waste places, pastures, open woods, cultivated ground.

Range: Throughout.

Comments: The Speedwells are a large group with more than 20 species in our area. The common name reflects the speed with which they spread. The species name of this plant is from the Latin for "belonging to ploughed land" and indicates that the weed is a frequent invader of lawns and gardens.

523 Common Speedwell
(*Veronica officinalis*)
Snapdragon Family (Scrophulariaceae)

Description: *Prostrate, mat-forming plants* have spike-like clusters of pale lavender or blue flowers arising from the leaf axil.
Flowers: about ⅕″ (5 mm) wide; petals 4; stamens 2.
Leaves: ¾–2″ (2–5 cm) long, opposite, elliptic, toothed, downy.
Height: creeper, with flower stalks to 3–10″ (7.5–25 cm) high.

Flowering: May–July.

Habitat: Dry fields, open woods.

Range: Nova Scotia south to North Carolina; west to Tennessee and Wisconsin; north to Ontario.

Comments: This weed is native to the United States, the British Isles, Europe, and Asia. Its species name means "of the shops" and probably indicates that it was at one time sold for its reputed diuretic and astringent properties.

126 Thyme-leaved Speedwell
(*Veronica serpyllifolia*)
Snapdragon Family (Scrophulariaceae)

Description: *Short, narrow clusters* of white or pale
blue flowers with darker stripes are at
the tops of creeping or erect stems that
form mats.
Flowers: about ⅛" (4 mm) wide; petals
4, 3 of them rounded, the lowest
narrower; stamens 2.
Leaves: ½–⅔" (1.3–1.6 cm) long;
mostly opposite, ovate, minutely
toothed.
Height: 2–10" (5–25 cm).

Flowering: April–July.

Habitat: Roadsides, meadows, damp open
woods.

Range: Throughout, except Texas and
Oklahoma.

Comments: This small plant is often found in
lawns. The variety *humifusa* is
distinguished by its bright blue
flowers. The genus name is said to be
derived from the Greek words *vera*,
"true," and *eicon*, "image," alluding to
a legend concerning the true image of
Christ received by St. Veronica, for
whom the flower was named.

133 Culver's Root
(*Veronicastrum virginicum*)
Snapdragon Family (Scrophulariaceae)

Description: *Dense, narrow, cylindrical, spike-like
clusters* of small, white, tubular flowers
are at the top of an erect stem over
whorled leaves.
Flowers: about ¼" (6 mm) long; petals
4, united, the lobes nearly symmetrical;
stamens 2, *extending beyond the petals*.
Leaves: 2–6" (5–15 cm) long;
lanceolate, sharply toothed; the upper
ones whorled in groups of 3–9, the
lower ones opposite.
Fruit: ovoid capsule.
Height: 3–6' (90–180 cm).

Flowering: June–September.

Habitat: Moist woods, thickets, meadows.

Range: Vermont and Massachusetts to northwestern Florida; west to Mississippi, Louisiana, and eastern Texas; north to Manitoba.

Comments: The genus name, a combination of *Veronica* and the suffix *astrum* ("false"), describes this plant's resemblance to the Veronicas. It is the only species in the genus. It can be grown easily in wildflower gardens. The root contains a powerful emetic and cathartic.

NIGHTSHADE FAMILY
(Solanaceae)

Herbs, shrubs, vines, or trees with often showy flowers, generally in branched clusters.
Flowers: usually radially symmetrical; sepals 5, united; petals 5, united; stamens usually 5, sometimes fewer. All these parts attached at base of ovary.
Leaves: simple, alternate.
Fruit: berry or 2-chambered capsule.
There are about 85 genera and 2,300 species in tropical and warm temperate regions, especially in Central and South America. Several are poisonous, but others supply foods such as chili, bell pepper, tomato, potato, eggplant, and groundcherry. Tobacco comes from the family. Petunia, Painted-Tongue, and Butterfly Flower are grown as ornamentals.

---

86 Jimsonweed
(*Datura stramonium*)
Nightshade Family (Solanaceae)

Description: A tall, stout, smooth plant with a greenish or purplish stem and *trumpet-shaped white or violet flowers.*
Flowers: 3–4″ (7.5–10 cm) wide; 5-lobed, angular and tubular green calyx, about half as long as the 5-lobed, funnel-shaped corolla.
Leaves: to 8″ (20 cm) long, ovate, irregularly lobed.
Fruit: *prickly, egg-shaped capsule,* 2″ (5 cm) in diameter.
Height: 1–5′ (30–150 cm).
Flowering: July–October.
Habitat: Waste places, fields, and barnyards.
Range: Throughout.
Comments: A rank-smelling plant, introduced from tropical America, it is easily distinguished by its large, trumpet-shaped flowers and spiny fruit. All parts

of the plant are very poisonous. Cattle and sheep have been killed by grazing on it, and children have been poisoned by eating the fruit. Touching the leaves or flowers may cause a dermatitis in susceptible persons. The common name is a corruption of "Jamestown" where the plant grew near the colonists' homes. Two southern species are Angel Trumpet (*D. wrightii*), with white flowers up to 8″ (20 cm) long, occurring along Florida roadsides; and Entire-leaved Thorn-Apple (*D. metel*), with violet-tinged, often double flowers, one within the other, reaching a height of 7′ (2.1 m). The latter is found from Florida to Texas.

---

273 Clammy Ground Cherry
(*Physalis heterophylla*)
Nightshade Family (Solanaceae)

Description: *Bell-shaped, greenish-yellow flowers* with purplish-brown centers are solitary on stalks in the leaf axils. *Plant sticky-hairy.*
Flowers: ¾″ (2 cm) wide; corolla 5-lobed; stamens 5, with yellow anthers.
Leaves: 1–4″ (2.5–10 cm) long, alternate, ovate to heart-shaped, with few teeth on margins.
Fruit: yellow, tomato-like berry enclosed in an *inflated, papery, green calyx.*
Height: 1–3′ (30–90 cm).
Flowering: June–September.
Habitat: Dry woods and clearings.
Range: Saskatchewan to Quebec; south through New England to Georgia; west to Texas; north to Minnesota.
Comments: The leaves and the unripe fruit of this plant are poisonous but the ripe fruit can be made into jams or pies. Animals have been poisoned by feeding on the plants but generally avoid them unless other forage is scarce. The Ground

Cherries, with 18 or more species, have bell-like flowers with colored centers and inflated "bladders" around the fruit. Virginia Ground Cherry (*P. virginiana*), is very similar but usually not viscid. The cultivated Chinese Lantern-plant (*P. alkekengi*), has white flowers and a showny inflated orange calyx in fruit.

79 Common Nightshade
(*Solanum americanum*)
Nightshade Family (Solanaceae)

Description: A smooth plant with few-flowered lateral clusters (umbels) of *small, white, star-like, drooping flowers.*
Flowers: ⅓" (8 mm) wide; petals 5, curved backward; stamens 5, forming yellow central core.
Leaves: 2–4" (5–10 cm) long, thin, ovate, pointed, wavy-toothed.
Fruit: black berry.
Height: 1–2½' (30–75 cm).
Flowering: June–November.
Habitat: Cultivated and disturbed areas, open woods.
Range: New England south to northern Florida; west to eastern Texas; north to North Dakota.
Comments: This native species often appears in open ground. The leaves and berries contain a poisonous alkaloid, solanine, and although the toxic quality of the fruit seems to disappear with ripening, it is best not to eat them. Other similar species with small white flowers include Cut-leaved Nightshade (*S. triflorum*), with deeply dissected leaves, that occurs in Minnesota, Iowa, Kansas, and westward, and Hairy Nightshade (*S. villosum*), with very hairy stems and yellow or red berries.

80 **Horse Nettle**
(*Solanum carolinense*)
Nightshade Family (Solanaceae)

Description: *Star-like, white or pale lavender flowers*
with yellow centers are in lateral
clusters on a *prickly, erect stem.*
Flowers: ¾–1¼″ (2–3.1 cm) wide;
petals 5; stamens 5 with *yellow,
elongated anthers forming central cone.*
Leaves: 3–5″ (8–12.5 cm) long, rough,
elliptic-oblong, coarsely lobed, and
covered with prickles.
Fruit: yellow, tomato-like berries, ¾″
(2 cm) across.
Height: 1–3′ (30–90 cm).
Flowering: May–October.
Habitat: Fields, waste places, gardens.
Range: Southern Ontario to New England and
New York; south to Florida; west to
Texas; north to Nebraska.
Comments: A coarse, native, deep-rooted perennial,
it is considered a weed by some, yet the
flowers are attractive. Deep hoeing is
needed to eradicate the underground
stems, and gloves must be worn while
handling the plant. Its foliage is not
eaten by cattle. This plant is not related
to the true Nettles. Silverleaf Nettle
(*S. elaeagnifolium*), a very similar plant
with silvery foliage, occurs in the
western United States east to Missouri
and is adventive further east. Buffalo
Bur (*S. rostratum*), an annual with
bright yellow flowers, is naturalized
from the Western United States as a
weed in fields.

448, 653 **Bittersweet Nightshade; Climbing
Nightshade**
(*Solanum dulcamara*)
Nightshade Family (Solanaceae)

Description: A *climbing plant* with loose, flattish
clusters of drooping, blue or violet,
star-shaped flowers with a *yellow "beak"*
in the center.

Flowers: ½" (1.3 cm) wide; corolla
5-lobed; stamens 5, the yellow anthers
forming a central cone.
Leaves: to 3½" (8.8 cm) long, halberd-
shaped, with 2 basal lobes.
Fruit: shiny green berries that turn
bright red.
Height: vine, with stem 2–8'
(60–240 cm) long.
Flowering: May–September.
Habitat: Thickets, clearings.
Range: Throughout.
Comments: An introduced vine, it has distinctive
lobes at the bases of the leaves. The
leaves and unripe fruit contain the
alkaloid solanine. Although sometimes
called Deadly Nightshade, the plant's
toxin is not fatal; however, the berries
are attractive to children and can cause
poisoning if eaten in quantity. The
name Bittersweet comes from the fact
that portions of the plant first taste
bitter, then sweet. The plant was used
in England to counteract witchcraft.

BUR REED FAMILY
(Sparganiaceae)

Aquatic or marsh herbs with grass-like leaves, and small flowers densely crowded into globose heads in or above the axils of bract-like leaves.
Flowers: unisexual; petals and sepals absent or represented by a few chaffy scales; stamens usually 5; pistil 1.
Leaves: alternate, positioned on opposite sides of stem and therefore 2-ranked, sheathing stem at base.
Fruit: seed-like, many together in bur-like masses.
There is one genus with about 15 species occurring in temperate and cool regions of the Northern Hemisphere, Australia, and New Zealand.

---

41 Bur Reed
(Sparganium americanum)
Bur Reed Family (Sparganiaceae)

Description: An erect, *grass-like, aquatic plant* with zig-zag stalks bearing *ball-like heads* of tiny green flowers.
Flowers: sepals and petals represented by chaffy scales. Female flowers with 1 stigma; male flowers with 5 stamens. Female flowers in heads 1″ (2.5 cm) wide, on stem below 5–9 smaller heads of male flowers. Male flowers wither and die after pollen is shed. Pistil of female flower has 1 stigma.
Leaves: to 3′ (90 cm) long, 2–4½″ (5–11.3 cm) wide; keeled beneath, flat, soft textured, partly submerged.
Fruit: Female heads form bur-like green masses of beaked, seed-like fruits.
Height: 1–3′ (30–90 cm).
Flowering: May–August.
Habitat: Shallow water, muddy shores.
Range: Throughout.
Comments: The Bur Reeds represent an important group of emergent plants that are partly in and partly out of the water; they

frequently form dense stands along the edges of shallow lakes and ponds. The seeds are eaten by waterfowl and marsh birds, and muskrats feed on the entire plant. The Great Bur Reed (*S. eurycarpum*), reaches a height of 7' (2.1 m), has 2 stigmas, not 1 as in the rest of the group; it is widely distributed. Floating Bur Reed (*S. fluctuans*), has a floating stem, and floating ribbon-like leaves; it is found in cold ponds and lakes across Canada and New England west to Minnesota.

CATTAIL FAMILY
(Typhaceae)

Aquatic or marsh herbs with creeping rootstocks, long, narrow leaves, and tiny flowers crowded in terminal spikes, with the male (staminate) ones at the top and female (pistillate) below. Spikes above bracts, which fall early.
Flowers: sepals and petals merely hair-like bristles; male flowers with stamens 2–5, usually 3; female flowers with a single, stalked ovary.
Leaves: sword-like, on opposite sides of the stem and therefore 2-ranked, with bases sheathing stem.
Fruit: 1-seeded nutlet.
There are about 18 species in one genus, which occur in temperate and tropical regions.

---

309 Common Cattail
(*Typha latifolia*)
Cattail Family (Typhaceae)

Description: This tall, stiff plant bears a yellowish, *club-like spike* of tiny, male flowers extending directly above a brownish cylinder of female flowers.
Flowers: calyx and corolla represented by bristles. Male and female flowers on separate spikes, each to 6″ (15 cm) long. Female flowers with 1 stalked pistil; male flowers usually with 3 stamens. Male flowers fade after pollen is shed, leaving bare stalk.
Leaves: up to 1″ (2.5 cm) wide and taller than the stem, sword-like, flat, sheathing the stem.
Height: 3–9′ (90–270 cm).
Flowering: May–July.
Habitat: Fresh water marshes.
Range: Throughout.
Comments: By its creeping rootstocks, this typical marsh perennial forms dense stands in shallow water and provides a favorable habitat for red-winged blackbirds, as

well as other marsh birds, and muskrats. The latter can cause extensive "eat outs," creating areas of open water in the marsh. The rootstock is mostly starch and edible; it was ground into meal by Indians, and the early colonists also used it for food. The young shoots can be eaten like asparagus, the immature flower spikes can be boiled and eaten like corn on the cob, and the sprouts at the tip of the rootstock can be used in salads or boiled and served as greens. The closely related Narrow-leaved Cattail (*T. angustifolia*) has narrower leaves, up to ½" (1.3 cm) across, a narrower fruiting head, less than ¾" (2 cm) wide, and a gap between the male and female flower clusters.

NETTLE FAMILY
(Urticaceae)

Leafy herbs, or in tropical regions shrubs
or trees, often with stinging hairs,
watery juice, and small, greenish,
clustered flowers, often in leaf axils.
Flowers: bisexual or unisexual; sepals
4–5; no petals; stamens as many as
sepals. All these parts attached at base
of ovary.
Leaves: mostly opposite, toothed,
simple.
Fruit: seed-like.
There are more than 40 genera and
about 500 species widely distributed
but most common in tropical regions.

24 False Nettle
(*Boehmaria cylindrica*)
Nettle Family (Urticaceae)

Description:	Tiny greenish flowers are in small, head-like clusters, arranged in continuous or interrupted spikes in the axils of opposite leaves. *Plant lacks stinging hairs.* Flowers: less than $\frac{1}{12}''$ (2 mm) long; male flowers usually in interrupted spikes, with calyx 4-parted, stamens 4; female flowers mostly in continuous spikes up to $1\frac{1}{2}''$ (3.8 cm) long, with calyx 2–4 toothed, tubular. Spikes often terminated by clusters of leaves. Leaves: 1–3" (2.5–7.5 cm) long, ovate to ovate-lanceolate, coarsely toothed. Height: $1\frac{1}{2}$–3′ (45–90 cm).
Flowering:	July–October.
Habitat:	Moist or shady ground.
Range:	Ontario to Quebec, south to Florida, west to Texas, north to Minnesota.
Comments:	This species differs from Clearweed (*Pilea pumila*), the other member of the Nettle Family lacking stinging hairs, in that it does not have a translucent stem and is taller.

23 Wood Nettle
(*Laportea canadensis*)
Nettle Family (Urticaceae)

Description: Clusters of small, greenish flowers are
in the leaf axils on a stout *stem with
stinging hairs;* female flowers are in
loose, elongated clusters in upper axils;
male flowers in shorter clusters in lower
axils.
Flowers: about ⅙″ (4 mm) long; female
with 4 sepals, 1 pistil; male with
5 sepals, 5 stamens; petals absent.
Leaves: 2½–8″ (6.3–20 cm) long,
alternate, thin, ovate, long-stalked,
coarsely toothed.
Fruit: dry, seed-like, crescent-shaped.
Height: 1½–4′ (45–120 cm).
Flowering: July–September.
Habitat: Low woods, streambanks.
Range: Manitoba to Quebec and Nova Scotia;
south to Florida; west to Mississippi,
Oklahoma, and Missouri.
Comments: The flowers of the similar Stinging
Nettle (*Urtica dioica*), are in tighter,
slender axillary clusters and the leaves
are opposite and have heart-shaped
bases.

21 Clearweed
(*Pilea pumila*)
Nettle Family (Urticaceae)

Description: A small, *translucent-stemmed* annual with
short, curved clusters of inconspicuous,
greenish-white flowers in the leaf axils.
Plant lacks stinging hairs.
Flowers: about ⅙″ (4 mm) long; female
flowers with 3-parted calyx, 1 pistil;
male flowers with 4-parted calyx, 4
stamens.
Leaves: 1–5″ (2.5–12.5 cm) long;
opposite, ovate, conspicuously veined,
coarsely toothed.
Fruit: dry, seed-like, green (often
marked with black).
Height: 4–20″ (10–50 cm).

Flowering: July–October.
Habitat: Moist, shaded places.
Range: Throughout.
Comments: The distinctive clear stem, soft and
with a watery look, is responsible for
the common name. It is restricted to
shady areas, where it may form a
continuous cover over moist soil.
P. fontana, very similar but with dull
black "seeds," occurs from western
New York south to Florida, west to
Nebraska and North Dakota.

22 Stinging Nettle
(*Urtica dioica*)
Nettle Family (Urticaceae)

Description: A 4-angled stem, covered with many
bristly, stinging hairs, has slender,
branching, feathery clusters of minute
greenish flowers in the leaf axils.
Flowers are unisexual, with either male
or female on a given plant, or on same
plant with males in upper leaf axils,
females lower.
Flowers: about $\frac{1}{12}$" (2 mm) long; petals
absent; calyx 4-parted; stamens 4.
Leaves: 2–4" (5–10 cm) long, opposite,
ovate with heart-shaped bases, coarsely
toothed, bearing stinging bristles.
Height: 2–4' (60–120 cm).
Flowering: June–September.
Habitat: Waste places, roadsides.
Range: Throughout.
Comments: This Nettle should not be handled, as
it contains an acid that can cause a
severe, burning skin irritation.
However, the very young shoots and
top leaves may be cooked and served as
greens or used in soups and stews. The
family and genus names come from the
Latin *uro* ("I burn").

VERVAIN FAMILY
(Verbenaceae)

Herbs, shrubs, or trees usually with flowers in spike-like or branched clusters or in heads.

Flowers: bilaterally symmetrical; sepals 5, united; petals 5, united, forming a corolla with a slender tube and an abruptly flared top; stamens usually 4, attached to corolla. Corolla attached at base of ovary.

Leaves: opposite or whorled, simple.

Fruit: often separates into 4 hard nutlets, each 1-seeded.

There are about 75 genera and 3,000 species mostly of tropical and warm temperate regions. Teak is a highly prized furniture wood. Vervain, Lantana, Lippia or Frog Fruit, and Chaste Tree or Vitex are grown as ornamentals.

---

550 Rose Vervain
(*Verbena canadensis*)
Vervain Family (Verbenaceae)

Description: An erect or reclining plant with a hairy stem and a dense, terminal, flat-topped cluster of pinkish lavender, *tubular flowers with flaring corolla lobes.*
Flowers: ½–¾" (1.3–2 cm) wide; petals 5, notched; stamens 4; pistil with 4-lobed ovary.
Leaves: to 3" (7.5 cm) long, opposite, palmately veined, ovate to lanceolate, coarsely toothed or lobed, with partly winged stalk.
Height: 6–18" (15–45 cm).
Flowering: April–October.
Habitat: Sandy or rocky prairies and roadsides.
Range: Virginia south to Florida; west to Texas; north to Iowa; and westward beyond our range.
Comments: A showy southern Vervain, it is especially good for rock gardens and tolerant of northern climes. A

somewhat similar species, Small-flowered Verbena (*V. bipinnatifida*), has a bristly-hairy stem and finely divided leaves with stiff hairs. It occurs in fields and along sandy roadsides from North Carolina south to Florida, west to Texas and north to the Dakotas. Stiff Vervain (*V. rigida*), with toothed, lanceolate leaves and a more elongated flower cluster, occurs from North Carolina south to Florida and west to Texas.

147 Vervain
(*Verbena halei*)
Vervain Family (Verbenaceae)

Description: An erect, rough, hairy, square-stemmed plant with *long, narrow spikes* of small, white, tubular flowers.
Flowers: about ¼" (6 mm) wide; corolla 5-lobed; stamens 4; pistil 1, with 4-parted ovary.
Leaves: to 4" (10 cm) long, opposite, coarsely toothed or cut, sharp-pointed.
Height: 2–4' (60 –120 cm).

Flowering: June–September.

Habitat: Rich thickets, wood edges.

Range: North Carolina to Florida; west to Texas and beyond; north to Oklahoma.

Comments: Often considered a weed, it is not as attractive as its blue counterpart, Blue Vervain (*V. hastata*). The very similar Pink Vervain (*V. scabra*), of the southern United States has pale pink flowers.

629 Blue Vervain
(*Verbena hastata*)
Vervain Family (Verbenaceae)

Description: Stiff, *pencil-like spikes* of numerous small, tubular, blue-violet flowers are at the top of a square, grooved stem and its branches.
Flowers: ⅛" (3 mm) wide; flaring petals

5; stamens in 2 pairs of different lengths; pistil 1, with 4-lobed ovary.
Leaves: 4–6″ (10–15 cm) long, opposite, lanceolate, doubly toothed, rough-textured.
Height: 2–6′ (60–180 cm).

Flowering: July–September.

Habitat: Damp thickets, shores, roadsides.

Range: Throughout.

Comments: An attractive perennial, it has flowers on showy candelabra-like spikes. Bumblebees are among the important pollinators. In ancient times the plant was thought to be a cure-all among medicinal plants and the genus name is the Latin for "sacred plant." Hoary Vervain (*V. stricta*), to 10′ (3 m) tall and with flowers ½″ (1.3 cm) long, is most abundant in the Midwest and occurs sporadically eastward. Narrow-leaved Vervain (*V. simplex*), has narrow leaves and lavender flowers ⅓″ (8 mm) long; it is a southwestern and midwestern species.

VIOLET FAMILY
(Violaceae)

Rather dainty herbs with perky,
colorful flowers in the United States,
but often shrubby and less showy
elsewhere.

Flowers: bilaterally symmetrical or
radially symmetrical; sepals 5, separate;
petals 5, separate, the lowermost often
largest and bearing a backward-
projecting spur; stamens 5, loosely
united with one another around the
ovary.

Leaves: alternate, simple but sometimes
deeply lobed.

Fruit: berry or explosively opening
capsule.

There are about 22 genera and 900
species found nearly throughout the
world. Many species of Violets,
including Pansies, are cultivated for
their attractive flowers.

18 Green Violet
(*Hybanthus concolor*)
Violet Family (Violaceae)

Description: *Greenish, drooping,* irregular flowers are
in groups of 1–3 on short stalks arising
in the leaf axils.
Flowers: ¼" (6 mm) long; sepals 5,
linear, about as long as petals; petals 5,
the lateral ones narrow, the lower one
longer and somewhat swollen at base;
stamens 5, united around ovary; pistil
club-shaped.
Leaves: 3½–6½" (8.8–16.3 cm) long,
elliptic, tapering at both ends,
untoothed or slightly toothed.
Height: 1–3' (30–90 cm).

Flowering: April–June.

Habitat: Rich woods, ravines.

Range: Ontario to Connecticut and New York;
south to Georgia; west to Mississippi
and Kansas; north to Wisconsin.

Comments: This flower, the only member of the

genus in the East, only vaguely resembles other Violets, but its 5 connate stamens and clublike pistil are characteristic of the family. The generic name is from the Greek *hybos* ("humpbacked") and *anthos* ("flower") and probably refers to the drooping flowers. The species name, "of one color," reflects the green of both the sepals and petals.

65 Sweet White Violet
(Viola blanda)
Violet Family (Violaceae)

Description: A fragrant, white Violet with leaves and flowers on *separate, reddish stalks* rising from underground stem. Runners present.
Flowers: about ½" (1.3 cm) wide; petals 5, the upper ones *bent backward and twisted;* lower petal purple-veined.
Leaves: up to 2½" (6.3 cm) wide; ovate with heart-shaped bases, dark green, shiny, sharp-pointed.
Fruit: purplish, ovoid seed capsule.
Height: 3–5" (7.5–12.5 cm).
Flowering: April–May.
Habitat: Rich woods.
Range: Quebec south through New England to Maryland and upland to Georgia; west to Tennessee, Ohio, Indiana, Illinois, Wisconsin, and Minnesota.
Comments: Very similar to the Northern White Violet (*V. pallens*), but the latter grows in wet woods and beside brooks, has a greenish seed capsule, and does not have the reddish stems.

64 Canada Violet
(Viola canadensis)
Violet Family (Violaceae)

Description: *Fragrant, white flowers* bloom on slender, purplish, stalks which also bear the

heart-shaped, finely toothed leaves.
Flowers: ¾–1″ (2–2.5 cm) wide; petals
5, the inside white, outside purple-
tinged, base yellow.
Leaves: 2–4″ (5–10 cm) long.
Height: 8–16″ (20–40 cm).

Flowering: April–June.
Habitat: Woods.
Range: Saskatchewan to Quebec; south to
Maryland and upland to South
Carolina; west in mountains from
Alabama to beyond our range; north to
North Dakota.
Comments: This Violet is found mainly along
southern Canada, the northern part of
the United States, and in mountains
elsewhere. It grows well in wildflower
gardens if planted in a cool spot.

595 Dog Violet
(*Viola conspersa*)
Violet Family (Violaceae)

Description: This low plant has *leaves and flowers on
same stalk.*
Flowers: about ¾″ (2 cm) wide; 5 light
bluish-violet petals, the 2 lateral ones
slightly bearded, the lower one with
purple veins and a spur ⅙–⅕″
(4–5 mm) long.
Leaves: to 1¾″ (4.5 cm) long; round,
heart-shaped, weakly scalloped; leaf-
like stipules in leaf axils *finely toothed.*
Height: 2–6″ (5–15 cm).

Flowering: March–July.
Habitat: Meadows, damp woods.
Range: Nova Scotia south through New
England to Maryland and uplands of
Georgia; west to Alabama; north to
Minnesota.
Comments: The Long-spurred Violet (*V. rostrata*),
is very similar, with pale blue flowers,
darker blue centers, and spurs ½–1″
(1.3–2.5 cm) long; it is found from
Quebec south to West Virginia and in
the uplands to Alabama, west in the
Great Lakes area to Wisconsin.

Prostrate Blue Violet (*V. walteri*), a
southern species, is densely hairy.
Hooked-spur Violet (*V. adunca*), is a
northern species occurring as far south
as New England in dry rocky habitats;
it is very similar to Dog Violet.

597 Common Blue Violet
(*Viola papilionacea*)
Violet Family (Violaceae)

Description: This smooth, low plant has *flowers and
leaves on separate stalks.*
Flowers: ½–¾″ (1.3–2 cm) wide; blue
to white, or white with purple veins;
petals 5, the lower one longer and
spurred, the 2 lateral ones bearded.
Leaves: to 5″ (12.5 cm) wide; heart-
shaped with scalloped margins.
Fruit: 3-valved capsule.
Height: 3–8″ (7.5–20 cm).

Flowering: March–June.

Habitat: Damp woods, moist meadows,
roadsides.

Range: Throughout.

Comments: In addition to the normal flowers there
are often flowers near the ground that
fail to open, but their whitish fruit
produces vast quantities of seeds. Violet
leaves are high in vitamins A and C and
can be used in salads or cooked as
greens. The flowers can be made into
candies and jellies. The Marsh Blue
Violet (*V. cucullata*), a similar species
of very wet habitats, has dark blue-
centered flowers borne well above the
leaves. The Sister Violet (*V. sororia*), is
also similar, with hairy leaves and
stems.

598 Bird-foot Violet
(*Viola pedata*)
Violet Family (Violaceae)

Description: This smooth plant has deep blue-violet
flowers and *deeply-cut leaves on separate
stalks.*
Flowers: often 1½" (3.8 cm) wide,
larger than most Violets; petals 5,
beardless, the lower one whitish, veined
with violet, grooved and spurred;
stamens 5, with *orange anthers*
conspicuous in throat of flower.
Leaves: 1–2" (2.5–5 cm) long,
fan-shaped, with linear, toothed
segments.
Height: 4–10" (10–25 cm).
Flowering: March–June.
Habitat: Dry, sandy fields, wood openings.
Range: Throughout most of our area.
Comments: A most beautiful Violet of dry, upland
sites. Its showy, light violet-blue
flowers, distinctive "bird's-foot"-shaped
leaves make it easy to identify. It is
pollinated by bees and butterflies. The
bicolored form of this species, with its
2 upper petals a deep violet and the
lower 3 a lilac shade, has been
considered the most beautiful Violet in
the world.

274 Downy Yellow Violet
(*Viola pubescens*)
Violet Family (Violaceae)

Description: A *softly hairy plant* with *leaves and
yellow flowers on the same stalk.*
Flowers: ¾" (2 cm) wide; petals 5, the
lower 3 with dark purple veins, the 2
lateral ones bearded.
Leaves: 2–5" (5–12.5 cm) wide, heart-
shaped, hairy, scallop-toothed; usually
one basal leaf.
Height: 6–16" (15–40 cm).
Flowering: May–June.
Habitat: Rich woods.
Range: Quebec to Maine; south to Delaware

and upland Virginia; west to
Tennessee, Missouri, Nebraska, and
Minnesota.

Comments: Among the numerous yellow Violets
the hairy nature of this species is
distinctive. Other stemmed species are
the Smooth Yellow Violet
(*V. pensylvanica*), with non-hairy foliage
and 1–3 heart-shaped basal leaves; the
Three-part-leaved Violet (*V. tripartita*),
a southern and western species with
3-lobed leaves; and the Prairie Yellow
Violet, (*V. nuttallii*), with lanceolate
leaves. Our only "stemless" yellow
Violet (with flowers and leaves on
separate stalks) is the Round-leaved
Yellow Violet (*V. rotundifolia*), with a
small flower and roundish basal leaves.

YELLOW-EYED GRASS FAMILY
(Xyridaceae)

Herbs with grass-like basal leaves and
erect, leafless stalks bearing flowers in
axils of leathery bracts which form
globose or cylindric heads.
Flowers: calyx bilaterally symmetrical,
with 2 keeled or winged lateral sepals
and a broader anterior sepal which is
sometimes absent; corolla radially
symmetrical, with 3 spreading lobes;
stamens 3, often 3 more sterile
stamens. All these parts attached at
base of ovary.
Leaves: very narrow, on opposite sides
of stem and therefore 2-ranked.
Fruit: capsule.
There are 2 genera and about 40
species, found in tropical regions, many
in Florida.

269 Yellow-eyed Grass
(*Xyris iridifolia*)
Yellow-eyed Grass Family (Xyridaceae)

Description: A tufted plant with *flat, linear, Iris-like
leaves* and a floral stalk terminated by a
reddish-brown, oval head with *scale-like
bracts* enclosing yellow flowers.
Flowers: about ½″ (1.3 cm) wide;
petals 3; stamens 6, 3 normal and 3
tufted, sterile.
Leaves: 16–32″ (40–80 cm) long,
about ½″ (1 cm) wide.
Height: 2–3′ (60–90 cm).
Flowering: July–September.
Habitat: Wet peat or sand.
Range: North Carolina south to Florida; west
to Texas.
Comments: This large southern species is one of
more than 15 in our range. They are
grass-like, wetland plants with
distinctive cone-like heads of
overlapping scales in which the flowers
are set. The different species are very
similar and distinguishing

them is difficult without a technical manual. The smaller, widespread Slender Yellow-eyed Grass (*X. torta*), grows to a height of 1' (30 cm) and has erect, narrow, twisted, needle-like leaves, and tufts of hairs on the notches of the scales which make up the flower head.

CALTROP FAMILY
(Zygophyllaceae)

Herbs or shrubs, rarely trees, with flowers borne singly or in branched clusters.
Flowers: usually bisexual, radially symmetrical; sepals usually 5, separate; petals 5, separate; stamens 5, 10, or 15, often with scale-like appendages on stalks. All these parts attached at base of ovary.
Leaves: opposite, pinnately compound.
Fruit: usually 5-chambered capsule.
There are about 30 genera and 250 species, mostly in warm temperate or tropical regions. Creosotebush is the common shrub on Southwestern deserts. The densest of woods, Lignum Vitae, is obtained from a tropical tree.

248 Punctureweed; Caltrop
(*Tribulus terrestris*)
Caltrop Family (Zygophyllaceae)

Description: A trailing plant with yellow flowers on short stalks in the axils of paired, pinnately compound leaves.
Flowers: ½″ (1.3 cm) wide; sepals and petals 5; stamens 10.
Leaves: ¾–2½″ (2–6.3 cm) long, one of each pair larger than the other; oblong leaflets up to ⅔″ (1.6 cm) long.
Fruit: splits into 5 segments, each ending in a *sharp spine*.
Height: creeper, with stem 1–3′ (30–90 cm) long.
Flowering: June–September.
Habitat: Dry waste places, open ground.
Range: Southern New York south to Florida; west to Texas and beyond north to South Dakota.
Comments: Introduced from Europe, this plant is a troublesome weed, especially southward. The spines on the fruits are very sharp and will injure animals if present in hay. In addition, there

appears to be a toxic substance in the plant which causes animals eating it to become sensitive to sunlight and develop swellings and dermatitis on unpigmented portions of the body.

Part III
Appendices

GLOSSARY

Achene A small, dry, hard fruit that does not open and contains one seed.

Alternate leaves Arising singly along the stem, not in pairs or whorls.

Annual Having a life cycle completed in one year or season.

Anther The sac-like part of a stamen, containing pollen.

Appressed Pressed closely against.

Aquatic A plant growing in water.

Awn A bristle-like appendage.

Axil The angle formed by the upper side of a leaf and the stem from which it grows.

Banner Uppermost petal in a Pea flower; also called the standard.

Basal leaves Leaves at the base of the stem.

Bearded Bearing long or stiff hairs.

Berry A fleshy fruit with one to many seeds, developed from a single ovary.

Bilateral symmetry In flowers, one that can be divided into two equal halves by only one line through the middle; often called irregular, or bilateral.

Bisexual A flower having both female (pistil) and male (stamen) parts.

Blade The flat portion of a leaf, petal, or sepal.

Bloom A whitish, powdery or waxy covering.

Bracts Modified leaves, usually smaller than the foliage leaves, often situated at the base of a flower or inflorescence.

Bulb A short underground stem, the swollen portion consisting mostly of fleshy, food-storing scale leaves.

Calyx Collective term for the sepals of a flower, usually green.

Capsule A dry fruit with one or more compartments, usually having thin walls that split open along several lines.

Carnivorous Subsisting on nutrients obtained from the breakdown of animal tissue.

Catkin A scaly-bracted spike or spike-like inflorescence bearing unisexual flowers without petals, as in the willows.

Clasping A leaf whose base wholly or partly surrounds the stem.

Claw Narrow, stalk-like base of a petal.

Column In Orchids, a structure formed by the union of stamens, style, and stigma.

Compound leaf A leaf divided into smaller leaflets.

Corolla Collective term for the petals of a flower.

Corona A crown-like structure on some corollas, as in the Milkweed Family.

Creeper	Technically, a trailing shoot that takes root at the nodes; but used here to denote any trailing, prostrate plant.
Cross-pollination	The transfer of pollen from one plant to another.
Deciduous	Shedding leaves seasonally, as do many trees, or the shedding of certain parts after a period of growth.
Dioecious	Bearing staminate and pistillate flowers on different plants of the same species, as in the willows.
Disk flower	The small tubular flowers in the central part of a floral head, as in most members of the Sunflower Family.
Dissected leaf	A deeply cut leaf, the cleft not reaching to the midrib; same as a divided leaf.
Drupe	A stone fruit; a fleshy fruit with the single seed enveloped by a hard covering (stone).
Embryo	The small plant formed after fertilization, contained within the seed and ready to grow with the proper environmental stimulation.
Emergent	An aquatic plant with its lower part submerged and its upper part extending above water.
Epiphyte	A plant growing on another plant but deriving no nutrition from it; an air plant.
Filament	A thread; the slender stalk of a stamen.
Follicle	A dry fruit developed from a single ovary, usually opening along one line.
Fruit	The ripened ovary or pistil, often with attached parts.
Gland	A small structure usually secreting oil or nectar.

Glandular Bearing glands.

Head A crowded cluster of flowers on very short stalks, or without stalks as in the Sunflower Family.

Herb Usually a soft and succulent plant; not woody.

Hypanthium A cup-like base to a flower; composed of the united and modified bases of calyx, corolla, and stamens. Sepals, petals, and stamens grow from the rim of the hypanthium.

Inferior Ovary Ovary positioned below sepals, petals, and stamens, which seem to grow from the top of ovary.

Inflorescence A flower cluster on a plant or, especially, the arrangement of flowers on a plant.

Involucre A whorl or circle of bracts beneath a flower or flower cluster.

Irregular flower A flower with petals that are not uniform in shape but are usually grouped to form upper and lower "lips;" generally bilaterally symmetrical.

Keel A sharp ridge or rib; in a Pea flower, the two lowest petals united and resembling the prow of a boat.

Lanceolate leaf Lance-shaped; i.e., much longer than wide and pointed at the end; technically, the widest portion below the middle (but in this book may also refer to a leaf that is widest at middle or above).

Leaflet One of the leaf-like parts of a compound leaf.

Legume A dry fruit developed from a single ovary, usually opening along two lines, as in the Pea Family.

Ligule A projection at the base of the leaf blade in grasses.

Linear Long, narrow, with parallel sides, as in the leaf blades of grasses.

Lip petal The lower petal of some irregular flowers, often elaborately showy, as in Orchids.

Lobed Indented on the margins, with the indentations not reaching to the center or base.

Monoecious Having both staminate (male) and pistillate (female) flowers on the same plant.

Node The place on the stem where leaves or branches are attached.

Ocrea Stem-sheathing leaf bases of members of the Buckwheat Family.

Opposite leaves Occurring in pairs at a node, with one leaf on either side of the stem.

Ovary The swollen base of a pistil, within which seeds develop.

Ovate leaf Egg-shaped, pointed at the top, technically broader near the base (but in this book the term is also used for leaves broadest at the middle).

Ovule The immature seed in the ovary that contains the egg.

Palate A rounded projection of the lower lip in two-lipped flowers, closing or nearly closing the throat.

Palmate Having 3 or more divisions or lobes, looking like the outspread fingers of a hand.

Pappus A bristle, scale, or crown on seed-like fruits of the Sunflower Family, as on the fruits of Dandelions, and Thistles.

Parasite A plant deriving its nutrition from another organism.

Pedicel The stalk of an individual flower.

Peduncle The main flowerstalk or stem holding an inflorescence.

Perianth The calyx and corolla or, in flowers without 2 distinct series of outer parts (sepals and petals), simply the outer whorl (as in the Buckwheat Family and others).

Petal Basic unit of the corolla, flat, usually broad, and brightly colored.

Petaloid Petal-like, usually describing a colored sepal.

Petiole The stalk-like part of a leaf, attaching it to the stem.

Pinnate leaf A compound leaf with leaflets along the sides of a common central stalk, much like a feather.

Pistil The female organ of a flower, consisting of an ovary, style, and stigma.

Pistillate flower A female flower, having one or more pistils but no functional stamens.

Pod A dry fruit that opens at maturity.

Pollen Spores formed in the anthers that produce the male cells.

Pollen sac The upper portion of the stamen, containing pollen grains; the anther.

Pollination The transfer of pollen from an anther to a stigma.

Pubescent Covered with hairs.

Raceme A long flower cluster on which individual flowers each bloom on a small stalk all along a common, larger, central stalk.

Radial symmetry In flowers, one with the symmetry of a wheel; often called regular.

Ray flower The bilaterally symmetrical flowers around the edge of the head in many members of the Sunflower Family; each ray flower resembles a single petal.

Receptacle The base of the flower where all flower parts are attached.

Regular flower With petals and/or sepals arranged around the center, like the spokes of a wheel; always radially symmetrical.

Rhizome A horizontal underground stem, distinguished from roots by the presence of nodes, often enlarged by food storage.

Rose hip A smooth, rounded, fruit-like structure consisting of the cup-like calyx enclosing seed-like fruits.

Rosette A crowded cluster of leaves; usually basal, circular, and appearing to grow directly out of the ground.

Runner A stem that grows on the surface of the soil, often developing leaves, roots, and new plants at the nodes or tip.

Saprophyte A plant lacking chlorophyll and living on dead organic matter.

Sepal A basic unit of the calyx, usually green, but sometimes colored and resembling a petal.

Sessile Without a stalk.

Sessile leaf A leaf that lacks a petiole, the blade being attached directly to the stem.

Sheath A more or less tubular structure

surrounding a part, as the lower portion of a leaf surrounding the stem.

Shrub A woody, relatively low plant with several branches from the base.

Simple leaf A leaf with an undivided blade.

Spadix A dense spike of tiny flowers, usually enclosed in a spathe, as in members of the Arum Family.

Spathe A bract or pair of bracts, often large, enclosing the flowers.

Species A fundamental category of taxonomic classification, ranking below a genus.

Spike An elongated flower cluster, each flower of which is without a stalk.

Spur A slender, usually hollow projection from a part of a flower.

Stamen The male organ of a flower, composed of a filament topped by an anther; usually several in each flower.

Staminate flower A male flower, that is, with anthers and without pistils.

Standard An Iris petal; also the upper petal or banner of a Pea flower.

Stigma The tip of the pistil where the pollen lands.

Stipules Small appendages, often leaf-like, on either side of some petioles at the base.

Stolon A stem growing along or under the ground; a runner.

Style The narrow part of the pistil, connecting ovary and stigma.

Superior ovary An ovary in the center of a flower, with

all parts attaching to receptacle near the base of the ovary.

Succulent Fleshy and thick, storing water; a plant with fleshy, water-storing stems or leaves.

Tendril A slender, coiling structure that helps support climbing plants.

Toothed Having a sawtooth edge.

Tuber A fleshy, enlarged part of an underground stem, serving as a storage organ (e.g., a potato).

Umbel A flower cluster in which the individual flower stalks grow from the same point, like the ribs of an umbrella.

Undulate Having a wavy edge.

Unisexual A flower of one sex only, either pistillate (female) or staminate (male).

Whorled A circle of three or more leaves, branches, or pedicels at a node.

Wing In plants, a thin, flat extension found at the margins of a seed or leafstalk or along the stem; the lateral petal of a Pea flower.

PICTURE CREDITS

The numbers in parentheses are plate numbers. Some photographers have pictures under agency names as well as their own. Agency names appear in boldface.

342, 362, 395, 396, 397, 399, 404,
427, 444, 446, 447, 461, 471, 472,
524, 548, 559, 563, 572, 573, 575,
616, 625, 655, 657)
James A. Cunningham (64, 70, 125,
128 left, 135, 187, 198, 200 right,
324, 352, 378, 434, 477, 503, 629)
Thase Daniel (146, 272, 293, 385,
424, 614, 615)
Kent and Donna Dannen (1)
Ed Degginger (58, 99, 129 right, 139,
201, 209, 231, 367, 368, 426, 565,
583, 624)
Jack Dermid (82, 151, 652)
John Earl (379)
John Ebeling (205)
Bob Eikum (90)
Frances Eikum (326)
George Elbert (46, 142, 509)
Harry Ellis (5, 27, 54, 55, 66, 67, 75,
87, 123, 124, 127, 134, 136, 153,
169, 194, 214, 238, 274, 301, 316,
358, 412, 443, 528, 556, 580, 603,
628, 631, 647)
Harry Engels (244)
Jon Farrar (179, 584)
Mary Ferguson (114, 297)
P. R. Ferguson (292, 462)
Richard B. Fischer (122, 296, 339,
579)
Albert Gates (390)
John H. Gerard (224, 225, 533)
Joseph Giunta (623)
Lois T. Grady (401, 403)

Grant Heilman
Grant Heilman (31)
Hal H. Harrison (414) Alan Pitcairn
(39 left) S. Rannels (243, 369) Runk/
Schoenberger (41)

Elizabeth Henze (290, 417, 521)
Cecil B. Hoisington/Vermont Institute
of Natural Science (6, 267)
Charles Johnson (7, 12, 15, 16, 20,
47, 80, 81, 83, 104, 118, 152, 154,
167, 175, 176, 178, 197, 215, 245,
246, 248, 268, 282, 284, 286, 288,
289, 313, 314, 315, 333, 341, 349,

361, 372, 375, 381, 394, 442, 449,
453, 460, 468, 476, 478, 483, 510,
515, 519, 535, 537, 538, 543, 544,
545, 546, 547, 551, 562, 564, 576,
577, 578, 596, 606, 608, 637, 638,
644)
Stephen J. Krasemann (541)
Dwight R. Kuhn (364 right)
Carl Kurtz (14, 86, 408, 536)
Mary LeCroy (4, 285)
Ken Lewis (23, 24, 50, 143, 155, 156,
181, 199 right, 303 left, 317, 328,
336, 480, 558, 566, 571, 645)
John A. Lynch (111, 157, 199 left,
200 left, 255, 257, 270, 299, 365
right, 371, 383, 458, 514, 561, 595,
613)
John MacGregor (3, 11, 51, 56, 102,
112, 129 left, 164, 172, 227, 229,
253, 287, 376, 386, 387, 389, 393
right, 422, 469, 495, 497, 499, 594,
607, 633)
Hershal L. Macon (130 left)
Anne McGrath (2)
Robert K. McIlvin (464)
William A. Niering (97, 101, 242,
344, 400, 433, 588)
C. W. Perkins (331, 474, 488, 557,
618)

Photo Researchers, Inc.
(71) A. W. Ambler (36, 141, 322,
330, 411, 481) Charles R. Belinky
(451, 609) Gale Koschman Belinky
(437) Anthony Bleecker, Jr. (621) Tom
Branch (416, 554) Ken Brate (132,
168, 247, 254, 265, 275, 409, 428,
435, 448, 534, 630) Louise K. Broman
(40 left, 622, 632) Jules Bucher (26)
Richard L. Carlton (604) Patricia
Caulfield (311, 312, 348) Stephen
Collins (300, 388, 445, 523) Alford
W. Cooper (540, 610, 639) Kelly Dean
(121, 220 left, 405) Townsend P.
Dickinson (373) R. W. Dimond (438)
M. dos Passos (69) Robert J. Erwin
(84, 600) H. F. Flanders (450) Glenn
Foss (393 left) Zoltan Gaal, Jr. (193)
Michael P. Gadomski (59, 210) Patrick

W. Grace (91, 332) Farrell Grehan
(277, 526, 585) Milton J. Heiberg
(589) Robert C. Hermes (522) Harold
W. Hoffman (239) Harold Hungerford
(60) Russ Kinne (321, 398) Ruth
Laming (137) Jesse Lunger (346, 382)
Michael Phillip Manheim (452) S.
McKeever (269, 520) P. J. McLaughlin
(421) Frank J. Miller (587) Irvin L.
Oakes (211, 303 right, 391, 479, 593)
Charlie Ott (230) Richard Parker (17,
18, 30, 40 right, 42, 72, 107, 119,
145, 147, 148, 171, 173, 180, 182,
183, 184, 186, 188, 204, 251, 259,
298, 323, 325, 366 right, 418, 419,
530, 531, 550, 635, 636) Constance
Porter (128 right, 350, 467) Lawrence
Pringle (109, 306 right) Noble Proctor
(35, 38, 57, 108, 131, 133, 213, 216,
232, 249, 261, 302, 337, 345, 353,
365 left, 420, 555, 582, 590, 626,
634) Louis Quitt (161, 482) Leonard
Lee Rue III (217) Delbert Rust (105)
Gregory K. Scott (592) Alvin E. Staffan
(43, 334, 359, 410, 441, 581) John K.
Terres (574) Mary M. Thacher (100,
226, 258, 407, 518) Katrina Thomas
(347) V. E. Ward (206) Jerome Wexler
(29, 33) Jeanne White (439, 440, 484,
567) Roy Whitehead (68)

Susan Rayfield (19, 21, 22, 37, 79, 89,
113, 195, 223, 235, 262, 264, 283,
305 right, 354, 355, 402, 406, 413,
456, 465, 466, 485, 490, 502, 516,
529, 539, 560, 591, 650)
Dorothy M. Richards (8, 98, 115, 263,
370, 392 right, 654)
Edward S. Ross (392 left)
Leonard Lee Rue III (53, 305 left, 306
left, 549, 656)
Mary S. Schaub (34, 553)
Werner W. Schulz (74, 159)
John Shaw (278)
Caulion Singletary (103)

Tom Stack & Assoc.
G. M. Brady (496) Michael P.
Gadomski (525) J. Madeley (640) Al

Nelson (511) Lynn M. Stone (617) P. Urbanski (602)

Alvin E. Staffan (76, 94, 106, 117, 150, 160, 163, 191, 202, 208, 221, 252, 273, 280, 320, 340, 356, 360, 380, 384, 415, 436, 469, 470, 487, 489, 504, 517, 527, 568, 586, 597, 598, 605, 611, 619, 620, 646, 648)
David M. Stone (294, 505, 512, 542, 653)
Lynn M. Stone (63, 260, 494 right, 513)
Ed Streekman (48, 120, 170, 174, 192, 256, 281)
Arthur Swoger (219, 291)
Larry West (423 right, 486, 491, 493 right, 498, 649)
Dale and Marian Zimmerman (149)
Jack Zucker (92, 641, 642)

INDEX
Numbers in boldface type refer to color
plates. Numbers in italics refer to pages.
Circles preceding English names of
wildflowers make it easy for you to keep a
record of the wildflowers you have seen.